D0309025

POLAND'S ~~S~~ DEFEN~~CE~~

~~A~~USTRALIA TAKES UP ARMS

INCESSANT AIR RAIDS

EXPIRY AT 5 P.M. YESTERDAY

AT ONE WITH GREAT BRITAIN

LL AND
KEY

Correspondent
...ced last night
...ad decided to
...nt and set up a
...s of the War
...ecember, 1916.
...is colleagues in
...eir resignations
...enable the new
...o effect.
...the following
War Cabinet

...of the Treasury
...AIN

...n Affairs

...f Defence
...LORD CHATFIELD

...LL
...A

last night that
...d the following
...not in the War

...of Home Security

...nion Affairs

...pointments will
...e.

...RIENCE
...inistry, who are
...abinet, are Mr.
...lankey.   Mr.
...previously held
State. He now
...s First Lord of
...returns to the
...outbreak of the

...has never held
...ut he brings to
...ence and know-
...many ways use-
...e last War he
...Committee of
...was also Secre-
...set up by Mr.
...d the Imperial
...stablished later.
...st year he held
...Secretary to the
Committee of
...rk of the Privy

...also a member
...cated the office
...n he has held

ANGLO-FRENCH DECISION CHEERED

From Our Correspondent
WARSAW, SEPT. 3

The German invasion, as far as can be observed at present—reports are scanty and hard to confirm—seems to have two separate aims, apart from terror. Towns and villages of strategic importance for communications are being bombed, and military offensives are being directed so as to pinch off certain cities commanding wide areas.

A *communiqué* issued on Saturday night states:—" The German Government with the Dutch Legation in Warsaw as intermediary proposed to the Government of Poland that air bombing should be restricted to military objectives. The Poles accepted, and yet on Sautrday the Germans bombed the following 'open' cities: Lublin, Radomsko, Trudziadz, Radom, Tomaszow, Bydgoszco, Torun, Pacanow, Sieradz, Mielec, Tranobrzeg, Rzesznow, Grodno, Poznan, Chelmno, Alexandrow, Krakow, Luck, Piotrkow, Lodz, and Debice. Several of these places were bombed on Saturday many times. In addition, villages, farms, and even farmcarts were attacked. The total casualties on Friday and Saturday are estimated at 1,500 killed and wounded, including many women and children."

Other big cities which have been bombed and where the damage is still uncomputed are Gdynia, Dzialdowo, Kutno, Wielun, Czestochowa, Jaslo, Krosno, Lwow, Biala Podlaska, Brest Litovsk, Kobryn, and Zambrow. The strategic importance of Poznan, Lodz, Cracow, and Grodno, which have been bombed, is obvious.

A general reduction in air attacks throughout Poland has been noticed, and also in Upper Silesia. Katowice and Cracow were only slightly bombed on Saturday. The British and French Consuls were asked to leave Katowice, from which the civil population has already been evacuated in trams and farm carts and on foot. The Cracow wireless station has been put out of action by bombs, and the telephone service with Katowice was temporarily cut off.

The heaviest fighting is in Polish Upper Silesia, where the Germans are pouring in through the "Moravian Gate." The attack is obviously aimed to cut off Katowice from Cracow, and hence thrusts have been made at several points—Rybnik, Olza, Kaczyce, Cieszyn (Teschen), and Zakopane. Katowice has been heavily bombed, and the local Nazis have added to its difficulties. The town is still held by the Poles, who are nevertheless manoeuvring on a careful defence plan between Cracow and Katowice.

Communication with Katowice after being cut off was re-established later. It was then stated that bands of local Nazis, reinforced by a Freikorps from Germany which had crossed the frontier, had attempted risings. The Poles, however, have the situation well in hand there. One band of 20 young men was taken out from Katowice and shot. Two other bands were driven through the streets to the jeers of the crowds with bayonets pointed at

PARIS, Sept. 3.—An official *communiqué* states that M. Coulondre, the French Ambassador, was received by Herr von Ribbentrop at 12.30 p.m. to-day. The Ambassador asked whether the Minister was in a position to give a satisfactory reply to his communication of September 1. Herr von Ribbentrop replied negatively.

In consequence M. Coulondre, having recalled for the last time the heavy responsibility assumed by the Reich in engaging in hostilities against Poland without a declaration of war and in not following up the suggestion of the French and British Governments, declared that as from to-day at 5 p.m. the French Government would find itself obliged to fulfil the obligations undertaken towards Poland, which were known to the German Government.

After his call on Herr von Ribbentrop M. Coulondre sent a Secretary of Embassy to the Wilhelmstrasse to obtain his passports. Members of the German Embassy in Paris have asked for their passports from the Quai d'Orsay.

War preparations were more obvious in Paris to-day. The underground is running a skeleton service both by day and by night and will remain the normal means of passenger transport. The streets are plastered with notices showing where air raid shelters are situated and how many people they can hold.

Since the "state of siege" was declared on Friday Paris has been under the control of the Military Governor, General Billotte. Almost all theatres are closed owing to the mobilization of actors. The strictest black-out conditions are insisted on. As an additional precautionary measure against air raids, weather forecasts are no longer being given.

A decree published in the *Journal Officiel* abolishes the weekly day of rest, and thus institutes a seven-day week in all State establishments and all concerns working for France's national defence.—*Reuter.*

JAPAN NEUTRAL

REPORTED ASSURANCES TO BRITAIN

SHANGHAI, Sept. 3.—It is understood that the Japanese Government have given assurances to the British Government of Japan's neutrality in the present European war.—*Reuter.*

TOKYO, Sept. 3.—Mr. Toshio Shiratori, the Japanese Ambassador in Rome, who was known to have been one of the staunchest advocates of a Japanese military alliance with the Axis Powers, has been recalled by his Government.

The Domei Agency states that Mr. Shiratori himself asked for this step to be taken "on account of his poor health." It is understood that a successor will be appointed as soon as possible.—*Reuter.*

ROME, Sept. 3.—It is officially stated here that the Japanese Ambassador is being recalled to report on the European situation. Japanese circles in Rome, however, do not hide the fact that the recall is due to the attitude of the Japanese Government towards the Axis Powers after the signing of the Russo-German Non-Aggression Pact.—*Reuter.*

MR. MENZIES' BROADCAST

From Our Own Correspondent
MELBOURNE, SEPT. 3

Mr. Menzies, the Australian Prime Minister, announced this evening that Australia was at war with Germany.

News of the outbreak of hostilities between Germany and Poland found the Federal Ministers dispersed, pending a meeting of the Cabinet at Canberra to-morrow. Mr. Menzies went to Colac, in western Victoria, on Friday afternoon, intending to address a meeting and to spend a week-end with a friend, completing his Budget speech; but having heard the news on his arrival at Colac he spoke only a few minutes before returning to Melbourne, where he summoned the available Ministers towards midnight. It is a coincidence that Mr. Menzies should have happened to be at Colac in such circumstances, for in 1914, on the eve of the last War, Mr. Andrew Fisher, then Commonwealth Prime Minister, addressed a meeting there, and made his famous statement that Australia was with Great Britain to the last man and the last shilling.

It was 3 o'clock on Saturday morning before the Ministers dispersed. Mr. Menzies, after a brief broadcast explaining that he had had no official confirmation of newspaper reports and promising a further broadcast when the situation was clarified, visited Sir Winston Dugan, who as the Governor-General's deputy, signed a proclamation declaring that a danger of war existed, and thus bringing into operation certain advanced plans in the war book. Mr. Menzies then indicated that if during the night Great Britain entered into a state of war, a proclamation declaring the Commonwealth to be in a state of war would be made.

CENSORSHIP IMPOSED

The Cabinet met yesterday afternoon. A special edition of the *Gazette* last night announced that a censorship had been imposed on all inward and outward communications by telegraph, telephone, cable and wireless, the post, and short-wave broadcasting. Mr. Menzies explained that the Commonwealth had been advised that the United Kingdom had taken similar action, and that uniform action throughout the Empire was most desirable.

The city was strangely quiet after the receipt of the first news. People apparently hurried home to listen to broadcast bulletins delivered at short intervals throughout the night.

Mr. Menzies, in his broadcast, said that having regard to the way in which negotiations were being conducted, it was clear that war could come about only if Germany wanted it. To dismiss possibilities of a settlement and to accompany acts of aggressive warfare with statements about honour and dignity, as if dignity weighed for anything where millions of human lives were at stake, was a crime against humanity. If this crime had really been committed, as he feared it had, then the British peoples would go to war with a clear conscience, confident in the righteousness of their cause and feeling with absolute assurance that justice, reason, and honest dealing could

London at War

By the same author

THE DUCHESS OF DINO

ADDINGTON

THE BLACK DEATH

KING WILLIAM IV

MELBOURNE

DIANA COOPER

MOUNTBATTEN

THE SIXTH GREAT POWER:
BARINGS, 1762–1929

KING EDWARD VIII

HAROLD WILSON

ed. THE DIARIES OF LORD
LOUIS MOUNTBATTEN 1920–1922

ed. PERSONAL DIARY OF ADMIRAL
THE LORD LOUIS MOUNTBATTEN
1943–1946

ed. FROM SHORE TO SHORE:
THE TOUR DIARIES OF
EARL MOUNTBATTEN OF BURMA
1953–1979

London at War

1939–1945

Philip Ziegler

SINCLAIR-STEVENSON

WOR/95/ 4536 4/95

HCL

942.1084 ZIE

First published in Great Britain in 1995
by Sinclair-Stevenson
an imprint of Reed Consumer Books Ltd
Michelin House, 81 Fulham Road, London SW3 6RB
and Auckland, Melbourne, Singapore and Toronto

Copyright © P. S. & M. C. Ziegler & Co. 1995

The right of Philip Ziegler to be identified as author
of this work has been asserted by him in accordance
with the Copyright, Designs and Patents Act 1988

A CIP catalogue record for this book
is available from the British Library
ISBN 1 85619 384 5

Phototypeset by Intype, London
Printed and bound in Great Britain
by Clays Ltd, St Ives Plc

Contents

List of Illustrations

Abbreviations Used in Text

AFS	Auxiliary Fire Service
ARP	Air Raid Precautions
ATS	Auxiliary Territorial Service
BEF	British Expeditionary Force
CEMA	Council for the Encouragement of Music and the Arts
DA	Delayed action bomb
ENSA	Entertainments National Service Associations
LCC	London County Council
LDV	Local Defence Volunteers
MCC	Marylebone Cricket Club
MoI	Ministry of Information
NAAFI	Navy, Army and Air Force Institutes
PLA	Port of London Authority
REME	Royal Electrical and Mechanical Engineers
RSPCA	Royal Society for the Prevention of Cruelty to Animals
UXB	Unexploded bomb
WAAF	Women's Auxiliary Air Force
WRNS	Women's Royal Naval Service
WVS	Women's Voluntary Service

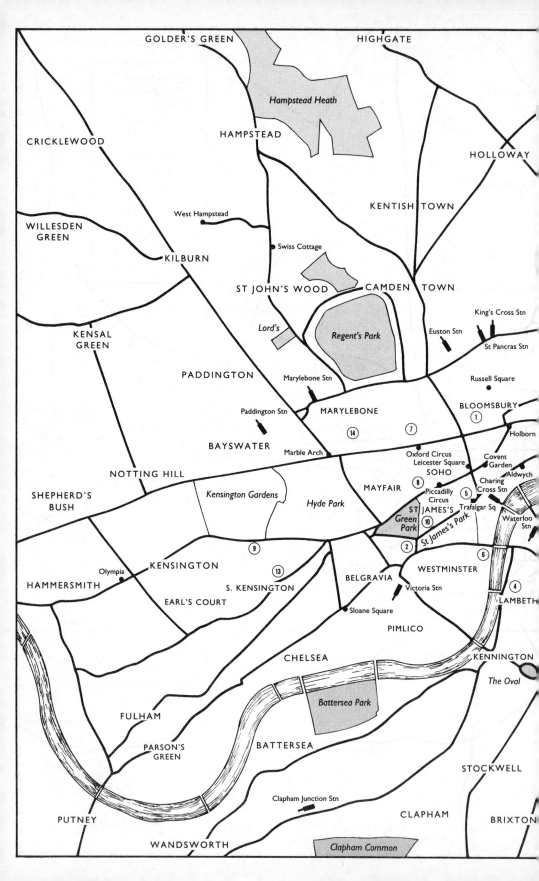

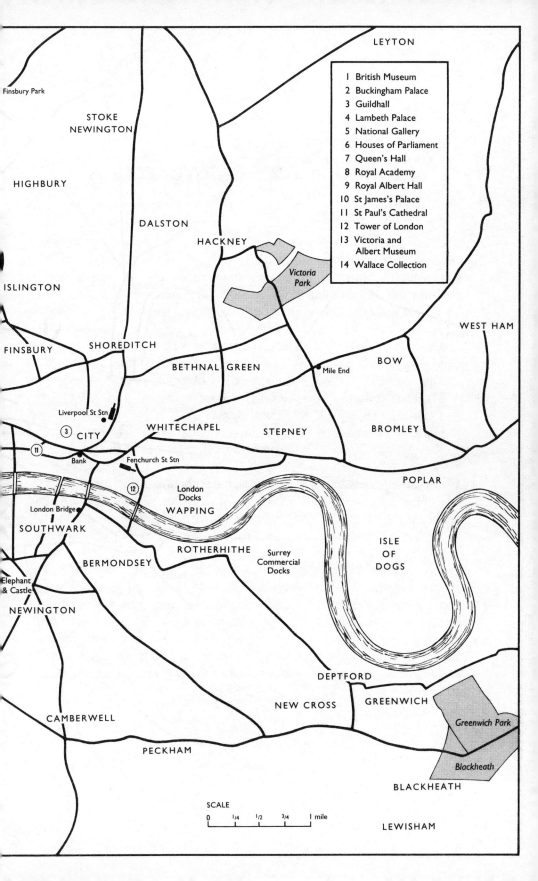

LEYTON

1	British Museum
2	Buckingham Palace
3	Guildhall
4	Lambeth Palace
5	National Gallery
6	Houses of Parliament
7	Queen's Hall
8	Royal Academy
9	Royal Albert Hall
10	St James's Palace
11	St Paul's Cathedral
12	Tower of London
13	Victoria and Albert Museum
14	Wallace Collection

Finsbury Park

STOKE
NEWINGTON

HIGHBURY

DALSTON

HACKNEY

Victoria
Park

ISLINGTON

WEST HAM

FINSBURY

SHOREDITCH

BETHNAL GREEN

Mile End

BOW

Liverpool St Stn

③ CITY

WHITECHAPEL

STEPNEY

BROMLEY

⑪

Bank

Fenchurch St Stn

POPLAR

⑫

London
Docks

WAPPING

London Bridge

SOUTHWARK

ROTHERHITHE

Surrey
Commercial
Docks

ISLE
OF
DOGS

BERMONDSEY

Elephant
& Castle

NEWINGTON

DEPTFORD

GREENWICH

NEW CROSS

Greenwich Park

CAMBERWELL

PECKHAM

Blackheath

BLACKHEATH

SCALE

0   ¼   ½   ¾   1 mile

LEWISHAM

Table of Comparative Values

THE POUND STERLING was decimalised in 1969; previously it had been divided into 20 shillings (20s) and 240 pence (240d). A shilling, which comprised 12 pence, was written 1/-; one and a half shillings would have appeared as 1/6d. The main units in the old currency, with their equivalents in new pence, were:

1 farthing (¼d)	-	just over 0.1 of a new penny.
1 halfpenny (½d)	-	just over 0.2 of a new penny.
1 penny (1d)	-	just over 0.4 of a new penny.
Sixpence (6d)	-	2½ new pence.
1 shilling (1/-)	-	5 new pence.
Half a crown (2/6d)	-	12½ new pence (a crown had been worth five shillings, hence the name).

Comparisons between the values of currencies at different periods are often misleading and always need cautious handling, but the latest figures from the Bank of England (for which I am indebted to Sir Peter Petrie) suggest that if the pound sterling in the summer of 1994 be taken as purchasing £1 worth of goods, the corresponding unit in the summer of 1939 would have bought 25.4 times as much. Inflation rose sharply in late 1939 and in 1940, but the purchasing power of the pound calculated on the same basis stabilised at a little under 20 at the beginning of 1941 and remained between 19.8 and 19.5 for the rest of the war. As a rough-and-ready guide, figures should be multiplied by 25 at the beginning of the war to arrive at the contemporary purchasing power, and by 20 from the beginning of 1941.

Introduction

MY AMERICAN PUBLISHERS first suggested I should write this book. They had been responsible for a very interesting study of Washington during the Second World War, and thought that it would be a good idea to accompany it by a book about a city closer to the firing line. At first I was doubtful. The subject had been covered before, and though I was confident that there would be plenty of new material I was not sure that I would find it easy to steer a course between the gullible acceptance of all the legends peddled about wartime London and a revisionist determination to reject the lot of them.

I soon found that I had mis-stated the problem. The subject was so vast, the material emotionally so super-charged, that *everything* was true. Individual stories might not be verifiable, yet in essence every legend illustrating the courage, the self-sacrifice, the dignity, the humour of Londoners under fire could readily be substantiated. But so could every charge of snobbishness, selfishness, the spirit of *sauve qui peut*. London between 1939 and 1945 was a theme bursting at the seams with spectacular vitality. It was one of the great stories of the world. Like all great stories it had its seamy side. As in all great stories the web of often contradictory detail sometimes concealed but never obliterated the simple, powerful drama that underlay them.

As a biographer, it was Londoners rather than London that most concerned me. So far as possible I have told the story through the words of contemporary Londoners, written in diaries or letters or taken from conversation. The diaries – published – of prominent personalities such as Harold Nicolson or Hugh Dalton, or – unpublished – of Lord Woolton or Euan Wallace have been of great value, but I have relied even more on the letters or diaries of ordinary people: George and Helena Britton, a retired couple living in Walthamstow and writing weekly letters to their daughter in California;

Hilda Neal, who ran a small typists' shop in South Kensington; Gwladys Cox, a middle-aged widow from West Hampstead. No less useful have been the records of Mass Observation, that regiment of skilled eavesdroppers who recorded the comments of Londoners throughout the war.

I have been able to add little by way of personal record. As a boy on my way to school I frequently traversed London and towards the end of the war I sometimes spent a night there, but such bombs as I heard fell on or around Southampton. I cannot claim, even in a small way, to have shared the experiences of the capital. Perhaps it is just as well: human memories are frail and I suspect that after fifty years I would have edited or enhanced my recollections beyond recognition. Not everyone is so fallible. Since I began work on this book I must have spoken to several thousand people – 3000 at least – who had some direct experience of wartime London. To list them all would take several pages and serve little purpose. I hope they will accept this as a statement of my gratitude.

All books pose problems of delimitation; a study of London during the Second World War sets some particularly complex challenges. First, what is London? Before the war the Greater London or Metropolitan Police area covered 700 square miles; the Greater London Town Planning or London Transport area 2000 square miles; the County of London 116; the City of London 1; the London Telephone area 1200; the London Postal area 232; the London Electricity District 1840; the Metropolitan Water Board area 573; the London Main Drainage area 159. With war still more entities were created: the London Civil Defence Region, for the purposes of the Fire Watchers Order, comprised the administrative County of London; the county boroughs of Croydon, East Ham and West Ham; all county districts situated wholly or partially within the Metropolitan Police district with the exception of the borough of Watford, the urban districts of Caterham and Warlingham, the rural districts of Hatfield, St Albans and Watford.

When people referred loosely to 'London' or 'Londoners', which of these did they have in mind? Almost certainly none. They knew what they meant by London, but did not seek to define it. To be a Londoner was and is more a state of mind than a question of geographical location. If pressed, I would probably fall back on the traditional LCC definition of Greater London as being any area within fifteen miles of Charing Cross, but I am aware that I have been guilty of inconsistencies and occasional transgressions of my own rule. I know what *I* mean by London and hope that readers will excuse some blurring of its exact demarcation.

Another problem is to distinguish between those things that pertain exclusively to London and those of wider application. It would be absurd to describe wartime London without mentioning rationing or the radio show *ITMA*, yet both of these were experienced as vividly in Glasgow or rural Devon. I have not excluded anything on the grounds that it was as much national as local, but have so far as possible described it as it seemed to those in London. It is possible that a Glaswegian or a Devonian would have had the same reaction, but the voices I record are those of Londoners.

My debt to published books is obvious. In the introduction to the bibliography I have tried to pick out those which I found of special value. Every book I list, however, every newspaper cited, every official document studied at the Public Record Office, is in some way reflected in my work.

I am particularly grateful to those who allowed me to see manuscript diaries and letters, either written by themselves or retained in their possession. Three institutions were above all helpful to me: the Imperial War Museum, with its invaluable collection of manuscripts as well as printed books and photographs; the Mass Observation Archive at the University of Sussex; and the *Evening Standard*, which tolerated my presence over many weeks as I grubbed page by page through their back numbers. I know well that I have only scratched the surface of the mountain of available material. Even from the notes that I compiled this book could have been three times as long; a collection of many volumes would be needed to cover every facet of life in London during the six years of war.

My greatest debt is, of course, to the inhabitants of wartime London. No one could have done the work necessary to write a book of this kind without emerging with a profound respect for their patience, courage and determination. I hope we will never have to endure again what they went through between 1939 and 1945. I hope, if we did, that we would conduct ourselves as well.

1

The Greatest City

LONDON IN 1939 was the greatest city in the world. 'Greatest' is a word of singular imprecision. It can mean everything or nothing. In this case it means, if not everything, then at least something close to it. If a Lithuanian, a Peruvian, an Indian, had been asked to name the world's leading city, it is inconceivable that they would have named any of London's rivals. In almost every sense, it *had* no rivals.

No one disputed that it was the largest. The size of its population varied according to the definition of its boundaries, but 'Greater London' in the most usual sense of the phrase was home for 8.2 million people. Next largest was New York, with 6.93 million. Only one other British city, Glasgow, had a population of over a million. In a pamphlet issued to American troops posted to Britain, the US Army used a different measure, crediting London with 12.5 million inhabitants, 'the size of greater New York City with the nearby New Jersey cities thrown in. It is also more than a quarter of the total population of the British Isles.'

London was growing too, probably as fast as any of the other great cities of the world. The explosive development of the urban centres in the less-developed countries – Cairo, Calcutta, Mexico City – was still an unimagined horror. The population of Great Britain rose by more than five million between the First and Second World Wars. Of these one-third lived in London or worked there. Over the same period 1.25 million houses were built to accommodate the ever-growing multitude of those whose life centred on the metropolis.

London was not *a*, it was *the* metropolis; Edinburgh and Cardiff might think of themselves as capitals but in any significant sense they did not stand comparison. London handled more tonnage than any other port in the world; a quarter of the country's imports passed through the Port of London, nearly twice the amount handled by the second port, Liverpool. Few thought of London as a manufacturing city, yet the value of its factories' output was larger than that of any of the industrial cities of the Midlands or the North.

The wealth of the world flowed through the City of London, that tiny, congested area between the docks and East End and the affluent West End. The stock exchange, the banks, the insurance companies, the heart of that intricate web by which money travelled freely to every part of the globe, was to be found in 'the square mile' of narrow, crooked streets and – give or take the churches and a handful of the palaces of Mammon – mainly undistinguished buildings. Only a few people actually lived there, but every morning hundreds of thousands flowed in from Greater London and farther out, to keep the financial wheels in motion. Directly or indirectly, more than half the world's international trade was financed through London.

It was the seat of government: legislature, executive and judiciary. As much could be said of Berlin or Moscow, but London was also the capital of the British Empire. The Secretary of State for the Dominions exercised only the most residual powers when it came to the 'Old Commonwealth' – Australia, New Zealand, South Africa, Canada – but the Secretaries of State for the Colonies and for India and Burma were ultimately responsible for the running of these vast territories. The House of Lords in its judicial capacity was the supreme court of appeal from all parts of the Empire. London, the newly arrived American troops were told, is 'the combined New York, Washington and Chicago, not only of England but of the far-flung British Empire'.

Intellectually, London University (barely a century old when the war broke out) lacked some of the antique glories of Oxford and Cambridge, but with the London School of Economics, the School of Oriental and African Studies, Imperial College and all its other component elements, it ranked among the leading universities of the world. In St Paul's and Westminster, London possessed two of the oldest and most distinguished public schools; its grammar schools – Alleyns, Battersea, Haberdashers' Aske's – were as renowned if not as fashionable. Musically it was among the best; its theatre was incomparably the richest in its variety and the skills of its players, directors and stage designers. The National Gallery and the British Museum were only the more notable in a complex of similar institutions which made London the most diverse and abundant of civilisation's treasure houses.

Not merely was it the greatest port; it was the focal point of a network of communications which connected all parts of the country by road and rail. Geographically it was far from being the centre – myriad cross-country journeys were possible – but from the time of the Romans the assumption had been that most serious travel would begin or end in London. Voyagers from Perth to Plymouth or Norwich to Aberystwyth would probably have found it convenient to plot their courses not as the crow flew but by way of London. More recently it had become the hub of a mesh of airways which increasingly provided an alternative means of travel between the larger and more distant British cities as well as internationally.

London was the royal capital. The royal family had Windsor as the Bourbons had Versailles, but when King George VI and Queen Elizabeth were on duty it was at Buckingham Palace that they would most often be found. The King had been crowned in Westminster Abbey, it was there or in St Paul's that dignitaries celebrated or mourned on state occasions. The crown jewels rested secure some three miles down the Thames in the Tower of London. 'All these buildings have played an important part in England's history,' the American servicemen were told. 'They mean just as much to the British as Mount Vernon or Lincoln's birthplace do to us.' This was an understatement: these buildings *were* British history, as much at the roots of national life as Notre-Dame in Paris, the Acropolis in Athens, the Colosseum in Rome, yet unlike the last two in that they were active institutions, playing a role in the day-to-day transaction of affairs.

London was cosmopolitan; far less so than it has become over the last fifty years but more diverse than any other city of the British Isles, even the great seaports like Liverpool or Bristol. There were some 430,000 practising Jews in Britain, of whom almost a quarter lived in London. Nine-tenths of the inhabitants of Stepney were immigrants or the children of immigrants and the vast majority were Jewish. Black and brown faces were comparatively rare but by no means freakish, especially in the East End, and there was a lively Chinese community around the docks. In Holborn clustered a sizeable and largely homogeneous society of Greeks and Cypriots;

in Finsbury there was a settlement of Italians, providing many of the waiters and restaurateurs who served Soho and the West End. To the racial cocktail had recently been added more than 50,000 German, Austrian and Czech refugees from fascism, largely Jews, but of a different social and intellectual background to the communities already established in the East End.

London was rich. Between 1921 and 1937 the number of motor cars owned by Londoners rose by 180 per cent; annual casualties on the roads of the capital were greater than the British military losses in the whole of the Boer War. Directly or indirectly, London generated a quarter of the nation's wealth. Londoners paid higher prices for their fuel, their food, their accommodation, but they earned more too; overall, the standard of living was among the highest in the country. It had suffered in the depression, but not so severely as other areas; even in 1932 only one worker in eight had been out of a job, compared with one in four in Scotland and the North and a shocking one in three in Wales. Now the depression was in the past, rearmament was stimulating the economy, it was boom time again.

But it was not all riches. The *New Survey of London Life and Labour*, published in 1934, showed that for every three families which had lived below the poverty line at the end of the nineteenth century, only one was similarly afflicted in the mid 1930s, but the statistic was more a reflection on the horrors of late Victorian London than a testimony to the improved conditions of the present. For most of those in work London provided a reasonable livelihood; for the lowest paid or the unemployed conditions were dire indeed. Crowded into mean and ill-built houses which often had only an outdoor lavatory and the most inadequate lighting, which were cold and damp in winter, hot and smelly in summer, the poorest 10 per cent of the London population was preoccupied above all by the grim task of keeping alive. Very few starved, but there were many housewives who were uncertain where the next meal was to come from, let alone how to provide nutritious and varied fare for the family. Nobody walked the streets naked, but many wore clothes that were discoloured and threadbare. In the less fortunate parts of the East End there was an under-privileged proletariat which seemed trapped for ever in the most degrading poverty. To the Marxists, to the more nervous social scientists and civil servants, to foreign observers concerned to estimate the people's will to resist attack, it seemed the conditions must be ripe, if not for revolution then at least for a sullen refusal to cooperate in the defence of the nation.

To those concerned with such matters London was special in another way; it was a prime, *the* prime target, for aerial attack. 'This concentration in 750 square miles of about ... one fifth of the population of Britain,' wrote Professor Richard Titmuss in his *Problems of Social Policy*, 'was expected to be the target of massed assault by the enemy's bombers. The theory of a "knock-out blow" which the enemy would aim at the country's nerve centre influenced many of the early plans, and explained much of the birth and development of the wartime emergency services.' A blow at London would be a blow simultaneously to the brain and to the heart, which might leave the limbs twitching for a while but would effectively destroy the capacity to resist. The conviction that this must be equally apparent to the Germans – or to any other putative enemy for that matter – obsessed those charged with the defence of Britain. London in 1939 was not merely the greatest city in the world; its rulers believed it to be the most threatened and the most vulnerable.

2

'The bomber will always get through'

MANY LONDONERS HAD already experienced bombardment from
the air. On 31 May 1915, a German airship had appeared unexpectedly over London and dropped a ton of bombs. So far as could
be seen, its load fell at random, killing seven and wounding thirty-
five. From then until mid 1918 the attacks continued. They fell into
three phases. The airships continued to be a menace for eighteen
months or so, but they were slow and vulnerable. Gradually the
defences improved their technique. Fewer Zeppelins got through to
central London and more and more bombs were scattered over the
countryside or into the gravel-pit at Bernard Shaw's Heartbreak
House. Losses among the raiders became unacceptably high. In
1917 the Germans switched to daylight attacks by conventional
bombers. The fiercest raid was on 13 June, when fourteen Gothas
flew over the East End, killing 162 and injuring 426.

The total of deaths from bombing in London throughout the war
was only 670, but the psychological shock of this relative carnage was
great. One bomb fell on a council school in Poplar, killing fourteen
children. This incident, more than any other, fostered the doctrine
of dispersal: as far as possible children, the elderly and the physically
handicapped should be evacuated from the likely target area and,
within that area, steps should be taken to prevent people congregat-
ing at cinemas, football matches, even churches. It could, of course,
be argued the other way: if people were dispersed throughout the
city, they would provide more targets for the bombers. This thesis
was advanced from time to time, but the potent image of children's
bodies dragged from a shattered school won the day. The dispersal
doctrine became official policy.

Once again defences began to make it difficult for the bomber to
penetrate over London; the emphasis switched to attacks by night

whenever the moon permitted. In February 1918 Freda Dudley Ward was walking through Belgrave Square when an air-raid warning sounded. She took refuge in a nearby house, found a dance in progress, was spotted by the Prince of Wales and danced with him for the rest of the night. So, in its way, a German bomber changed the course of royal history. The incident was exceptional; most of the raids were directed against dockland and the East End. When the moon made a raid seem a probability many East Enders would trek to the relatively safer areas to the west or, more often, take shelter under railway arches or in the stations of the Underground. More than ten thousand people used to crowd into a single tube station; on one occasion in February 1918 a third of a million Londoners went underground. Sometimes it proved hard to persuade them to emerge the following morning. From such incidents stemmed another theory that was to haunt those responsible for planning; that a 'deep shelter' mentality might grow up and result in paralysis of will among those who succumbed to it. In 1937 the future Lord Woolton was appointed to a committee considering the case for building deep shelters and adapting tube stations for use in time of war. He began in favour of the proposition, but was convinced by expert evidence that people who took refuge in this way 'would grow hysterical with fear and would never surface to perform their duties'. With the benefit of hindsight it is hard to find evidence for such a theory but at the time it seemed that the experiences of 1917 and 1918 pointed inexorably in that direction.

1918 saw the end of the war that was to end wars, and most Londoners pushed the horrors of air attack to the backs of their minds as something that could not possibly recur. It was May 1924 before a sub-committee of the Committee of Imperial Defence began any serious study of air-raid precautions. Its chairman was Sir John Anderson, an enormously able but uninspiring public servant who was to play a major part in civil defence at the beginning of the war. His group can hardly be said to have tackled the problem with electrifying energy, but its conclusions were to provide the basis on which London went to war in 1939. What is now most striking about its deliberations, indeed about all discussions of civil defence in the years before the war, is the background of apocalyptic gloom against which they were conducted. 'The bomber will always get through,' Stanley Baldwin told the House of Commons in 1931, and it was the assumption of all so-called experts that, though it might be possible to inflict heavy casualties on the attacker, there was no effective defence against onslaught from the air.

Not merely would the bomber get through, once there it would strike with devastating effect. Anderson's committee took it for granted that London would be the immediate target when war broke out: 2000 tons of bombs, they believed, would be dropped in the first twenty-four hours, 150 in the second, 100 a day for the next month or so. Each ton would cause fifty casualties, a third of which would be fatal. Within a month the death roll would have mounted to 28,000. The bombardment of Barcelona in the Spanish Civil War provided grounds for fresh calculations. The figure of fifty casualties per ton was not amended, but the probable strength of the attack was vastly augmented. The Air Staff were now contemplating an all-out attack on London in which 3500 tons of bombs would fall in the first twenty-four hours; by the time the all-clear sounded, 58,000 Londoners would have been killed. 'We thought of air warfare in 1938 rather as people think of nuclear power today,' wrote Harold Macmillan in his memoirs, while Bertrand Russell sought to curdle the nation's blood when he predicted (in *Which Way to Peace?*) that London would be 'one vast raving bedlam, the hospitals will be stormed, traffic will cease, the homeless will shriek for peace, the city will be a pandemonium'.

The storming of hospitals and shrieks for peace were a feature of many nightmare predictions propagated at the time. To cap their vision of Londoners refusing to emerge from their troglodytic security in the Underground, the authorities assumed that the first raids would generate mass panic and probably widespread and destructive rioting. War would be 'a terrible shock to the country', the normally sensible writer and politician Harold Nicolson wrote in his diary. 'The bombing of London by itself would provoke panic and perhaps riot.' At about the same time the Committee of Imperial Defence was taking the view that the maintenance of public order would be the most difficult problem, and that large numbers of troops would have to be assigned to the task.

Of course nobody told the Londoners that they were expected to suffer so badly and to react with such tempestuous dismay. Until the Munich crisis in the autumn of 1938 made the outbreak of war an urgent probability, few Londoners concerned themselves with events on the continent or Britain's foreign policy. BIG FIGHT EDITION, proclaimed the *Daily Express* on the day the Germans marched into Austria, but the fight was between two heavyweight boxers: the Englishman, Tommy Farr, and the American, Max Baer. On the same day a group of black-shirted supporters of the Fascist leader, Oswald Mosley, assembled around the statue of Eros in Piccadilly Circus and celebrated the German achievement 'with raised arms and placards and leaflets'. Miss Andrews, a retired schoolmistress up for the evening from Tonbridge, watched apprehensively, expecting a set-to between the demonstrators and the gathering crowd, which consisted mainly of rugger enthusiasts in London for the Scotland–England match. 'They weren't feeling politically minded at all,' however, 'and merely gazed benignly on the Fascists, who were soon gently but firmly broken up by half a dozen mounted police.' She did not know whether to be irritated by the crowd's frivolity or approving of their tolerance: 'It could have been seen nowhere but in England,' she concluded.

Public apathy stemmed partly from disbelief – surely not even politicians could be so silly as to start another war? – partly from helplessness. They could do nothing effective to reduce the risk of war, so why worry? A similar sense of futility overcame the Battersea Council when they were invited to send representatives to discuss the protection of the civil population against air attack. There could be no defence against high explosive or gas attack, they concluded, and they could not be expected 'to assume the responsibility or be saddled with the cost of matters outside their normal range of functions'. Probably they shared the general belief that by talking about war one made it more likely to come about. When a Harrow housewife in 1936 took a course of anti-gas lectures, she was severely criticised by several of her friends; it was people like her who made wars, she was told. When gas drill was introduced in Southgate, the Wood Green Women's Arbitration Committee protested to the borough council. To educate the public in this way would 'create war mentality and panic'. It would 'have a harmful effect upon the plastic minds of children' and 'convey the impression that the obligation entered into by governments not to resort to war' would not be honoured.

Pacifist convictions underlay many of these reactions. Pacifism had its apotheosis in the by-election in East Fulham in October 1933. A Tory majority of 14,521 was overturned in a Labour victory by 4840. In his maiden speech the new member, John Wilmot, described his platform as having been based on 'a passionate and consistent desire for peace'. Three years later Baldwin admitted that it was this by-election, fought, as it was, 'on no issue but the pacifist', which had convinced him that rearmament was impossible. But the mood was transitory. In 1934 Arthur Salter persuaded the Bermondsey Borough Council that they should refuse to cooperate in any air-raid precautions; two years later the council set up a committee to consider what precautions should be taken. They did not succumb totally, however. When a national register was established for the purposes of national service, Salter saw this as a prelude to conscription and urged the council to boycott the operation. They agreed, and instead supported a No Conscription League, with its headquarters in Bermondsey town hall, charged *inter alia* with the provision of advice to conscientious objectors.

Little by little Londoners reluctantly accepted that something had to be done and even – though this was harder – that they might have to be the ones to do it. One of the first overt manifestations of this new awareness came in February 1938. 'Great doings in Paddington last night,' reported the *Daily Express*. 'Mythical enemy bombers wrecked houses, ripped (in theory) fifteen foot craters in the road and sprayed the Borough with mustard gas . . . Girls who had been "burned" by mustard gas were rushed to the first-aid station in Paddington Central Baths. The first thing to do is to remove contaminated clothing. The organisers had previously warned "casualties" to wear bathing costumes underneath.' For most of the participants the exercise was no more than a harmless lark, for some at least of the bystanders it seemed a silly waste of time, but it marked a step in the capital's acceptance of the likelihood of war.

The Munich crisis finally jolted all but a hard core of unregenerate ostriches out of their complacency. Throughout 1938 tension had increased as the German government protested about the alleged ill-treatment of German nationals in the Sudeten area of Czechoslovakia and demanded cession of the province. Neville Chamberlain, who had become Prime Minister on Baldwin's resignation in 1937, was convinced that a settlement could and should be reached, even at the price of Czech surrender. Twice in September he flew to see Hitler to plead with him to relax the rigour of his position. At the same time the Czechs were told, privately but with some brutality, that they could expect no help unless they surrendered the disputed territories. By the last week in September it seemed that Chamberlain's efforts had been in vain: the Czechs refused to cut their own throats; a German invasion appeared inevitable; so far as the man-in-the-street could tell, this would probably be followed by a declaration of war by Britain and France.

The crisis, sudden in the eyes of most Londoners, exposed with alarming clarity the inadequacy of the capital's preparations. In theory, the resources of the regular fire services should have been substantially reinforced by an army of auxiliaries. In June 1938 the head of London's fire services, Aylmer Firebrace, and the Leader of the London County Council (LCC), Herbert Morrison, had jointly appealed for volunteers to join the Auxiliary Fire Service (AFS). Only a handful came forward. At the same time £5 million had been allocated for the improvement of fire-fighting supplies. By the end of September most of this was still unspent and the bulk had been earmarked for 24-inch pipes to run between the Thames and the Grand Union Canal, a provision which proved almost useless when the blitz began. Plans included the assumption that 3000 emergency fire appliances would be needed for the London area; by the time of Munich 99 were available.

Other branches of civil defence were equally unready. When the Edmonton air-raid wardens arrived at their assembly point in Church Street on 24 September they found the premises locked and no key available. Eventually they forced their way in; there was no lighting, no furniture and the place had not been cleaned for weeks. F. R. Barry, then a Canon of Westminster, decided to take a first-aid course so that he could help in the emergency which seemed imminent. The first lecture was devoted to the treatment of snake bites. Another clergyman, the Revd J. G. Markham of St Peter's, Walworth, called on the Town Clerk to establish what was being done to protect his parishioners. He found that on the official list there were only four names of potential wardens to care for 11,000 people; two of them were teenage girls, all were untrained. He offered to enrol volunteers in his church, but was told no forms were available; he suggested that his crypt would make a suitable shelter, the offer was accepted in principle but nothing was done to make the necessary alterations. Walworth was unusual in the fecklessness of its officials but other town clerks had little to boast about.

At least things now began to happen. George and Helena Britton, a retired middle-class couple living in Walthamstow, went to the cinema near their home. Towards the end of the performance the manager came on to the stage and asked all ARP wardens to report to their depot as soon as possible. 'That made me feel very uneasy,' wrote Mrs Britton. 'I knew something was on.' But the number who answered the call to duty was encouraging. They may, like their colleagues in Edmonton, have found the depot locked when they got there, but once the machine was launched it gathered pace. Nobody quite knew what they were preparing for, but there was a new readiness to envisage the worst and try to guard against it. In Fulham the Coroner's Court and the mortuary were cleared to make room for the influx of bodies which would follow the first raid; in Townmead Road troops moved into the power station and set up machine guns on the roof to ward off low-flying aircraft. 'On all sides I hear of rigorous preparations for ARP in big offices,' a typist from Putney, Vivienne Hall, wrote in her diary. 'The Banks have drilled their staffs to perfect order at a given signal to "take cover", the LCC have instructed their staff at County Hall very carefully in their actions and duties in the event of an air-raid.' In her office, 'alas, we have done nothing!!' The most overt sign of London's will to resist was to be seen on Westminster Bridge. A subaltern and his platoon arrived with an anti-aircraft gun, which they proceeded to set up. A policeman walked across to remonstrate. 'Don't worry, old boy,' said the subaltern. 'There's no danger. She won't go off.'

Almost as conspicuous a sign of preparations, and that most often referred to by those seeking to evoke the atmosphere of the time, was the digging of trenches in the parks and other open spaces. The Home Office asked local authorities in densely populated areas to provide trenches that could accommodate up to 10 per cent of the population. These were intended for people caught out of doors, but some of the public declared their intention to leave their houses when the warning sounded and head for the parks, in the touching

belief that anything constructed by the authorities must be superior
to what they could contrive for themselves. The first trenches ran
thirty to forty yards in a straight line. These would be a death trap,
Professor J. B. S. Haldane, the chairman of the ARP Co-ordinating
Committee, pointed out in the rather unlikely forum of a Foyles
literary lunch; if even the smallest bomb fell at one end of a trench,
the blast would kill all the occupants. The point was taken, and
future trenches zig-zagged across the park. Even this was not enough
to satisfy the doubters; an old lady in Enfield, observing a trench
under construction in the town park, was asked if she would use it
in a raid. 'What! Go down there?' she replied robustly. 'Not me!
Conditions in that would be worse than outside!' By the end of
September a million feet of trench had been dug; within a few weeks
most had several inches of water in the bottom and were crumbling
at the edges.

Though the sight of trenches carved across the normally sacred
parks convinced Londoners that the danger was real, there was still
an air of artificiality, even of carnival, about the proceedings. In
Bethnal Green volunteers were set to filling sandbags to stack
around the more vulnerable public buildings. The work, remarked
a local official, produced 'such an air of gaiety and so many sightseers that the atmosphere was . . . more akin to children playing
with their spades and buckets on one of the popular seaside beaches,
than to the potential horrors of total war'. But not everything was
so merry. 'All our ideas about raids were dominated by Poison Gas,'
wrote the Revd J. G. Markham. In the lectures he attended gas was
treated as the main threat, with incendiary bombs second and high
explosive a poor third. The horror of this weapon captured the
public imagination; it was taken for granted by many Londoners that
within hours of the outbreak of war their city would be enveloped in
a cloud of searing poison that would blind them, burn their skin
and tear out their lungs.

'Under the spreading chestnut tree,' the children were singing,
'Neville Chamberlain said to me, "If you want to get your gas-
masks free, join the blinking ARP!" ' They were all to get their
gas-masks free. On the last Sunday in September loudspeaker vans
toured the streets calling on everyone to proceed to given points to
be fitted with a mask. In Walthamstow, as in many other boroughs,
the schools were chosen as assembly points. Mrs Britton at first

refused to go; it would be a waste of time, the masks would be no use; 'but Dad said we *must* do what we could to protect ourselves and he would go, so I thought, well if a war does come, Dad will be giving me his and that won't do, so I must go'. She was not alone in her scepticism, but on the whole Londoners agreed with Dad that one must do what one could to protect oneself. In Westminster the public were exhorted by posters, car loudspeakers and announcements at football matches, cinemas and churches, to make their way to one of the fourteen centres opened for the fitting of masks. Within a few days more than 90 per cent of the inhabitants had been equipped.

Some proved impervious to persuasion. Usually such recalcitrants simply failed to turn up, but a few delighted in overt defiance of the authorities; in Croydon one man refused to benefit by a scheme which did not also offer protection to his dog. Mistakes were made; the need for the larger sizes of mask was over-estimated, with the result that the supply of the smaller models was exhausted before the demand was met. Nor did the fitting always run smoothly. Markham's first task as a warden was to help with this. 'One old lady was most concerned with my efforts to pin the tapes of the gas-mask round her hair as it proved to be a wig, which was inclined to slip askew, or even leave her head, as I took the mask off. I had a moment of struggle with her, as she tried to hold on to her wig and I tried to remove the mask.' But by the time the Munich crisis was over the vast majority of Londoners had been furnished with the means to survive – or so it was hoped – an attack by gas.

Children posed a problem. 'Pay attention, now. This has to fit you so you can use it – just like a pair of shoes,' Mrs Briggs of Flood Street, Chelsea, urged her children. If they behaved well, the instructor rewarded them with a peppermint drop. The smaller children were issued with Mickey Mouse gas-masks. Four-and-a-half-year-old Barbara Roose was delighted with hers, but her eighteen-month-old brother Geoffrey screamed hysterically when incarcerated in the coffin-like container provided for the very young. His mother pulled him out: 'That's it! Hitler can do his worst but my son never goes back into that thing. We can both hide under the blankets.' Elsewhere the shortage of 'baby-bags' which could be fitted over an infant's head and shoulders caused angry scenes; in

Fulham Town Hall one man made such an uproar that he had to be arrested.

Unless they were actually engaged in digging trenches or queueing for a gas-mask, most Londoners behaved as at any other time. Nine months after the declaration of war a dramatic fall in the conception rate became apparent; perhaps because it passed so quickly, the Munich crisis put no comparable brake on procreation. There seems to have been some reluctance to indulge in unnecessary extravagance. When buying aspirins from a chemist Vivienne Hall remarked that she supposed the shop must be doing a roaring trade in materials needed for first aid. They were losing far more in sales of beauty products, came the gloomy reply. 'The situation *must* be bad for the ladies to lose interest in their beauty aids,' she commented archly. West End shops reported abnormal sales of groceries, while George Beardmore, who worked for an insurance company in the City, noted with evident satisfaction: 'Today we spent 25/-* on sugar, rice, corned beef and Marmite which we have stored against the day when these things will be difficult or even impossible to obtain.' But though there was some hoarding and a few shops ran short of basic foodstuffs, it did not amount to panic buying. Londoners phlegmatically went about their business: uneasy, certainly; casting furtive glances at the sky; but on the whole concluding that there was nothing much they could do about it.

One thing they *could* have done was to leave London, or at least ensure that the infirm, the elderly and the children were evacuated. Harold Nicolson walked through Trafalgar Square on 28 September 1938. His companion looked with disapproval at the boys and girls feeding the pigeons. 'These children ought to be evacuated at once,' he said, adding for good measure, 'and so should the pigeons.' The Munich crisis came and went but hardly a pigeon stirred. The theory had originally been that people would organise their own evacuation and the authorities would confine their role to encouragement and advice. A booklet circulated early in 1938 suggested that 'children, invalids, elderly members of the households, and pets, should be sent to relatives or friends in the country if this is possible'. It was

*A Table of Comparative Values on page xii shows the impact of inflation since 1939 and the conversion rate to decimal currency.

not until May of that year that the LCC accepted it had a duty to evacuate at least the children, and the mothers too if children were too young to travel with a school party. When the risks of war began to seem pressing, Herbert Morrison urged the Home Secretary to give the LCC authority to provide the necessary transport. There was some reluctance on the government's part, but eventually arrangements were made for the evacuation of 637,000 children. On 28 September the first contingent of 1200 infants from nursery schools and 3100 physically impaired children left London.

But that was as far as it went. At the Mary Datchelor Girls' School in Camberwell a parents' meeting had been called and the LCC's scheme explained. 'The absence of fuss and panic, the amazing trust in us, the steady calm with which parents carried out all the arrangements, . . . the confidence which we felt in the plan made for us by the LCC and worked out down to its smallest detail,' wrote one of the mistresses ' – all these things forged a new bond of trust and understanding, not only between the members of the school community, but also between us and the Authorities.' A year later, that bond was to prove its worth but now the need passed. Evacuation was first postponed, then cancelled. The teachers of Mary Datchelor's were profoundly relieved; some at least of the children, deprived of an adventure into the unknown and an enjoyable disruption of workaday routine, felt they had been deprived of a promised treat. Few adult Londoners had not felt despair as war approached and gratitude as the risk diminished. In the House of Commons, at the end of August, Nicolson had noticed the change of mood when it seemed that diplomacy might after all avert disaster: 'The House is therefore more cheerful than it has been for weeks and looks at the anti-gas doors being fitted downstairs and the sandbags being heaped on our basement windows with amusement.' The amusement did not last long; throughout September the mood in London had grown blacker, and Hitler's image was booed when he appeared on a cinema screen; men who had been accustomed to raise their hats as they walked past the Cenotaph now did so even when travelling in a bus; a couple of hundred yards away a crowd of spectators stood each day outside 10 Downing Street, waiting for the worst. Men and women streamed to the Soldiers' Corner in Westminster Abbey: typists from Whitehall, clerks, nurses off night duty in their white aprons and caps. Among them, unattended and unrecognised, had been Mrs Neville Chamberlain.

Then, on 28 September, her husband had made his dramatic announcement that he had been invited to fly to Munich to meet Hitler and make one final bid for peace. A few feared that there was treachery in the air, the Czechs were to be sacrificed to save the skins of the British and French, but most Londoners were conscious only of hope renewed. And when Chamberlain came back clutching his precious piece of paper and proclaiming peace in our time, there were few who questioned the price that had been paid. Bernard Kops, a boy in Jewish Stepney, saw a woman brandishing a newspaper. 'It sounded as if she was shouting "Piss in our time". I wondered what on earth she was talking about.' He soon found out and was assured that Chamberlain was a hero. Somebody said he was 'partly a Yiddish fellow. Anybody we revered had Jewish blood somewhere.'

Yet doubts there were – doubts as to the permanence of the settlement as well as its morality. Shelagh Morrison-Bell, daughter of a Tory MP, was at first as enthusiastic as Bernard Kops. On 1 October, she recorded, she saw 'a most touching sight. As I passed the Horse Guards' Parade I saw a large crowd, so I stopped. It was Mrs Chamberlain making her way to Downing Street with policemen all round her and everyone surging round her and shaking her hand *in complete silence*. Everyone's heart was too full to speak and Mrs Chamberlain was finding it very difficult herself not to cry. The silent gratitude of the crowd for the wife of the saviour of civilisation was terribly touching.' But within forty-eight hours second thoughts began to obtrude. 'It can't really mean a thing . . . Can we trust Hitler? Do we fancy a close pact with a Jew-baiter and religious persecutor?'

3

'Smells, paints, steel and black material'

THOUGH SHELAGH MORRISON-BELL was ahead of the public mood, 1939 saw a steady growth in those who accepted that the so-called settlement had provided no more than a breathing space. For a while the appeasers rejoiced over the victory won by their champion, Chamberlain. The Archbishop of Canterbury enraged his chaplain, Canon Don, by alluding to 'the so-called crisis of September, as much as to say, "I cannot conceive what all the fuss was about." ' Superficially most Londoners seemed to share the Archbishop's myopia. Charles Ritchie, a young Canadian diplomat, arrived from the United States to find the capital 'less concerned with the likelihood of war than the Washington I had quitted. We were permitted, even encouraged, to hope that the danger had passed. Whether anyone fully believed this is another matter.' He was shrewd enough to detect the disquiet just below the surface. At almost the same moment the London correspondent of the *New York Times* reported that he found the capital's 'nervousness more acute than anyone could remember at the time of crisis in the previous September . . . The Stock Market was peculiarly volatile.' Rumours were flying everywhere, wrote Beverley Baxter in the *Sunday Graphic*. 'Have we gone a little mad in Britain?' To those who frequented neither the stock exchange nor West End clubs, but a pub in Lambeth or a Women's Institute in Shepherd's Bush, the people seemed far from volatile and the rumours more likely to concern football matches or film stars than the incidence of war. But the nagging uncertainty was there.

In March the Germans took over the rump of Czechoslovakia. At a luncheon party Charles Ritchie heard a fellow guest say, 'It may seem cynical, but I really cannot get excited over this. I do dislike all this sentimentality about the Czechs.' This point of view, commented Ritchie, seemed to be general among 'the people one meets at dinner'. Even among the 99.99 per cent of Londoners whom Ritchie did not meet at dinner, the majority would probably have tacitly condoned German aggression provided it was not towards the West. Yet the inarticulate mass of the population, who still prayed for peace and dreaded war, was beginning to feel that its hopes were vain. It might be a matter of weeks, months, even years but, unless there was a dramatic and unexpected change of heart among the German leadership, war had become inevitable. Robert Bruce Lockhart, journalist and former diplomat, noticed that Londoners seemed more resigned to war than they had been in September 1938; men 'who had cheered Munich now even refused to drink German wines and German beers'. Covent Garden put on Smetana's *Bartered Bride* in a well-intentioned gesture of solidarity with the victimised Czechs, but marred the occasion by allowing it to be sung in German.

The visitor to London in the summer of 1939 could have been excused for missing this undercurrent of opinion. The wealthy and well connected seemed as preoccupied as usual with the delights of the London season. Ritchie observed in wonder the parades of debutantes, the feathered and flowered hats: 'The London season seems unrealistic in the face of anti-gas precautions and evacuation orders. Snobbery must indeed be a lusty plant that grows even on the edge of the precipice.' But it was not only in the gilded ghettoes of Kensington and Mayfair that talk of gas or evacuation was rarely heard. The leaflets which cascaded through the letter boxes of every London home, warning and advising about the threats ahead, were largely ignored; immediately before war broke out only 17 per cent of those living in Hampstead and Highgate and 14 per cent in Fulham could recognise the signal for an air-raid warning. The authorities were as reluctant as any citizen to admit the inevitability of war. A revue called *Going Gay* ('gay', in those far-off, innocent days, meaning no more than light of heart) featured two unspecified European dictators who 'on saluting in farewell made vulgar noises to each other' – the Lord Chamberlain's department took exception to a discourtesy likely to offend certain of Britain's European neighbours.

There was a conspiracy of silence, but as the summer wore on it became tattered. Cliff Beard, a schoolboy in Edmonton, remembered the approach of war as a mystery, discussed *sotto voce* by his parents as being unsuitable for children's ears. He understood vaguely that war would be a bad thing, but could not help finding the concept agreeably exciting. The influx of refugees from the continent made it increasingly difficult to ignore what was going on. Since 1933 some 29,000 refugees from Germany had been admitted to Britain, of whom all but 4000 had remained. Most, particularly those prominent in the worlds of art and science, had stayed in London. The Warburg Institute and Library, for instance, moved *en bloc* to London and found a temporary new home in Thames House near the Houses of Parliament. A Free German League of Culture had been founded in Hampstead in 1938. The intellectual life of the capital was immeasurably enriched by this inflow of new knowledge and new ideas, but the Home Office, conscious as ever that it was the guardian of Britain's gates, played a grudging role. When twelve Jews from Czechoslovakia arrived at Croydon on 29 March 1939, the immigration authorities declared that, as they were sponsored by no recognised refugee organisation, they must be sent back. The Czechs protested that this would condemn them to the concentration camps and almost certain death, the pilot refused to take off, public opinion was roused; in the end the British Committee for Refugees agreed to act as sponsors and they were granted visas for three months.

On the whole, once in, the refugees were made welcome. There were grumbles about jobs being lost to cheap continental labour and parasites battening on the British taxpayer, but sympathy was the more usual reaction. On 16 February, however, came a presage of things to come. The main front-page story of London's *Evening Standard* bore the headline: HITLER'S GESTAPO EMPLOYING JEWS FOR SPYING IN ENGLAND! A member of the Gestapo, it seemed, had admitted that his organisation had 400 agents in Britain. Some of these were Jews, who had been bribed or blackmailed into spying on the country which had offered them refuge. The fear preoccupied many Britons that the foreigners within the walls would turn and rend them; Churchill in his history of the Second World War wrote that there were 20,000 organised German Nazis in England at the time: 'It would only have been in accord with their procedure in other friendly countries that the outbreak of war should be preceded by a sharp prelude of sabotage and murder.'

Though the ponderous personality of the Regional Commissioner, Sir John Anderson, failed to invest the process with any conspicuous urgency, a great deal was going on in London to prepare for war. Most of the planning took place within the walls of official buildings, whether those of government or the LCC, but some activity at least was apparent to the average citizen. Shortly after the Munich crisis, for example, the boroughs were asked by the Home Office to turn the open trenches in the parks into permanent shelters, lined and roofed with steel or concrete and covered with three feet of earth. Some complied; in Clapham the work had been completed by the end of the year. Others were more dilatory. In January 1939 the *Evening Standard* sounded the alarm. If you were in central London and the sirens went, it asked, where would you run for cover? Not into the trenches in Hyde Park certainly; they had not been touched since the previous autumn and anyone rash enough to take refuge in them would be up to his or her waist in mud. Not into the nearest building because, except in those rare cases where a specially constructed shelter had been provided, it would probably collapse when the first bombs fell. Not into the Underground, for that would be closed. Plans for deep shelters had been shelved, the blueprints for evacuation had been allowed to gather dust. Worst of all, 'Nobody knows how many gas-masks still work'; many were said to have deteriorated through damp or heat.

So far as public shelters were concerned, the *Standard* had a point. The government, as a matter of policy, was still opposed to the provision of deep shelters or the use of the Underground. As for surface shelters, it saw its role as being to advise, to encourage, to provide some modest financial support, but on the whole to leave the work to the local authorities or private individuals. Public response was unsurprisingly patchy. Some work was done. The senior boys at Bishopsholt School in Hillingdon spent part of their summer holidays digging a large shelter trench along the side of the playing field. In Lambeth Palace, the crypt of the chapel was shored up for use as a public shelter which it was hoped would be proof against anything except a direct hit from a large bomb. 'It is lamentable to think that after 700 years of peaceful existence the crypt should now have to be transformed into a place of refuge from the terror of the skies,' wrote Canon Don mournfully. Across the river the Queen visited the shelters and gas-proof rooms being prepared in the basement of Buckingham Palace. Steel girders converted five hundred yards of corridor space below the building into a virtually impregnable redoubt.

The government seemed more ready to prepare shelters for its own high command than for the citizenry. Alexander Cadogan, Permanent Under Secretary at the Foreign Office, complained that he was constantly having to shift personnel to and fro to allow access to the new 'War Room' being constructed in the basement; in early January the *Evening Standard* reported 'furious drilling and clanging' in King Charles Street and beneath the quadrangles of the Treasury and Foreign Office. The Central Telegraph Office in West Norwood had to make do with 'great steel shutters' for protecting its windows from blast, but the price in noise and inconvenience was hardly smaller: 'We live in an atmosphere of smells, paints, steel and black material intensified by the heat,' wrote one of the secretaries, Irene Byers.

Most members of the public were expected to make do with what they could rig up at home. The Anderson shelter, called after Sir John but owing nothing to his inspiration, was simple to manufacture and erect and remarkably cheap: two curved sections of corrugated steel bolted together at the top and sunk three feet into the ground, with an entrance protected by a steel shield and earth embankment. It was recommended that the roof should be covered with at least eighteen inches of soil; some users supplied more, many less. The result offered protection for up to half a dozen adults against virtually anything except a direct hit. The most noticeable design flaw, which quickly became apparent, was that the shelters were not provided with drainage. Many of them flooded at the first onset of rain and endless baling-out was needed to keep them habitable. Another problem was that they could be installed only in houses with a garden; in the cramped East End such luxuries were rare. Nevertheless, hundreds of thousands of Londoners availed themselves of the offer of a free Anderson (from October 1939 those with an income of more than £250 a year had to pay a small amount).

'Big Hearted' Arthur Askey and Richard 'Stinker' Murdoch, heroes of the BBC's most popular pre-war comedy series, *Band Waggon*, received their Anderson shelter in the summer of 1939. They bickered acrimoniously over how to put it together but finally concluded: 'Big and Stinker must agree, Now they've joined the ARP.' Most Londoners eschewed do-it-yourself, but the contractors whom the LCC employed for the installation work seem sometimes to have been singularly disaffected. The workmen who did the job for George and Helena Britton in Walthamstow 'talked of the different MPs who had interests in the firms who made the shelter, also that they did not believe anything they read except the *Daily Worker*. One had been in the last war and said, "Whatever happens, I'm not doing anything this time," and the others said it was all a dirty filthy business, and didn't want anything to do with it.'

The beneficiaries in this case were almost equally disgruntled. 'Our air-raid shelter arrived yesterday and made Mother feel quite ill for a time,' wrote Mrs Britton. Three men had been in the garden for the best part of two days digging a hole to put it in. 'My personal opinion is that the whole performance is merely a dodge to put the population in a complacent vein and so save them getting out of hand.' Irene Byers's mother was still more sceptical when the men arrived to install a shelter in their garden in West Norwood: 'Mum doesn't want us to have an Anderson. She says it would be better to be bombed in the warm than to get pneumonia.' It would not be long before both Mrs Britton and Mrs Byers were profoundly grateful for their Anderson, which saved the lives of many thousands of Londoners when the air attacks began.

Some people believed a superior product could be acquired privately. Glazier and Sons of Savile Row advertised in *The Times* their special brand of bomb-proof shelter, designed by 'a pre-eminent technical expert who has made a careful study of the actual conditions of aerial warfare in Barcelona'. Others evolved their own solutions. John Geer was a teenager living in Woolwich, whose father was convinced the main danger came from flying glass. Mr Geer turned the coal hole into a shelter by bricking up the outside door and breaking a hole through to the scullery. There the family was to sleep, with only a thin slate roof between them and the raiders overhead.

The authorities themselves rarely engaged in the work of building shelters. In January 1939 the Croydon Borough Council went it alone and approved the conversion of a car park into a shelter that would take 30,000 people. It was a bold move, since the work would cost £300,000 and the Home Office showed no sign of wishing to make a contribution. This was not only meanness; there was real uncertainty about the kind of shelters that should be built. When some months later the Finsbury Council also decided to go ahead with the construction of underground shelters, Haldane told Anderson that they were courting disaster. If a half-ton bomb were to fall in the entrance to an underground shelter it would kill everyone inside. 'I do not suggest that you should put 7000 people inside a Finsbury shelter, let off a bomb and see if it kills them all,' wrote Haldane magnanimously. 'It is a matter for scientific investigation.' The trouble was that scientific investigation was a lengthy business, and though the Munich settlement might have bought Britain a little time, that time was running out. It was not until war was imminent that the government accepted its responsibilities and took over as public shelters a number of solid buildings, vaults and cellars. At the same time it urged local authorities to begin a programme of building surface shelters able to accommodate up to fifty people each. Even then the government stuck to its conviction that the Underground would be needed to handle casualties and other abnormal traffic and should not be used for shelter.

When it came to civil defence, the government proved more effective. Not everyone agreed. It was displaying a woeful lack of energy, complained the Chelsea Borough Council – a particularly unkind cut since Samuel Hoare, the Home Secretary, was their local member. Anderson had come in for some harsh criticism, and a group of ARP workers refused to meet him because he had evaded their questions at a rally at the Albert Hall the previous night. When he got back from a holiday in January 1939, he was threatened by mutiny; according to the *Evening Standard*, several of his own officials had joined in the chorus of abuse: 'They said they had not yet been asked for their advice, even though Sir John Anderson had now been in charge for eight weeks.'

It was more a matter of style than substance. Anderson was in fact constructing a sound organisation which was to withstand the batterings of the blitz, but he lacked the public relations skills to demonstrate this to his own subordinates, let alone to the outside world. His responsibilities were daunting: he was in charge of the Metropolitan Police District, the City and the remainder of the counties of Hertfordshire, Essex, Surrey and Kent. He was appointed in September 1938 and at once named Harold Scott, the Chairman of the Prison Commission, as his Principal Officer. Scott stayed with the prisons until February 1939 and then took over, styling himself Administration Officer, 'a title that I invented to indicate that my powers were more extensive than those of Principal Officers in other regions'. Sir George Gater, the Clerk of the LCC, was appointed Chief ARP Officer and Sir Philip Game, the Commissioner of Metropolitan Police, doubled as Chief Executive Officer so as to maintain order in the whole area. The region was divided into a number of groups, and then into boroughs, which were the principal operational unit of civil defence, each with its own report and Control Centre, located usually in the town hall. The borough in its turn was divided into districts containing about 10,000 people and a score of wardens' posts. Most posts were manned by three to six wardens, though some were considerably larger.

Scott considered Caxton Hall and other large buildings as headquarters for the fledgling organisation and finally opted for the Geological Museum in South Kensington. This had the advantage of being steel-framed, spacious and easily accessible. To the outsider the choice seemed eccentric since the walls were largely glass, but by a curious freak of chance, scarcely a pane of glass was broken throughout the war.

Two Regional Commissioners, Sir Ernest Gowers and Admiral Evans, were then appointed (a third, the politician Euan Wallace, joined them in May 1940). Gowers was a senior civil servant, scholarly and a skilled administrator, whose *Plain Words*, a fierce assault on the dragons of gobbledygook and jargon, was to rejoice the heart of every lover of well-written English when he published it after the war. Evans was a naval hero, noisy, extrovert, endlessly good-humoured, who appeared the first morning on horseback and never ceased to delight and outrage his colleagues by his extravagance and informality. He was the front man; it took him almost a year to visit all the 95 boroughs or local authorities within the region, but where he had been he was never forgotten. Scott was occasionally infuriated by Evans's propensity for ignoring rules and cutting red tape but admired and liked him and saw how much he would contribute to morale when the bombardment started.

The wardens were the front-line infantry, the men and women

on whose courage and determination would depend the fate of the capital. 'Thanks largely to the wardens,' wrote Evans with character- istic bluffness, 'all that rot about standoffish "Don't-speak-to-me- without-an-introduction" Englishmen has gone with the wind. The Wardens' Service, to my mind, is the greatest community movement we have ever seen.' But first the service had to be assembled. In Fulham, according to one report compiled for Mass Observation,* recruitment was slow except at moments of crisis. Volunteers tended to be male, middle-aged and middle class; the unskilled working class provided the fewest, probably more because of transport prob- lems and the physical strain of their daily occupations than for lack of patriotism. Patriotism, in fact, was rarely specified as such by those asked their reasons for joining the service: 'To do my bit', 'To be in it somehow or other', were the most common replies. In Bromley, where the target for recruitment was 1000, the service was still 350 short by early 1939. A vigorous recruiting campaign was launched and, at a public meeting held at St Andrew's Church Hall, Burnt Ash Lane, the wardens dressed up in their yellow gas- proof oilskins with boots and respirators. This evidently exercised strong appeal – forty members of the audience signed up there and then. The eventual target was a force of 200,000 wardens for the whole of London, of whom some 16,000 would be full-time and paid (an ungenerous £3 a week). All over the area recruitment stepped up as the year wore on, but there was still a shortfall when war came.

Almost imperceptibly the tempo quickened, until by the late summer a hectic busy-ness was apparent all over London, as if an ant-heap had been stirred by some giant foot. 'We are all blacking- out, stuffing up cracks, laying in sand etc,' the writer Rose Macaulay told her sister. 'I think this is a good thing, as it gives people something they feel useful to do, and may actually diminish effects of raids, and therefore lessen fear and prevent collapse of nerves in crowded districts.' Sand bulked large in many such activities, whether placed to hand for extinguishing fires or crammed into bags to protect doors and windows. The Geological Survey identified twenty sites in the region where large deposits of sand were readily

*Some information about this remarkable organisation will be found in the
  bibliography.

accessible and every mechanical digger within fifty miles was hired to dig out the precious substance. In Hyde Park, the site of the 1851 Exhibition was excavated to a depth of forty feet; on Hampstead Heath, wrote Scott, the diggers created 'a miniature Cheddar Gorge, which glowed in the sunshine of that wonderful autumn in warm lines of ochre, orange and red'. A stream of heavy lorries transported the sand to distribution points around the area; among them were observed 'a small Austin car with a tiny trailer attached. Beside the driver sat his small daughter. When their turn came they drew up beside the giant drag, received a great dollop of sand on their trailer, and drove happily away.'

Rose Macaulay's view that vigorous self-help would insulate the citizen against the horrors to come co-existed with a secret belief, held by many of those in authority as well as ordinary Londoners, that their efforts were to little purpose. The Dean of St Paul's, in the summer of 1939, sought guidance on whether the cathedral doors should be opened during raids so that it could serve as a shelter. For a long time no answer was forthcoming, then a harassed official rang to say, 'I don't think it matters much what you do. If there is a raid tonight we expect 30,000 casualties.' (The Dean also sought advice on how to camouflage the dome, but 'no genius arose able to make it resemble a farm yard, or a hay rick'.)

In May the Fulham ARP Committee ordered the digging of long trenches in the cemetery of Sheen to accommodate the thousand or so corpses expected to need disposal after each raid, while in the LCC it was assumed that there would not be enough timber for coffins – mass dumping of the dead in lime pits or even in the Channel was envisaged. The Mental Health Emergency Committee reported that psychiatric casualties might exceed physical by three to one; three to four million people would suffer from hysteria or other neurotic conditions. But the consoling voice of common sense was still to be heard. When the officers of the Home Publicity Division met to discuss action to counteract panic resulting from air-raids, 'Lady Grigg said that the most comforting thing – at least where women were concerned – was to have a cup of tea and get together to talk things over. This was agreed to be a most valuable suggestion.'

For ten days during the Munich crisis, and then again in August

1939, Londoners' travel was disrupted by work under the Thames. Somebody had calculated that a single bomb penetrating the tunnels between Charing Cross and Waterloo could lead to the flooding of half London's Underground system – from Shepherd's Bush to Liverpool Street, from Euston to Clapham Common. No one dared predict whether trains would act as a cork or be swept along by the flood, but all agreed that the damage would take a year at least to repair. Twenty-five flood gates were therefore installed, with other safety devices on water mains and sewers. As it turned out, it was not until September 1944 that an underwater tunnel was penetrated, but the precautions proved their worth when only a section of 200 yards was affected.

More visibly, the first barrage balloons appeared over London shortly after Munich; sixty-two feet long and twenty-five in diameter, the 'blimps', as they were usually called, were designed to fly at up to 5000 feet and thus force the German bomber to a height where aiming would be difficult. Forty were initially deployed, of which five promptly broke adrift. One dragged its cable across an electric railway, causing a half hour's delay. 'London's Air Death Web', a journalist called them; Londoners gave them more prosaic names – Flossie and Blossom, Chelsea's first two blimps were christened.

Chelsea was one of the first boroughs to experience a full-blooded civil defence exercise; 400 wardens were on duty and the Control Centre at the town hall was manned. It was an occasion to test the imagination. Imaginary shelters were designated by roped-off enclosures, and eight minutes after the siren sounded in Sloane Square imaginary bombers scattered imaginary bombs around the area and fire engines dashed off to deal with imaginary fires. In Peter Jones, the department store, everyone took cover, except for one uncooperative customer who announced that if no one would serve her she would take her business elsewhere. She stormed out but was corralled by a warden and confined to one of the imaginary shelters in the square. There she might have seen the recumbent form of long-term Chelsea resident and writer, Frances Faviell, who had been designated a casualty and was being swathed in bandages. Beside her stood her housekeeper, holding the family dachshund. An officious warden pointed out that dogs were not allowed in shelters, but the housekeeper retorted that real dogs were allowed into imaginary shelters and, anyway, what was the warden going to do about it? 'Lot of tommy rot! Won't be no air-raids here. All this silly play-acting,' Frances Faviell heard her fellow casualties grumble. 'They had voiced the thoughts of many who believed what they wanted to believe. There would be no air-raids on England! It was unthinkable.' A little later, in Battersea, at a similar exercise, a 'bombing car' drove around the area with a warden throwing out different coloured tennis balls: yellow and green denoting gas; red, high explosive; those with red stripes were incendiary bombs.

It was all good fun, and even the wardens sometimes failed to take it altogether seriously. An incident closer to the real thing occurred on 4 August when a gas main exploded and blasted a crater fifty yards wide at the corner of Godliman Street and Knight-rider Street in the City. A block of offices collapsed, hundreds of windows were broken and debris was blown as far as Cannon Street station, more than 400 yards away. The photographs of the damage gave a new seriousness to the exercise held a week later when eight formations of 'enemy' bombers attacked London. Everyone was asked to stay up till 12.30 a.m. so as to ensure that the blackout was working properly; people made a party of it and surged around the streets savouring the new experience. Superintendent R. K. Smith, in charge of the West End division, climbed Marble Arch to inspect the blackout and commented, 'London looked like a Gruy-ère cheese with a candle behind it.' The RAF pilots pointed out that no object was served by blotting out the lights of London when the ways to its centre were clearly signalled by trains and cars. The signals were not clear enough for George Hitchen, a bus driver, who was so tired after driving through a night of blackout that he announced he would do better to join the army. 'You stick to your bus, love,' advised his wife. 'At least they won't be firing things at you, even if there is a war.' It was a remark Mr Hitchen was to remember fifteen months later when his bus was almost destroyed by blast. The operation was deemed a success: 'The keenness of the defenders,' announced the Air Ministry, 'aided by the blackout and the commendable efficiency of the Observer Corps throughout the intensive air attack, saved London from destruction.'

In another exercise on 17 August, 150 French bombers, flying in arrowhead formations at a height of 1500 feet, 'raided' the capital. Spitfires, diving at 400 mph, swept down on them. The main attack was deemed to have been frustrated, but some raiders returned that night. *A Midsummer Night's Dream* was being played in the open-air theatre in Regent's Park. Puck's speech, 'Captain of our fairy band', coincided with the searchlights and the hum of aeroplanes. 'Puck threw back his head,' recorded the writer F. Tennyson Jesse, 'gazed at the skies and said, "Lord, what fools these mortals be." And, believe me or not, in the little silence that followed . . . the hyenas laughed from the Zoo.'

By now there can have been few Londoners who did not privately accept that the count-down to war had begun. On 24 August Parliament passed the Emergency Powers (Defence) Act, and in the next few days a host of new regulations affected every facet of national life. The Tory MP and diarist Chips Channon contrasted the mood with that of the Munich crisis. 'I suppose it is like getting married,' he reflected, 'the second time it is impossible to work up the same excitement. Certainly London is quiet and almost indifferent to what may happen. There is a frightening calm.' There were fewer sightseers around Downing Street; what crowds there were included many Czech and German refugees. 'Gosh, but you people are cool,' said Louis Kopling from New York. 'One would never think there was an emergency. I arrived from the States last Monday. There was far more excitement over there.'

Shades of the prison house began to close. The television service went off the air, allegedly because its signal would make life easy for incoming German bombers. Val Gielgud, writer, producer and brother of the actor, John, was working on his first film for television – Somerset Maugham's *The Circle*. At noon on 1 September he was told that the television headquarters at Alexandra Palace was closing down immediately. As he put down the phone a messenger arrived with some props: two tennis racquets and some balls. 'I have occasionally wondered what happened to them,' he wrote. 'If they were ever collected, or if they remain there to this day, forgotten relics of a dead world.' At the same time the BBC announced that radio programmes would be restricted to a single channel.

Housewives were advised by the *Evening Standard* to lay in a reserve stock of food. 'This is not a matter of mere self-interest,' they were assured. 'It will lighten the burden on transport in the event of war.' Not many complied. Those who had stockpiled at the time of Munich did not feel inclined to look foolish a second time and, whatever the *Standard* might say, to hoard seemed vaguely unpatriotic. People were more concerned about what if anything they could do to help. 'Squads of women' were working in shifts in Lord Derby's house in Stratford Place, making nightshirts for hospitals. Lady Crewe, who was in charge, announced that the work would probably 'be extended later to include the making of bandages and swabs'. The young had different priorities. Hundreds of couples flocked to the register offices to try to arrange a rapid marriage; the registrars worked overtime to cope with the queues.

Those with designated tasks took up their duties; police leave was cancelled, driving tests were suspended since the examiners were 'temporarily engaged on special defence duties'. For those with nothing to do – the old, the sick, the children – the question of whether or not to leave London became urgent. Hospitals began to clear their wards: St Thomas's had 600 patients; 300 mild or convalescent cases were at once sent home; 150 were designated as too ill to move; the rest were prepared for evacuation to Brighton in case of war. Plans had been made to move the parliamentarians to Stratford-on-Avon: the Commons to the theatre, the Lords to the conference hall. Two clerks had earlier been sent down to find accommodation, and came to the conclusion that Members could be asked to sleep in double rooms but not in double beds. Now MPs were told of their possible destination and even issued with luggage labels. Businesses similarly prepared to move to safer areas, some even began to send papers and key staff to the country. 'Will the air-raids really be as bad as we have been led to believe?' Vivienne Hall speculated. 'Will our office stay as at present in the City or will we start making evacuation arrangements as every other large office now has done?'

The first grindings of the mighty machine which was to evacuate four million mothers and children really brought home to Londoners the imminence of war. The intention was to get them out within four days, accepting that for some of that time London might be under heavy attack. What happened to the evacuees at the other end was a secondary consideration. The scheme, suggested the Socialist and pioneer sociologist Margaret Cole in the *Evacuation Survey*, failed to appeal because it was drawn up 'by minds that were military, male and middle-class'. Only males would have assumed so confidently that wives would be happy to desert their husbands and only the middle classes could have supposed that children would happily be parted from their parents. The criticism was not wholly unfair but the evacuation scheme assumed that London would be the victim of ferocious, all-out assault, and that if the children remained they would die in their tens of thousands. If such an attack had come, little would have been heard of the discontent of wives and children; as it was, there was plenty of time for everyone to dwell on the shortcomings of the scheme.

Evacuation was never intended to be anything but voluntary: 'Obviously it would be completely unjust, and indeed impossible, to go down to the homes of the people and begin driving the people out of them,' said the Minister of Health. Families who were not able to tolerate the idea of separation could always show their feelings by staying put. The majority did not. 'Keep calm,' was Herbert Morrison's parting message to an early wave of evacuees who left on 1 September. 'Keep a cheerful British smile on your face . . . Good luck, and a safe return to dear old London.'

The lights were going out all over Britain. Harold Nicolson left his club after dinner and was startled to find 'a perfectly black city. Nothing could be more dramatic or give one more of a shock than to leave the familiar Beefsteak and to find outside not the glitter of all the sky-signs, but a pall of black velvet.' To many wardens the blackness was far from perfect: 'Put out that light' was a constant refrain as they roamed the city in search of chinks left by unpractised hands. The move towards wartime conditions was under way, even though war was not declared for another two days. Charles Ritchie, dining at his club, Boodles, noted with mild surprise that all but two of the waiters had been called up and that, for the first time in history, members were not required to put on evening dress. 'Telegrams are not delivered,' he complained, 'telephones not answered, taxis do not run. I suppose once the war gets under way we shall get back to more normal conditions.'

4

The First Alert

AT 11 A.M. ON 3 September the plaintive voice of Neville Chamberlain informed the nation that it was at war. At 11.27 the air-raid sirens in London announced that a raid was imminent. In fact a stray French aircraft had blundered into Britain's defences and triggered a false alarm. To a population inured to the idea that war must mean devastating bombardment from the skies, however, the alert seemed confirmation of their expectations.

Few who heard the warning in London that day ever forgot where they were or what they were doing. 'My wife commented favourably upon the German promptitude and precision,' remembered Winston Churchill, 'and we went up to the flat top of the house to see what was going on. Around us on every side . . . rose the roofs and spires of London. About them were already slowly rising thirty or forty cylindrical balloons. We gave the Government a good mark for this evident sign of preparation and as the quarter of an hour's notice which we had been led to expect we should receive was now running out we made our way to the shelter.' That afternoon they went to the Westminster flat of their son-in-law, the comedian Vic Oliver, where they drank to victory in champagne.

The reactions of the populace at large were not dissimilar. People showed a disconcerting inclination to stand around gaping at the skies when they should have been taking cover. At a house in Fulham the owners opened the windows, turned off the gas at the mains, fetched their gas-masks and sallied out to see what was going on. 'All along the street people were standing at their gates, and many decided it was a practice, but the wardens ordered people indoors, though hardly any followed their instructions. Curiosity in many cases overcame fear; people stood together at their open front doors or looked up at the sky with a curious blend of apprehension and interest in this new menace from the sky.'

The fear was there, though usually well concealed. For Virginia

Cunard, a young woman who was to find that war was a liberation from the shackles of her class and her family, the first alert was terrifying – nothing was ever so bad again. Gwladys Cox, a widow living in modest comfort in West Hampstead, went directly to the shelter. 'My knees were knocking together with weakness,' she wrote in her diary, 'while I stifled a strong desire to be sick. I was not exactly afraid, but nervous that I should be afraid; startled and bewildered; glimpsing dimly that, already, all my known world was toppling about my ears.' It put the fear of God into us, testified an auxiliary fireman from Whitechapel, 'I've never been so frightened in all my life.' Expectation of a gas attack was one of the most potent causes of alarm. The German-Jewish refugee who worked as a maid in Theodora FitzGibbon's London home insisted on donning her mask as soon as the siren sounded. 'The flaps of rubber around her cheeks made loud farting noises as she breathed.' Theodora FitzGibbon ventured: '*Keinen gas. Nehmen Sie es ab*,' in her best schoolgirl German. The maid was unimpressed and kept it on. People took refuge in mundane activities. Stanley Rothwell, historian of Lambeth during the war, put on the kettle for a cup of tea. The Greek family who lived in the flat above him protested that only the English would be so unfeeling as to drink tea at such a time. 'Might as well do that as to wail,' Rothwell observed phlegmatically. But he was far from feeling calm: 'I believe that if the Germans had raided us then, panic would have defeated us. We were not prepared. We could not believe it would happen.'

On the whole the veneer of composure was carefully preserved. In Holland Park when the siren sounded people stepped up their pace but showed no panic. Only when police on bicycles rode by calling 'Take Cover!' did passers-by 'begin to run frantically . . . People in streets diving for any open door they can see.' Most Londoners felt that running, frantic or not, was bad form. Canon Don was halfway over Westminster Bridge and decided that he must take shelter in the House of Commons 'and if need be die with the Speaker in the Mother of Parliaments'. But he would do so with dignity: 'I must not run so I walked fast.' Those taking refuge in public shelters queued up politely and avoided any impression of hysteria. At the Clapham Congregational Church in Grafton Square, the Revd A. Halfpenny was so engrossed in his sermon that he missed the siren altogether; his audience did not, they shuffled uneasily in their pews, but stuck it out.

The wardens in Fulham seem to have been less successful than most in shooing their parishioners into the shelters. Raich Carter, the Sunderland footballer, rushed out of the Russell Hotel to see what was going on, but was at once chased back and, with the rest of his team, made to sit on the floor on the third storey, believed to be the safest level for flying glass. In Walworth the public even began to climb down the ladders into a half-constructed and roofless public shelter. Angrily, a warden tore down the Air Raid Shelter notice which the Borough Engineer had prematurely displayed.

Once within the shelters, imagination ran riot. At the BBC Joseph Macleod, the news reader, was driven from his studio by the internal alarm system, 'the loudest, most ear-tearing, most soul-lacerating things I had ever heard'. Immured in the concert hall, he and his fellow refugees began to hear bangs and bumps, some distant, some much nearer. There was a debate about the direction of the bombing but all agreed that London was under severe attack. Macleod emerged uncertain whether he would find Portland Place a mass of rubble or the devastation in some other part of London. Instead, all was calm. 'I can only suppose that the bumps and bangs were the shutting of different doors.' Even without auditory aids, rumour could do an impressive job. Constantine FitzGibbon, who was later to write a classic history of the blitz, was rung up by a young woman shortly after the all-clear. There had been an appalling raid, she reported; Chelsea, where she lived, was inviolate but the East End was in ruins. Thousands were dead.

That evening the siren went again. George Jellicoe, a young naval officer, was staying at Claridges. He dutifully filed down to the shelter, then, at the entrance, realised he had forgotten his gas-mask. For a moment he hesitated, wondering whether to turn back into what he feared might at any moment become an inferno. A footman volunteered to collect the mask for him and Jellicoe, to his eternal shame, accepted. He made up for it by spending the follow-ing day of precious leave filling sandbags outside the hotel. One false alarm was stimulating; two perhaps a joke; more seemed intolerable. Alexander Cadogan was woken by a siren at about 3 a.m. on 4 September: 'Went down to basement. Damned nuisance. All clear after about half an hour.' Next day it happened again, and so it

went on, 'Another of these "electrical defects". It's an outrage!'
When the 3 a.m. alarm was heard at Lambeth Palace, Canon Don
hurried to the Archbishop's bedroom. He found Lang already up,
'fumbling his way into a purple cassock. I exhorted him to hurry
and mentioned the desirability of inserting his teeth.' Once arrived
in the crypt, Lang 'took a seat at a safe distance from his fellow
refugees and sat miserably for a while, protesting that he had been
dragged to this dungeon quite unnecessarily'.

As each warning seemed more likely to be a false alarm, so fear
waned and irritation grew at the waste of time, the inconvenience
and most of all the loss of sleep. But the prevailing sentiment of
those first few days was one of unity in the face of peril; everyone
was in it together and had to make the best of it. At the Central
Telegraph Office on 4 September Irene Byers recorded, 'Everybody
and all familiar things and jobs seemed so unreal; we even spoke
differently to each other as if we should soon be parted, perhaps for
ever – uncanny but understandable . . . Had that strange but familiar
feeling which always comes with any crisis that we are all *one* just
belonging to one another.' It was a feeling that became even more
familiar when London confronted its real crisis a year or so in the
future.

5

The Phoney War

'I SUPPOSE,' Charles Ritchie had written, 'once the war gets under way we shall get back to more normal conditions.' He was right, but it took a little time. The life of London in the months after the declaration of war was shaped by the conviction of the authorities that devastating air-raids would come quickly and that large groups of people would provide an easy target for the enemy. The moral was obvious: send away everyone who could be spared and discourage those who remained from gathering together.

There were, of course, limits to what could be done if the life of the capital was not to be drastically impaired. The stock exchange was closed, ostensibly to allow it to perfect its air-raid precautions, in fact because the authorities hoped the brokers would disperse and carry out whatever business was still possible from some provincial city. The stockbrokers, in top hats and with their gas-mask cases slung over their shoulders, milled around Throgmorton Street, making informal bargains and reminding Anthony Weymouth, the writer and broadcaster, of the royal enclosure at Ascot. The exchange was open again within a week. The banks were shut for only a day, while the National Safe Deposit in Westminster did roaring business as Londoners queued to put their valuables in what they hoped would be security.

Places of entertainment seemed an easier target for the government. First instructions were that nothing should be allowed to open unless it could be deemed essential to national life. 'It is interesting that churches are specifically excepted by government regulations from the places in which large numbers of people are likely to congregrate,' wrote the journalist and future politician Tom Driberg with mild cynicism, ' – a sadly realistic reflection of the emptiness of some of them.' Cinemas had no such luck. At the Granada, Clapham, they took down the canopy advertising Q Planes and substituted, SORRY, WE'RE CLOSED. KEEP SMILING. REOPENING

SOON. The Embassy, Notting Hill Gate, did not even offer this hope: CLOSED UNTIL FURTHER NOTICE, it announced. 'Nearest cinema open, Aberystwyth, 239 miles' (Aberystwyth being the only local authority in England and Wales which ignored the official guidelines and allowed its cinemas to open).

Bernard Shaw described the closing of all theatres and cinemas as 'a masterstroke of unimaginative stupidity', but some managements were relieved to be able to close their doors with a clear conscience. Even popular successes such as Ivor Novello's *The Dancing Years* had been playing to thin houses as war approached and by 2 September the stalls were so empty that Novello invited the public from the gallery to occupy the vacant seats. The disappearance of many reservists from among the actors and stage hands posed another problem. At the Grand Theatre, Croydon, where an Edgar Wallace thriller was being rehearsed, six prompt scripts had to be left on stools around the stage to help newcomers, while the producer doubled (or perhaps quadrupled) as scene-shifter, propsman and front-of-house manager. When the management felt confidence in the future of a show – as with Emlyn Williams's *The Corn is Green* – the cast were sent on tour until the position was clarified. Others perished, as did Michel St Denis's London Theatre Studios, an admirable training centre for actors, which closed when its director left to join the French Army.

Anything that required external floodlighting – greyhound racing and speedway in particular – was doomed until peace returned; 'for the duration' was a phrase of dread finality which was increasingly heard about this time. Wembley Stadium spent £300 painting its glass roof black; the police admitted that it was one of the best blacked-out places in town, but it had to close down just the same. The cricket season was anyway petering out at the end of the summer, but the immediate future of football seemed unpropitious: Arsenal and Queen's Park Rangers, for example, were clubs where almost all players volunteered for the services. The manager of one of the most popular West End dance halls called in his staff after the declaration of war and explained the situation: 'We all went into the ballroom and started taking the glass tops off the tables and clearing the room, making it ready as an air-raid shelter.' One of the few institutions to benefit was the public house, which even the most foolhardy government would hardly have dared to touch.

The West End pubs were doing a roaring trade, recorded Jane Gordon, wife of the author Charles Graves. 'All the men and women were singing "Tipperary" and the old war songs. Their voices sounded extraordinarily loud, coming out of the dark.'

Such privations could not last. 'Londoners are facing boredom,' wrote Tennyson Jesse. 'We have doubtless a few thousand people who would panic badly in an air-raid, but I think it is more deadly to subject several million people to black boredom.' The people *must* have some means of recreation if their morale were to be kept high. Canon Don noted in his diary, 'The dangers of long hours of darkness with nothing to do are obvious.' A delegation from the Cinematograph Exhibitors' Association went to County Hall to plead with Herbert Morrison to reopen the cinemas. He received them in his dressing gown, affability itself, and promised to do what he could to help. He kept his word. But some features of London life were beyond resuscitation. The Tower of London was converted to a war headquarters and prison for enemies of the state; its moat was adapted as a vegetable patch. The sentries at Buckingham Palace deserted their rich red uniforms for dingy battle dress; the horse-drawn delivery van of Scott's, the hatters, remained as elegant as ever, but the liveried coachmen and footmen exchanged cockaded toppers for tin hats. The Opera House at Covent Garden, anyway only open for a three-month annual season, closed to reopen eventually as a dance hall. It was, Dame Ninette de Valois points out sadly, the only opera house in Europe to shut for the whole war. Rotten Row in Hyde Park remained empty, the riding schools unused, the horses diverted to more utilitarian pursuits.

Many houses were deserted. The Duchess of Sutherland retreated from Hampden House; Londonderry House and Holland House were put into mothballs. 'It is sad that the houses of the great will never again open their hospitable doors,' mused Chips Channon wistfully. The houses of the slightly less great closed as well; in Belgrave Square thirteen out of forty-five private houses were for sale, seventeen out of thirty-seven in Hyde Park Gardens. A rich Greek couple in Mount Street turned their house into a hostel for servicemen; the cook and butler were thrown in to help run it. The traditional pleasure of window-shopping was restricted even though there were still goods to covet; in Bond Street the luxury shops 'boarded themselves up so that the stroller has to squint at pigskin and emeralds framed as though they were peepshows'. Prunier's restaurant painted its sandbags blue to match its woodwork, while a Westminster antique shop had its blackout shutters decorated with a mural featuring antique furniture, the owner and her Pekinese dog. Many of the Mayfair galleries closed for good; their glass roofs were now a hazard, while their more valuable pieces seemed likely to sell better in provincial cities or the United States.

Guy Fawkes night on 5 November passed without a rocket or a bonfire to be seen; a few squibs inside were the most permitted. Six days later there was no formal Remembrance Day ceremony at the Cenotaph, though Sir Ian Fraser, the blind chairman of St Dunstan's, laid a wreath, as did an equerry on behalf of the King. The reason for the cancellation was officially that a siren could not be sounded to herald the traditional two minutes' silence; a middle-aged London housewife identified what was perhaps an underlying reason, 'How bitter all those men and women are going to be who lost sons and husbands all for nothing.' That must have been the feeling of the woman who interrupted the wreath-laying with a shout of 'Hypocrites!' and had to be removed by a policeman, screaming abuse and brandishing her cane.

Kew Gardens closed for a few days, presumably for fear of the cascade of glass that might follow a bomb near the palm houses. It was well frequented throughout the war; even in 1942 there were 1.25 million visitors. Much war work was done there, notably on rubber substitutes. Certain African plants and two types of dandelion seemed hopeful; one of the latter yielded 17 per cent rubber. The botanists concocted a palatable marmalade from green walnuts, grew belladonna, colchicum and digitalis, and experimented with potato eyes instead of seed potatoes, thus saving bulky transportation. Stinging nettles were enlisted to make paper from their fibre, chlorophyll from their dried leaves and artificial silk from their woolly stems.

The zoo suffered more lasting damage. Chloroform was used to kill the poisonous and constricting snakes and the black widow spiders, while the aquarium was drained, since a direct hit would have released 200,000 gallons of water. Some fish were eaten, some bottled for museums, some found new homes; the manatees were shot. The pandas, mating elephants and a few other animals were evacuated to Whipsnade; the carnivores remained, though when an alert sounded riflemen patrolled the cages in case a bomb led to escapes. The zoo was open again by mid-September. Demoralised chimpanzees, pining for lack of attention and forced to pose for propaganda photographs showing them doing their bit for the war effort, put on a spectacular display of gymnastics to greet the returning visitors; the worst sufferers from the closure had been the pigeons and sparrows which had been looking for the handouts they were accustomed to receive from their patrons. Like Kew, the zoo never lost its popularity, with 1.6 million visitors in 1943, compared with two million before the war, and almost as many animals on display, including Polly Anna, a young reindeer given to British sailors in Russia and brought back by submarine. Like Kew too, it tried to contribute to the war effort; on its front lawn people were taught how to keep fowls in a confined space or to rear rabbits, bees, pigeons and silkworms.

Trenches had already changed the faces of the parks; now deck-chairs were banned as being likely to impede access. After much protest they were allowed back in Hyde Park in the spring of 1940, though grouped in compounds so as not to get in the way. They had to yield place, too, to a rash of allotments – 6000 in the parks, 30,000 in the London area. Four acres of Greenwich Park were put under cultivation, eleven on Primrose Hill, thirty in Bushey Park. The gardens of Kensington Palace were turned over to cabbages, while allotments jostled for space with anti-aircraft guns and barrage balloons on Hampstead Heath. 'We see posters exhorting all and sundry to Dig for Victory,' Mr Britton told his daughter-in-law in California. 'I tell you the allotment holders have suddenly become very important people, although I hear that some of the ground which has lately been turned into allotments is absolutely hopeless.' This was certainly the experience of Mr Geer, who tilled a stony desert near the barrage balloon site on Plumstead Common in Woolwich. 'The results were abysmal, but it did give us hearty exercise,' his son John reflected. 'It was also good entertainment for the balloon crews.'

Ed Murrow, the American broadcaster who became something of a national hero during the blitz, toured London one rainy Sunday afternoon in October. The tailors' windows, he noticed, were devoted to uniforms, women's shops featured heavy wool evening dresses and sturdy shoes. Some exhibited 'a new kind of women's wear – a sort of cover-all arrangement with zippers and a hood; one-piece affairs, easy to put on. They are to be worn when the siren sounds.' Bands of white paint marked trees, kerbs, letter boxes, lamp-posts: 'I wonder if anyone knows how many gallons of white paint have been used in London?' The police, in tin hats rather than traditional helmets, had lost some of their dignified solemnity. The plinths of many statues stood empty and Charles I was enveloped in a brick-and-timber carapace, but Nelson still surveyed the scene from the top of his column: 'He seems almost out of place without a tin helmet and a gas-mask.' To Stephen Spender, London's warlike garb that first September gave the capital a festive air: 'The sandbags on the side walks, the strips of paper on the windows, the balloons in the sky, are all sufficiently new in the bright sunlight to be interesting and almost gay.'

London was suffering economically from the war. Sir John Simon's budget on 27 September raised income tax from 5/- to 7/6d in the pound and sharply increased duties on beer, wine, spirits and tobacco. No less had been expected; more had been feared. Retail trade actually increased in September, but the 6 p.m. curfew imposed on all except tobacconists, confectioners and newsagents was affecting the small corner shop which did much of its trade in the evening when the locals returned from work. Frenetic efforts were made to whip up trade: Mons. Vasco of Dover Street offered servicewomen a reduced price for his famous 'Hair Bubbles' short cut and perm by his 'Unique Machineless Steam-Point-Winding Perming Invention'. So as to 'ensure free movement in case of raids', Mons. Vasco assured his more timorous clients that he had 'strictly excluded from service all wired Permanent Waving Machines'. War-like toys abounded; Hamley's speciality was Build Your Own Maginot Line, an assembly of tiered dugouts with little soldiers performing a variety of military duties. But the children who might buy them, or goad their parents into purchases, were conspicuously absent; the toy fair at Harrods was a sorrowful sight, with only a handful of children brought up from the country for the day by anxious parents.

Sir John Simon urged patriots to spend less at Christmas and save for victory instead. Mass Observation reports suggested that, though a few were determined to spend heavily because this might be the last Christmas they would see, most were ready to heed the Chancellor. Early closing, anyway, made shopping difficult and the blackout rendered it disagreeable as well. At Marks & Spencer's in Romford only one door was in use. The congestion became so intense that the manager ordered all the exits to be opened and the lights in the front of the shop turned off. This caused panic – 'It's a raid! They're here!' – and a mass exodus. As Christmas approached, however, good resolutions faded and most people ended up buying as much as and spending more than usual. The goods could usually be found; David Greig, a poulterer in the Waterloo Road, reported large arrivals of turkeys including supplies from Hungary and Yugoslavia, though at prices 2d a pound above those of 1938. But as merchandise was exhausted the retailer found it increasingly difficult to procure replacements. Vivienne Hall thought the Harrods' January sale 'awful, the few things that were left were terrible and expensive'.

A free-spending Christmas presaged a black New Year. People had dissipated their savings; even by the beginning of October Miss Hall was congratulating herself on being still in work when 'so many girls and men around me have either lost their jobs because their firms have closed down or are in fear of losing them through lack of business'. Everyone in the theatre seemed to be out of work, many for only a month or two, some for far longer. In his insurance office George Beardmore noted in his diary that the staff of seventy was almost entirely idle, 'We play cards and read newspapers from 10.30 a.m. . . . Unemployment is today an even greater threat than Hitler.' Hitler would put matters right in time; the demands of war would make unemployment a distant spectre; but in 1939 it loomed disconcertingly large. The doctors, particularly the Harley Street specialists, found the going as hard as anyone. Their patients had gone away and 80 per cent of the lessees of fashionable consulting rooms were said to be looking for new tenants. 'The long, rather narrow street which has been called "the valley of the shadow of death" was now an empty thoroughfare,' wrote Anthony Weymouth.

Though the small shopkeepers were under pressure, it was becoming evident, especially if they dealt in food and drink, that the balance of power was shifting in their favour and against the customer. They were figures of importance, to be ingratiated, even fawned upon. It was necessary to register with a retailer if a shopper was to be sure of obtaining essential supplies; once registered, it was difficult to change without moving to a new area. Prices of staple products rose sharply in the first months of the war and by the time price control was introduced in November 1939 the poor were already hard pressed. Bacon and butter were rationed at two and four ounces a week respectively, but so many did not buy their allocations that the allowance of both was doubled. 'Strange to relate, the increase did not cause any great depletion of stocks,' wrote Mr Britton bitterly. 'Of course, the government thought that, as the people couldn't afford to purchase four ounces of butter a week, they would jump at the chance of being able to purchase eight ounces. Now the stocks of margarine are falling in an alarming manner and they are talking of rationing that.' There was inevitably some hoarding: when the rationing of sugar was imminent, consumers were urged to buy only their usual supply, 'but that seems an incentive to some people to grab all they can so that they can be a little better off than the other fellow,' wrote Britton. Even before price controls were introduced, the public were on the look-out for profiteering. In Spitalfields a grocer was nearly lynched for selling for 1/2d a tin of salmon marked 11d. Shops were picketed by the Stepney Tenants' Defence League if malpractice was detected.

Petrol rationing was expected in mid-September. 'It was a great sight last Friday night to see the cars queueing up for miles round each garage to fill up before midnight,' Rose Macaulay told her sister. 'And then after all it was put off . . .' It was only put off by a week. Petrol rationing transformed the appearance of London. People hoarded their tiny allowance for weekends or essential journeys; trams, trolleys and tubes were packed; the roads largely deserted. Petrol for London Transport was cut by a quarter when war broke out; 800 central London buses were withdrawn, leaving the streets still emptier, the trains more crowded. A fleet of buses was converted to run on gas, but it was some time before this brought relief to the hard-pressed traveller. A third of London's taxis was taken over by the Auxiliary Fire Service, leaving less than 5000 on the road. They were allowed only three gallons of petrol a day and gave up cruising in search of passengers, yet they still earned almost as much money as before. Their lot became even happier when more than half London's motorists decided not to relicense their cars at the end of 1939. Now it was garage space that was at a premium. Those who had kept their cars on the road used up their last reserves of petrol in a foray at Easter 1940; from then on the day of the private motorist was all but done.

It was a cold winter in 1939/40 and there was a shortage of coke and coal. Tennyson Jesse reported with delight that two sacks had just been delivered. 'There is, believe me, no more beautiful sound than that of coke being emptied out of a sack into your yard when you have given up hope.' At the other end of the thermometer the Stop-Me-And-Buy-One ice-cream salesmen disappeared, since the refrigerating machines were needed for the transport of blood. They came back temporarily in the spring, when the need to ferry blood seemed less pressing, then vanished again when ice-cream ran out.

They say the war has not started yet, mused Vivienne Hall, yet nearly everything cost more; the 'small intimate things' were difficult to get; clubs and societies had closed, travel was difficult, 'friends I saw frequently have disappeared'. Her whole life had changed for the worse. And yet for some there were compensations. London had never been more beautiful than in that first winter, thought Jane Gordon. 'There was a fresh tang in the air, which was no longer laden with petrol fumes, and for the first time we knew how enchanting the city looked by moonlight.'

In the meantime life had returned to London's entertainment world, filtering back from the remoter limbs towards the heart. The impresario C. B. Cochran had from the start refused to believe that the ban could continue for long, announcing his plans for the autumn in a defiant letter to *The Times*. His confidence was justified when the Golders Green Hippodrome opened a few days later. The play was *The Importance of Being Earnest*; the remarkable cast included John Gielgud, Edith Evans, Peggy Ashcroft, Gwen Ffrangcon Davies and Jack Hawkins. The stars arrived carrying gas-masks. 'We are all delighted to be back at work,' said Gielgud. 'It won't last long for some of us. Jack Hawkins and I are waiting to be called up and many more stars are in our position.' Hawkins went, Gielgud did not. The authorities concluded that good actors might be more useful on the stage than in the services and ruled that they could obtain exemption provided they were not out of work for more than two weeks at a time. Laurence Olivier and Ralph Richardson were among the many younger stars who preferred not to use this dispensation, but enough stayed on to keep productions going.

A crop of other suburban theatres – in Streatham Hill, Richmond, Wimbledon – joined the Hippodrome in the first wave of re-opening; six West End theatres followed after eleven days of closure; fourteen more on 28 October. They were allowed, by then, to stay open till 11.15 p.m. Edith Evans's appearance at Golders Green must have been fleeting, since the revue in which she starred, *Diversions*, was the first new production to open in the West End. The only new play that year with any pretension to seriousness was J. B. Priestley's *Music at Night*, 'played in lighting as murky as a blackout and progressing entirely through the spoken thoughts of the actors with occasional interruptions from the dead,' wrote Mollie Panter-Downes in the 'Letter from London' she contributed to the *New Yorker* magazine. Most managements, probably wisely, felt that blackouts and voices from the dead were the last thing Londoners wanted: Jack Hulbert and Cicely Courtneidge in a musical, *Under Your Hat*, or the long-running *Me and My Girl*, which featured the 'Lambeth Walk', were safer fare.

'The theatre is said to be reviving here – meaning that more are opening – mostly "legs and lavatories",' commented Tennyson Jesse loftily. Legs were acceptable, breasts less so. Diane Raye, the American striptease artiste, was denounced as a 'wartime curse' and a 'national scourge'. The British were hypocrites, she retorted; they flocked to see her at the Victoria Palace where she had earned £600 in four weeks – 'and that ain't hay!' More ambitious productions were to be found in the theatre clubs which abounded on the West End's fringe: the Actors' Company, for instance, headed by Alec Guinness, Marius Goring and George Devine, put on Guinness in his own adaptation of *Great Expectations*.

Some theatres went over to war work. Drury Lane became the headquarters of ENSA, the Entertainments National Service Association, where Basil Dean organised entertainments for British forces, wherever they might be. Drury Lane looked dreary beyond words, noted Anthony Weymouth. 'Occasional single lamps lighted one through the entrance hall. The grand staircase . . . was in semi-darkness.' In the room in which Sheridan had written *The School for Scandal* the Controller of ENSA, Sir Seymour Hicks, seventy years old and old beyond his years, wrangled with Dean. Despite their discord, Drury Lane spawned a remarkable flow of diversions for the troops, most mediocre, some ghastly, a few extraordinarily good.

Ballet dancers were not given the same exemption as actors; partly, it was supposed, because the management feared that the prejudice against 'effete' male dancers might be strengthened if they were excused military service. Within a few months the entire male company of Sadler's Wells was in the services. The situation was saved by boys of fifteen or sixteen and a handful of South Africans and Australians, notably Robert Helpmann. With Ninette de Valois at the prow and Margot Fonteyn emerging into splendid maturity, Sadler's Wells throve, as did Marie Rambert and the Ballet Club at the Arts Theatre. Indeed, it seemed that London could not have enough dance to satisfy its craving for (in Arnold Haskell's phrase) 'the need for *re*-creation, in the Greek sense of the word'.

Recreation, in the English sense of the word, was more often sought in the cinema. Here again, permission to reopen was given grudgingly and piecemeal; first for the suburbs; then for inner London, but with a curfew; finally, in December, for unrestricted showing. Authority to reopen the inner London cinemas was given on the 9 p.m. news on 15 September; by 8.30 the following morning the chairman of the Granada group was touring his cinemas, chiding those laggards who still proclaimed themselves closed. Greta Garbo in *Ninotchka* – the film remembered for the fact that Garbo laughed – was one of the first great wartime successes; *Goodbye, Mr Chips* reduced Vivienne Hall to such floods of tears that she emerged praying no friend would see her blotched and swollen eyes, 'but I enjoyed the film immensely'. The war as yet was little in evidence in the feature films, though newsreels were filled with German tanks rolling across the Polish plains or gallant British lads preparing themselves for battle. The plummy resonance of the announcers seemed curiously reassuring, their platitudinous bromides invested with the sanctity of eternal truth.

The orchestras were as badly hit as the ballet companies; the BBC Symphony Orchestra losing thirty of its 120 players before it moved, with many other sections of the BBC, to less vulnerable premises in Bristol. Concerts resumed on 24 September, Charles Hambourg conducting the London Symphony Orchestra at the Queen's Hall, with pianist Myra Hess as soloist. It was March 1940 before the Albert Hall was reopened for evening performances, its audience limited to 5000 against 10,000 capacity. The National Gallery, its pictures decanted into a disused slate quarry in North Wales, provided an unexpected venue for some of the capital's most memorable concerts. Myra Hess asked the Director, Kenneth Clark, if she could give a lunchtime concert in the deserted rooms. You must give one every day, replied Clark. The first was little advertised and it seemed unlikely that many would come; when the doors were opened, there was a queue all the way along the north side of Trafalgar Square. Myra Hess played Beethoven's 'Appassionata' and her own arrangement of Bach's 'Jesu, joy of man's desiring'. 'I confess that in common with half the audience, I was in tears,' wrote Clark. 'This was what we had all been waiting for – an assertion of eternal values.' The Home Office rule was that not more than 200 people should gather together, but nobody seemed to mind when audiences grew much larger. One thousand were there a few weeks later when 'City workers, shop assistants, shoppers, ARP workers, soldiers, Bloomsbury intellectuals and the Lord Chancellor, Lord Caldecote, flocked to the National Gallery for the lunchtime concert. Many were turned away. Sir K. Clark helped people find seats and apologised for the poor quality of the few pictures left on the walls.' A canteen was later added, to provide food for those who would otherwise do without lunch. The actress and monologist Joyce Grenfell was one who regularly helped cut sandwiches.

But it was a need to dance that above all consumed every level of London society in those first months. The large public dance halls were full as never before: the Streatham Locarno had 800 people on the floor and 256 in the balcony on a Saturday night; the Jitterbug Marathon at the Paramount, Tottenham Court Road, attracted 1400 – well above the pre-war average. The colour, the light, the company, the noise, seemed irresistible to old and young alike. One elderly couple used regularly to come up from Croydon by car. With petrol rationing, the manager assumed he would see them no more; they arrived by bicycle. There were more dance bands playing in the West End than before the war; even the most sedate restaurant found it necessary to have a small orchestra.

Customers want to dance, said Ed Murrow: 'Places are jammed nearly every night. People come early and stay late. Uniforms and civilian clothes are about evenly divided, but practically no one wears formal evening dress. That's a change.' Only the most credu-

lous would have supposed that London had lowered all its class
barriers, but some of the stuffiness had disappeared. At the Café de
Paris, the *Evening Standard* gossip columnist observed, 'a democratic change has come over London night life. The dancers . . .
bore the stamp of districts as far afield as Wimbledon and their
clothes were as heterogeneous as at any bargain counter. There was
far more vitality than before the war.' At Quaglino's, 'Only a few
women wore full evening dress. "I may not be an officer," chanted
a corporal in a Savile Row uniform, "but at least I'm a gentleman." '

At the Café de Paris the *chanteuse* Inge Anders sang the first hit
song of the war, the idiotic 'We're going to hang out our washing
on the Siegfried Line'. At the Café Anglais Harry Roy's band performed what it hoped would also be a hit:

> God Bless You, Mr Chamberlain,
> We're all mighty proud of you.
> You look swell holding your umbrella,
> All the world loves a wonderful feller – so
> God Bless You, Mr Chamberlain!

When first played this apparently met with enthusiasm and calls for
an encore, but it proved shorter lived even than the ill-fated 'Siegfried Line'. The Revd John Palmer, of St Katherine's, Rotherhithe,
fared little better with his Rotherhithe Roll, intended to rival the
Lambeth Walk.

> We like a lark down in Rotherhithe,
> It's a cheery place to be,
> For they are not too posh in Rotherhithe,
> For the likes of you and me.

Neither the words nor the actions, which involved 'a good deal of
knees bending, slapping your partner, and walking around with your
thumbs stuck in your waistcoat', caught on with the public, but at
least Palmer was not left looking as silly as the other two lyricists
when the war went disastrously wrong a few months later.

The vicar would have thought them indecently posh at the Grosvenor House Hotel when Queen Charlotte's birthday dinner-dance
took place with most of the traditional ritual. One thousand guests,
including 150 debutantes in white (except for one in purple), celebrated Leap Year 1940. At midnight the men were issued with

favours: one side was red and bore the words, 'Stop. Do not propose'; the other was green and marked, 'Go ahead. You may propose'. Mr Palmer would have been equally ill at ease dining with the newspaper proprietor Lord Kelmsley. John Colville, one of Chamberlain's private secretaries, recorded the occasion. 'We none of us dressed (to show it was wartime) but in every other respect it might have been a party of pre-war days; all the rooms were open, there was a galaxy of footmen, the dinner was fast and excellent, and wine flowed like water. Vulgar, perhaps, in these days, but certainly a pleasant relapse into a gilded past.' The gilded past was in evidence, too, when Winston Churchill's son, Randolph, married nineteen-year-old Pamela Digby* 'in a panoply of jingling spurs and swords'. Only Lord Londonderry wore a top hat, but Lord Stanley of Alderley made up for this with his 'long, tightly-buttoned frock coat'.

In Mayfair or Rotherhithe, the Café de Paris or the Streatham Locarno, there was the same urgent determination to eat, drink and be merry; for though one might not actually die tomorrow, it seemed unlikely there would be much scope for merriment. The West End was as crowded as ever, wrote Vivienne Hall in her diary, 'people jostling each other in good-natured tolerance and everyone determined to have a good time, despite the fate hanging over us'. It was not all so good-natured. Servicemen were exploited in cheap 'clubs' where they paid exorbitant amounts to sip fruit cordial with a hard-faced 'hostess'. Sometimes they showed their disappointment by understandable violence. An army of harlots moved in to take advantage of the blackout and the prevailing mood. Two officers of the Public Morality Council, prowling around Soho, were solicited by thirty-five women in just over a hundred yards. That was at midnight; even at 4 a.m. seven women were still on duty. Observation in twenty-one streets showed 'there are French and Italian women, and some German women, a large number of English and a goodly number of Welsh and North Country women'. The police paid little attention, confining themselves to intervening in the not infrequent cases that a prostitute's activities led to noisy altercation.

Spectator sports had fallen prey to the same embargo as cinemas or

*Still refulgent today as Mrs Pamela Harriman, American Ambassadress in Paris.

theatres, and by the time it was possible to reopen, many of the most important arenas were no longer available. Arsenal's football ground had been turned over to civil defence and it was forced to share facilities with Tottenham Hotspur; Twickenham was transformed into allotments; the Oval cricket ground became a camp for prisoners of war; sheep grazed and vegetables were planted on the courts at Wimbledon. But football at least soon got restarted; the London clubs decided to organise their own internal league.

'Selfish and foolish,' the chairman of Norwich Football Club angrily described them. 'I have repeatedly told them that they would draw better gates out of London.' But how to get there and find players able to spare the time? the manager of Fulham retorted. Against his better judgment, he had arranged two matches with Portsmouth but 'though they are still a long way off, I am already worrying about them'. London attendances were not too bad; for its Boxing Day match against Arsenal, Crystal Palace applied for and obtained permission to admit 15,000 spectators to the ground instead of the usual ceiling of 8000. Greyhound racing was resumed at Wembley on 16 September; the last race had to be held at five o'clock. At Haringey several thousand were left outside when the attendance limit was reached, they stormed the entrances and many got in free before the police restored order.

Some of the museums also reopened, though usually only a few rooms. Most of their precious treasures had been evacuated. This was the case, too, with many of the statues: George III from Cockspur Street, the Burghers of Calais from Victoria Tower Garden. Irving, outside the National Portrait Gallery, was given a brick shelter. Eros left Piccadilly Circus. A few hundred yards from the Burghers, Richard Coeur de Lion remained on watch outside the Houses of Parliament. He was to suffer wounds when the blitz came. The Imperial War Museum opened its doors in February 1940; it exhibited the signed Munich document, the promise of peace in our time. Certain galleries of the British Museum also reopened, but only for a few hours on Saturdays and Sundays, and for 300 people at a time.

Those using the Museum Reading Room were treated rather better. It resumed service in mid-September, but at first was little used. Some of the regulars were missing: the charming old black man who had been engaged for many years on a history of Liberia;

the French priest who had been at work even longer on a study of the Roman Catholic Church. Other libraries either closed or cut back their facilities; and since some of those which stayed open did not get around to blacking out, the hours of access were limited. Borrowings fell heavily – in Battersea and Chelsea by over 40 per cent – but by the end of October were back at 80 per cent of their pre-war level. A Mass Observation report shows that fiction was most in demand; with do-it-yourself books on gardening, cooking and embroidery running a close second. Books on politics languished, both in libraries and bookshops; *Mein Kampf* was a conspicuous exception, being asked for all round the country (though probably as little read as most of those turgid tracts which from time to time come into fashion). Christina Foyle felt that the blackout had been a great stimulant to reading, of light fiction particularly, but also of Dickens, Thackeray or Trollope – 'It is many years since we have sold so many copies.'

The Ministry of Information, based in London University in Bloomsbury, and the BBC, a little farther west in Portland Place, provided the hives around which otherwise unemployable intellectuals buzzed busily. The Ministry of Information (MoI) in particular ('*L'état c'est MoI*,' was the joke of those who deplored its protean distension) offered a haven to a miscellany of literary figures. It was a depressing time for these displaced and aimless wanderers. For a few weeks, months even, the publishers upon whom they depended seemed to have suffered a collective loss of nerve; few new books were commissioned, many under contract were cancelled or postponed. To the publishers it seemed that the loss of nerve was as apparent among the writers; the quantity and quality of new typescripts declined. 'How can I write with the world in this state?' was a question the publisher Geoffrey Faber heard several times as the war began. The authors lapsed into catatonic gloom; by the time they emerged the *Cornhill Magazine, Criterion, London Mercury, New Stories, New Verse* and several other of the capital's literary magazines had ceased publication.

It was Cyril Connolly who sounded the trumpet of resurgence. In January 1940 he founded the defiantly highbrow *Horizon*, a magazine deliberately intended to be at odds with its times and to challenge the national mood. 'Our standards are aesthetic,' he proclaimed, 'and our politics are in abeyance ... So far this is a war without the two great emotions real to so many of us. It is a war which awakens neither Pity nor Hope.' Writers were supposed to write, Connolly believed; they had no business soiling their hands with propaganda or lending themselves to the purposes of war. The paper was edited from Stephen Spender's flat in Bloomsbury; Spender remembers Connolly working by the window, 'occasionally glancing up to see whether any German aeroplanes were coming over, for, during the "phoney war" period, there were constant false alarms, and we expected a raid which would demolish whole districts of London'.

John Lehmann recalls a party he gave shortly before he sold *New Writing, Horizon*'s rival, to Allen Lane of Penguin. Rosamond Lehmann helped officiate, Guy Burgess made sardonic comments, William Plomer and Joe Ackerley arrived 'like mischievous twins whispering malicious asides to me about their fellow guests', George Orwell was 'full of friendliness and stimulating talk'. David Gascoyne pushed himself 'as if panic-stricken into a corner'. John Banting, the painter, explained the mural he had recently painted, but not many fellow painters were in the company: Victor Pasmore was a reluctant soldier, Piet Mondrian had left for the United States, Ben Nicholson and Barbara Hepworth for Cornwall. For Lehmann, the party was possessed by a spirit of impermanency, of a crumbling and transitory society – 'Goodbye, goodbye, a dark bat in my bowels telling me it was goodbye for a long time.'

On the whole, communal life in London was now reassembling rather than disintegrating further. Evacuees of every kind had left the city, but by early 1940 many were back. For the purposes of evacuation, Britain was divided into three parts: potential target areas, from which children and other vulnerable groups were to be removed; 'neutral' areas, where things stayed as they were; and 'reception' areas to which evacuees were despatched. Some areas contrived to be neither one thing nor another; Uxbridge, for example, was classified as a neutral area but provided temporary shelter for City firms such as Lloyds Insurance.

At the time of Munich, 80 per cent of London parents had said they wished their children to be evacuated in case of war. By August 1939 the proportion had dropped to 66 per cent. In the event under half took advantage of the scheme. When it came to the point, some parents decided they could not bear to be parted from their children, others felt that, after all, the bombers might never come and it would be better to wait and see. Nevertheless, the evacuation was strikingly well conceived and smoothly carried out. The day before the operation began, Automobile Association scouts raced around the suburbs, unveiling bulletin boards which announced that most of the principal routes in and out of town had been designated one-way for the next few days. The majority used the railways, however; a threatened strike was called off in recognition of the crisis and London buses carried 230,000 evacuees to the main termini, some drivers going for thirty-six hours without sleep. Evacuation from Dagenham and other riverside boroughs was by the boats of the General Steam Navigation Company.

'It was a lovely sunrise,' recorded John O'Leary, the historian of Dagenham, 'as the last boat slipped her moorings soon after eight o'clock into the golden haze of the river. One personal impression – an awful silence. The children did not sing.' Mass Observation reports tend to record happy, well-ordered children singing ' "Under the Spreading Chestnut Tree", full voices and with a swing in it'. When Euan Wallace, the Transport Minister, went to Hornsey station to see how his railways were coping, he found everyone cheerful, in spite of the fact that 825 people were being packed into space intended for a maximum of 800. Bernard Kops would have agreed with O'Leary. The leaves seemed very green as he and his fellow schoolchildren marched away from Stepney: 'This was the place where we were born, where we grew up, where we played and sang, laughed and cried. And now all the grey faces as we passed were weeping. It was strangely quiet.' No panic, but 'a sort of calm desperation', was Vera Reid's impression of the crowds at Paddington when she rushed back to London to take up her duties with the WVS. Two babies were tied by a strap to a large suitcase, presumably while their parents sought information. They wailed disconsolately, but most of the tears were shed by the mothers who watched their children go.

These were the official evacuees; all over Kensington and other more affluent areas cars waited as children, elderly aunts, canaries and dogs were loaded up. Paddington lost 29,000 adults in a few days: businessmen, civil servants, students. Mrs Catchpole had provided lodgings for eight civil servants and two bank clerks; within a week all had left to join their evacuated offices. So far as the children were concerned, two serious difficulties arose. The first was due to negligence. The evacuation was efficient, but the organisation in the reception areas was woefully inadequate. Children were bundled from pillar to post; families were broken up; hopelessly unsuitable matches of host and guest contrived. The seeds of many premature returns to London were sown in these first few days. The second was less culpable. The authorities had expected almost all children to leave London; when they did not, no facilities were left to cater for them. Two-thirds of the schools had been taken over for civil defence, most of the teachers went with their pupils to the country, school doctors and nurses were reassigned. Jean Stafford was five when war broke out, just beginning to read at St Mary's Church School in Ladywell. At once 'half-time schooling started – or, rather, hardly any time schooling'. She at least had somewhere to go, elder children roamed the streets: juvenile delinquency rose by more than 40 per cent in the months after war began.

Within a few weeks the drift back from the country had begun, and things got worse. At first it was mainly the mothers who had accompanied their children to the country but worried about their deserted husbands. 'The father is tired of living alone and is really acting selfishly,' said an official dismissively. Little sympathy was shown towards the renegades, especially if they had returned against their husbands' wills. One mother, who had come back from Worthing after only three days, complained to the magistrate at Tower Bridge that her husband refused to support her. 'You had no business to return after you had been evacuated by the government for your own safety,' retorted Mr Bernard Campion. 'My advice to you is to obey your husband.' But soon the children were pouring back as well. Florence Speed, a forty-year-old writer from Brixton, heard two women talking on a bus. 'Government or no government, I'm going to bring my children back tomorrow,' exclaimed one of them. Her ten-year-old daughter was being monstrously misused, made to dress her little brother and wash a blackberry stain from her shirt. 'Foolish, disgruntled woman,' was Florence Speed's lofty comment.

By mid-October 50,000 mothers and children were believed to have returned; a month later the figure had more than doubled. In an effort to stem the flow, the authorities began to organise special trains with cheap fares, on which mothers with children far away could visit them; the scheme applied only to journeys costing more than £1, which caused much indignation among those whose children had been sent to Kent or Sussex. At Christmas a publicity campaign was launched on the theme, 'Keep them happy, keep them safe', but many children still came home for the holidays and often stayed. By January 1940 the situation was patently out of hand; at least 200,000 children, of whom getting on for half were returned evacuees, were in London needing education. Some sort of stop-gap was provided by the Scouts and Guides. At first those bodies had expected to close with the departure of their members. After the first wave of evacuation, one scout leader from Chiswick wrote sadly, 'We knew what Hamelin City had felt like after the Pied Piper.' Only three members of the pack were left. But soon more than half were back. 'We have chosen a beetroot red scarf to be our war scarf, and new chums will be invested with their own pack colour,' wrote the scout leader exultantly. But there were limits to what he or any of his colleagues could do. It was schools that were needed.

Still the authorities resisted popular demand, arguing that if they gave in they would make the situation worse by encouraging the return of yet more evacuees. Earl De La Warr, the Minister of Education, claimed that the failure to reopen schools was primarily the fault of Herbert Morrison, who was deliberately going slow while trying to make it seem the government was responsible: 'He has never been very keen on education and prefers to spend his exchequer grants on items which give a better political return.' The fact that many school buildings had been taken over by civil defence and few of those available were equipped with adequate shelters was at least as important a factor. By November, though, so many children were back that De La Warr agreed some schools might reopen in the vulnerable area, though hopefully stressing that 'the government decision must not be taken as an all-clear for a return'. By 11 January only fifteen of the LCC's 900 schools were open, but once started the process was irreversible. Another forty reopened the following week and public clamour grew for speedier action. On 12 February 1000 angry parents stormed a meeting of the Croydon Education Committee and won a promise that schools would reopen as soon as shelters were available; £7000 was voted for this work. Inch by inch the authorities gave ground, allowing clergy or parents as a halfway house to organise their own schools if not more than six children were gathered together, then twelve, then two groups of twelve under one roof.

The returned children were euphoric. 'London was, for me, like a return from exile,' remembered John Geer. 'My pet cat met me at the gate, the neighbours welcomed me and the sun shone . . . The vicar arranged a class in his house, using local retired people with some teaching experience to help out. We learnt odd subjects such as Esperanto and Monopoly, all very enjoyable.' Those who had been running wild in London were almost as glad to be back in school. 'I was tired to death of kicking about around home,' admitted one Fulham boy. 'Except when the snow was on the ground and I could have some snowballing, there was nothing to do.' In January the 600 boys of Dulwich College had returned from their temporary exile in Tonbridge, the first public school to join the homeward flow. By the spring it was believed that almost 400,000 children were in London, most of those old enough receiving some education. Making the best of a bad job, the government sought to register them for a new evacuation scheme, to be implemented if serious air-raids started, a move opposed by Euan Wallace, who argued that people would not be any more likely to stay away on the next occasion and there was little point in the authorities subsidising 'a series of free trips to the country'. After a week, 10 per cent of parents had enrolled their children; 10 per cent had refused to do so; 80 per cent had done nothing. Only 800 out of a possible 10,000 in East Ham were on the new list. The proportion crept up, but never got anywhere near the government's hoped-for total.

The government could not control the London children, but it could do what it wanted with its own employees. 'Plan Black', for use in emergency, would have moved the whole administration out of London; 'Plan Yellow', which was at once put into effect, evacuated those ministries (or parts of them) which could function just as well outside the capital. Meanwhile the Faraday Building, a concrete block near St Paul's, was transformed into a redoubt where the Cabinet could retreat if need arose and the Prime Minister run the war in greater security than Downing Street could provide. By Christmas 15,000 civil servants had been exiled to different parts of the British Isles, with another 5000 scheduled to leave soon. The civil servants, marooned in such spas as Bath or Harrogate, and their wives, abandoned in London, stormed at this cruel treatment, but the government did not relent. Indeed, as the influx of returning children jammed every station, 3000 officials of the Ministry of Health found themselves packed off by special train to north-west England. Those left behind paid for the luxury by working extravagantly hard; most senior civil servants were at it from 9 a.m. to 9 p.m. and many had camp-beds in their offices to save themselves a trek home through the blackout. Given a chance, the government would probably have sent the MPs into exile too, but the members were having none of this. Reluctantly they accepted they should sit only three days a week. Ministers felt this an excellent idea, which would make it easier for them to get on with their work, but back-benchers thought they were being unreasonably gagged and made their displeasure plain.

Hospitals were evacuated not so much to protect the patients as to make way for the flood of air-raid casualties which was hourly awaited. When Guy's received the fateful telegram 'Clear Hospitals', all but twenty-seven immobile patients were bundled off to Brighton by train or Green Line buses converted into ambulances. Doctors, students and nurses followed, leaving only a skeleton staff: 'We who remained,' wrote Dr Bishop, 'looked upon ourselves as a doomed garrison.' A company of the Queen's Regiment was billeted near the hospital, allegedly to protect the building from being stormed by panic-stricken civilians in the event of an air-raid. Doomed or not, the staff soon found themselves underemployed and bored. The sports grounds were closed and the younger members of staff solaced themselves with noisy parties. Meanwhile the London public suffered; the editor of the *Daily Express*, Arthur Christiansen, trailed from hospital to hospital in search of someone to set the leg he had broken in the blackout. Gradually it was realised that something had to be done to cater for the civilian sick; out-patient departments were reopened and by the spring of 1940 sixty or seventy in-patients had infiltrated Guy's. Even so, only half the clinics in London catering for eye, ear or throat conditions had reopened and a mere eight dentists were doing hospital work compared with a pre-war fifty-nine.

By the end of the year 3453 large firms had left London; three months later 700 had returned and several of the others, including such giants as ICI, were thinking of doing the same. The net exodus had still been massive, however, and was matched by that of the trades unions. Ernest Bevin, boss of the giant Transport and General Workers' Union, was an exception; he refused to leave London and urged his colleagues to return – 'He declares that he will not scuttle from Transport House, he will not go until he is driven out.'

Mrs Catchpole, the landlady from Paddington, was not the only person to deplore this exodus; house agents were in despair. 'It's really appalling the number of houses which are to be let or sold,' complained Anthony Weymouth. 'Almost every day I see removal vans; they are never bringing furniture in, always taking it out.' Myriads of TO LET signs besmirched the main shopping streets, and any reasonable offer would be accepted: one notice read, 'Rent will be adjusted to takings.' By March 1940 the population of Chelsea had fallen from 57,000 to 36,000, a third of the rateable properties stood empty. 'London is fast becoming a distressed area,' protested the local MP, Sir Harold Webb. 'I have reached the conclusion that London's losses already outweigh possible losses through an air-raid.' The mathematical basis for this assumption remains obscure, but in February the Mayor of Kensington concurred that the cost of evacuation was crippling, in his borough 14 per cent of properties were empty as opposed to a pre-war average of 5 per cent.

Yet things were looking up. Within a few weeks of Sir Harold's objurgations a house agent in Bayswater was reporting that he had fewer flats on his books than in August 1939 and that business premises were also being sought. The big houses stood empty but furnished flats were soon snapped up. The traffic had begun to thicken even earlier. In November it had been possible to stroll across Piccadilly with hardly a glance to left or right; now, wrote Tennyson Jesse a month later, 'London is so jammed with traffic you can hardly move.' By January many private cars had disappeared, but the people were there in increasing numbers, 'some with the most curious excuses such as, "Of course, *I* should never have left London, my dear, but I simply had to go and help a wretched friend out with her evacuees!" '

It was business as near usual as possible in London in the spring of 1940. The government viewed the people's mood with some dismay. To preserve *sang froid* was all very well, but not if it implied a blinkered reluctance to confront the dangers ahead. How would the Londoner cope if the phoney war became reality?

6

'Universal darkness buries all'

A GREAT DEAL had been done to prepare London for all-out war. The foundations of the capital's civil defences had been laid in the year bought by Munich; with the declaration of war the pace quickened. At first the expectation of imminent attack lent urgency to the work. 'The city is convinced, beyond any doubt, that we shall have a week-end of raids,' wrote Vivienne Hall in her diary on 22 September, 'everything points to it, they say; there are dozens more balloons up, there are hundreds and thousands of enemy planes massing on the Holland frontier, the moon is just right and everything is perfect.' The weekend passed, other weekends passed, and the hundreds and thousands of enemy planes failed to arrive. It was a relief, and yet Londoners were left feeling curiously let down – like party-givers who had rehearsed endlessly how they would deal with uninvited guests and were left feeling silly when no gatecrashers arrived.

The declaration of war provoked a rush to join the ARP. Even a borough as traditionally anti-war as Bermondsey vigorously organised its ARP, the unkindest cut for the pacifists coming when the Labour Institute was requisitioned as a wardens' post. When numbers were at their highest, nearly one Londoner in six was involved in some way with civil defence. The fact that its headquarters were in the Geological Museum was supposed to be a deadly secret. A covey of journalists invited to inspect it was first taken on a mystery tour in a blacked-out bus. One of the visitors unkindly pointed out that a notice headed 'Geological Survey' was still prominently displayed. This was hurriedly removed, but a similar visit a few weeks later revealed that the cloakroom towels were marked 'Geological Museum'.

The training was at first equally amateurish. Volunteers in Fulham complained of incompetence and waste of time. 'We finished the gas course and never heard any more,' protested one. 'I sort of lost heart when they didn't ask me to continue with the first aid.' 'There should be more to do,' was another grumble. 'We're left on the shelf now.' Facilities were sometimes primitive. The wardens of Post 25 in Edmonton complained that their floor had not been concreted, the only light and heat came from paraffin lamps and stoves, there were condensation and noxious fumes. They were told that the Home Office allowance of £8.16.9d per post was not enough to allow concreting or the installation of electricity, they must either man the post or be dismissed, didn't they know there was a war on? Morale slumped; it had become a 'war of yawns' for thousands of ARP workers, Mollie Panter-Downes told her *New Yorker* readers, 'who spend their nights playing cards, taking cat naps, and practically yearning for a short air-raid'.

Worse still, after a brief period of popularity, the wardens, in the eyes of the public, became, if not villains, at least self-important nuisances. Their enforcement of the blackout, in particular, led to their being considered spies on their fellow citizens, coppers' narks. One warden was hit by a well-aimed boot while patrolling near World's End. Usually they were doing no more than their duty but some let authority go to their heads. 'They got very important and officious,' remembered Jean Stafford, a housewife in south London. 'Nobody liked them, they were always regarded as the lowest form of life.' Anxious to avoid any charge of nepotism, the Enfield Council resolved that relations of councillors or council employees could not hold any paid job in civil defence. This was rescinded when the Home Office ruled that efficiency alone should be the criterion for employment. Almost at once the *Enfield Gazette* demanded an enquiry into allegations that nepotism was rife and plum jobs were being handed to council insiders. Even the authorities seemed infected by the public resentment. When an ARP worker told a London magistrate that he had been 'called up', the magistrate rebuked him sternly, 'You were not called up. You volunteered. There are too many people in the AFS and ARP.'

Protests about the cost multiplied; the ratepayers of Barnes complained that ARP volunteers were paid £10 to £20 a week while holding comfortable daytime jobs. Nearly £100 had been spent on providing radio sets at wardens' posts. In Chelsea the council insisted it could not afford to strengthen one post with steel supports, seeking to sweeten the pill by offering a grant of £7.10/-

towards the funeral expenses of any warden killed on duty. All nine ARP posts in the J division of Hendon closed because the householders who had provided the premises refused to do so any more. By December the boroughs had 9000 paid wardens, averaging nine to a post. The Ministry proposed that this should be cut to six, and 1500 stretcher bearers and 4000 members of the rescue service laid off for good measure. Harold Scott was horrified; London, he insisted, would be the first target if bombardment began and to reduce its defences below an essential minimum would be disastrous false economy. He prevailed, but refugees from a demoralised service continued to flow to industry and the armed services. The government professed concern, but it was not until the blitz had begun that London wardens were ordered to stay in their jobs.

Much the same pattern applied to the fire services, the increasing professionalism of the auxiliaries being matched by growing public discontent at their expense. Sydney Kear joined the AFS at the outbreak of war, but after a few months sickened of inactivity and asked to be allowed to rejoin his stockbroking firm. Permission was given on the understanding that he would return to duty as soon as need arose. In January 1940 the AFS was amalgamated with the London Fire Brigade proper. This caused much distress to the Fire Service Union, which was as intensely conservative as most similar organisations. Firemen stormed at the dilution of their elite by rank amateurs, snubbed the newcomers and in some cases refused even to instruct them. Only the spirited intervention of John Horner, the General Secretary, ensured that the former auxiliaries were given tolerable treatment. The 5000 women who had joined the AFS fared even worse; they were allowed to do little driving – even of the taxis which had been requisitioned to tow trailer pumps – and were assigned to cook, wash up and scrub floors. More than one hundred a week were resigning in protest at the beginning of 1940. The descent from hero to public nuisance was even more vertiginous than in the case of the ARP workers. 'At the outbreak of war,' wrote the novelist and auxiliary fireman Henry Green, 'firemen were second only to fighter pilots in public esteem, stood drinks by elderly gentlemen, eyed lovingly by pretty girls. But a few months later, an old lady said in front of everyone, "Army dodgers, that's what you are!" ' A six-year-old girl peeped through the door of a fire station in Chelsea, was invited in, and told her hosts, 'My daddy says you're a waste of public money.'

The false alarms that had punctuated the first weeks of war gradually died away; they still occurred but became a rarity. Not all was peace; in Heston boys warbled the alarm signal so convincingly that people took fright and complaints were made to the police. For the most part, however, London was a place of unwonted silence. Under the Control of Noises (Defence) Act, the unauthorised sounding of sirens, factory hooters, whistles and noisy rattles was forbidden; church bells joined the list in June 1940.

Observation posts were installed on many of the taller buildings; Wimbledon introduced a particularly efficient system which was to stand it in good stead when the bombers came: specially trained wardens could pinpoint a bomb or fire to within fifteen yards in a matter of seconds. Ambulances were at first less professional. A trainee driver, Nancy Bosanquet, was given so little equipment that she carried her own scissors and a bottle of brandy – 'It makes me feel very dashing – like a buccaneer with his rum.' After a cursory test, another driver, Nancy O'Connor, was provided with an ancient car which constantly broke down and lost water from its radiator almost as fast as it was filled; it behaved, she commented, as if 'it had ceased work years before and deeply resented being dragged from honourable retirement'. On the Thames the Port of London Authority put together an armada of little boats to act as ambulances, messengers and patrol vessels. One of them was *Water Gipsy*, a boat belonging to A. P. Herbert, the MP and writer. 'I think we shall have to abandon the Thames,' the First Lord of the Admiralty, Winston Churchill, told him gloomily. 'I belong to a service which means to see that we don't,' protested Herbert.

It was the blackout which impinged most forcibly on the life of the average Londoner. Alexander Pope had said it all in *The Dunciad*.

Nor public flame, nor private, dares to shine;
Nor human spark is left, nor glimpse divine!
Lo! thy dread empire, Chaos! is restored;
Light dies before thy uncreating word:
Thy hand, great Anarch! lets the curtain fall;
And universal darkness buries all.

For many Londoners it was the first time they had encountered real darkness except when safely in bed. The experience was often daunting. Evelyn Waugh's fictional Guy Crouchback left Bellamy's Club with his brother-in-law, Box-Bender. They stepped out 'into the baffling midnight void. Time might have gone back two thousand years to the time when London was a stockaded cluster of huts down the river, and the streets through which they walked, empty sedge and swamp.' Roads which people could have sworn they knew intimately became impenetrable mysteries. Virginia Cunard, venturing from the Underground station at Piccadilly Circus, was lucky enough to encounter a thunderstorm, and profited from each lightning flash to run as far as she could, pausing for the next flash before resuming. Irene Byers lost all sense of direction outside the Central Telegraph Office where she worked. 'I stood still, panic-stricken, then said firmly over and over again to myself, "I know this street absolutely well – don't be such an ass – walk forward quietly and you will come into Newgate Street." ' She obeyed her own instructions and got to the station, but 'I felt damp with per-spiration and quite exhausted.' Such extreme reactions were prob-ably experienced only once or twice, but few became entirely habituated to London's gloom.

According to the writer and feminist Vera Brittain, some managed in time to acquire a sixth sense – 'half way between the sense of touch and the sense of smell' – which enabled them to pick their way between lamp-posts and sandbags. More did not. For the majority it was a matter of minor inconvenience – a black eye, a skinned knee. The South Mitcham Residents' Association complained about the sandbags heaped outside the police station, which proved an unac-ceptable hazard for silk stockings. For some it was more serious; by December, with the longer nights, there were forty fatal accidents involving pedestrians every day, eight times as many as in pre-war London. The authorities were initially unsympathetic. When William Windsor was knocked down and killed in Epping, the coroner ruled with some brutality, 'I am convinced that a man of eighty-two has no right to be out at that time of night.' 'Billy Brown of London Town', whose rhyming injunctions to the good citizen seemed omnipresent, wrote,

Billy Brown's own highway code

For blackouts is 'Stay off the Road'.
He'll never step out and begin
To meet a bus that's pulling in.
He doesn't wave his torch at night,
But 'flags' his bus with something white.
He never jostles in a queue
But waits and takes his turn. Do you?

But Billy Brown's jingle indicated a retreat by the authorities. Before mid-October he would not have been allowed a torch at all, even after that date the bulb had to be shrouded in a paper cap. By the New Year the police were noticeably more relaxed in their application of the law: no longer would a mother be fined for turning on the light for a second in an uncurtained room when her baby had a fit. Cars were allowed to use one screened headlamp and West End shops could cast a discreet glow – up to twenty-five watts – on objects at the back of their premises. Just before Christmas 'glimmer lights' were turned on in some of the larger streets: 'It will not be a cheerful light,' said Anderson, 'but strong enough to help people find their way about.' Mrs Hagborg of Sutton was meanwhile earning 1/- a time painting keyholes with white luminous paint; each keyhole took five to six minutes, so she made a reasonable living while the work lasted.

In spite of such palliatives the blackout remained unpopular. Mass Observation scouts reported twice as much grumbling on this subject as on any other. The time it wasted was particularly resented; a Pinner housewife claimed it took her more than half an hour to black out her house every day; ten to fifteen minutes were commonplace. Public zeal was as much responsible as officialdom for maintaining the full rigour of the law. There was overt opposition to the introduction of 'glimmer lights', and when entrance lighting was installed at the public shelter in Bethnal Green, it was deliberately sabotaged. Grotesque overestimates were made of the visibility of lights from 5000 or more feet above the ground. A German-Swiss resident of Kensington was accused of using his cigar to signal to the (non-existent) enemy: 'He was puffing hard to make a big light and pointing it at the sky,' said a porter. Eighty-three-year-old William Hance of Kentish Town showed a light and found his house surrounded by an angry crowd shouting, 'Smash the door down!' A policeman got in and turned off the light, Hance turned it on again, whereupon the crowd became so indignant that he had to be taken into custody for his own protection. There were many cases of wardens or even members of the public taking the law into their own hands; one warden, seeing an exposed light in a shop window, drew a pistol and shot it out. Police Constable George Southworth saw a light shining on the fourth storey of a house in Harley Street, clambered up a drainpipe to reach it, slipped and fell to his death.

While in Bellamy's, Crouchback and Box-Bender heard talk of crimes committed in the blackout: 'So-and-so had been sandbagged in Hay Hill and robbed of his poker winnings.' There were plenty of such incidents in real life; one gang haunted the neighbourhood of the big railway stations, masquerading as roistering drunks, embracing passers-by, picking their pockets, and knocking them unconscious if they resisted. But this never became an epidemic. On the contrary, so many extra reserve policemen were on duty that would-be footpads hesitated to tackle an invisible passer-by who might turn out to be equipped with whistle, cudgel and tin hat.

The richer the household, the worse the standard of the blackout. In the first weeks of war 80 per cent of middle-class homes showed some light; this improved but the proportion remained notably higher than in working-class districts. As for the civil servants, on 9 November the War Office showed four lights, the Admiralty seventeen, the Home Office thirty-five. This was partly because there were more and stronger lights, larger windows, less fear of the officious air-raid warden, but also suggested that at more sophisticated levels of society there were doubts whether the blackout had much point. It was far worse than Paris, grumbled the journalist James Lansdale Hodson. 'There's more light on the roads of our British defensive positions than in London's environs. This travelling back from work in the evening unable to read the paper – is it necessary? Does any sense lie in depressing and irritating people unduly?' An experienced fire-watcher told him that even on the darkest night the Thames was visible as a silver ribbon, while railway signal lights could also be seen for miles. Many of the precautions on which the authorities insisted, not merely in the field of blackout, were adopted as much for reasons of public morale as for their intrinsic usefulness, and it was not surprising that some of the more independent-minded treated them with levity if not disdain.

*

They may have wondered, for instance, whether it was really necessary to close the subway which connected the Palace of Westminster with the Underground station across the street. Was it supposed that a German armoured car would batter down the perfectly serviceable grille which already protected members from the incursions of the public? Once inside the parliament buildings there was austerity but no extravagant security. 'I came out into the semi-darkness of the inner lobby and the greater darkness of the outer,' wrote Anthony Weymouth. 'This part of the House is now lit only by electric candles which are placed on the floor and illuminate about one square yard around. For the rest it is blackness.'

Lord Stanhope, Lord President of the Council, announced that the gas-proof rooms on the ground floor were now ready. If they were full, peers could sit in the ministers' new rooms but would have to wear gas-masks. No attempt was made to provide members with deep shelters; inside the Palace of Westminster as outside, the government's dictum was observed: deep shelters were undesirable; cellars, basements and surface shelters would provide all the protection needed. Frank Lewey, Mayor of Stepney, had been protesting about this policy for years but achieved nothing; deep shelters were expensive, he was told, they took time to make. 'In the background of it all was a suspicion that anyone asking for them must be a fool (because London would never be raided) or a coward (fancy being afraid of the Germans!) and so nothing was done.'

A lot was done, on the other hand, to provide public shelters on or near the surface. The work was hurried, cheaply carried out and often shoddy. The standard shelter consisted of brick and lime mortar walls, resting unsupported on the surface of the road with a nine-inch slab of reinforced concrete deposited on top. They were to become known as the 'Morrison Sandwich' shelters, a grim joke derived from the fact that blast sometimes sucked the walls outwards, leaving the occupants as the meat in a sandwich between roof and ground. The public received them with some scepticism; they were even more doubtful about the trenches in Hyde Park which had now been sandbagged and covered over. Gwladys Cox was told that the real purpose for these shelters was to act as burial grounds after the raids; she was also assured in confidence that there was a factory in Willesden busily employed in making cardboard coffins.

The brick walls of the public shelters at least *looked* solid; the sandbags, which played a ubiquitous role in every shelter, deteriorated with alarming speed. One shelter in the Finchley Road had to be rebuilt after only three weeks as the sandbags on which it partly depended had disintegrated; they sprouted grass, were said to be infected with fleas and succumbed quickly to the attentions of mischievous small boys or even the high heels of passing women. In Bond Street they were sprayed with concrete and painted in bright colours; this improved their appearance but did little to make them more effective. But these setbacks did not curb the enthusiasm of the authorities; the 'miniature Cheddar Gorge' which Scott had encountered on Hampstead Heath that summer had by the late autumn become, in Gwladys Cox's eyes, a Grand Canyon in miniature: 'I had not seen such a sight for twenty-six years, not since I had watched the excavations of the Panama Canal in October 1913.' Private contractors did a roaring trade; filled sandbags cost between £4.5/- and £5 a hundred, empty ones cost 3d each.

As well as building public shelters, the authorities selected basements and other suitable parts of existing buildings and adapted them for use in air-raids. The Westminster City Council claimed to have inspected more than 14,000 such sites. Their activities did not always please the proprietor. A shelter in the Strand bore an official notice stating that it could accommodate 150 people in addition to the sixty-four already working in the offices above. The owner of the building appended an indignant postscript: 'We disclaim all responsibility for disappointment and danger to life and limb that must follow for persons misled by the above notice. Our air-raid shelter is regarded as insufficient for our staff.' The basement of the publishers Allen and Unwin, where they kept their stock, was requisitioned as a shelter. People flocked in whenever an alert sounded and helped themselves to books. One well-dressed lady took four copies of an expensive art book and tried to sell them to Bumpus, the celebrated bookshop just down the road.

Sandbags were omnipresent too in private shelters. The Anderson was still the favoured device, but in densely populated Pimlico, where only 235 suitable gardens existed, 8000 coal cellars were cleared and strengthened by the local authorities. Heavy rains in the late autumn produced the inevitable result for the Andersons and some at least of the cellars. The women of Romford marched on the town hall bearing placards reading, 'Sink or swim in Romford shelters', and 'Is pneumonia better than bombs?' In Fulham, disillusionment was so marked that more than 1000 householders applied to have their Andersons removed. The council offered sympathy and some advice on drainage but did not act on the requests, which anyway stopped abruptly when the threat of air-raids became more real in the summer of 1940.

Anti-aircraft guns and searchlights began to obtrude wherever space permitted: 'I love searchlights,' wrote Tennyson Jesse, 'because they are the only things connected with war that look serene and even benign.' Serene and benign were terms that might equally have been applied to the barrage balloons, which by the spring of 1940 were the most conspicuous signs of London's readiness for attack. Sometimes as many as 1000 balloons were deployed over the area; at the end of October they disappeared briefly, then reappeared, their stylish silver painted a dirty green. Balloons, as well as their crews, were adopted by the neighbourhood they served and often given nicknames: the balloons at County Hall were called the Bishop of London and Herbert Morrison; 'They call that the arch-blimp,' said Archbishop Lang, pointing to the balloon tethered in the garden of Lambeth Palace. The arch-blimp ran amok and trailed its wire over Lambeth Palace Road, to the peril of passers-by.

The threat of gas was still much emphasised by the authorities. Pillar boxes were painted in squares of bilious yellow which changed colour if poison gas was around and were said to be as sensitive as chameleons. The *Sidcup Times* featured a prominent photograph of the Women's League of Health and Beauty practising deep breathing exercises while wearing gas-masks. It was never a crime to venture abroad without a mask, but at first social pressure to carry one was considerable. At Unilever House top executives were hardly allowed to cross a corridor without their mask; two soldiers, condemned to death for murder, were about to leave the dock at the Old Bailey when a policeman pointed sternly at the ground where their forgotten masks were lying. But there were rebels even in the early days: H. G. Wells refused to carry his, so did the editor of the *New Statesman*, Kingsley Martin. Soon, to do so became unfashionable; as early as 9 October a London park-keeper complained that he had been jeered at by small boys for carrying his mask.

The statistics tell the story. On 6 September on Westminster

Bridge 71 per cent of the men and 76 per cent of the women carried masks; by 30 October the figures were 58 and 59; by 9 November a mere 24 and 39. Other regulations, too, lost favour as the phoney war made them seem increasingly unnecessary. The windows of tubes and buses were criss-crossed with sticky tape to guard against blast. People tended to pick away at this so as to establish where they were. 'I trust you'll pardon my correction, That stuff is there for your protection,' chided Billy Brown of London Town on the ubiquitous posters. 'I trust you'll hear my explanation,' an impatient passenger wrote below, 'I can't see the bloody station.'

By the spring of 1940 many owners were regretting the holocaust of pets that had occurred at the outbreak of war. Of half a million dogs and one and a half million cats in Greater London, 400,000 (mainly cats) were destroyed in the first few days of war; the furnaces of the RSPCA had to be damped down at night because of the blackout, so could not cope with the demand. Eighty thousand dead pets were removed to a secret mass grave in east London. One by-product of this massacre was that some districts of London were threatened by a plague of rats and mice, 'so now the authorities are begging people to keep their pets if possible,' noted Gwladys Cox with some satisfaction. Surviving pets were at risk from other causes. 'Watch your cats!' warned the *Daily Express*. There had been an epidemic of organised cat thefts, particularly of Persians. 'There is a shortage of cat pelts in the fur trade.' A perennial grievance for dog and cat owners was that their pets were not allowed into the public shelters. The ARP Advisory Committee adorned Hyde Park with white posts, chains and leads to which dogs could be moored while their owners sheltered in the trenches.

As the fear of imminent attack died away, the paranoiac suspicions of treachery assumed more reasonable proportions. In the first weeks of war any flicker of escaping light, any noise not readily explicable, was taken as evidence of enemy activity. Anthony Weymouth was chatting to the foreman of a group digging trenches in Hyde Park, wondering whether there might be material for a BBC talk. He asked how many people the trench would hold and whether it would be gas-proofed. Suddenly a large woman in black erupted, ' "What right 'ave you to tell this man wot you're a-telling 'im? 'Ow d'you know 'e ain't a German spy?" Her voice was raucous, her manner belligerent. It crossed my mind that she was the type out

of which the sans-culottes of the French Revolution were made.'
Weymouth retreated with as much dignity as he could manage.
Security extended everywhere. It was said that Pen Ponds in Rich-
mond were to be drained to block the landing of German seaplanes:
'Isn't that going a little far? They can't drain the Thames,' com-
mented George Beardmore in his diary.

Many of the German and Austrian refugees who had fled to
Britain in the late 1930s were victims of the initial frenzy. Some of
the Germans in London were known to be Nazi sympathisers; in the
excitement of September 1939 the only prudent course seemed to
be to round up everyone and separate sheep from goats at leisure.
Olympia in West Kensington and the Royal Victoria Patriotic
Asylum on Wandsworth Common were used as staging posts,
though most internees were moved rapidly out of London. Eugen
Spier, a German-Jewish liberal and refugee, was arrested on 1 September and taken to Olympia, where he was the first to arrive
apart from Baron von Pillar, a notorious Nazi sympathiser. By next
morning he found that another hundred Germans had arrived,
almost all of von Pillar's persuasion. It seemed to him so extraordinary that he should be included in such company that he concluded it must be a charade, 'staged by the British authorities for
the purpose of testing my reliability. Obviously such a test would be
essential before undertaking any important work which the authorities might call upon me to render in the fight against Nazi-ism.' He
was soon disillusioned; he was not even interrogated before the
internees were bundled into buses and taken off to a former Butlin's
holiday camp at Clacton.

Most Londoners felt it proper that all German nationals should
be rounded up, even if a few innocent did suffer as a result. A
priest who had himself been imprisoned in Buchenwald before being
allowed to leave Germany was arrested in Edmonton; the vicar
protested, but few of his parishioners supported him. Suspicion of
aliens, however, always knew some bounds; when the German priest
was released after a few weeks and returned to Edmonton, the
decision was accepted cheerfully. It was always possible to bend
the rules: Eve Molesworth, thanks to a husband working in the
Foreign Office, was able to keep her Italian maid with her until
1943 and then spirit her back to Italy. Anna Freud, daughter of
Sigmund and herself a psychoanalyst, had her wireless confiscated

but was allowed to live at home and travel freely – 'And there are thousands like me,' she told the American journalist Ralph Ingersoll. Londoners believed in spies but also found the concept slightly comic. The most celebrated German agent was Funf, whose endearing incompetence and heavily accented inanities were prominent in Tommy Handley's radio programme, *ITMA*.

A contrast to 1914 noticed by Florence Speed, a writer from Brixton, was 'the absence of flag-wagging and the lack of hate. There is no animosity against the Germans. The general opinion is just "poor devils".' This benevolence was far from invariable even in 1939 and did not long survive the beginning of the blitz. Advertisements for domestic help sometimes specified, 'No Germans need apply', while the conductors of buses through West Hampstead – where it was popularly believed many Germans were still at large – would call out, 'Alight here for Finchley Strasse!' Rules, the restaurant in Maiden Lane, advertised itself as 'English and proud of it'. But there was no persecution. In the First World War dachshunds had been kicked in the streets and their owners had put them down or secreted them in the country; in 1939 Frances Faviell heard a few small boys shout 'German Sausage!' at her dachshund, but that was the extent of it.

Prejudice against Germans was irrationally compounded with anti-semitism; an unattractive element of London life which was to become more apparent a year later, but even in 1939 surfaced from time to time. Gwladys Cox was complaining about profiteering to a 'sprightly little middle-aged woman' in West Hampstead and exclaimed, 'And to think this is a Christian country!' 'Christian?' came the indignant reply. 'Jew rather! The place is entirely run by Jews. There are 25,000 in Hampstead alone. *And don't they eat!* Always nibbling bananas or chocolates.'

Belligerent patriots in the public house were more likely to inveigh against the conscientious objector than the Jew. 'Conchies', to them, were cowards, shirkers, almost traitors. Sir Edward Phipps, a London magistrate, voiced their views at a tribunal considering requests for exemption from national service, when he described the applicants as 'these miserable creatures', and interrupted their evidence with a cry of 'What tosh!' The strongly Labour Council of Bermondsey evidently shared his opinion; they dismissed all employees who were conscientious objectors, even though this cost some their pensions. A. R. Gardener of Thurrock was exempted on condition he would continue to work with the AFS; he gladly accepted, only to find that the other members of his trailer pump crew were not prepared to work with him. Sidney Greaves was imprisoned at Wormwood Scrubs for refusing to do any sort of war work; he found the warders treated him as scum: 'People who were in for robbery with violence got much more respect from them.' But not everyone was so unsympathetic: David Markham, a conscientious objector working with the Old Vic, was treated with contempt by Edith Evans and Athene Seyler but protected by the director, Tyrone Guthrie, and encouraged by Sybil Thorndike and her husband, Lewis Casson.

Even in court the voice of tolerance was sometimes heard. Six officials of the Peace Pledge Union were prosecuted for exhorting the public not to fight. The case was dismissed on the grounds that 'This is a free country. We are fighting to keep it a free country, and these gentlemen, fortunately for them in my judgment, are living in a country where they can express their pacifism, or their non-pacifism, with perfect freedom.' London had one of the worst records in the country for granting exemption to conscientious objectors; one judge even urged that God was clearly no pacifist 'for he kills us all in the end'. But the standards varied from borough to borough. Overall only about 4 per cent of those who applied obtained unconditional exemption; in Fulham, in January 1940, the figure was 1.5 per cent; in Southwark in the same month 20.8 per cent.

The first enemy plane to fly over the outskirts of London ventured up the Thames estuary on 20 November 1939. It was greeted by heavy anti-aircraft fire and turned tail. The first wartime bomb came three months later, but not from the Germans. The police were warned in February 1940 to be on their guard against a possible IRA campaign; there had already been bombs in Birmingham and it was feared the capital would be the next target. It was; on 2 March a bomb went off in Bayswater outside Whiteley's store. Four days later there was another explosion in Park Lane outside the Grosvenor House Hotel – 'it did little damage and injured no one,' recorded Hilda Neal, who ran a typists' agency in South Kensington. 'Alarming, though, for wardens on duty.' The wardens, in fact, took modest comfort from the incident: the Westminster Bank had some windows blown in but those protected by strips of gummed paper proved inviolate.

The war seemed remote from London in those first months. The sinking of the old battleship, the *Royal Oak*, at Scapa Flow was the first item of news to shake public complacency, inspiring mingled dismay and dissatisfaction. 'All those men dying for nothing like that. We might as well make peace and be done with it,' was one response recorded by a Mass Observer, but more common was frustrated anger, 'If we wanted to we could smash them to bits in two minutes. There's something wrong with the organisation at the top.' The hunger for action and, still more, for glory was shown vividly when three British cruisers, the *Exeter*, *Achilles* and the *Ajax*, took on the German pocket battleship, the *Graf Spee*, in the mouth of the River Plate and eventually forced her to scuttle. Britain rejoiced and when, two months later, the crews of the two ships marched through the City to the Guildhall, London waxed hysterical. 'The best fun in the world,' wrote Tennyson Jesse, 'the crowds were such as there have not been since that heavenly summer of King George's Jubilee ... People kept on running forward and touching the men as they passed. One white-haired old man kept on clapping them on the shoulder or shaking them by the hand and saying "Well done, boy" and so on.'

Such moments of exaltation were rare, but inaction bred a dangerous confidence. The German bombers had not come because they could not come; London had been made impregnable. Interviews in Kilburn towards the end of October showed that two-thirds of the women and half the men believed there would be no raids on the capital. 'I wouldn't go out of London for £100,' said one. 'We're so well protected here.' Others had reservations. We were told we would be destroyed when war came, mused Vivienne Hall, 'now that this has been shown to be untrue we are apt to think that it will never be so. Pray heaven it won't, but I feel we mustn't be too confident.' The authorities shared her doubts and feared that public complacency today increased the risk of panic tomorrow or the day after. Frank Whipple, a reserve policeman recruited early in 1940, was trained to use a rifle. He asked innocently who was expected to be the target. 'You'll use them on Londoners if you have to,' he was told. 'If they get out of control when the bombings come, you'll have to use them.'

To his potential victims, panic or any cause for it seemed remote. Londoners had accepted at the outbreak of war that they might soon be dead. They had realised that if the sea routes were cut they might go hungry or even starve. They were ready to be terrified or agonised by grief. They had never expected to be bored. Yet boredom is the word that occurs most frequently in reports on the capital's morale. The blackout, evacuation, the general dislocation of life had been damaging, wrote Harold Nicolson; 'The Government had not foreseen a situation in which boredom and bewilderment would be the main elements.' Londoners were 'waiting, always waiting', complained the would-be actress and trainee Bohemian Theodora FitzGibbon. 'Waiting for news, for buses, for trains . . . Waiting for bombs that never fell; gas. Waiting for casualties in dreary improvised rooms. Worst of all, waiting in queues: for foods, for forms to be filled in, for things that would never happen. The misery of doing nothing, waiting to be told what to do. Maybe. It became known as the Great Bore War.' A feeling of pointlessness stifled the fervour of September 1939; the British had gone to war to defend Poland, Poland had been crushed, what was it all for now? Mass Observation found war weariness rife at the beginning of 1940, particularly among women. How could the war end? Was the country doomed to a dismal stalemate that would last an eternity?

Few Londoners openly, or even privately, argued for a negotiated peace. 'Don't get the idea these people are discouraged or defeated,' Ed Murrow told the Americans. 'They are confident of winning this war somehow or other.' But a war in which patience proved to be the supreme virtue was not to their taste. The British were accustomed to imperialist wars with plenty of flag-wagging and patriotic fervour, Mollie Panter-Downes wrote in the *New Yorker*: 'So far there is little of either, and people talk as though the war were some tiresome chore.' The result was frustration and impatience. 'Why don't they begin fighting?' asked a man in a north London pub. 'Is it a war or isn't it? Everyone's losing heart, that's it.' In November a London landlady was asked what she had been doing all day. 'Oh, nothing much,' she replied, 'just waiting for this war to start.'

The politicians were unable to dispel this lassitude. By-elections showed an electorate resolutely determined not to be enthused. There was a respectable turnout at Silvertown, in the docks, where a highly popular Labour candidate crushed Communist and Fascist opposition, the Conservatives standing to one side, but this was an exception. In Southwark less than a quarter of voters turned out, and only thirty people mustered outside the town hall to hear the result. Churchill was the only minister who could kindle any excitement; his appearance on a newsreel in late November was loudly clapped, but 'a very youthful looking Duke of Windsor' received even more applause. The last by-election of what could still just be described as the phoney war came in North Battersea early in April 1940. Even fewer voted than in Southwark. Only a tiny proportion of those who were asked favoured the immediate ending of the war but a Mass Observer reported, 'Bewilderment and apathy are, if anything, on the increase. Grumbling also increasing, particularly among women and on economic grounds.'

Easter had fallen two weeks before. Londoners seemed resolved to show that, if the government were not interested in waging all-out war, they would do no better themselves. Last reserves of petrol were used up before cars were put away, and 70 per cent of the usual pre-war traffic headed for Brighton. Innumerable bicycles clogged what was left of the roads and the trains out of London were packed with holiday makers. It was two-way traffic; civil servants and office workers who had been moved out of London took advantage of the break to visit family and friends; special trains brought 1600 from Blackpool, 700 from Morecambe. Of the 1400 Prudential Company employees deported to Torquay, 1000 found their way back to London for Easter. The Bank Holiday fair on Hampstead Heath boasted most of its peacetime glories; only the organs on the merry-go-rounds were mute on the somewhat far-fetched ground that they might have been confused with air-raid sirens. It was the last fine flourish of peacetime London: the merry-go-round had barely departed, the last employee of the Prudential Company had hardly made his reluctant way back to Torquay, before the real war began.

7

'The world's centre'

ON 9 APRIL 1940, the day after deck-chairs reappeared in Hyde Park, five days after Neville Chamberlain told the world that Hitler had missed the bus, the Germans invaded Norway. The effect on public opinion was dramatic; Euan Wallace noted that interest in the war had been keenly stimulated, 'it has also stimulated apprehension, the numbers of people carrying gas-masks in Piccadilly Circus having trebled . . .' A month later it was the turn of Belgium, Holland and France. The Dutch army capitulated on 15 May, the Belgians on 27 May, by 22 June France too was out of the war. In the meantime, in one of the most dramatic scenes the House of Commons ever witnessed, Chamberlain had been deserted by so many of his followers that he felt bound to resign. In his place came Winston Churchill at the head of a coalition government. He was to remain in office until the war was almost over.

'We want action, and Churchill's the man,' said an artisan from Stepney; 'I've complete faith in Churchill. He knows what he's doing,' said a plumber from Notting Hill; 'Our Prime Minister is really the greatest man we have ever produced in all our long history – except perhaps for Alfred the Great,' concluded Vere Hodgson, a welfare worker from Holland Park. Churchill represented the nation more completely than any other prime minister of the twentieth century but in the capital he was above all a Londoner; even though he might be seen only by a handful of the people his presence was a source of comfort and of inspiration, his absence a cause for vague disquiet. When his voice came over the radio in a noisy Fleet Street pub, there was an instant hush: 'All eyes were glued on the loudspeaker,' wrote the American journalist Quentin Reynolds, 'almost as if the listeners believed that by concentrating they could see Churchill's face.'

In fact the voice may well have been that of the actor Norman Shelley, who was hired from time to time to repeat on radio speeches which Churchill had previously delivered in the House of Commons, but the impersonation was good enough to satisfy the listeners. Churchill had no rival: not the King, though George VI became more and more respected as the war continued; not Herbert Morrison, though the 'soft-hearted suburban Stalin', as Michael Foot memorably described him, had been a champion of Labour London for many years and was now Churchill's Home Secretary. Not everyone joined in the worship: 'I'm no friend of Churchill. If it wasn't for him we'd have peace now,' exclaimed a woman of forty angrily. But she was one of a tiny minority; for most Londoners in the summer of 1940 Churchill was the unquestioned hero.

It is an article of patriotic faith that Britain in 1940 was united as never before or since in a mood of resolute defiance. Like most generalisations, it requires qualification. Like, indeed even more than, most generalisations, it is in essence true. Surveys of public opinion prepared for the Ministry of Information and presented each week to the Cabinet describe a mood of belligerency and resolve. But the picture was not wholly rosy. People were not frightened but they were depressed, women more than men, said the report of 22 May, a few days before the evacuation from Dunkirk.

Rebecca West for one believed that people were frightened too. Every evening she would walk with her husband in the rose garden in Regent's Park. 'Under the unstained heaven of that perfect summer, curiously starred with the silver elephantines of the balloon barrage, the people sat on the seats among the roses, reading the papers or looking straight in front of them, their faces white. Some of them walked among the rose-beds, with a special earnestness looking down on the bright flowers and inhaling the scent, as if to say, "That is what roses are like, that is how they smell. We must remember that, down in the darkness." Most of these people believed, and rightly, that they were presently to be subjected to a form of attack more horrible than had ever before been directed against common man. Let nobody belittle them by pretending they were fearless. Not being as the ox and the ass, they were horribly afraid. But their pale lips did not part to say the words that would have given them security and dishonour.' The last sentence seems a trifle melodramatic; it is hard to think what words, honourable or dishonourable, could have won security for the Londoner at this juncture. But Rebecca West and the Ministry of Information would at least have agreed that even if some such magic incantation had existed the average Londoner would have scorned to invoke it.

Opinion in the capital was more volatile than in the rest of the country, the Cabinet was told, Londoners were more on the lookout for sudden changes in the progress of the war. 'London therefore needs a firmer and more stable background tone, instead of a less-integrated and more emotional, changeable tone.' A sudden loss of heart could be provoked by the most insubstantial causes; on 27 May observers reported 'serious defeatist talk in Fulham working-class and ARP posts due to rumour of King and Government about to go to Canada.'

It was above all Churchill who supplied the firmness and stability, though the unidentified expert from the MoI might have faulted him as injudiciously emotional. His speech of 4 June, in which he pledged, 'We shall fight on the beaches, we shall fight on the landing grounds, we shall fight in the fields and in the streets, we shall fight in the hills, we shall never surrender,' transformed the mood of the nation. 'This speech filled us all with a quiet determination to be as courageous as possible,' wrote Joan Veazey, young wife of a Kensington curate. 'I intend to stick by my Man and to guard our little bit of England, even if it is a little bit broken.' Churchill's pugnacity and refusal to contemplate anything except ultimate victory gave exactly the lead that was wanted. When the preacher at St Martin-in-the-Fields took a pacifist line, Mrs Churchill stalked out in protest. 'You ought to have cried "Shame",' said Churchill, 'desecrating the House of God with lies!' The remark was splendidly irrational, and splendid irrationality was badly needed. The mood prevailed. A dockyard worker recorded that the moment the collapse of France became known, 'men of all ages were trying to enlist, asking when they could fight and how they could drill and get arms'. A grandmother kept an old sword in the corner of her room; 'she was going to slash any German that came in'.

The fact that Britain had lost all her allies seemed reason for satisfaction. As the commissionaire at one of the Service clubs said to a rather downcast member, 'Anyhow, sir, we're in the Final, and it's to be played on the Home Ground.' The remark seems improbably picturesque, but it was the sort of thing people *were* thinking and saying at the time. Mrs Byers felt relief that Britain was now on its own and could 'really get on with the job'. She hesitated to voice this thought when she went to work, but heard it 'again and again from our folk all over the office. They are fighting mad and not in the least afraid.' Eric Sevareid, another American journalist who was in London at the time, saw nothing surprising in this somewhat blinkered vision of the future. After all, he commented drily, since the Londoner 'had never thought of London as anything but the world's center, it did not surprise him that the world's attention was now fixed on London. The average Londoner . . . found nothing particularly novel about the alignment of forces; he was hardly conscious that it had ever been anything but himself against the Boche.'

Blind confidence in victory was not invariable. In Westminster Abbey for a Service of Intercession Churchill sensed the fear 'not of death, or wounds, or material loss, but of defeat and the final ruin of Britain'. From Greenwich and Deptford came reports that the 'possibility of our not being victorious is now being considered by some people'. But this was not seen as a reason for opening negotiations with Germany, let alone for surrender; in a by-election at Bow and Bromley on 12 June only 6 per cent of those asked favoured peace at any price; the 'Stop the War' candidate gleaned a derisory 506 votes. Most people are still hopeful, Vivienne Hall noted in her diary, and only one or two 'announced gloomily that we might as well put our heads in a gas oven as the Germans would be here any minute'.

George Orwell, then working discontentedly in the BBC, remarked that people still talked little about the war; when he went into a pub to hear the news he found that the barmaid had not intended to turn on the radio. This would not have been surprising six months before, or even a year later, but a Mass Observation survey showed that in the summer of 1940 almost everyone in London with a radio listened to the news, usually twice a day and sometimes five or six times. Otherwise the casual observer would have seen little sign of crisis in London's streets and parks; the crowds still milled around Speaker's Corner, listening to orators from the National Secular Society and the New and Latter House of Israel and amiably heckling orators from the Peace Pledge Union; hundreds more boated or bathed on or in the Serpentine. There were pockets of frenzied activity, as in Stornoway House where Lord

Crowds in Downing Street on 1 September 1939. A high proportion of those present were Czech or German refugees (p. 33)

Parents were trained in the use of gas-masks with small children. Few of the latter proved as cooperative as the enthusiastic victim illustrated above (p. 17)

Women in Kensington fill sandbags. 'I think this is a good thing,' remarked Rose Macaulay, 'as it gives people something they feel useful to do' (p. 29)

Anderson shelters were supposed to be covered by eighteen inches of soil, as in this case in Clapham. 'When old 'Itler comes over, we'll 'ave to shout, "Don't destroy it, there's such lovely marigolds!" ' joked a Stepney gardener (p. 100)

Colonel Trotter, ARP Warden in Holborn. During the phoney war wardens, in the eyes of the public, became, if not villains, at least self-important nuisances (p. 65)

Mothers see off their evacuee children from Waterloo. Almost at once the return flow would begin

Downing Street, defended by a sand-bagged pillbox

The statue of Charles I in Whitehall

Piccadilly early in 1940. Eros has disappeared, and most of the private cars, but the flower women are still selling their wares

A break in training. 'It did thrill me to see all those men doing their bit. Elderly men, they deserve a bit of a snooze on Sunday afternoon, but there they were, all of them' (p. 106)

The zoo reopened by mid-September 1939. The chimpanzees celebrated the return of the visitors with a spectacular display of gymnastics, though it seems improbable that many of them joined in the war-effort as in this somewhat contrived picture (p. 44)

The Home Guard take over at Buckingham Palace,
relieving regular troops for more active duties

Boy Scouts join in Home Guard training, mounting
an attack on a gasworks and meeting stiff resistance

Home Guard and Wardens in Whitehall

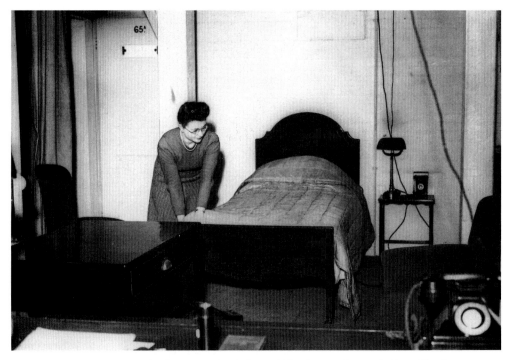

Churchill's austere bedroom in the Cabinet War Rooms beneath King Charles Street. During raids he was as likely as not to be above ground, seeing what was going on (p. 137)

Beaverbrook was creating the Ministry of Aircraft Production and work went on seven days a week from 8.30 a.m. to 2 a.m. but most Londoners were slow to switch to the tempo of all-out war. When J. T. Murphy joined a London engineering works in July he found a conspicuous lack of the 'Dunkirk atmosphere'; everyone worked at their own pace and the unions rigorously enforced the traditional rules and restrictions. Nor was overtime, when it existed, necessarily devoted to martial causes; the *Daily Telegraph* reported, 'For the second week in succession the Crown Office and the College of Arms have had to work at top speed in the preparation of patents of peerage.'

Though the mood was patriotic there was little strident jingoism. A headmaster in Woolwich set his boys and girls to saluting the flag, singing 'Land of Hope and Glory' and marching around the playing field to chauvinistic tunes, but he was considered mildly comic by most who witnessed his activities. The same tolerant indifference was shown towards the 'group of bearded intellectuals' who remained seated in a West End bar when 'God Save the King' was played. A couple who tried to leave the Hammersmith Palais de Danse during the national anthem were checked by the commission-aire but the rest of the audience affected not to notice. The govern-ment seemed almost deliberately to avoid whipping up enthusiasm. General Raymond Lee, attached to the American Embassy, noticed the excitement provoked by the spectacle of a tank lumbering up the Strand and marvelled at the failure of the authorities 'to understand the advantages of a reasonable amount of publicity'. Not that a military presence was always welcome; a barman in Notting Hill complained that soldiers were 'a perfect nuisance hanging round the customers cadging drinks. They spoil our regular trade.' Nor were even patriots necessarily delighted by displays of unbridled fervour. *Music While You Work* was initially a great success when introduced at Schneider's factory in Stepney but enthusiasm soon dwindled: 'We didn't want to hear "God Save the King" a hundred times a day. It's killing – honestly.'

'The British people are still very calm and resolute and show no signs of fear,' wrote Hilda Neal early in June. Calm resolution is the impression given by many commentators, foreign as well as British. An American journalist, Bill Stoneman of the *Chicago Daily News*, turned on Lady Diana Cooper and exclaimed, 'Don't you realise what's going on? The Germans are rolling like burning lava over the whole world. Burning lava!' Those listening thought his vehemence exquisitely funny, and he was known from then on as 'Lava' Stoneman. But Londoners were not blind to their danger, thought another American journalist, Vincent Sheean. 'In fact the English all knew that they stood upon the brink of death, but being conditioned in their own style, preferred not to state it too often or too strongly.' In July Raymond Lee called for reports on the state of morale from American consuls around the country. 'It was high everywhere and no consul but thought the people would see the thing through.' The only possible weak spot, he rather surprisingly concluded, might be 'the City's commercial men'.

Through the summer and autumn of 1940 London lived in day-to-day expectation of invasion. Quentin Reynolds, who had arrived shortly after Dunkirk, was disconcerted to see how the people went about their normal business 'as if death might not drop from the sky at any moment'. In fact, the people were doing quite a lot outside the normal line of business to cope with death if it arrived, but a cultivated *sang froid* seemed the appropriate response in public. 'Invasion? That would be a *great* bore!' was the bland comment of the Foreign Secretary, Lord Halifax. No doubt he went on to complain that it would interfere with the cubbing. Hitler had proclaimed 15 August as being the day he would dictate peace terms in London. The Overseas League gave a tea dance on that date to celebrate the fact that he was not able to attend.

Where defeatism existed it was most often among those who had been given no part to play. A Home Office report referred to 'nests of defeatism in London' among Local Defence Volunteers who were not being trained or armed, or women who had been registered as possessing special qualifications and then left idle. As the machinery of war gathered pace such grumbles died away; subversive talk of a more forthright kind was rarely heard. A commercial traveller going by tube to Edgware heard people saying that it was time we caved in to Hitler, who had anyway done a good job dealing with the Jews. 'They were probably fascists,' he concluded in dismay. Equally unusual was the report put to the Cabinet that in certain working-class districts there was 'increasing dissociation of leaders and led. Many women say about Hitler: "He won't hurt us, it's the bosses he's after. We'll probably be better off when he comes." ' If 'many women' did say this, their voices left few ripples on the smooth surface of public opinion. Almost every report, oral or written, contemporary or recollected in tranquillity, records a London in which the old reasons for discord survived, but which was united in its determination to resist the potential invader.

The government was more concerned about rumours that might weaken the will to resist. It was itself partly responsible for creating the climate in which such rumours flourished. There were some things which, for excellent reasons, could not be told the public, but many more which were concealed to save time or embarrassment or just from love of obfuscation. People felt they were being kept in the dark and speculated wildly about the true facts and the reasons for hiding them. 'There's a lot we don't know,' a Mass Observer overheard in Stepney, 'I've got a feeling there's something brewing . . . They're not keeping quiet for nothing, take it from me,' and then a few days later, 'We don't know all what's going on. I reckon there's things we don't know about.' This was true not only of the East End. 'There is too much quack, quack, quack,' complained Hugh Dalton, the Minister for Economic Warfare. 'I think it is probably worst in the clubs of the West End, where not only are conversations overheard, but it is noted who goes with whom, and on this basis inferences drawn and gossip continually embellished.' At best this was harmless sensationalism, at worst there was a deliberate will to stir up dissension. Mrs Watson of Empire Court, Wembley, told anyone who would listen that at Dunkirk officers of the BEF had fought to be evacuated before their men. A neighbour reported her to Scotland Yard and asked that she should be warned and reprimanded.

How far Scotland Yard, or the authorities in general, should try to curb excesses of this sort was a question which perplexed those responsible. For the most part they were content to let the public carry the burden. They would heartily have approved of the Kilburn café proprietor who took exception to a customer announcing that Hitler would win the war within a month: 'I shut him up sharp. Kicked him out. I've often done that. I won't have them in here talking treachery.' But not everyone could be relied on to act with such robustness, and the law sometimes felt bound to intervene. The organising secretary of the Women's Peace Campaign was jailed for a month for saying in Hyde Park that the British ought to lay down their arms. At Chatham a shipwright who said that Hitler would win and that £1 notes would be worth 1/- a hundredweight was fined £10. But such action smacked of repression, and sometimes teetered into absurdity. A man who drank 'To Hell with Hitler!' was accused of saying 'Heil Hitler!' A fracas followed and he was fined 5/- for insulting behaviour. The 'Rout the Rumour Rally' in Hendon Park was certainly well intentioned: 10,000 people gathered to hear Jack Warner tell funny stories, Will Fyffe sing 'Loch Lomond' and Harold Nicolson make a patriotic speech. But the mood was one of 'vague good-humoured curiosity'; it seems unlikely that a single rumour received even a glancing blow, let alone was killed, as a result of this extravaganza.

A related problem facing the authorities was whether to discourage people from listening to the broadcasts from Germany by Oswald Mosley's former lieutenant, William Joyce, better known as 'Lord Haw Haw'. Most people laughed at him; some were enraged – 'He makes my blood boil!' said a Lambeth housewife, 'I feel inclined to smash the set, saying what he does about England.' But the propaganda was insidious, the effect cumulative, and another Lambeth woman spoke for a substantial minority when she remarked, 'I think he's very good . . . he's very interesting, and a lot he says is true.' Harry Davey, a small child living in the Elephant and Castle, remembers that his family would rather have missed even *ITMA* than Lord Haw Haw. What he said was taken seriously. If he seemed to threaten a raid, then preparations were made for a night in the shelter. The government would have preferred people not to listen, but knew the uproar that would ensue if it tried to enforce a ban and wisely let things be. The angry public reaction to revelations that Ministry of Information investigators were listening to their conversations and reporting on morale showed how sensitive people were to any suggestion that they were being spied on. 'Cooper's Snoopers', as the investigators were christened, were denounced and their activities hurriedly curtailed.

The Home Morale Emergency Committee concerned itself particularly with the question of how the British – in particular the Londoner – would react to aerial bombardment. It made some sensible recommendations about the need to tell the public more about ARP services, and thus increase its confidence; as well as some less helpful injunctions to West End actors to keep people cheerful, lead community singing and generally turn the theatres into centres of innocent merriment. But the Committee really knew little of what was going on. What now seems evident yet was far from clear at the time is that morale in the late summer was lower than it had been a few months before, but that this was not because the Londoner was oppressed by fears of invasion or an imminent blitz. On the contrary, it was the lack of activity which caused the drop in morale. 'I wish he'd try invasion, and have a scrap and get it over with,' said a sixty-year-old woman in Fulham. 'It's this waiting that gets you down.' In Stepney, where unemployment was still high and economic pressures added to the general malaise, Mass Observers believed that 'behind it all can be detected a longing for something to happen'. But an analysis of London opinion at the beginning of September based on censored mail suggested that overall morale was still 'outstandingly good'. The phrase 'Our Island Fortress' was used more often and with more gusto than any other; the conviction that it was a privilege to be in Britain in 1940 was expressed in many letters – 'I would not be anywhere in the world but here, for a fortune,' wrote one Wembley correspondent. Letters to friends or relatives abroad originated mostly from the middle or upper classes and the members of the Morale Committee might have argued that they provided few clues to the state of mind in the poorer areas. It was reactions in the working-class districts that most concerned them. But here too there did not seem particular cause for worry. Reports from areas outside London which had been regularly bombed showed that morale was significantly higher as a result; as bombs began to fall in the East End in the weeks before the real blitz began Home Office reports showed that drunkenness was down, absenteeism less common, there was an 'improved condition of morale'.

The six months before the blitz began were a difficult time for many Londoners. Nationwide, prices had risen by 19 per cent over the previous twelve months; wages by only 11 per cent. In London both figures were marginally higher, and the variation between areas was dramatic. In Islington in July 1940, for every working-class family whose income had increased in real terms, three stayed the same and three were worse off. Since the per capita income of the majority was only £1.10s. a head, deprivation was inevitable. 'What we haven't got, we go without,' said one housewife, 'I go without food to give it to my husband.' There was some bitterness: 'It's the poor people that fight the war, not the rich. They call on us to fight and we aren't fed well enough.' The government saw the dangers of disaffection and tried to head it off. Bob Boothby, Parliamentary Secretary at the Ministry of Food, called for less luxurious dishes in restaurants; it had already happened, said a restaurateur regretfully, in the past he had sold £20 worth of caviare a night, now it was £1 a week. At the LCC-run British Restaurants a three-course meal including soup, braised tongue and a pudding cost only 9d. The Minister of Food, Lord Woolton, was photographed tucking in with relish. 'Those who want luxury feeding in these days are outsiders,' he remarked.

Not everyone would have accepted Woolton's definition of an outsider. Chips Channon dined with Loelia, Duchess of Westminster, the day Holland and Belgium were invaded. 'We all felt the dinner to be so excellent,' he wrote in his diary, 'that we wanted to keep the menu in an album, as an archaeological specimen showing that this was the meal that we, in England, were fortunate enough to enjoy even after six months of war effort.' It was still possible for the rich to live in great comfort without breaking the law, and some chose to do so; it was not unknown for customers to storm out of expensive restaurants because they wanted larger portions of cream and sugar and had decided to seek them elsewhere. But for most, including many who could well have afforded to live better, austerity was increasingly the rule. Raymond Lee returned to London after several months to find 'One gets only a lump of sugar and a thin little flake of butter. No more iced cakes. Fewer kinds of cheese. Only six pages in the newspaper. All paper is saved.' The sugar ration was reduced to eight ounces a week in May; butter to four ounces in June; tea, margarine and cooking fats were rationed in July. Tinned milk was a rarity, much prized for its storage qualities. 'Great shortage of eggs in London,' noted Vere Hodgson. 'I shall have to switch over to baked beans.'

An appeal for anything aluminium to help build aeroplanes resulted in the accumulation of mountains of dubiously valuable scrap; the royal family contributed miniature kettles and tea-pots given to the two princesses by the people of Wales. The shortage of goods meant that trade languished. A shop selling leather goods survived almost entirely on repairs; a radio shop abandoned the hire purchase system used for most of its sales: 'With everyone moving about we can't take the risk. There's no safeguard.' The bigger shops, which could make up here what they lost there, survived best; a large dress store in the Mile End Road reported that things were bad but 'not as bad as we'd expected. The spirit of the people is good and they try to carry on as much as possible in the usual way.' Bright colours were out of favour, blacks and sombre browns or greys were in fashion. But a woman selling lingerie in a small shop a few hundred yards away was in despair: 'I have never in all my life experienced or thought of experiencing such a terrible season. We don't have a customer all day, hardly. It's heartbreaking.'

Efforts to keep things going as in peacetime were often surprisingly successful. The Royal Academy had 400 more exhibits at its summer show than in 1939. 'El Greco-like' portraits by Augustus John were generally admired and only some searchlight scenes and 'The Homecoming of HMS *Exeter*' by Charles Cundall reminded viewers that a war was on. In August attendance figures at the zoo soared to 18,000 a day; most museums were closed but Hampton Court was vastly popular; 13,000 went to Lord's cricket ground to see an inter-services match; the main dance hall at Richmond was so well patronised that it was decided to open an extra night a week. Newspaper sellers were not allowed to prepare new posters, but made out by using old ones: HEAVY GERMAN LOSSES could serve on almost every occasion. Much ingenuity was devoted to presenting goods as if they had a martial value: 'First Aid in Wartime for Health, Strength and Fortitude. Wrigley's Chewing Gum', proclaimed an advertisement on the sides of London buses.

But even a cursory inspection often showed that beneath the veneer of normality the strains were showing. The Bachelors' Club appeared to thrive, but more than half its 700 members were away on national service. Every member left in London was asked for an extra £14, thus doubling the annual subscription. Even more drastic, women were admitted to certain parts of the club, though an attempt was made to preserve the proprieties by insisting that, to merit the privilege, they had to have been presented at court.

Every optimistic forecast by shopkeepers, restaurateurs, club secretaries, was qualified by the provision that all might change if air-raids started. People still hoped that they would not. The well-informed General Lee told his wife, 'I consider it extremely unlikely that any attack will take place on London.' Possibly he was trying to put her mind at rest; he did not subscribe to the hopeful hypothesis that at the last moment Hitler would shy off and move eastwards: 'That is very British. I can't see how he can change his direction now.' But of one thing he was sure: if Hitler did turn towards the Balkans, 'in a month's time England would go off sound asleep again'.

If the raiders came, the city they attacked would be more cosmopolitan than ever in the past. 'London is an extraordinary place in this pause between battles,' mused John Lehmann, 'on the streets and in the pubs you see Canadian, Australian, New Zealand soldiers; French sailors, air-officers, légionnaires; Dutch officers, Norwegian and Dutch sailors, Poles and Czechs ... It quickens one's interest and excitement in the moment; it seems almost impossible to contemplate that one should fail them all.'

Mingling in Kensington Gardens with the debris of half a dozen continental armies, Charles Ritchie 'had the sense of swimming in the full tide of history'. It was not by accident that so many foreign troops were congregated in London; the government believed that seeing Dominion troops in particular would boost the spirits of the people. Surveying them the American journalist Ben Robertson was reminded of Daniel Boone's stockade in Kentucky with the Indians at the gates: 'London, the greatest city in the world, had become a frontier town.' Londoners did feel reassured by the presence of allies from so many parts of the world, but their welcome was not invariable; the censorious were quick to find the visitors rowdy and obstreperous. 'What did make me fed up,' admitted a middle-aged woman in Notting Hill, 'was seeing a drunken Australian being carried into a taxi by two tommies. I can't think why they didn't leave the pig in the gutter.'

The Free French were among the most numerous and certainly the most conspicuous. When Charles de Gaulle arrived in London in June 1940, he was struck by the 'look of tranquillity, almost indifference' he observed wherever he went. He was at first unequivocally admired by the British; Vere Hodgson thought him a hero, 'His voice is thrilling, and his answer to Pétain made me shiver in my chair.' It seemed to have less effect on his fellow countrymen. On 19 July 800 members of the French Embassy left for Paris, leaving a rump behind. M. Corbin, the ambassador, was one of the few to rally to de Gaulle.

Though Londoners admired him, they were less certain about his followers. There were moments at which their hearts went out to the Free French volunteers, as when on 14 July, Bastille Day, they marched through the streets and sang the 'Marseillaise' at the foot of Foch's statue in Victoria. An English crowd accompanied the fervent singing of the French with a noisy wordless rumble. But on less emotional occasions Londoners had reservations; the man in the street felt that the Free French were representatives of a defeated nation who had let Britain down once and, given the chance, would no doubt do so again; the insider doubted their discretion even more than their fighting qualities. They 'do not present a pretty picture', remarked Oliver Harvey, a senior official at the Foreign Office. 'They fill the restaurants of London with their gossip and intrigue. So bad is their propensity to chatter that we cannot confide to them any of our secrets.' They cut a dashing figure in the eyes of many young girls, but this merely reinforced the doubts of the less glamorous British; the places where they congregated – the York Minster pub in Soho or their canteen in the Astors' house in St James's Square – were considered to be, if not dens of vice, then at least dangerously louche. Their propensity to squabble among themselves was evident only to a few, but de Gaulle's intransigence and the fact that he was anathema to many genuine French patriots gradually became apparent to a wider circle. On the whole Londoners preferred the Poles, who were quite as colourful, less convinced of their superiority and a great deal readier to learn English properly.

London found civilian refugees harder to accept. Most people were torn between feelings of pity for the dispossessed, hospitality towards guests, resentment of those who would take much-needed food and, in time, no doubt jobs as well, and suspicion of aliens who talked unfathomable tongues and had strange and probably nasty habits. George Orwell went to Victoria Station to see the first arrivals. 'One refugee woman was crying, or nearly so, but most seemed only bewildered by the crowds and the general strangeness. A considerable crowd was watching and had to be held back by the police to let the refugees get to the street. The refugees were greeted in silence but all sailors of any description enthusiastically cheered.'

Twelve large halls were opened for the reception of Dutch and Belgian refugees, Earls Court and Crystal Palace among them. Private hotels around Kensington, Paddington and Bloomsbury were set aside and the Strand Palace turned into a caravanserai. 'The vast lounges are thronged with a population of small, dark, well-dressed Latin, Slav, Mongolian, Semitic beings,' wrote a somewhat supercilious observer, 'established in groups around tables with the air of nomads who pitch a wandering tent without being a day's march nearer home.'

Many Londoners remembered an earlier wave of refugees. 'If they are anything like the Belgians in the last war, they are a dirty lot,' exclaimed the owner of a small Paddington sweetshop, adding handsomely, 'but, poor things, they can't help it.' Cricklewood was an area to which many of them were despatched, but nearly half the local inhabitants proved reluctant to offer them shelter. 'I'm not taking any, because I don't think it right,' said a woman of twenty-five, 'especially now the king's turned on us.' 'Who's paying for them?' asked an air-raid warden. 'If it's our government, it's a bloody shame.' But both these misanthropes in the end relented and agreed that they would do what they could do to help – 'They're victims, I suppose.' Home Intelligence Reports told of growing hostility to aliens in Richmond, with Belgian children excluded from local play groups; while in Dulwich and Hammersmith there were cases of Belgian refugees being booed in the street.

The 12,000 or so Gibraltarian refugees, mainly Maltese in origin, were particularly resented, though it was grudgingly admitted that they were at least part of the imperial family. Many of them were installed in two blocks of luxury flats near Lancaster Gate. Rachel Ferguson, a Kensington resident guilty of the most bigoted snobbishness, abused them roundly: 'Of course, one was sorry for them,' she declared, but after that perfunctory expression of sympathy she proceeded to denounce their faddiness, their 'savagely primitive' personal habits, their 'flair for conversion of any place into which they were put into a slum'. With nothing to do all day and lavish subventions from the government, 'they infested the shops and bought up the few comparative luxuries (ham was one of them), at which we domestically ridden and largely servantless householders got no chance'. It had been wrong to billet them in an area where they could have no rapport, 'physically, financially or psychically'.

They would, she concluded crushingly, have been more at home in Soho. Luckily for the Gibraltarians, not everyone was so bleakly hostile: the local scouts adopted many of the 650 children and enrolled them in their local troops. The Kensington troop at first reminded the scout master of the Demon's Chorus from *The Dream of Gerontius*, but he persevered and in the end established a happy and successful unit.

It is easy to be struck by the uncharitable comments and to forget how many people there were like the scout master, how many decent, hard-working, kindly Londoners who sacrificed time, energy and often sorely needed food and clothes to make the lot of the refugees more tolerable. On the whole, though, London's response was nothing to be proud of. Kensington hauteur was matched by the abuse of the working classes in the East End: 'Bleeding French!', 'Stinking Dutchmen', 'There's all of us 'ere, we want work, but they give these bastards the jobs', 'Why should we have to keep them? They're all Jews – always getting something for nothing.' There are too many such remarks recorded, from too many parts of London, to leave any doubt that the capital was rich in racist bigots who were singularly short of charity.

Excuses could be found in the atmosphere of the time. As the Germans overran Western Europe there had been many reports of sabotage and treason. Some at least of these were well founded, particularly in Holland, where local sympathisers had linked up with enemy paratroops. With invasion a probability it would have been astonishing, indeed irresponsible, if the British had not looked suspiciously at the potential enemy in their midst. Spy fever was fanned by the arrest of a cypher clerk from the American Embassy, Tyler Kent. Kent, who had been passing secrets to the Germans, was known to be in touch with extreme right-wing British political figures. How many others might be involved? The threat was real, though it did not add up to much. The head of MI5 remarked blandly that he had been surprised by his success in rounding up German spies at the outbreak of war: 'I am greatly disappointed in what the Germans have managed to do. They are not in the same class as in the last war.'

MI5's belief that few if any German spies remained at liberty did not stop a vigorous round-up of German nationals soon after Churchill came to power, including some who had been arrested in

1939 and later released. The first ruling was that all German men between the ages of sixteen and sixty were to be apprehended. This disturbed some who pointed out that there might be spies aged sixty-one, not to mention Mata Haris. Two thousand aliens were picked up at London addresses in an early morning swoop on 16 May; ten days later 1500 women were added to the bag. Hampstead was a favourite target. The methods used by the police do not seem to have been particularly sophisticated; a constable simply walked into the public library and called for all Germans and Austrians to step outside. The operation may have eased pressure on the library's newspapers, but does not seem to have contributed notably to national security. It was perceived as a great success, however. Florence Speed from Brixton recorded in her diary that in the round-up secret papers had been found giving instructions for sabotage at key points: 'It does look as if *all* aliens should be interned just to make sure.'

Aliens were the prime target for public suspicion. 'If we were 100 per cent British we should be all right,' reflected Vere Hodgson. 'It is the Fifth Column we fear.' But some 100 per cent British were to be feared as well; the Special Branch of Scotland Yard had prepared a list of people to be taken into custody as soon as the amended Defence Regulations had been passed by Parliament. In the last week of May they struck; 1600 British citizens were arrested, including the leader of the British Fascists, Oswald Mosley, a Tory MP, Captain Ramsay, and a retired admiral. Gradually most were released but there were still some 400 in custody by mid-1941, including the Mosleys, installed in modest comfort in a flat in Holloway Prison.

'C class' aliens, those not felt to require internment but still of interest to the security services, were subject to a curfew from midnight to 6 a.m. This produced some odd results. The Prime Minister's son-in-law, Vic Oliver, an American entertainer, urged his audience at the Hippodrome, 'Please laugh a bit quicker, ladies and gentlemen, because I've got to be home by midnight', but in fact he had an exemption allowing him to be out until 4 a.m. So did most people who had a reasonable need to be away from home. Siegfriede Samitz was less fortunate, she was imprisoned for a month for being found in Vincent Square at 1.30 a.m. 'The thing I object to most is that you were out late at night with British soldiers,' said the magistrate; leaving some uncertainty whether it was the 'late', the 'British', the 'soldiers' or her unspecified activities which caused the most offence. Hotel managers in Hampstead, Hendon and Golders Green acted as unofficial watchdogs, reporting the movements of alien guests. One 'extremely wealthy woman' was found to have stayed at eleven different addresses. 'That was a good catch,' said the police appreciatively.

When Italy entered the war on 10 June 1940, an army of predominantly harmless foreigners was transformed into the enemy. A large number of Italians ran or were employed in restaurants and hotels. At the Ritz and Carlton Italian waiters were suspended in mid-shift without waiting for the police to act. A clean sweep of Italian residents quickly followed, including many who had spent most of their lives in London as well as some pimps and petty gangsters whom the police had wanted to put inside for years. Prominent figures in London society, like the Quaglino brothers or Ferraro, the popular maître d'hôtel at the Berkeley, disappeared abruptly. Victor Toliani, an Italian waiter who had lived in London since childhood, was marched away with a group of his compatriots. 'Look at the dirty Germans! Spit at them!' a teacher enjoined his charges. They obliged, but it was the charge of being German that hurt Toliani most. He was not the only one to suffer abuse. Mrs Celetti, wife of a King's Road restaurateur, said that the police had been correct and courteous but the people, including some of their former patrons, had 'behaved with unexpected violence'. In Soho Italian restaurants hopefully put notices in their windows proclaiming themselves '100 per cent patriotic British' or, in the case of a spaghetti house, 'British Food Shop', but this did not prevent a mob stoning some of them and doing a little looting. George Orwell walked through Soho to assess the damage and found only three shops with their windows smashed, but there were others throughout London. Orwell concluded that 'the low-down, cold-blooded meanness of Mussolini's declaration of war at that moment must have made an impression even on people who as a rule barely read the newspapers'.

The instinct that led louts to throw bricks through the windows of ice-cream shops or spaghetti houses did engender a brief madness in London. Cecil Beaton, trying to photograph some bomb damage a week or so before the blitz proper began, was set on by 'a little man with ferret eyes and a pointed red nose' who claimed the

Ministry of Information would disapprove. A newspaper seller joined in and Beaton was taken to a police station where he was cautioned for 'provoking the antagonism of the crowd'. The wife of the Speaker of the House of Commons, Mrs Fitzroy, saw a man who looked foreign standing outside Westminster Abbey looking at a map, and at once summoned a passing constable. She was outraged when the policeman said it was no business of his. A seventy-year-old man in Hendon stood watching workmen excavating a gas main. A passer-by asked what the men were doing. ' "Looks as if they're digging a hole," I said. Well, it wasn't right, was it, asking a question like that. *I* knew what it was, of course, but I wasn't going to tell him.'

Such instances were absurd but harmless; there was a real fear, however, that spy fever might get out of hand. 'The Fifth Column hysteria is reaching dangerous proportions,' Home Intelligence commented in June. Cecil Beaton had merely been inconvenienced, others were threatened with the loss of their jobs or even their liberty. The *Enfield Gazette* reported complaints that an alien had been employed in an important ARP centre: 'We are glad to be able to state that the employment of the person in question has now been terminated.' In the same borough half a dozen other people were discharged or transferred because they were 'pacifist, fascist, communist or conscientious objector'. Nobody was martyred, but Londoners exposed an ugly intolerance which ill became the champions of democracy.

Fortunately most patriots had other preoccupations. The programme for the building of public shelters was broadly complete by the end of July. Londoners thought little of them. 'They smell so, they're so dirty,' said one discontented East Ender; the children used them as playgrounds, complained another, 'Empty bottles, broken toys, it all goes in them. It's a real annoyance.' More serious were the doubts of another critic, who looked scornfully at a Stepney shelter, 'Much good it may do us! I'm afraid to blow as I go by, in case I knock it down.'

Her fears, it seems, were sometimes shared by the authorities; the public shelter at Waterloo Station bore an unpromising notice threatening that people using it did so 'entirely AT THEIR OWN RISK'. While the danger of raids still seemed remote, some councils had taken to keeping the public shelters locked to prevent vandalism and the theft of fitments; by mid-August most of them were open again, though Wandsworth kept the keys in a glass case, to be broken open only in case of emergency, while Wembley appointed wardens to open the doors when the sirens sounded. On the whole the public put more faith in shelters adapted from the crypts of churches. In St Martin-in-the-Fields, thousands of coffins were removed at the cost of £6000 to make way for shelterers. The verger, Mr Ambler, boasted that he had personally unscrewed the lot. Didn't he find it a gruesome job? he was asked. Not at all, he replied, 'after a week's work it was as easy as opening a tin of sardines'. Many of the bodies had been in perfect condition when the coffins were opened, though exposure to the air led to their quickly crumbling. For the churches the cost of such operations was serious; heating and lighting the crypt of St Martin's cost more than £100 a quarter, so the rector, William McCormick, wrote articles for the magazine *John Bull* to raise the money.

The Communist *Daily Worker*, followed more temperately by the *News Chronicle*, *Daily Mail* and *Evening Standard*, pressed for the immediate provision of deep shelters. The authorities remained opposed and ARP lecturers were instructed to point out the dangers. 'What happens if the doors get blocked?' asked a warden in the Mile End Road. 'Then people won't be able to get up from the bowels of the earth and will just have to remain there with RIP written on top.' At a London engineering works the Communist shop-stewards threatened a strike if deep shelters were not provided; the management offered strong semi-surface shelters and the men voted down their leaders to accept the compromise. The idea that tube stations might serve as shelters was still flatly rejected by the authorities. When an alert sounded at Camden Town at the end of August, a Mass Observer saw officials gather around the entrance to the Underground and ask everyone who sought entry whether they were *bona fide* travellers. One woman admitted she was not – 'she stares rather blankly and stumbles out again'. The public would not be so docile when the bombs began to fall.

'There's nothing like an Anderson shelter,' the Mile End Road lecturer had concluded. By July half London's householders had a private shelter, most of them Andersons. Early raids had proved them remarkably successful, able to resist a 50kg bomb falling six feet away and a 250kg bomb at twenty feet. In spite of the damp and discomfort, many were becoming quite attached to their shelters. One in Stepney had a crop of flowers growing from its earth covering. 'When old 'Itler comes over, we'll 'ave to shout, "Don't destroy it, there's such lovely marigolds",' joked the proprietor. This Anderson accommodated the neighbours as well, 'We 'ad a practice the other night and we didn't 'alf 'ave a lark. We lay down on the floor and all the men could see our bloomers! Laugh? You'd have died.' In spite of such inducements, some men took a loftier line. A Mass Observer heard one woman pleading for a shelter while her husband argued that the kitchen would be quite as safe. 'Better to be properly protected,' she persisted. 'We're staying in the kitchen, my good woman,' he concluded imperiously.

Many remained strikingly indifferent to the rules laid down for their protection. George Orwell was amazed by the numbers who still confused the alert with the all-clear, 'and this after ten months of war and God knows how many explanations'. In spite of urgent injunctions after the fall of France, less than a quarter of Londoners carried gas-masks, a spot check in Holborn showed that only one in ten had troubled to get their mask tested. Among the young, to refuse to carry a mask was a sign of virility. Colin Perry, an eighteen-year-old awaiting call-up, longingly eyed a pretty girl in a café. 'But wait! She carries a gas-mask and to lunch! Horrors! No girl of mine would display so frightening a taste. But wait! Maybe I should appreciate the gas-mask as a truly feminine instinct and consequently I should loom the more manly as I never carry one? No, I don't admire that instinct.'

Everywhere last-minute preparations were put in hand. A fortified control room in the Natural History Museum, linked by underground passage to the civil defence headquarters in the Geological Museum, was opened in August. Peering through the boards which encompassed what was then the designated site for the National Theatre in the Brompton Road, Harold Nicolson saw six enormous tanks filled with water: 'We are evidently prepared for vast fires when the raiders come over; it is comforting to know there will be *some* water if the mains burst.' Stirrup pumps were in such demand that no London store could provide them. The idea of a 'Housewives' Service' – a loose organisation of women ready in a raid to give help to wardens by providing hot drinks, blankets or first-aid –

was first tried out in Barnes, then spread to Wandsworth and to Hampstead, where by July 400 housewives were registered. A recruiting drive was launched to bring London's ARP back to full strength, while members of the AFS who had returned to civilian jobs were summoned to rejoin. But there were still doubts whether the wardens would be up to the task. A brief raid on Kilburn a few days before the blitz began led to complaints that the wardens had sat around playing cards and avoiding danger: they 'don't do their job and are always first into the shelter', complained an indignant woman.

The LCC would not have agreed. A survey of civil defence satisfied them that the organisation was sound and could meet any demand made on it: 10,000 men at 100 depots had been equipped and trained for rescue work; 112 auxiliary ambulance stations supplemented the twenty permanent stations of the London Ambulance Service; the AFS included about 20,000 whole-time auxiliaries and operated 2250 appliances. Vere Hodgson, practising first-aid in Putney, was made to crawl through thick smoke, climb a ten-foot wall and drag an insensible person down a flight of stairs. Her gas-mask had to be fitted with an attachment to keep out a new arsenic gas. 'The calm way we now take these things is such a contrast to our pre-war fright. Of course, we're still really frightened but we have got a grip on ourselves, thank God!' Meanwhile on the Thames A. P. Herbert was training the crew of *Water Gipsy* to act as part of the PLA River Emergency Service. At the cry 'Lady Astor Overboard!' the steward abandoned his duties at table and dived into the water. Ten minutes later, in dry clothes, he resumed serving dinner. The readiness of the general public was less impressive. An enquiry in Streatham, Cricklewood and Kilburn showed that, though people were more knowledgeable than in September 1939, there was still much 'apathy, disinterest and uncertainty'. Thirty-eight per cent had taken no ARP precautions in their houses; less than 10 per cent had tried to make a room gas-proof, at least a quarter had no idea how to cope with an incendiary bomb.

Euan Wallace, who had become senior Regional Commissioner when the job was turned down by Herbert Morrison, hurriedly inspected as much as possible of his ramshackle empire. Walthamstow was the star turn: 'A model of its kind . . . keen, efficient and well-equipped', while a 'very remarkable gentleman', Mr Ellard

Styles of Leyton, won the individual trophy. Mr Styles, an engineer by profession, had converted his house into the Wardens' District HQ, built a heavily protected dugout under his lawn, and had worked twelve hours a day since the beginning of the war for no pay and precious little recognition. Wallace had some sharp things to say about the individual boroughs. Uxbridge went in for fancy uniforms: 'A tremendous impression of alertness and efficiency was given at HQ, but I came away doubtful whether it was much more than skin deep.' Greenwich was sharply divided 'into what are known locally as the "slums" and the "snobs". The former provide the keenest and most efficient wardens' service.' The slums did well in Shoreditch too – 'a Borough where the poverty of most of the inhabitants has been fully offset by keenness and team spirit'. But West Ham was 'the weakest spot in the Region . . . the whole affair is rather Pickwickian'. Stepney confused Wallace most, since the fact that the population was predominantly Jewish had caused some concern. He was pleasantly surprised; the stretcher parties in particular, though 'a villainous lot', seemed 'disciplined and efficient'. The area, he concluded, 'probably represents the greatest possibility of panic . . . It might on the other hand cover itself with glory.' Clement Attlee, MP for Stepney, insisted on visiting his constituency by night. An over-bright torch used by a member of his party led to a fracas and the Deputy Prime Minister almost ended up in the police station. 'If any War Cabinet ministers wish to go visiting after dark under the auspices of the London Region, I propose to insist in future that they should take their own detectives,' wrote Wallace drily.

There was little response to pleas to evacuate the children. The vast majority of evacuees had returned by the late spring of 1940; among the private schools, Dulwich and Colet Court were already back, St Paul's Girls' School was on the point of returning. The government set out to reverse the trend. 'It would clearly be wise to remove the east-end children first and let those in the areas where there is presumably better protection wait till later,' commented Euan Wallace: an admirable sentiment, but one which assumed readiness on the part of East End parents to fall in with the government's plans. There were 94,000 London children registered for evacuation by 1 June, nearly double the figure of a month before but still well under half those eligible. 'The children don't want to go,' said a lady working at the Haverstock Hill evacuation office. 'Particularly in the case of the 12–14 year olds, they refuse to go to safety while their mothers face raids.' More pertinently, they had been once already, had returned, and were not to be had for mugs again. But as Europe crumbled some sense of urgency did return. In mid-June 180 special trains departed in six days, carrying over 100,000 children. A further 4000 followed on 3 July. 'We have to anticipate that the war will get nearer and nearer,' said Malcolm MacDonald, Minister of Health. Parents were required to sign a certificate promising that they would not bring their children back until told to by the government. But it did no good. By the end of August 2500 children a week were returning. On 5 September, two days before the blitz began, the London School of Economics announced its decision to return from Cambridge to Houghton Street. By then there were 520,000 children of school age in the metropolitan area.

It seemed in the summer of 1940 that there was precious little to stop invasion. Colonel Meinertzhagen of the War Office spoke gloomily to Alexander Cadogan about the ease with which the Germans could descend on London. 'I think it must be more difficult than he makes out,' wrote Cadogan, adding, however, that Anthony Eden had just reported on a tour of Kent and Sussex 'which certainly makes it seem that the Germans can take a penny steamer to the coast and stroll up to London!' On 14 May Eden announced the creation of a citizen army – the Local Defence Volunteers, who in July were more picturesquely renamed the Home Guard.

The new force began unpropitiously with innumerable volunteers, no organisation, no facilities for training and, above all, no weapons. The result was frustration. After three weeks Chelsea's volunteers had not even been asked to parade. General Sir Hubert Gough was asked to take the matter in hand. He found that the list of recruits was held by the senior officer responsible for the Home Guard in south-west London, who refused to hand it over without the approval of the Commissioner for Police, who in turn needed the permission of the GOC, London District. When this was sorted out, Gough was advised to form his volunteers into groups of fifty, issue them with batons and march them around Chelsea in the hope that this would boost local confidence.

Harold Nicolson and Kingsley Martin, opting for private enterprise, decided to get hold of a pair of blunderbusses 'and try to shoot a German or two as they marched up Gower Street'. They would have been lucky to find even the most ancient firearms. The Marylebone Company of the Home Guard made do with forty-eight pikes borrowed from the Drury Lane Theatre, where they had been used in patriotic tableaux. In dockland one platoon manufactured hand grenades out of potatoes with razor blades inside them, a weapon that would certainly have maimed the volunteers pitted in training against them but might have been less effective against a German tank. A week after the Home Guard was created Scotland Yard descended on the gun shops and removed their wares, but it seems the aim was more to prevent the weapons falling into the hands of a Fifth Column than to equip British troops. Anyway, the infantry returning from Dunkirk without their rifles would have had first claim.

The difference between the rural and urban Home Guards, the farmer and broadcaster A. G. Street concluded, was that the former were pre-war territorials returned to life, the latter unashamed irregulars. Pilfering and ingenious adaptation filled many of the gaps in the equipment of the London Home Guard, but nothing could supply the missing weapons. For the first months of their existence the Home Guard looked and felt absurd, as they drilled with wooden rifles or practised street-fighting with non-existent Sten guns. They earned some derision; two teenagers in Stockwell were fined £1 for telling members of the Home Guard that they were playing at soldiers. But on the whole they were respected, even though there were private doubts about what would happen if they met the Germans in battle.

They were as eccentric as they were irregular. The London Home Guard abounded in anomalies and odd formations. It was based on units with strong local loyalties and intimate knowledge of their areas. The Buckingham Palace Guard was given special dispensation by the King to wear the badge of the Grenadier Guards. Men of the 9th County of London Battalion were allowed to wear black gaiters because they had blackened them before the order came to retain the original colour. The 24th City of London Battalion wore a leading seaman's anchor on their left sleeves as they were recruited from the staffs of master lightermen and tug owners. No. 2 Company of the 1st County of London (Westminster) Battalion was half composed of peers and members of the House of Commons; seventy-six-year-old Lord Jessel was the most ancient among the many veterans who attended every parade. The newspaper proprietors at first opposed recruiting among their staffs on the ground that ARP already occupied as much time as could be spared from normal duties, but they were overborne by popular demand. Two hundred volunteers from *The Times* alone enrolled in the first few weeks and eventually their proprietor, John Astor, became commander of the 5th City of London (Press) Battalion, and converted his Rolls-Royce into an armoured car to help him in his task.

The BBC was considered a prime target for saboteurs, and a Home Guard unit was recruited to protect the buildings and relieve regular soldiers for other duties. There were four posts to maintain and 168 men needed to man them – which, with only 181 volunteers available, meant much juggling of rosters and long hours. Val Gielgud once found himself on duty for twelve hours without a break – 'His Shakespeare-like face with its pointed beard does not go well with the accoutrements of the soldier,' wrote Anthony Weymouth. With steel doors fitted with spy holes impeding progress in every direction, armed men at the entrances, an intricate system of graded passes, the defences seemed impregnable, but Sir Stephen Tallents, the controller of public relations, who had a flat nearby, was still able to toddle over in pyjamas and dressing-gown and reach his office without being challenged.

American citizens had been advised by their Embassy to return home unless their business made it essential to stay in London. Many decided it did and defied their neutral status by forming a Mobile Defence Unit, affiliated to the Home Guard and armed with weapons privately imported from the US. Organised by the millionaire anglophile Charles Sweeny, and commanded by Brigadier Wade Hayes, who boasted four rows of medals and whose service went back to the Spanish-American war, this unit took over the guarding of London District HQ one night in eight. When they finally stood down in 1944 every member attended the last parade, even though one of them had to totter from his sick bed with his uniform over his pyjamas.

Sixteen hundred men enrolled in Marylebone, of whom 400 were ex-officers; in Bermondsey the figures were 1000 to only sixty. George Orwell speculated whether 'there has been any tendency to avoid raising LDV contingents in very poor districts where the whole direction would have to be in working-class hands'. That does not seem to have happened, though control of the force was firmly in the hands of retired regular officers, nearly all veterans of the First World War. Lieutenant General Sir Douglas Brownrigg – Zone Commander with the Home Guard rank of Colonel – believed that the veterans were invaluable for the initial training but found it hard to assimilate new ideas or adjust themselves to the street-fighting role which the Home Guard would probably have to undertake. But he did not think that rigidity of ideas was necessarily related to old age. His Lieutenant Colonel deputy (better known as Admiral of the Fleet the Earl of Cork and Orrery) had to retire when he became sixty-eight in October 1941. Brownrigg deplored the ruling: 'Some men have never been young,' he declared, 'whilst others never grow old.' The following year the retirement age was lowered to sixty-six. The 1st County of London Battalion lost one duke, one earl, one canon and six holders of the DSO. Whether efficiency improved as a result is uncertain, but there was much chagrin among the rejects and the gain to morale of seeing the elderly rallying to their country probably outweighed any benefit to be had from shedding them. 'It did thrill me to see all those men doing their bit,' said a seventy-year-old from Hendon. 'Elderly men, they deserve a bit of a snooze on Sunday afternoon, but there they were, all of them. I think it was very nice indeed.'

With images of *Dad's Army* in mind it is easy to portray the Home Guard as gallant but absurd; old buffers who would have been contemptuously swept aside by the invading Germans. They were never intended for pitched battle, but in street-fighting they would by no means have been useless. It took some time to make them an effective force. In June 1941 Orwell complained that no real training had yet been done, 'no specialised tactics worked out, no battle positions fixed upon'. His criticisms were confirmed a few weeks later when the first big call-out of the Home Guard in London District exposed alarming deficiencies in transport and 'total ignorance of elementary military principles'. On a local basis, however, many units were becoming surprisingly efficient in a limited range of skills. Partly this was the work of the journalist Tom Hopkinson and an expert in irregular warfare, Tom Wintringham, who despaired of official methods and decided to take Home Guard training into their own hands. They asked Lord Jersey if they could borrow his stately home and park at Osterley; of course, he said, though he hoped they wouldn't blow up the house as it had been in the family for some time. The painter Roland Penrose was enlisted to teach camouflage; a veteran of the Spanish Civil War gave instruction in destroying tanks; a senior Boy Scout instructor took on stalking. Applications to join the courses poured in. The War Office first tried to close the school, then accepted defeat and took it over. Stephen Howarth, a chartered accountant working with Hoare's Bank, went to Osterley for a two-day course in August 1940. He was lectured on unarmed combat by a cripple who stood about 4ft 9ins. 'Forget the playing fields of Eton and the Marquess of Queensbury,' bellowed the instructor, 'and remember that no way is too dirty to kill a German.' Attack from behind with a knife was advocated, 'If you have to do it from the front, slit him up the stomach – but he'll squeal. He won't if knifed from behind.'

Such refinements were additional to the Home Guard's most substantial role – to take over guard duties and release regular soldiers to fight invading Germans or to carry the war overseas. Progressively, too, Home Guard units were allowed to man anti-aircraft guns. In July 1942 a rocket gun, operated by Home Guards, opened fire in the outskirts of London. A kill was claimed but not given much credence; the historian of the Home Guard, Charles Graves, dates their first probable victim as being brought down in January 1943. They played a useful part, too, as an organised force able to help out civil defence in times of emergency. Often they were called out to police heavily bombed areas or clear the way for ambulances and fire services, but cooperation with such bodies was not always close. One Home Guard on sentry duty saw a heavily booted figure approaching. 'Halt or I fire!' he cried. 'Fire!' answered the man defiantly. The Home Guard decided nevertheless to use his bayonet, but while he was still trying to get it free, realised that his interlocutor was a fireman warning him that his headquarters was ablaze.

The plan for the defence of London envisaged an outer, anti-tank line with deep trenches, barriers, pill-boxes and road blocks running around the outer suburban frontiers; a second line encompassing Enfield, Harrow, West Norwood and Wanstead; a third line, to be occupied wholly by regulars, which followed the Thames, embraced Ealing, passed through Golders Green and returned to the Thames via the Brent; and a final, inner redoubt manned by crack units of the Royal Marines or Guards. Ben Robertson arrived in London in June 1940 to find that the traditional white leather breeches and red coats had disappeared. 'Soldiers were stretching barbed wire along the streets, barricading buildings, digging trenches.' Signposts and street names were taken down and the destination boards removed from buses to confuse the enemy (and, incidentally, reduce to impotent fury any visitor or Londoner who had strayed from his familiar patch).

Mrs Britton in August still found little outward evidence of war, though around her local pub 'they are building little erections about four feet cube of brick and cement which I believe are intended to be a nuisance to any hostile tanks that might get so far'. She sounded somewhat sceptical about the value of these excrescences. Her doubts were shared by Churchill, who minuted indignantly, 'What was the reason for attempting to put an anti-tank obstacle across St James's Park? Who ordered this?' The enterprise was abandoned; 'the soldiers have changed their minds,' recorded Euan Wallace. They changed their minds, too, about draining the lake in the same park. The work was half done when the civil defence authorities indignantly pointed out that the water constituted an essential reserve for the fire-fighters. The power station in Chelsea was laced around in barbed wire: 'Looks easy to me, if one had pliers, to snip it,' commented another sceptic, Hilda Neal. Yet however ineffective such precautions might have proved in practice, they manifested a will to fight. London, they proclaimed, would be no Paris; the Germans would have to fight their way, street by street, house by house. What resistance would have been offered was mercifully never established, but Londoners were to have ample opportunity to show their courage and their determination against another threat.

The first bombs on the London Region fell on 8 June on open country at Addington. A fortnight later bombs fell in a field at Colney. A goat was killed. It was on this occasion that Greater London heard its first alert of 1940. In Notting Hill 13 per cent of the population failed to wake up, of those who did 17 per cent of men and 3 per cent of women stayed in bed. One in three made a cup of tea. But it was not until August, when the Germans began to attack the airfields around the capital, that Londoners first heard the sounds of heavy bombardment. As reports had come in of attacks on the south coast towns the conviction had grown that London would remain inviolate. 'Look at Clacton! Look at Canterbury!' said a girl in Fulham. 'Of course London's safe enough, or the King and Queen wouldn't be here.' A woman in Stepney announced that she was bringing her son back from Woking, 'London is the safest place you can be, that's what I believe.' Surveys of public opinion showed that confidence was high all over London; in Silvertown concern was only shown when there were stories of raids in the West Country, where many local children had been evacuated. The authorities were alarmed at the complacency, but though they continued to urge Londoners not to bring their children home, they hesitated to point out how fragile the defences really were.

The proximity of war became ever more evident. On 11 August Anthony Weymouth chatted in the Lansdowne Club to a young RAF pilot with a bandage who had been in action earlier that day. 'Life is certainly exciting,' he commented, 'when a youngster can be shot down into the sea in the morning and be in a club in Berkeley Square the same evening.' On 15 August German bombers struck at Croydon airport. Sidney Chave, a laboratory assistant living in Upper Norwood, rushed to an upper-floor window to see 'a great column of black smoke right across Croydon and occasionally flames leaping high'. Wild rumours spread. All seventeen bombers had been shot down, Viola Bawtree was told by one of her friends in Sutton, and all had fallen harmlessly in the fields. This proved, she said, that a divine power was at work. Oh no, replied her friend, it showed the efficiency of the British pilots. 'What silliness!' Miss Bawtree wrote in her diary. Of course it was God's will! 'How can any airman know for certain first that he is going to send a plane down and second that it is going to fall according to his plan?'

As more areas of outer London were affected, morale remained high. The children were said to be in even better spirits than the adults, playing 'English and Germans' in the street with added zest. 'Everyone had a tale of how much worse it had been somewhere else – Croydon said Purley, Purley said Kenley, Kenley said Coulsdon.' One of the few grumbles was about the failure of the authorities to put a list of casualties on the notice board outside Croydon town hall. The porter said brusquely that there wasn't such a list and almost certainly wouldn't be one. If they put one up, 'so many people would see names that they knew and collapse on the spot that there would be a lot of confusion'.

Such trivial cases of panic as were reported occurred far from the scene of action. In Kensington four people on a bus lost their heads when a siren sounded; there was some jostling at the entrance to a public shelter underneath Swan and Edgar's in Piccadilly and an old lady was pushed over. The conviction that there would be no raids on central London was fast evaporating, but people were said to be more excited than apprehensive. When Wimbledon had its first raid on 16 August, killing fourteen and wounding fifty-nine, spirits were equally high; to such an extent that sightseers impeded the rescue work. Colin Perry rushed to the spot with his journalist father. 'Honestly, it's unbelievable,' he wrote. 'They are just having a look around like a child looks at a new toy. There will never be any breaking the British morale.' Unexploded bombs caused even less concern. A woman was found excavating one from her garden on the grounds that she wished to keep it as a souvenir; adopting a different approach, a railway employee looked pensively at the hole left near the line by a falling bomb, filled it in and carefully raked it over.

On 24 August the first bombs fell on central London, starting fires in the East End. Probably the bombing was accidental, but retaliatory raids on Berlin made it inevitable that the process, once started, would escalate dramatically. For the first few days and nights the raids amounted to little. 'It is perfectly clear that these night raids are intended chiefly as a nuisance,' concluded Orwell. Sleep was the principal victim, and frayed tempers the most obvious result: 'For the first time in twenty years [since the raids of the First World War] I have overheard bus conductors losing their tempers and being rude to passengers.' Mass Observers reported widespread complaints about sleeplessness and a sixty-five-year-old man complained that in his office everyone was snapping everybody else's head off. But on the whole Londoners congratulated themselves that they had managed well under what they fondly hoped was the worst the Germans could throw at them.

People developed their own techniques for dealing with daytime raiders; for shoppers in Kensington the shelters in Harrods were much favoured, 'where chairs are provided and first-aid workers unobtrusively but comfortingly hover about'; in Chelsea the Weymouths drew the wooden shutters and ate plums – 'We are getting accustomed to "going to ground" several times a day. We do it now as a matter of course. The human biped is a very adaptable creature.' At Lambeth, Canon Don complained on 27 August that the Archbishop maintained 'an air of Olympian detachment which is most irritating. He will soon be talking of "these so-called air-raids".'

The authorities knew that these 'so-called air-raids' were only a foretaste of what the Germans were likely to direct at London. They were still far from confident about the ability of Londoners to stand firm in the face of sustained attack and every report was anxiously scrutinised for evidence of panic or loss of heart. There were some early grounds for worry. 'The excess of raid warnings and gun-fire and bombs has seriously affected East End morale,' read a report of 26 August. 'They have an inkling of what it is like and they are sure they will get more.' In Neasden four days later an observer found many people on the verge of hysteria. A woman of forty trembled uncontrollably when the siren went, and wet her pants, bursting into tears. 'The much boasted calm of the British people cannot be relied on – not in the East End anyway,' reported the writer and Mass Observer Naomi Mitchison from Stepney. The novelty had worn off and morale was low. On Sunday a daylight alert had provoked panic in the Mile End Road. 'Everyone ran. No matter where, they just ran. Shelter! Quick! People running in all directions. People screaming. A woman with a baby in her arms fainted.' But once in the shelter calm was restored: 'It is only the first few minutes in which people lose control.' When a public shelter was found to be locked a warden urged people to keep calm. 'Keep calm, with them over our heads, and nowhere to go!' exclaimed a woman, but after a few moments of aimless running about and screaming the people decided there *was* somewhere else to go and proceeded towards it. Heightened nervousness was more often encountered than real panic. In the entrance to a shelter a man struck a match to light a cigarette. His neighbour blew it out.

'I'm doing it for your own good,' he explained. 'They're on us. They're right above. You don't know how big that looks from the air.'

Yet already people were adjusting to the growing violence. In Streatham, on 6 September, an investigator noticed that people seemed to be settling down well to the constant air-raid warnings, there was 'a strong tendency to grumble humorously about the raids'. In Stepney people cheered themselves up in the shelters with singing and dancing. The public tried to keep things going as usual. Vic Oliver played to full houses at the Hippodrome. When the sirens went, three-quarters of those present stayed on until one o'clock, some volunteering to entertain the audience with amateur performances. At the Queen's Hall, wrote Mollie Panter-Downes, 'a Wagner concert ran to greater length than *Götterdämmerung*, while the immortal Richard's compatriots droned somewhere in the vicinity'. Here too there was community singing and solos by members of the orchestra. If London be taken as Valhalla, then within a few days the Twilight of the Gods was to begin indeed.

8

'Blimey, we've lost the war!'

AT ABOUT FOUR O'CLOCK on Saturday 7 September Colin Perry was bicycling over Chipstead Hill. He heard planes overhead and glanced up to see whether they were fighters or bombers. 'It was the most amazing, impressive, riveting sight. Directly above me were literally hundreds of planes, Germans! The sky was full of them. Bombers hemmed in with fighters, like bees around their queen, like destroyers round the battleship, so came Jerry.' To the Revd Maurice Wood, watching aghast from near Big Ben, it was the 'majestic orderliness' of the bomber fleet that impressed him most. Seconds later the East End disintegrated. 'Blimey, we've lost the war!' thought Ted Harrison in Hackney as his world collapsed. What could have happened to London's vaunted defences? Had the RAF been driven from the skies? Where were the guns? Maxwell Hyslop from the Board of Education, bicycling through Richmond Park, saw in the distance an enormous mushroom of smoke. The fire must be near Hammersmith, he thought, and bicycled towards his home in Chelsea. Well, it must be around my house, he decided as he got closer, 'finally, when we got home, we realised it was ten or twelve miles away from us still'.

By night the docks were blazing furiously and hundreds of the mean houses that surrounded them were in shattered ruins. The crowd emerging from Gounod's *Faust* at Sadler's Wells saw a real hell reddening the sky to the east. The Surrey Commercial Dock was so fiercely ablaze that the Fire Officer signalled desperately: 'Send all the bloody pumps you've got; the whole bloody world's on fire.' There had been 1.5 million tons of softwood in the dock that morning; within twenty-four hours four-fifths of it had been destroyed. The heat from the fire blistered paint on a fire boat 300 yards away. By 8 p.m. the West Ham Fire Brigade alone had called in 500 extra pumps from other regions; by 11 p.m. 1000 pumps were battling with the conflagration in the Surrey Commercial and

London Docks. Ivy James, in the Isle of Dogs, smelt acrid fumes
and hurried to put her baby into a gas-proof container. It was several
hours before she learnt that a nearby paint store was on fire. ARP
wardens were overwhelmed by the scale of the disaster; most did
their ineffectual best; some gave up the struggle. 'Our brave warden,
who for months had been swaggering about in his uniform, tin
helmet cocked to one side, was cringing against the wall under the
concrete steps, sobbing,' wrote Mr Kyle of West Ham contemptuously. 'I never saw that man again.'

Meanwhile a few miles away in St James's Park, Lord Gort was
strolling with a friend, commuters were running for their trains,
others were reading their evening papers. General Lee penetrated
as far as Wapping to see what was going on, then returned to dine
with Mrs Lionel Guest: 'We had a magnum of champagne to celebrate the commencement of the real war.' The West End was not
left inviolate when the Germans returned that night; bombs fell on
Pont Street and Victoria Street, but the 247 Junkers which kept up
the bombardment until 4.30 a.m. and left more than 430 dead
concentrated on the docks of West Ham and Bermondsey, with
destruction spreading out over Stepney, Whitechapel, Poplar, Bow
and Shoreditch. Worst hit was Silvertown, a near-slum with many
small factories but housing 13,000 people, hemmed in by the
Thames, the River Lea and the docks. For many hours the area was
cut off from access overland by the inferno in the docks, paralysed
by the presence of more than a hundred unexploded bombs and
with what water supplies it still had contaminated by the breaching
of the main sewer.

Most of those with defined jobs to do performed them bravely
and to the best of their ability. For those left idle it was harder. In
the crypt of one Bow church, 'people were kneeling and crying
and praying. It was a most terrible night. I became unconscious,'
remembered Gladys Strelitz, from East Ham. Yet not far away in
Limehouse Ben Thomas found his old mother standing by her door.
'It's quite interesting to look at,' she explained. In the Troxy Cinema
the audience was trapped by the raid. The manager called on them
to sing 'There'll Always Be An England'. As he spoke, a bomb fell
nearby. 'I'm not so sure of that!' shouted a joker. There was much
laughter and the sing-song went on till after midnight.

In Chelsea the morning after the pubs were packed. 'Jokes were made to relieve the tension,' wrote Theodora FitzGibbon, 'beer mugs were put down more noisily to shut out other sounds. We were glued together by dread. All our eyes were rounder, the pupils enlarged, and although we laughed, our lips twitched with alarm.' Meanwhile Churchill visited the East End. Colin Perry followed him around. 'He looked invincible, which he is,' wrote Perry in his diary. 'Tough, bulldogged, piercing. He made his way through the smoke, through the City workers all crying "Good old Winston" – "Give 'em socks" – "Good luck" – and the culminating cry of "Are we down-hearted?" to the heaven-rising response of "No-o-o-o-o" which echoed around the City, around the world indeed. It was magnificent, tremendous, stirring, dramatic.' Harold Scott accompanied Churchill to Silvertown. 'Pessimists had predicted panic and bitterness in the East End, but I saw nothing of the kind,' he wrote. 'Smiles, cheers and grim determination showed already that "London could take it".' People sometimes see what they want or expect to see. Not everyone was so enthusiastic about the Prime Minister's expedition. But the prevailing mood as the East Enders surveyed the smoking ruins on 8 September was defiance and resolution.

When the Germans returned to pound the same areas night after night the spirit of exaltation burnt lower. 171 bombers hit the East End on the night of 8 September, killing 400. On 9 September 200 bombers came by day, 170 by night. Another 370 died. The following night saw the gutting of St Katherine's Dock in what at that date some believed the worst fire England had ever known. All the warehouses surrounding the dock were destroyed in four or five hours. Paraffin wax, skins and cobra wax were ablaze. Wax ran across the quays and into the docks where, lying on the water, it became a hard sheet. Seven floors were engulfed in a few minutes. Flames rose 200 feet. The survivors in the adjoining areas emerged wearily from the shelters to find that, even if their homes were still standing, there was no gas or electricity, often no water, no milk delivery, the neighbourhood bakery was in ruins. People were 'tight-lipped and strained', a teacher wrote to his friend. They were 'no longer ashamed of their fear, and the shelters are full to suffocation'.

Suffocation not just from overcrowding. The public shelters, particularly those which the public had adopted without official sanction, were foetid swamps in which every kind of disease should have flourished. 'They actually stank,' wrote a horrified curate's wife who accompanied her husband on a tour of them. 'In one very large shelter, which was made to hold about 300 persons, only two buckets or latrines were available and the result was that the whole floor was awash. The smell was so awful that we tied hankies around our mouths soaked in cologne.' Churchill enquired at a meeting of ministers what the smell was like in the larger shelters. 'Horrible,' said Woolton; too many unwashed bodies and too few lavatories. 'Oh, I see,' commented Churchill in one of his less tasteful jokes, *'esprit de corps.'*

The shelters often did not provide real protection. The notorious Tilbury shelter, part of the Liverpool Street goods station off the Commercial Road in Stepney, was covered only by flimsy arches. An official shelter accommodated 3000 but when this was full people overflowed into the loading yard of a huge adjacent warehouse. Sometimes as many as 14,000 people would doss down amid the cartons of margarine and other foodstuffs: cold, damp, and without even the most primitive sanitation. The trench shelters were little better. The first night of heavy raiding, 1450 people packed into the shelter in Victoria Park, Bethnal Green, crowded so tightly that the warden could not penetrate to see what was going on. The walls oozed damp, people were standing all night in two or three inches of water. Small wonder that social workers touring the shelters two or three nights after the blitz began should have found that 'in dockside areas the population is showing visible signs of nerves cracking from constant ordeals. Old women and mothers are undermining morale of young women and men by their extreme nervousness and lack of resilience.'

One obvious solution was to take refuge in the tube stations. Churchill favoured this. Was it true, he asked, that 750,000 people could be accommodated in the Aldwych section alone? It was not, but the system offered safety to many thousands. The authorities remained reluctant but on 8 September the public took the law into their own hands. A huge crowd assembled outside Liverpool Street Station and demanded entrance. Soldiers were called in to reinforce the beleaguered officials, but the crowd refused to disperse. What precipitated the change of heart is uncertain, but suddenly the doors were flung open. Bernard Kops was among those who surged through: ' "It's a great victory for the working class," a man said.

"One of our big victories." ' But as the crowd got underground working-class solidarity dissolved in a battle for space. 'What sort of victory had we achieved? Every family for itself now. Dignity and joy left the world, my world.' Once conceded, the right to shelter was not rescinded. 'London decided how the tube stations were to be used,' declared *Picture Post*. 'Officials are cooperating.' The authorities did their best to control numbers and keep sections of the stations clear, but effectively the tubes had become London's largest air-raid shelters. Fifteen miles of platforms and tunnels were put into use; on one record night 177,000 people were underground.

Even those were not entirely safe. Marble Arch was the first to suffer a hit, on 17 September; but the earliest serious incident occurred at Trafalgar Square when a bomb landed near King Charles I's statue, penetrated the surface and by ill luck exploded just above the escalator. The steel and concrete casing collapsed and an avalanche of wet earth engulfed the shelterers. Seven were killed. So little sign of damage appeared on the surface that the rescue services rushed by in search of more deserving cases. Two nights later the grisliest incident occurred at Balham, when the roadway caved in and water from the mains flooded the station below. Ballast, sand and water cascaded down and the station was submerged in slime. 'All you could hear was the sound of screaming and rushing water,' remembered an ARP worker, Bert Woolridge. 'People were lying there, all dead, and there was a great pile of sludge on top of them.' Sixty-four died, but even this toll was exceeded at Bank station in January 1940, when 111 people were crushed, killed by blast or thrown in front of an approaching train.

One of the most frequent complaints about those early raids was that nothing was being done to check the bombers. Hardly an anti-aircraft gun was heard. The reason was that the skies were being left open for the night fighters, but nobody told the public this. The effect on morale was calamitous, especially since few if any German bombers were being shot down. Anti-aircraft fire was little more effective until radar came to the rescue of the defence. In September 30,000 shells were fired for every enemy plane destroyed, though this dropped to 11,000 in October and a mere 4000 in January. Aircraft were forced to fly higher as a result of the barrage, but since this made it more likely that the bombs would miss docks or railway stations and hit civilian homes instead, the advantage to the average citizen was not immediately noticeable. But the people *wanted* gunfire. Canon Barry actually called on Churchill's parliamentary private secretary, Brendan Bracken, and told him 'this simply would not do . . . If this were allowed to go on there would be anti-war demonstrations which the Government might not be able to contain.' His intervention was not needed – ministers had already decided to withdraw the night fighters, bring in every gun available and let the gunners blaze away to their heart's content. ARP workers were supposed to have spread the word but the message rarely got through; to most the barrage came as a vast and deafening surprise.

It was as welcome as it was cacophonous. The guns made Barbara Nixon, an air-raid warden who later wrote an impressive book about her experiences, 'laugh for joy even at 3 a.m.'. People quickly learnt to distinguish the various types of gun: 'One very near that sounds like a thunderclap straight overhead, and the one that sounds like giant tympani,' Nancy Bosanquet wrote in her diary, 'and what is so nice is that they mask with their shouting, and their *yelling* and their *bawling*, the drone of planes, which is frankly horrible.' Home Office reports showed that morale soared 'to new levels of confidence and cheerfulness . . . "We'll give them hell now", is working man's comment heard today.'

A price was paid in sleeplessness. Mass Observers established that a third of London's population got no sleep at all on the night the barrage opened and even four nights later two out of three were sleeping less than four hours a night. The barrage was dangerous too, both in shrapnel and in unexploded shells plunging back to earth. The guns killed many more Londoners than they did German pilots. But even if the facts had been fully known, there would have been few who would have dispensed with this reassuring presence.

Between 7 September and 13 November 1940 London was the main, almost the exclusive, target of the German raiders – 27,500 high explosive bombs and innumerable incendiaries were dropped, not to mention oil explosive bombs and parachute mines. An average of 160 bombers attacked nightly: a figure reduced by bad weather – as on 2 November, the only raid-free night of the whole period – but greatly exceeded when the full moon and good weather coincided – as on 15 October when 410 raiders dropped 538 tons of high explosive bombs, killing 400 people. Throughout this period the authorities made steady if sometimes unacceptably slow progress in their task of helping the civilian population to endure this monstrous burden. A lot needed to be done.

It was not just the ARP workers and the fire-fighters who were unable to cope with the immensity of the disaster. In certain parts of London civil administration broke down, almost ceased to exist. West Ham was the most notorious example. A massive, permanent Labour majority with no effective opposition and an average age among councillors of almost sixty, had resulted in local government that was, at best, low in vitality, at worst corrupt and irresponsible. Even though the sodden, low-lying land made Andersons or trench shelters unsuitable, the council had done little to provide more adequate public shelters. It had obstinately refused to recruit conscientious objectors for civil defence work, even though some obviously well-qualified volunteers were thus rejected, and had ignored bodies like the Friends' Ambulance Unit because the Quakers were contaminated by pacifism. The consequence was that on the morning of 8 September virtually nothing was done to restore the machinery of everyday life.

Churchill found high spirits and the will to fight on; these existed indeed, but H. F. Grey, an East End policeman, saw crowds wandering aimlessly around, having no idea what to do or where to turn for help. Such control as there was came from the local ARP. 'There's some good people, sorting themselves out,' said a colleague of Grey's. 'Give 'em time and a system will emerge.' It did, but in the interval hideous mistakes were made. The worst came when over a thousand homeless were crowded into a disused school. Blankets and a minimal amount of food were provided but the coaches intended to evacuate the fugitives were misdirected and never arrived. For two days they awaited rescue; the second night the school was hit and more than 450 killed. Many of the councillors, meanwhile, had evacuated themselves, and there was little central direction to restore essential services or offer even a word of comfort to the victims. Food was hard to find, water unfit to drink, a blitzed jam factory provoked a plague of flies, the homeless were despatched on fruitless quests from one distant office to another. 'People wanted to be brave,' said a Mass Observation report, 'but found bravery was something purely negative, cheerless, and without encouragement or prospect of success.' Margaret Cole's devastating judgment cannot be challenged: 'It was more than bricks and mortar that collapsed in West Ham . . . it was a local ordering of society which was found hopelessly wanting, as weak and badly constructed as the single-brick walls which fell down at the blast.'

West Ham was the worst, but it was not alone. The weak and inefficient Stepney Council failed to exercise any control and it was left to private individuals to give a lead. Father John Groser broke into an official food store and distributed rations, bullied the local authorities and Whitehall, ordered coaches on his own initiative to evacuate the homeless. Another clergyman, 'Lex' Miller, set up an advisory service to help people find shelter and financial assistance. The councillors faced a daunting and largely unexpected challenge. Within a few weeks 40 per cent of the flimsy houses in Stepney had been destroyed. The shoddiness of their construction compounded the problem. The houses collapsed more easily but the lightness of the debris ensured that many survivors could be extracted. The council was prepared for mass burials; instead it had to provide shelter and counsel for an unexpectedly large number of dispossessed survivors. It failed to meet the challenge.

'This is the end. I'm clearing out now!' a fifty-year-old man told a Mass Observer. 'Is your house damaged?' she asked. 'No, but the wife's nerves are to pieces . . . She just cries all day. It's no good, she can't go on like this.' Within a few days most of those who found the bombing intolerable had fled the East End. Gwladys Cox in Hampstead recorded seeing 'numbers of strange looking people with babies, children and odd parcels of clothes and bedding straggling up West End Lane'. But the majority stayed put. Even from devastated Silvertown only 2900 accepted Malcolm MacDonald's offer of immediate evacuation, and many of these soon returned. Horror stories filtered back of the indignities and ill-treatment meted out to those who moved to other parts of London: the bombed-out family from Whitechapel made to sleep in a servant's room directly under the roof of a Belgravia mansion and forbidden to use the basement shelter. Exaggerated or not, such tales reinforced the conviction of the East Enders that they would do better to stay where they belonged.

Their determination was strengthened when, after five or six days of blitz, the bombing extended to the West End. The government was profoundly relieved, partly because it would give the docks a chance to recover; more importantly for reasons of morale. Attlee told Harold Nicolson, 'If only the Germans had had the sense not to bomb west of London Bridge there might have been a revolution in this country. As it is, they have smashed about Bond Street and Park Lane and readjusted the balance.' Jock Colville, motoring up from Chequers a few days later, passed his twice-bombed flat and noted sadly 'how many houses in Berkeley Square and Bruton Street are crumbled to dust'. One East End family, bombed out themselves, were said to have been offered a billet in a fashionable house. On being shown their room they looked out of the window, realised they were within a hundred yards of Buckingham Palace and exclaimed, 'Not on your life! This is too dangerous.' The palace had its first bomb on 13 September; the King and Queen were there at the time and would have been seriously injured had the windows been closed. That afternoon they visited bombed areas in the East End: 'The fact that they had had such a narrow escape in the morning made their reception even more enthusiastic,' wrote Euan Wallace.

It was a public relations blunder for the Germans. 'I'm glad we've been bombed,' said the Queen. 'Now I feel we can look the East End in the face.' Incidents such as this did not still complaints that it was the poor who suffered by far the worst privations while the privileged escaped relatively lightly. The facts made it too clear that this was indeed the case. But they removed the sharpest edge of bitterness from the East End's resentment. Often, too, they inspired an upsurge of indignant loyalty. 'Our King and Queen are contending with war magnificently,' wrote Colin Perry, 'carrying on here in their capital when they could be miles away in safety . . . This is the King and Queen of whom we are so proud.' Ed Murrow doubted whether the effect on the public had been as significant as some suggested: 'Minds have become hardened and calloused. It didn't require a bombing of Buckingham Palace to convince these people that they are all in this thing together.' It may not have been essential, but it helped.

People's minds were almost visibly hardening over those first sixty-eight days and nights. Celia Fremlin, a Mass Observer, visited a shelter in Cable Street, Stepney, at the very beginning of the blitz. 'They were screaming and saying, "I can't stand it, I'm going to die, I can't stand it!" Sometimes the women would be really hysterical, crying and falling on the floor.' Four nights later she returned. All was calm, stools had been brought, there was community singing, 'because, once you've gone through three nights of bombing and come out alive, you can't help feeling safe the fourth time'. Many coped by clinging to old routines and, whenever possible, maintaining traditional standards. When the War Office was badly hit, General Lee remarked that the only suggestion of disarray shown by Mr D'Arcy, the former Grenadier who acted as commissionaire, was that he forgot to put on his cockaded high hat to greet his visitor.

It was not the relentless pounding of the back streets but the blows struck at great monuments which most impressed the popular imagination. The fate of St Paul's was a perpetual concern. On the night of 12 September an 800lb bomb, 5.5 feet long and powerful enough to destroy the whole façade of the cathedral, landed in front of the steps, penetrated deep into the earth, but failed to explode. To remove it a team had to tunnel twenty-six feet through gas mains, electrical cables and a stratum of black mud into which the bomb receded further as they advanced. Finally they tethered it and drew it inch by inch to the surface. It was loaded on to a lorry more than three days after it fell, and rushed to Hackney Marshes. When exploded it made a crater a hundred feet across and broke windows half a mile away. The men who saved St Paul's were the first recipients of new honours – the George Cross and the George Medal – invented to reward civilians who performed acts of conspicuous gallantry. It was the King's idea and he announced it to the nation in one of his most successful broadcasts, thus reclaiming for a moment the limelight which Churchill's overpowering personality usually made his own.

One by one the familiar icons of London life were assailed. Madame Tussaud's was in ruins after only two nights of blitz; its cinema demolished and the rows of tip-up seats blown over the top of nearby Baker Street Station. Hilde Marchant was sent by the *Daily Express* to view the damage. A workman was picking up the arms and legs of waxworks and sorting them into stacks of left and right. 'Hitler's nose was chipped and Goering's magnificent white uniform was covered with black dust. Mary Queen of Scots had left her head on the executioner's block while her body was blown across the room into the tableau of Kings and Queens.' The Natural History Museum was set on fire in October. Its Botanical Gallery had kept most of its specimens on show and in the fire-fighting some of the seeds in the Herbarium were soaked and began to germinate, notably those of *Albizzia julibrissin* which had been collected 147 years before. Encouraged by this, the Keeper of Botany tried the same treatment on Nelumbium from the prehistoric peat beds in South Manchuria. 'All germinated within two days – an unwitting contribution by Hitler to the Museum's research.'

About the same time the Tower of London was hit and a bastion pierced. 'I was disappointed to find that they were not made of solid masonry but chiefly of brick, only faced with stone,' recorded General Lee. Another archaeological surprise was sprung by a bomb which fell near the Dell in Hyde Park, exposing a lead conduit pipe used to take water to the Palace of Whitehall during the reign of Edward the Confessor. The zoo was hit several times though never seriously; by the end of September the only casualties were some humming birds which had escaped and presumably perished. A zebra similarly made off but was rounded up the following morning. The director, Julian Huxley, was struck by the behaviour of the camels, which did not get up even when a bomb fell ten yards from their cage. The chimpanzees ignored bombs and guns but screamed at the sound of sirens. The Barbary sheep, which had run amok during the raids of the First World War, were mysteriously reformed characters; 'they could not behave better if we had given a course of lectures in ARP,' said a keeper. The cranes were less decorous, greeting the bombers with loud rattling cries and much flapping of wings.

The BBC too was hit several times, the worst incident being on 15 October when a bomb buried itself outside the Music Library, where it exploded after twenty minutes, killing six people. Bruce Belfrage was reading the news at the time; he paused to blow the dust off his script, then continued without a tremor: 'The expression of amazed indignation on Bruce's face was a sight to see,' recorded his fellow news reader, Joseph Macleod. Such *sang froid* was admirable, but the bland content of the bulletins did not satisfy everyone. ' "The material damage is *slight* and casualties *few!*" Change your record, the public are tired of it,' protested an angry listener. '10/- a year [the licence fee] for a lying machine, you won't get many

10/- from Londoners for lies, lies, lies. Take a day ticket on a London tram. Listen in to conversation. See how much confidence we have in the BBC. Look for your *slight material damage*. But of course you cannot see thousands of hearts broken, they are not *material damage*.'

West End clubland suffered severely. That Conservative redoubt the Carlton was badly hit. Part of the roof fell in and the club was filled with smoke, the smell of cordite and the dust of rubble. A few side lights remained intact, through the thick fog Harold Macmillan sighted 'the figure of Quintin Hogg escorting old Hailsham from the ruins, like Aeneas and Anchises'. 'We must get you out of this at once,' a fellow diner told Hailsham, 'I will call my car.' 'Excuse me, sir, have you seen your car?' the hall porter asked. It had been buried in the debris. Viewing the ruins next day Churchill could hardly credit that nobody had been killed; 'the devil looks after his own,' remarked one of his Labour colleagues cheerfully. The Naval and Military Club (Palmerston's old town house) was hit by three bombs and the fine suite of mid-eighteenth-century rooms demolished, but the grill room behind was barely touched and was serving lunches the following day. The Athenaeum got off relatively lightly, though John Lehmann arrived one day to find 'the liveried staff sweeping away debris, while disconcerted Bishops stepped as delicately as cats over a litter of broken glass'. He found, he wrote, that he experienced 'a shocked sense that this time the Nazis had definitely gone too far'.

Much survived. From his boat A. P. Herbert saw the river's most famous pub, the Prospect of Whitby, surrounded by blazing warehouses, and mourned its passing. Next day, 'perky and white', it stood there still. Much too was maimed but could still function. Sidney Chave walked down Oxford Street the day after it had been heavily attacked. Bourne & Hollingsworth was devastated, 'not a window remained and the interior was a shambles'. Waring & Gillow was closed by an unexploded bomb. John Lewis was a gutted ruin. Selfridge's and Peter Robinson had both been hit. It seemed that shopping in Oxford Street must be a thing of the past. Yet within four days nearly all were open again; Bourne & Hollingsworth had draped the ruins in Union Jacks and sales girls were serving a few yards from the great hole ripped through the centre of the shop. Only John Lewis defied repair, outside it lay a pile of plaster dress models, 'very pink and realistic, looking so like a pile of corpses that one could have mistaken them for that at a little distance. Just the same sight as in Barcelona,' reflected George Orwell, 'only there it was plaster saints from desecrated houses.'

The unexploded bomb (UXB) that had paralysed Waring & Gillow was only one of many. One in ten of the HE bombs that fell did not explode on impact; many by malfunction, some – DAs, or delayed action bombs – because they contained timing devices. By the end of the first phase of the blitz a backlog of 3000 such bombs required attention. Since each UXB necessitated diversion of traffic and the evacuation of nearby houses, they disrupted life infuriatingly. Many were never detected, some were stumbled on after weeks or months; from time to time they are still encountered today when sites are excavated. Sometimes they augmented the damage done by later bombs. On 26 September a bomb exploded on the corner of Denbigh Street and Belgrave Road, trapping people in a shelter beneath the pavement. A water main was ruptured, flooding the shelter. A gas main was set alight. Finally a UXB went off a few yards away, killing the officer in charge of the rescue operation.

Yet people got used to this lurking hazard. Frederick Leighton-Morris removed a 50kg bomb from his flat in Jermyn Street and tottered down the pavement with it. His intention was to dump it in St James's Park. He was arrested when he put it down on the pavement to have a well-earned rest. The magistrate praised his courage but fined him £100. You cannot decide, he was told, 'in which part of London a delayed action bomb should go off'. On appeal the fine was reduced to a more modest £5. Mr Leighton-Morris was exceptional in his doughtiness, but people in general learnt to treat UXBs with some indifference. Vere Hodgson noticed that when a large section of Hyde Park was cordoned off, with seats resting against the rope carrying placards marked BEWARE. UXB!, people were peacefully sitting on the seats and some had penetrated the barrier and were relaxing on the grass inside.

Parachute mines, in spite of their great size and devastating effects, were another hazard to which the public adjusted. As soon as one was seen falling, people would begin to move towards it: partly, perhaps, because they mistook the mine for a descending German pilot who needed to be lynched or apprehended; more probably because they wanted the silk of the parachute to make skirts or dresses. When mines fell into the Thames the Navy took over; A. P. Herbert remarked that he had never expected to see the boat race course swept by mine sweepers.

For the first few weeks of the blitz daylight attacks were a commonplace. They were never again as large as on the first day, but they still provided a constant and dangerous irritant. Gradually the RAF made such assaults unacceptably hazardous; daylight raids died away and by mid-October had become such a rarity that a siren was assumed to be a false alarm or, anyway, only of passing interest. The writer Naomi Royde-Smith noticed that in Piccadilly, where three weeks before an alert had led to a rush for cover, people now paid little attention: 'A soldier and his girl stood on a refuge in the middle of the street. They were showing each other snapshots.'

It took the authorities some time to realise that there were going to be many fewer dead and many more homeless than originally expected. No provision had been made for a stay of more than a few hours at the inadequate rest centres which had been set up; blankets were few, sanitation deplorable, reserves of clothing pitifully small. In theory there were 997 rest centres in the London area, able to cope with 132,000 people, but many existed only on paper or were empty buildings, usually schools, on which no work had been done. In the first six weeks of the blitz 16,000 houses were destroyed, 60,000 seriously damaged; more than 300,000 people needed rehousing. Of these many looked after themselves, but the demands on the rest centres were still far greater than they could accommodate. The horror of one Stepney rest centre, where 300 homeless slept on the floor, with ten pails or coal-scuttles to serve as lavatories, seven basins with cold water only, hurricane lamps for lighting, was mercifully not typical, but nor was it unique. Others were much better. 150 more fortunate East End homeless found themselves in a luxury block of flats in Mayfair, dining on trestle tables on the dance floor, the cooking and washing-up looked after by the regular residents. But though this too was not unique, it was encountered far less often than the treatment meted out to their fellow victims left behind in Stepney. Gradually, things got better. On 11 September the Lord Mayor launched a Mansion House Fund to relieve the suffering of the homeless, and supplies of clothing and other necessities were provided to supplement official provisions.

Two weeks later H. U. Willink, a lawyer turned Tory MP, was appointed Special Commissioner for the homeless. His main energies went into the repair of damaged houses, but he brought some order into the chaotic business of resettlement and relief and set up administrative and information centres to speed the work.

The system could only be as good as the people who operated it. It had been a mistake to put air-raid relief into the hands of Public Assistance, manned as it was by officials who were used to people on the dole and behaved with some hauteur when dealing with the public. F. R. Barry, who had been bombed out of his canon's lodgings in Dean's Yard, Westminster, applied for help 'to a spotty young man enjoying a brief authority. I found that interview most enlightening. "Address?" "I have no address at the moment." That was enough; we were homeless persons and could therefore be bullied and put in our proper places.' Barry could look after himself, but some of the homeless could not and either submitted to arrogant bureaucracy or preferred not to apply for help at all.

Bread, margarine, potted meat, corned beef, jam, biscuits and tea were at first the staple diet in the rest centres; sustaining, but after a few days inclined to pall. Some of the dispossessed were nevertheless touchingly grateful; a taxi driver remembered that the LCC was very good to him, providing 'as much boiled ham and bread and tea for breakfast as we could eat, and corned beef and hot potatoes for dinner'. Others were less easily satisfied. For these the Londoners' Meals Service provided some relief, building up a system which in the end served cooked food at 170 fixed centres and 190 mobile canteens. It did not offer *haute cuisine* but substantial and modestly varied meals: 'Roast shoulder of lamb, carrots and potatoes – huge portion – rice pudding, for 10d,' noted the writer Leslie Paul, after eating in an Emergency Feeding Centre. 'Cheaper than I can feed myself.' For those who could not afford even that, or whose money was buried in the rubble of their houses, the meals were free. Bureaucracy could make life difficult. The Ministry of Food was responsible for communal feeding centres where people paid, the Ministry of Health for Food and Rest Centres, where the homeless got their food free; in one south London school two sets of cooks produced two sets of meals for their respective clienteles. But such absurdities were gradually ironed out; on the whole the system worked well and progressively more smoothly.

For Londoners who did not have their house destroyed or seriously damaged – a vast majority – the blitz was frightening but, still more, an infernal nuisance. 'The telephone in London is war inconvenience number one,' concluded the American journalist Ralph Ingersoll. The rust which gushed from the taps at the Dorchester Hotel was an irritant but the telephone drove him to rage, especially when he knew that government communications of trivial importance were given automatic priority. At Claridges General Lee also deplored the shortcomings of the telephone, but was more put out by the absence of hot water. And these were luxury hotels; the average householders, without skilled artisans at their beck and call, were far worse affected. Yet with surprising speed the basic services were each time restored. No hot water for ten days, moaned Anthony Weymouth; virtually no telephone, 'but I suppose repairs will be carried out with the same matter-of-factness with which the buildings that have been destroyed are being tidied up'. It might take three days to get a letter across London yet, unless it had the misfortune to perish in transit, in the end it arrived.

Somehow, too, the buses and trains kept running. Four hundred buses arrived from Scotland to reinforce London's depleted fleet but even so it was necessary to impose a curfew, first at 11 p.m., then at 10.30. Late-night buses were almost empty, anyway; those running at rush hour, on the contrary, were hideously overcrowded – queuers would carry placards announcing their destination in the hope that some kindly motorist would offer them a lift. Bus drivers caught in a raid were told to use their discretion as to whether or not to carry on. Often they had to use discretion over the choice of route as well. This sometimes produced odd results: the vicar of St Paul's, Portman Square, boarded the bus of a driver who had been sheltering in the crypt of his church and said he wanted to go to Baker Street. Only when he arrived did the driver admit that he was supposed to be going in the opposite direction, to Knightsbridge. Leslie Paul took a No. 35 tram from Leicester Square. At Lambeth the road was blocked by a fire, so the driver decided to travel via Kennington. Halfway there it stopped; the track was rusty and no power was getting through. 'Nobody didn't say nothing about no diversions,' complained the driver, ' "Get as far as she will go", they said to me. That ain't very 'elpful when you come to think of it.' Paul abandoned ship and found a bus pointing in the right direction. It bowled along merrily at 30 mph. Where is it going? he asked the conductor. 'Dunno. Haven't the faintest,' was the reply. 'I'm certain everyone was enjoying that chaos,' commented Paul. 'After all, when you have run to schedule for countless years it must be fun not knowing how you will arrive. Or whether!'

The fun must have worn thin pretty soon, as it did for those who spent hours in unlit, unheated carriages crawling by train through London's suburbs. The worst day on the Southern Region was 17 October, when all the automatic signalling had been knocked out within two and a half miles of Waterloo. Commuters had better luck when a mine on a parachute twined itself around the main signal box at London Bridge. If it had gone off it would have closed the station for weeks, perhaps months; instead it was disarmed at dawn and services were uninterrupted. Stations were tempting targets and were often hit; the worst incident occurred not at a main-line station but at Sloane Square. 'I never saw such a mess,' wrote Alexander Cadogan. 'The new station one huge crater and, at the bottom, a train crushed under an avalanche of concrete blocks and steel girders. They think about thirty people killed.'

Once the commuter reached his suburban destination he found a world much nearer normality than anything he had left behind. At one time or another every outer suburb was bombed, some often, some heavily. Croydon, for one, had suffered severely before central London even experienced its first attack. But on the whole incidents were rare. Dereliction rather than destruction caught the eye. In his novel *The Avenue Goes to War*, R. F. Delderfield described a once prosperous street with its pre-war trimness lost, privet hedges run riot and lawns neglected or dug up for potatoes, 'To Let' and 'For Sale' signs everywhere, grass growing between the paving stones and even on the street. Though bombs fell only from time to time on Dagenham, the guns were thick on the ground and the shower of shrapnel was as lethal as in areas more regularly attacked. Since there were no deep shelters there was no way of escaping from the racket of the anti-aircraft barrage; in his history of Dagenham John O'Leary complained most of all about the noise.

In the centre of London, night-life, which by the late summer of 1940 had returned to near normality, now survived only fitfully and in hugger-mugger. Even the pubs were at first empty, especially in the East End, where superstition held that they were especially likely to be hit. Most theatres closed in the first two or three days of the blitz because managers did not believe that audiences would venture out. On 10 September a mere two West End theatres opened: the Coliseum, with *White Horse Inn*, and the Criterion, which in spite of being mainly underground presented a Farjeon revue only to half-empty houses. Three days later again and only the Criterion was left, though the Windmill offered a genteel nude show for every night of the war, sometimes to audiences of only two or three, once to a solitary soldier. The Windmill was justifiably proud of its record: Vivien van Damm, the general manager, and several of his staff were in the Home Guard; one special constable, four air-raid wardens, two firemen and ten first-aiders also worked in the theatre. During the worst of the blitz the Windmill closed at seven o'clock, but most of the chorus spent the night in its cellars, jealously guarded by van Damm.

Then, little by little, life began to return to the West End theatre. There was lunchtime ballet at the Arts, a farce at the Comedy, ending at 6.30 p.m., Shakespeare at the Vaudeville. When the blitz closed down night-time London the *Evening Standard* renamed its column from 'Lighter London' to 'Darker London'. On 28 October they announced that they were considering changing back again.

The cinemas never closed, though they too settled for an earlier schedule. At the Granada, Woolwich, on the first day of the real blitz, the exit doors were blown in. People began to leave, saw the broken glass and flaming incendiaries in the street and retreated inside. The manager urged them to stay and began a sing-song, which faltered until three usherettes, no doubt with thwarted stage ambitions, commandeered the microphone and began to sing 'Oh, Johnny!' That raid lasted only half an hour, but it set a precedent for many evenings when the cinemas provided entertainment and an illusion of security for several hours after the scheduled closing time, sometimes with two showings of the main film, three or four supporting films, two organ recitals and an impromptu cabaret. So popular did this become that people began to turn up for the last performance armed with blankets and pillows. The strain on cinema staffs became intolerable, and as the blitz wore on the public found itself gently but firmly shooed towards the nearest shelter. But the community spirit did not die. 'We became a brotherhood of the blitz,' claimed a cinema manager in Wandsworth. 'It was wonderful to see the way patrons helped each other with unfailing good humour and cheered up any timid souls among them,' said his opposite number in Edmonton. But the timid souls sometimes prevailed; the Union Jacks which Granada cinemas had flown were hauled down because patrons feared they would suggest to the Germans that the buildings were military objectives.

By mid-October many cinemas were almost full again; Hitchcock's *Foreign Correspondent* and *Rebecca* were two films which took as much money that week as they had in August. 'Customers will face the blitz if the cinemas will give them the right films,' declared the *Evening Standard*. Most right of all was *Gone With the Wind*. When this opened in April 1940 the management predicted optimistically that if there was no blitz it would run until the end of the year; blitz or not, it ran until the spring of 1944. 'Those queues in Leicester Square have been as much a part of the war pattern of London life as the sandbags and the uniforms,' wrote Guy Morgan, historian of the wartime cinema. Sometimes fire engines would be racing around the square and fires blazing within a few hundred yards, yet people waited placidly for the last performance.

The restaurants – at least in the West End – fared less well. Particularly at dinner, the tables were deserted. Dining at the Apéritif, Charles Ritchie noted 'groups of tired waiters muttering together in corners, the bartender brooding over his deserted bar'. This was not a reflection on the cuisine. The following night General Strong, later to be Eisenhower's Chief of Intelligence, dined at an equally empty L'Escargot and ate pâté de foie gras, a fillet of sole, and a roast pigeon washed down by Pomerol and old Armagnac. But during dinner a bomb fell in the street outside and ruptured a gas main; when he left there were no taxis and he had to walk home. It took more than food to tempt most people from their homes in such circumstances. The right cabaret still could, however; Inge Anders was singing to an almost full house at the May Fair restaurant less than a fortnight later.

The urge to preserve propriety often conquered fear. A girl having a bath was unscathed when the bath, with her in it, was blown upside down. When rescuers arrived to extricate her she refused to come out until she had been given something to cloak her nakedness. Afterwards she was so embarrassed that she would cross the road to avoid meeting the warden who had extricated her. Another warden crawled into a shattered house to rescue an old woman. Though it could only be a matter of minutes before the building collapsed, she insisted on grubbing around in what was left of her bedroom; 'I'm not going out without me corsets on; I never 'ave and 'Itler won't make me.'

However appalling the carnage of the night before, life carried on. After several hours in the shelters, Joan Veazey emerged in the early morning and saw 'people going to work on lorries, carts, in fact anything that moved had people holding on – just to get to their work. The Londoners were not going to give in.' Amazingly few of those whose work kept them in London deserted their posts and only a handful used the raids as an excuse for non-attendance. They would leave homes damaged by the previous night's raid; find what transport they could; if necessary walk for miles through shattered streets, stepping around craters and over fire hoses, diverting to avoid a UXB. In the end they would arrive.

Everyone had their favourite heroes. For a foreign diplomat it was the civil servants in Whitehall who somehow kept appointments and transacted business however chaotic the circumstances. To Bruce Lockhart it was the office girls who 'came early and left late to the cacophonous chorus of bombs and guns and sirens. Poorly paid, they never complained. They rarely, if ever, arrived late.' General Lee particularly admired 'the little tarts who wander about the streets of Mayfair. When everyone else is hurrying for the air-raid shelters, they are quite indifferent and continue to stroll unperturbed.' It never occurred to Londoners that they were being particularly brave; they just got on with it as their friends and neighbours were doing. Perhaps heroism is too strong a word, but the patience, the resourcefulness, the dogged determination of the working Londoner during the worst months of the blitz deserve profound admiration.

It took nearly two months before even the worst deficiencies of the public shelters were corrected. Sometimes the authorities were woefully dilatory; occasionally worse. When the committee of the Tilbury shelters approached the ARP with demands for basic facilities, they were charged by mounted police and their leaders taken to the police station. A similar ginger group for Swiss Cottage shelterers – who produced a newspaper called the *Swiss Cottager* – complained of 'shameful apathy' and 'indifference amounting almost to callousness'. But gradually things improved. Urgent practical as well as humanitarian reasons demanded it: there was every reason to fear that disease would ride rampant in the congested and unhygienic shelters. 'The foetid atmosphere of most of them was like the germ-incubation rooms of a bacteriological laboratory,' wrote Ritchie Calder, author, journalist and one of the most vivid reporters of the blitz, 'only the germs were not in sealed flasks, but hit you in the face in a mixed barrage.' Lice-borne typhoid was the most pressing threat, cerebro-meningitis a close second, and in dockland there was a fear that imported malaria-bearing mosquitoes would breed in the muggy atmosphere. That many would suffer and some die from influenza was taken for granted by doctors. Almost miraculously, the worst did not happen; health suffered in the shelters but there was no serious epidemic. By mid-October most shelters had sanitary closets and washing facilities were being introduced; where canteens and latrines existed, the two were separated. A month later hot food and drink was being supplied to 150,000 shelterers and capacity was increasing by 100,000 a month. Bunks were introduced, though in some shelters, as in Bethnal Green, this improvement led to near rebellion since it was felt they cut down the space available for dancing and card games. Soon West Ham shelters had a library of 4000 books, in Bermondsey amateur actors toured the shelters with a production of Chekhov's *The Bear*; by the end of the year the LCC was holding more than 200 classes in a diversity of subjects.

Shelters in churches were put in order more quickly, though in the long run they inevitably lacked the resources of official shelters. Churches were in fact hit as often as any other public building, but the conviction lingered that somehow they would be immune. The Roman Catholic church in Willesden Green had no crypt but still filled up whenever there was a raid; the priest slept on a camp-bed in the vestry and emerged to invoke the aid of the Virgin Mary if bombs seemed to be getting close. More typical was St Paul's, Portman Square, where a stout crypt offered reasonable security. About 150 people sat or lay on wooden benches around the walls; tea, coffee and sandwiches were for sale at low prices; when the noise was not too great the curate, Maurice Wood, played the organ to entertain the shelterers. Church shelters varied widely in atmosphere. St Martin-in-the-Fields specialised in drunks and down-and-outs, and the clergy also accepted responsibility for the 'Hungerford Club', a facility under the arches of Charing Cross Station where the meths drinkers, the lice-infested, the mentally subnormal – all those who could not cope with the demands of wartime London – could be registered and guaranteed food, medical attention and a bath. St Peter's, Eaton Square, reminded Leslie Paul more of a country church institute on club night: 'Knitting women, amber lemonade in glasses, the urn of tea, the genial vicar, the darts tournament.'

At Lambeth 200 people sheltered regularly in the crypt and Archbishop Lang would go there most evenings to take a simple form of family prayer; the shelterers were more comfortable than those stalwarts who stuck it out in the trench shelters in the Archbishop's Park even though, by mid-October, the water was often over their shoes. Nothing would shake the devotion of the committed trench shelterer. Henry Jenkins, a builder working on a surface street shelter, was asked if he would use it himself. 'Nah! Trenches for me every time.' But surely the church would be closer, it was suggested. 'Don't like it. Was on the job and didn't like it. Nothin' against it, mind you, but trenches for me every time.' Usually relations were excellent between civil defence and clergy, but there was sometimes friction, as at Walworth where the Revd J. G. Markham was ordered by the Borough Health Officer to cut capacity from 650 to 230. Markham refused to impose such a restriction himself; two burly sergeants and six constables arrived to do so for him, and by the time the alert went an indignant crowd was massed around the gates. Fortunately for them, the alert was a signal for the police to return to their station, whereupon the would-be shelterers pushed through the gates and took their usual places.

Not all was harmony in the public shelters. Gwladys Cox recorded a 'colossal row' in a West Hampstead shelter over the allotment of space; with practice, such problems were more quickly regulated but they still arose from time to time. There were always troublemakers; John Parsley, a milk roundsman, was fined £2 for 'being insulting in an air-raid shelter'. He and his friends were behaving so raucously that life for the other shelterers had become intolerable. Shelters developed a special character and cliques were formed:

one, where the elderly congregated, made children feel unwelcome; another, where Bright Young Things were in a majority, made the oldies ill at ease. It was partly the dread of such wrangling that led the great majority of Londoners to eschew public shelters altogether. There were plenty of other reasons, too: pride, inertia, love of privacy and the comforts of home, indifference to danger, reluctance to undertake what might be a long and uncomfortable journey. Even at the height of the blitz only one in seven Londoners left home. The Ministry of Home Security calculated that half the deaths and serious injuries could have been avoided if everyone had used tubes or public shelters, though since there would anyway not have been room for them all the calculation was of academic interest.

It was difficult to establish exactly who was sleeping where. Wardens dutifully enquired, so that they would know who needed rescue if a building was hit, but 'people thought we were interfering and nosy', said Betty Hudson, a warden in Kensington. The reasons were sometimes obvious: 'One woman said she slept with a gent and when pressed to give his name, admitted that she couldn't because it was never the same one.'

Luxury hotels provided an altogether superior service for their clients. The Dorchester, where several members of the government had taken up residence, boasted a gas-proof shelter protected by twelve feet of concrete; the hotel's brochure proudly proclaimed, 'Experts agree the shelter is absolutely safe against even a direct hit.' Those dining at the Hungaria were tucked up on camp-beds if the alert sounded while they were on the premises, and even served breakfast the following morning. At the Berkeley only humbler accommodation was on offer. The Edinburgh MP, Geoffrey Shake-speare, was caught there by a raid. 'After dinner a great transforma-tion took place. From every corner came waiters and waitresses, porters and page boys, carrying blankets and pillows, and lay down on the sofa seats where normally the public dined. My head lay on the feet of the giant night porter, who usually guards the entrance door . . . The porter snored loudly all night.' At three o'clock the all-clear went and the dishevelled guests went home.

At one stage about 4 per cent of inner London's population slept in the tubes. Though the authorities accepted they could not drive people back above ground they at first made their disapproval clear. Leslie Paul tried to leave the Underground station at Charing Cross when the all-clear went at 4 a.m., but was told by 'a gloating policeman' that he would have to wait another three hours. 'The spite of police and officials against the public for taking shelter in the tubes was the most unpleasant aspect of the whole affair.' Things looked up when Lord Horder was appointed to investigate conditions in shelters, including tubes. The improvements effected in the public shelters took place in the tubes as well. A compressed air system was installed to force sewage to a higher level where it could be discharged into the main system. The London Passenger Transport Board agreed at the end of October that bunks could be installed provided they did not obstruct genuine passengers. But no satisfactory solution was ever found for the mosquitoes which refused to hibernate because of the heat generated by the packed bodies, or for the fierce winds, now cold, now searingly hot, which blasted along the platforms and sent the bedclothes flying.

Henry Moore's drawings catch more vividly than any words the squalor and yet dignity of that strange troglodytic life. They constituted, said Herbert Read, 'the most authentic expression of the special tragedy of this war – its direct impact on the ordinary mass of humanity, the women, children and old men of our cities'. Moore, together with his friend Graham Sutherland, applied to take a course in precision tool-making at the Chelsea Polytechnic. Fortunately they were not accepted, and Moore engaged himself in a semi-detached relationship with the War Artists' Scheme which led him eventually to the tube shelters. 'I took care never to let them see my sketching,' he said. 'That would have been much too rude. People were trying to get a little privacy even down there.' Not everyone was so considerate. The tube shelters were considered by many Londoners to be in some way inferior; to use the tubes was to lose face. Mass Observers noted that those who went underground always felt bound to excuse themselves to others. Harold Nicolson's housekeeper, Mrs Groves, tried it once but did not like the company: 'Greeks, they were, sir, by the look of them. I never did hold with foreigners.' In some, the shelterers inspired extravagant hostility. Rachel Ferguson saw the queues outside Notting Hill Gate tube station. 'These were members of the save-your-skin brigade, in their panicked desire for life seeing nothing disproportionate in a day-long wait every day in the street . . . Demoralised and demoralising, they would have rejoiced the heart of any German.' The journalist

Sefton Delmer, when an American colleague praised the courage of Londoners, 'thought, with shame, of those able-bodied proletarians absenting themselves from their workshops while they lay on their mattresses in the Underground, publicly copulating on the platforms and blocking up the stations for those who had to go to work'.

Meanwhile Winston Churchill and his staff also went underground, behaviour which to Rachel Ferguson would no doubt have seemed wholly different from the ignoble self-preservation of the tube shelterers. The Cabinet War Rooms, housed in a warren of little chambers beneath the Cabinet Office at the end of King Charles Street, survive almost unchanged today and provide one of the most evocative reminders of what London was like during the blitz: cramped and dingy cells for typists and telephonists; the occasional bunk for the grander VIP; the Prime Minister's austere accommodation; the tiny cubby-hole with a lavatory-type catch marked 'Vacant' or 'Engaged' where Churchill would retreat to telephone President Roosevelt in Washington. The rooms were completed just before the blitz began; Churchill was apt to disappear above ground when raids were on so as to see what was happening, but the nerve centre of Britain's war was in these rooms and functioned without interruption whatever might be going on above.

In provincial towns, when the blitz spread beyond London, people would trek to the adjacent countryside to spend the night in safety if not in comfort. In London this was more difficult, but the caves in the hills around Chislehurst in Kent provided safer and more spacious accommodation than even the deepest Underground. Legend claimed that the caves had been excavated by druids, using the antlers of deer as tools; certainly they had been in use in Roman times. Bernard Darwin, the golfer and sportswriter, was going home by train late one evening. As the train drew into New Cross station he saw that the platform was crowded with people, massed four or five deep. Sixteen of them, mainly mothers with children, surged into his carriage. He was baffled by this Derby Day influx; only when they all got out at Chislehurst did he remember about the caves. At one point up to 5000 people would go there every night, special trains were provided, and facilities equal to those in any London shelter were developed to serve the transient population. A more modest trek was towards the West End, where the basements of the larger shops were much favoured. 'There is growing up quite a discrimination on the subject,' reported Ernest Brown, the Minister of Health, 'Dickens and Jones being generally held to be the best.'

The government still had doubts about the growth of a 'shelter mentality'. John Anderson favoured the closing of shelters until a red alert had been given and the eviction of shelterers once the all-clear had sounded. Wallace argued that this was impractical and would lead to rioting in areas like Stepney, while the Commissioner of Police, Philip Game, went even further and maintained that it was perfectly sensible to spend one's time in a shelter if one's duties did not require one to be anywhere else. Gradually their point of view prevailed and the fact that so many people were not content with surface shelters, coupled with a fear that heavier bombs would soon be falling, led to a change of heart on this front too. In October 1940 the government decided that some deep shelters must be provided. Work began on eight, each planned to accommodate 8000 people. The news that this was happening was heartening to Londoners; it might have been less so had it been realised that the first would not be ready until long after the blitz was over.

Evacuation was as much encouraged by the authorities as the use of the Underground was deplored. They had some cause to feel despair at what must have seemed to them the wilful short-sightedness of the London public. By 7 September, with the inevitability of the blitz becoming every day more apparent, there were still 520,000 children of school age in the London area. In September and October 35,000 unaccompanied children and about 90,000 mothers and children were evacuated; in November the figure dropped to 15,000, by December it was a trickle. Far fewer people left because of the bombing than had done on the declaration of war. Malcolm MacDonald, at the end of October, pleaded with parents to consider not just the danger from bombs but the threat to their children's health. A half-page advertisement in the *Evening Standard* was headed: MOTHERS! 'You'd give your life for your children,' it read. 'Won't you take this chance to get them away to greater safety and health? Here in London your children's minds and bodies are in danger of being injured for life. Yet you can send them out of London at once. Within a few days they can be in healthier, safer surroundings, living and sleeping as children should.'

The Ministry organised house-to-house visits so that pressure could be brought on reluctant parents. There was even talk of compulsory evacuation and, in February 1941, a few 'raid-shocked' children were actually packed off to the country under legislation which allowed the authorities to intervene if it was felt a child's physical or mental health were seriously at risk.

Many of the schools that had reopened early in 1940 now closed again, particularly in the East End. The children who remained, however, often seemed more resilient than was the case with adults. Naomi Royde-Smith's ten-year-old nephew was asked what he would do if he got home to find it destroyed by bombs. Well, he said reflectively, if his house had gone the same would presumably be true of the neighbours. In that case he'd try first the Warden's Post, then the First-Aid Post, then the police station; if all else failed he'd telephone Auntie Norah in Winchester. 'If we had as little trouble with adults as we do with children it would be all right,' commented a warden. 'Hitler'd pack up if he could see some of these London kids.'

Barbara Roose, an eight-year-old in Covent Garden, knew quite as well as any grown-up when danger was imminent and would ignore orders to take shelter until she judged the moment had arrived. 'The fact that people were being killed did not touch me as a child,' she remembered. 'I was selfishly glad that it wasn't us.' General Lee, on a visit to Stepney, found few children about but those who were, 'wild-looking and grimy outwardly, but full of vitality and enthusiasm. One youngster said, "Mister, let me take you to see the last bomb round the corner." '

The businesses that had never left London or had done so earlier only to return were reluctant to be driven out. Basil Dean made plans to evacuate ENSA to Hindhead and sent his accounts department ahead, 'but after a while we all seemed to catch our second wind, so I ordered all staff back to London, feeling secretly rather ashamed of myself'. Mr Potter, the fishmonger, shut up shop in Chelsea because so many of his clients had gone away, but such things happened only in the richer and more central residential areas. Most foreign ambassadors stuck by their posts though some, notably the American, Joe Kennedy, left every night for a safe billet in Windsor Great Park. Mrs Maisky stayed with her husband, the

Russian ambassador, and drove around with him while the bombs were falling.

The House of Commons dismissed any idea of quitting London but agreed not to announce the times of its sittings and to start its debates earlier in the day. Churchill still considered the Houses of Parliament a tempting target, offering little protection against bombs, and on 22 October he decreed that alternative accommodation must be found. Church House, a few hundred yards away, was deemed safer and the Commons met there for the first time on 11 November. Chips Channon found the acoustics awful: 'The atmosphere was gay, rather like the Dorchester. Outside in the cloisters, however, I ran into several clerics who seemed indignant that their building should have been taken for such lay purposes as law making.' The clerics did not have much to worry about; the new venue was not popular with members and was used rarely, though one State Opening was held there, on 11 November. Black Rod got lost, wandered fretfully about the building and had to be restrained from administering his traditional three thunderous knocks to a curtained glass door, which would undoubtedly have shattered under the impact.

The House of Commons was one of many buildings whose roof was endowed with spotters – nicknamed Jim Crows – who warned the people within if attack seemed imminent. This system was a particular favourite of Churchill's, who had been disturbed by the time wasted in offices and factories, where everything closed down if there was an alert. It worked well, notably in hospitals, where patients were sometimes put at real risk by unnecessary movement. A few hospitals which did not have to be in London but had survived the first evacuation now moved out; notably the City of London Maternity Hospital which transferred to Brocket Hall in Hertfordshire. The senior staff protested at the inconvenience involved and tried to get the director sacked; he had the last laugh when the hospital was hit only a few days after the evacuation. The only 'casualty' was a corpse which had been left behind in the morgue.

Londoners still had babies. Josephine Barnes, an obstetrician at University College Hospital, used to deliver them at home, driving around in the matron's car during raids with two mattresses strapped to the roof to guard against shrapnel. One delivery was made on

the floor of a room without blackout curtains, by the light of a
storm lantern.

The army of ARP wardens had been gravely depleted by the
demands of the armed services and industry before the blitz began.
In October 1940 the 10 per cent who were full-time professionals
were frozen in their jobs, part-time volunteers remained as a more
volatile though still powerful force. Many were elderly, some disabled, one in six a woman who was confined, in theory at least, to
operating the telephones or keeping the headquarters running.

'Here's old G is stone deaf; he's no use,' expostulated an exasper-
ated warden in north London. 'Old R can't hardly walk. The general's nearly eighty, and H can't walk without a stick. Talk to me
about the lame, the halt and the blind! Cor!' Wardens, according
to a Mass Observation survey in Kilburn, fell into two camps –
those who argued, 'If a warden can't patrol in gunfire, he's no use,'
and those who prudently declined to venture out if the going was
rough. Each group reviled the other. For a time, in Kilburn, the
timorous prevailed and wardens had a bad name: 'Not a single
warden did I see. There I was, alone in the house, the whole of the
top floor burning and not a soul to help'; 'By the time the wardens
came along, George and I had got it under control. They didn't do
a thing.' This was a temporary phase, however; by November the
weaklings had been weeded out and the wardens reinstated in public
esteem.

The public's attitude towards the firemen was subtly different.
With the advent of the blitz they had become heroes; a cartoon by
Donald Zec in the *Daily Mirror* showed a fireman and a warden
pelted with brickbats in 1939 and showered with flowers in 1940
above the caption, 'Local Boys Make Good'. But whereas the
wardens *were* local boys and for the most part perceived as amateurs,
firemen were less tied to a specific area and were considered more
professional. In the richer areas, particularly, they were classed with
the police or, perhaps more accurately, categorised as plumbers or
electricians to be called in when necessary. Hilda Neal, in Thurloe
Square, South Kensington, provided the firemen with tea after a
fire had been put out and was disgusted that no neighbour joined
her in the task. 'One woman even refused the firemen passage
through her flat – "a cursed woman", a girl warden called her.' In

fact, the Auxiliary Fire Service was in its origins quite as heterogeneous as the ARP, as is apparent in the memoirs of Henry Green, Stephen Spender, William Sansom and other unlikely firemen; but it had quickly been welded into a more coherent, professional body – as indeed it had to be if it were to survive the tests ahead.

Behind these front-line troops lay an army of part-time helpers. The Women's Voluntary Service (WVS) performed innumerable ancillary tasks which would otherwise have fallen to the wardens and fire-fighters or been left undone. The Housewives' Service, an offshoot of the WVS, turned the homes of its members into miniature canteens or first-aid posts. Part-time special constables took on police duties far more onerous than anything they had envisaged when they joined the Force. The boy scouts were frenetically active as messengers and orderlies. In Holborn tube station they led the community singing and conducted a Scouts' Own Service each night at midnight; they helped out on exercises with the Home Guard; a Croydon troop checked fire buckets and tested stirrup pumps in the local hospital; one startled scout found himself nursing a new-born baby while a harassed nurse disappeared on other duties. In Hackney the girl guides did similar work; a volunteer was required to head, tail and gut a hundred herrings. One scout volunteered to help in a civil defence exercise and was lowered in a stretcher from the second storey of a 'bombed' house. Euan Wallace, who was observing the operation, was so horrified by the risks that he insisted only dummies should be used in future rehearsals.

Civil servants of a literary bent and retired admirals, poet firemen and crippled wardens, housewives and boy scouts: London's battle was fought by an army of amateurs. Not surprisingly, there was at first some incompetence and disorder. But though the forces of civil defence sometimes bent under the strain, they never broke. In the first sixty-eight days of the blitz they grew steadily tougher, more efficient, more resilient. There were those who said that London could never have survived another two months of unbroken onslaught. Mercifully the test was not applied, but the record of those charged with London's defence suggests that they would have passed with honour. London in mid-November 1940 was better equipped to withstand attack than it had been on 7 September. Many people had reason to be proud of that achievement.

9

'A real community'

ON 14 NOVEMBER 1940, the Luftwaffe turned its attention to Coventry. There had been major raids on provincial cities before this; on 25 October for instance 170 people had been killed in Birmingham, but the Coventry raid was of a new and terrible intensity.

It introduced something of a respite for the capital. In the next two months London had only six important raids and a handful of minor ones. It was a desperately needed breathing space. At first there seemed little reason for optimism; the night after Coventry was destroyed bombs fell on all but one of the metropolitan boroughs and 76 of the 95 boroughs in the London region; 142 people were killed and Westminster Abbey, the National Portrait Gallery, Wellington Barracks and the giant GPO sorting-office at Mount Pleasant were among the buildings damaged.

Shortly after that raid London lost the little-loved American ambassador, Joe Kennedy. 'I did not know London could take it,' he remarked on his return to Boston, presumably intending it as a compliment, but going on to say that democracy in Britain was finished and the same fate might befall the United States if it were drawn into the war. In his place came John G. Winant, who said on arrival, with apparent sincerity, that there was no place on earth he would rather be; whose wife was shortly to join him; who scorned Kennedy's bolt-hole in Windsor and set up in a flat adjoining the Embassy in Grosvenor Square. By the time he arrived, the capital had endured its most severe test of the war so far, the great fire raid of 29 December 1940.

In fact, the raid was not great by the standards of some of its precursors. On at least five earlier occasions more incendiaries had been dropped. Its greatness lay in its timing. The twenty-ninth was a Sunday, the first Sunday after a Christmas when London had been left in peace. The offices, warehouses and churches in the City were locked and deserted, the fire-watchers snugly at home. The area was therefore unusually vulnerable, and to compound the danger the Thames was at such low ebb that fireboats were unable to manoeuvre near the site of the fires and many locally based pumps were out of range of the water. The result was the nearest London ever got to the fire-storms which were later to consume Dresden and a great part of Hamburg. Nearly 1500 fires were started, the great majority in the City of London, and these combined in two mighty conflagrations, the worst of which ravaged half a square mile between Moorgate, Aldersgate, Cannon Street and Old Street. Twice Fire Brigade control centres had to be abandoned, the occupants in one case escaping through a network of tunnels under burning buildings. B. J. Rogers watched aghast from the roof of the Bank of England: 'The whole of London seemed alight! We were hemmed in by a wall of flame in every direction. It wasn't just big fires here and there, but a continuous sheet of flame all around us. We rather got the wind up, as it looked absolutely out of control, and we thought if it did reach us, how were we going to get away?'

The Bank survived. So, amazingly, did St Paul's, though the streets around were ravaged and twenty-eight incendiaries hit the cathedral. One lodged halfway through the outer shell of the dome and began to melt the lead. It was beyond the range of stirrup pumps and the dome seemed doomed; then it somehow fell outwards onto the parapet and guttered out. The Faraday Building, the Cabinet's private refuge, survived too, with John Anderson and Ernest Bevin among those who saw the flames draw so close that the military contemplated blowing up adjoining buildings in order to protect it. But the Guildhall was badly damaged, eight Wren churches destroyed, the Port of London reduced to a quarter of its capacity. In all, 163 died, a tiny figure given the scale of the catastrophe; sixteen of these were firemen and 250 more firemen were detained in hospital.

Two days later Charles Graves visited the still smouldering ruins. 'Numbers of City workers walked about with dazed and stunned looks. They were the people who had arrived the previous morning and found that their place of employment was gutted and were coming back on the following day simply because they had nothing better to do.' Some may have been so bemused but more were probably hoping to find someone in authority who would tell them how and where to carry on with their work. For Anthony Weymouth, who was there a day or two later, the remarkable thing was that 'the life of the City seemed to be going on just as usual. There was just as much traffic; and people were passing to and fro on their business.' Mrs Byers too surveyed the desolation around her badly damaged office. 'There is not the slightest feeling of defeat in the air or on the faces of the clerks and shopkeepers, only a stern and grim determination to hold on to the end – Hitler's end.' But no one could survey the desolation without feeling dismay if not despair. Robert Herring came back from Sheffield the day after the raid and walked aghast through the smouldering ruins. 'The air felt singed. I was breathing ashes . . . The air itself, as we walked, smelt of burning. Gritty, it grated my lungs. I felt cannibal – inhaling, with each breath, skeleton cinders.'

The horse having bolted, the authorities busily locked the stable door. The failure of City firms to protect their premises finally convinced the government that fire-watching must be made compulsory. Every factory or business house was required to provide for its own protection and every street was asked to organise a roster. But though each business was instructed to guard against incendiaries, the individual was still expected to volunteer. This caused problems when employees felt that their first responsibility was to their own homes and families.

Nor were things necessarily better in big blocks of flats; in one West End building there were 550 tenants; one hundred were needed to provide an adequate service; nineteen men and twenty-two women volunteered. In Shawfield Street in Chelsea the fire-watching party consisted of a widow with two sons of seventeen and sixteen, an elderly couple with a son of sixteen, and a retired and arthritic chef with an invalid daughter. This was not due to slackness or cowardice on the part of the remainder; all other residents had left. Yet the Shawfield Street team were in no way discomfited by their inadequacy; on the contrary, they complained to the town hall when 'people from another street without even badges, and without invitation', arrived and extinguished an incendiary which 'they themselves had been perfectly capable of dealing with'. Such demarcation disputes were not uncommon. The ARP swiftly and efficiently put out a fire on the roof of a flat rented by the Canadian diplomat and future Prime Minister, Lester Pearson, but ignored appeals to deal with another in the adjoining mews – 'Sorry, but that's outside our district; Squad 216 must deal with those.' 'Good old red tape!' commented Pearson resignedly. In fact the inhabitants of the mews soon disposed of the fire themselves.

On 5 January 1941 a bomb damaged the prison at Wormwood Scrubs. When war broke out it had been decided to reduce the London prison population by releasing many who had only a short time to serve. The Scrubs, Pentonville and Brixton were cleared of almost all their occupants and the remaining prisoners sent out of London or concentrated at Wandsworth and Holloway. This did not last long: the number of convicts and prisoners on remand swelled inexorably; the provincial prisons returned their London visitors as a disruptive element; political internees had to be housed, sometimes for several months or longer; conscientious objectors who had been convicted for refusing to do anything that might help the war effort were usually imprisoned at Wormwood Scrubs. After some experimentation it was decided that during raids prisoners should be confined to their cells. 'Subsequent experience regularly proved the soundness of this decision,' concluded the report of the Commissioner for Prisons. One governor even claimed that the prisoners liked it, many slept peacefully through raids without being aware of them: 'There is no doubt that the protection of a cell keeps up the morale.' The recollections of one convict at Wormwood Scrubs are rather different. 'I remember during air-raids there was panic in the prison because we were all locked up,' wrote the conscientious objector Sidney Greaves. 'If the prison were hit there was no way you could get out. Prisoners would bang plates, jerries, mugs, anything; it was an enormous noise. There was nothing you could do . . . It was very disturbing to be in that position.'

The relative infrequency of raids in January and February caused vague disquiet. Was this the prelude to something even worse? Were the Germans saving their strength for the moment of invasion? Or were they weakened by their losses and British raids on Germany? In some areas the number of wardens was cut and grumbles about their expense and uselessness were once more heard. When raids did come, as in Hendon on 13 February when a single plane dropped its cargo without the warning having sounded, the effects seemed the more dreadful for being so unusual. The bomb – or bombs; one woman claimed she knew it was a stick of bombs lashed together because she heard the clanking of the chains as they fell – must have been exceptionally powerful; it destroyed 100 houses, killed sixty inhabitants, seriously injured 200 more. The failure to give a warning, presumably because the bomber was taken to be a reconnaissance aircraft, caused much public indignation: 'It was the *unexpected* surprise which seems to have disturbed people,' commented a Mass Observer. 'Another factor may, of course, be the lull and the consequent de-conditioning.'

The incident inspired greater hostility towards the authorities than the more sustained destruction of 1940. So did the bomb which four days later fell on the public shelter in the archway under London Bridge Station. A water main was fractured and many of the sixty-three deaths were by drowning. Home Office records show much bitterness against those who had allowed the archway to be used as a shelter. People who had become conditioned to the blitz 'have now lost some of their toughness and indifference', concluded the report. They were soon to have a chance to re-grow their carapace as the frequency and scale of raids began to mount again in March. One landmark which perished at this stage was the Queen's Hall in Langham Place. With it went all the double basses, violins, oboes and harps of the London Philharmonic. Somehow the orchestra scraped together replacements and found another hall in which they played the following afternoon. They moved their regular base to the Coliseum; and in June the Albert Hall, which had been occupied only by six firemen since its closure in July 1939, was reopened for a season of promenade concerts.

Inevitably incidents of this kind, involving celebrities and famous buildings, gained more attention than innumerable less glamorous tragedies. A prime example was the bombing in March of the fashionable nightclub, the Café de Paris. 'It was a gory incident,' admitted Barbara Nixon, 'but the same week another dance hall a mile to the east of us was hit and there were nearly 200 casualties. This time there were only 10/6d frocks and few lines in the papers ... Local feeling was rather bitter.' With the Café de Paris, as with the sinking of the *Titanic* some fifty years before, it was the instant transition from luxury, glitter, apparent stability to shocking destruction which caught the imagination. Martin Poulsen, the enterprising manager, had been accumulating champagne throughout 1940 and claimed to have 25,000 bottles in stock. 'Good times are just around the corner,' he announced, and on 5 November, after a long closure for decoration, he reopened what he advertised as 'the safest and gayest restaurant in town, 20 feet below ground'. At first he lost £500 a week, by mid-December he was in profit, New Year's Eve was the biggest night the Café had enjoyed since 1927. But the safety was a myth – two bombs penetrated the roof, one failed to explode, the other killed the band leader 'Snake Hips' Johnson and many of the staff and guests.

'It was full of aliens, and if any restaurant had to be hit that was the one to catch it,' remarked Charles Graves disagreeably. Betty Baldwin, the former prime minister's daughter, who was a survivor, would not have agreed – 'The men, almost all in uniform, seemed extraordinarily handsome, the young women very beautiful, the whole atmosphere one of great gaiety and youthful charm.' Nor would Barbara Roose's Uncle Tom, a dustman who was on the spot and who had tears running down his cheeks as he spoke of 'young men in uniforms carrying out their dead girl-friends'.

Both Betty Baldwin and Uncle Tom were sickened by the looters who prowled around the floor of the shattered nightclub, ripping open handbags, tearing rings off the hands of the dead and the unconscious. There was an epidemic of looting during the blitz, so serious that Scotland Yard set up a special squad to deal with it. Some of it was organised: gangs would send out spotters during the raids, who would report promising incidents to their headquarters and summon a team to the spot before the wardens or firemen (still less the police) had heard what was going on. More was casual. With youth clubs closed and families often divided, under-employed teenagers were particularly prone to snap up whatever unconsidered trifles they might chance on. Some were younger still. Four boys, two of eleven, two of ten, were sentenced to be birched for stealing from a bombed house. Leslie Paul thought the punishment harsh. 'I can excuse a ten-year-old who wondered whether, in this orgy of destruction, he might not salvage something precious for himself. Indeed, it would seem a kind of sanity.' Many of the cases of so-called looting were little more reprehensible than picking up a coin which had fallen in the gutter and failing to hand it in to the police. Verily Anderson, in St John's Wood, helped herself to a nursery fireguard which had been lying for weeks on a nearby bombed site. As she stepped into the street she ran into a policeman, who shook

Italy's entry into the war provoked louts to throw bricks through the windows of restaurants or cafés run by Italians (p. 97)

By mid-1940 many buses and cars had been adapted to run on gas

Those privileged enough to drive cars were sometimes accused of scorning those less fortunate, but in fact most people helped out by offering lifts

The railings come down in Berkeley Square. 'I regard this ruthless tearing up of old iron railings . . . as a barbaric piece of Socialism,' wrote an indignant MP (p. 182)

Anything containing aluminium was collected for the war effort, usually to rust for months or years in unsightly heaps

Father John Groser, one of the heroes of the blitz, took over in his area of
Stepney when the Council failed to exercise control. Here he is talking to a
group of parishioners at a Mobile Feeding Canteen (p. 120)

Shelterers on the platform and, less usually, on the tracks at Aldwych
Underground Station

An old man asleep in an empty
sarcophagus beneath Christ Church,
Spitalfield.
A photograph by Bill Brandt

Queueing up for water at a standpipe near the Elephant and Castle,
the morning after London's last great raid

Getting to work. For Bruce Lockhart the heroes of the blitz were above all the office girls, who 'came early and left late to the cacophonous chorus of bombs and guns and sirens. Poorly paid, they never complained' (p. 132)

The hole left by an unexploded bomb near St James's Park

John Lewis was one of the few Oxford Street stores to be so badly damaged as to be beyond repair (p. 124)

A dress shop bravely reopens, even though its windows are broken and its stock much damaged

The Guildhall the morning after the great fire raid of 29 December 1940

Salvage work at the Café de Paris. 'It was full of aliens, and if any restaurant had to be hit that was the one to catch it,' remarked Charles Graves disagreeably (p. 148)

his head in disappointment. Visions of prison flashed before her eyes and she offered herself for arrest. ' "It's not that, miss," he said. "I've had my eye on it to take home after dark for my own toddler." "Take it," I said, holding it out to him. "No, miss," he said sadly. "You got it first." '

That was the innocent end of the spectrum. Many were the victims who returned to their bombed homes to find that looters had struck. Gwladys Cox was back at her burnt-out flat in Hampstead within a few hours of the fire being extinguished. 'Under my bed, my trinket box was lying open . . . It had been taken out of the dressing-table drawer, which had been forced, and everything of the least value removed.' Gladys Strelitz found her windows blown out, the house ransacked, 'and all the bed linen and everything stolen and, well, we were full of despair.'

The heavy-rescue men and demolition squads were particularly prone to mix business with pleasure by helping themselves to objects from the houses they worked in; nearly half the arrests made by the police were of civil defence workers. A Mass Observer found that some demolition men took up the work specifically with this in mind. 'Even those who are not primarily concerned with what they can find are not averse to taking something when it turns up. The press campaign and the heavy sentences for looters don't seem to worry them.' So far as heavy sentences were concerned, the law's bark was at first worse than its bite. In theory looting from bombed premises was punishable by death or penal servitude for life, but when it came to the point far lighter sentences were handed out. Herbert Metcalfe, the Old Street magistrate, told a man who had broken into the electricity meter in a bombed house that, if he offended again, he would be sent to the Old Bailey and, no doubt, hanged, but he then discharged the accused on probation (as it happened, a few weeks later, the man went home drunk, fell downstairs and broke his neck). Sir Gervais Rentoul similarly menaced a west London looter who had stolen a masonic emblem from the dead licensee of a pub; in this case the offender at least got six months. But the rising tide of looting caused such concern that by 1941 sentences of five years' penal servitude were becoming more common. The police drafted in extra patrol cars and set up a special squad of plainclothes detectives to mingle with civil defence workers and catch the looters red-handed. Sometimes, too, the police took the law into their own hands; in his novel *Caught*, Henry Green described their manhandling a looter, 'most of his clothes torn off, heels dragging, drooling blood at the mouth, out on his feet from the bashing he had been given'.

One of the more remarkable features of London life during the blitz was the way in which, beneath a veneer of violence and perpetual crisis, most people pursued their day-to-day avocations as if all was as usual in the world. On the night on which the Café de Paris was hit, 150 debutantes, dressed in white, were curtseying to the cake in the ballroom of Grosvenor House. The red light shone to indicate raiders overhead, the floor shuddered from nearby bombs, but for Charles Graves the only flaw in the evening was that 'the spectacle was rather robbed by the absence of actual Royalty cutting the huge cake'. All over the London region in a multitude of pubs, clubs, church halls, women's institutes, people placidly played whist, got on with their knitting or talked about the weather.

Life went on, too, in other ways. For Christmas 1940 people seem to have put aside the doubts about the propriety of spending which had possessed them the year before and resolved to buy whatever they could find and – more or less – afford. Oxford Street had the atmosphere of a pre-war Christmas, reported the *Evening Standard*. The pavements were congested, women had flocked in from the suburbs, and 'the shops were doing business that was described as "not at all bad" '. There was not much *in* the shops, noted General Lee gloomily on Christmas Eve, 'but to try to buy anything today was like swimming against Niagara'. Though merchandise such as silk stockings and French scent had almost vanished, there was, in fact, still a surprising amount in the shops, especially by way of food and drink. 'Many thousands of finest Xmas turkeys from Norfolk, West of England, Northern Ireland,' announced one of the more expensive wholesalers. Mince pies and Christmas puddings were hard to find, fruit cake impossible. There were no crystallised fruits, toffees or boiled sweets but plenty of liqueur chocolates and a few drums of Chinese figs and Turkish delight. Wine and spirits were plentiful, brandy rare. Soap was the most popular present. There was rationing by price. Sidney Chave in Upper Norwood found fruit too dear to be contemplated; chickens also priced high; meat plentiful but limited in type and quality.

There was little attempt to see in the New Year with the fervour shown at Christmas. Tom Driberg was one of forty or fifty people who assembled rather sheepishly on the steps of St Paul's. A policeman pointed out that fires were still smouldering in the area and asked mildly if they could not celebrate somewhere else. By way of response, a woman led the people in the singing of 'Loch Lomond'. A fire engine clanged by just as the hour boomed out. 'We sang "Auld Lang Syne" – shakily, out of tune, not in unison, but we sang it.' Then an old man who had previously deplored the fact that there was no service in the cathedral led his friends in singing 'Praise God, from Whom all Blessings flow'. A few days later Driberg was one of the observers at a peace convention at the Royal Hotel led by the lawyer and far-left socialist D. N. Pritt. Over 2000 delegates heard more or less routine denunciations of capitalism; praise for the Soviet Union; demands for a direct appeal for peace to the German people 'over Hitler's head', and a protest by a private soldier who disliked having to salute when drawing his pay. The audience was no doubt infiltrated by Special Branch men making notes on those who attended but the authorities – not without justification – congratulated themselves on allowing such a meeting to take place at a time of menacing crisis.

'The very soil of the city at this time seemed to generate more strength,' wrote Elizabeth Bowen in her novel *The Heat of the Day*, 'in parks the trees on which each vein in each yellow leaf stretched out perfect against the sun blazoned out the idea of the finest hour . . . All this was beheld each morning more light-headedly: sleeplessness disembodied the lookers-on.' It was upon an already exhausted and bemused population that two crushing blows fell in mid-April, together far worse than anything that had occurred before. On 16 and 19 April raiders killed more than a thousand people on each night, and 148,000 houses were damaged against an average of 40,000 a week in September and October 1940. Wednesday 16 April – 'The Wednesday' as it was thereafter known – was marked by the use of JU88 dive-bombers which 'caused a screaming sound in the air', wrote Charles Graves. 'Chandeliers, flares and flaming onions lit the sky with their yellow, white and red colours; a pall of smoke hung over Chelsea . . . So low did the dive-bombers come that for the first time I mistook bombers for taxi cabs, which is a very different thing from mistaking taxi cabs for bombers . . . It was the hell of a night.' The centre suffered most, but over Bromley a chandelier flare heralded a full-scale attack. The district had only 55 bombs during the whole blitz; 18 fell on 16 April and 74 people in Bromley died.

The morning after London looked 'bleary and disfigured', wrote Jock Colville. 'There is a great gash in the Admiralty, St Peter's, Eaton Square has been hit, Chelsea Old Church is demolished, Jermyn Street is wrecked.' With St Peter's had perished its gallant vicar, Austin Thompson, who had been standing on the steps urging passers-by to take shelter within when the bomb fell. The gash in the Admiralty gave some satisfaction to Winston Churchill, who announced in Cabinet that his view of Nelson's Column was now much improved. This was little consolation for the residents of Mayfair. Scarcely a window was left between Marble Arch and Grosvenor House, the waterlogged craters in Hyde Park suggested that the Tyburn stream had been breached by the bomb. 'I thought Londoners this morning looked as happy as though they had all the excitement of a cup tie!' wrote Woolton in his diary the morning after. There was no sign of fear, only a passionately expressed hope that there would be instant retaliation. He was selective in his viewing; there was no despair but much apprehension in London on 17 April.

That night there were 24,000 more people sheltering in the tubes. In Hackney even the surface shelters which had been deserted for several months were once more in demand. Lord Horder visited four East End shelters and found that in three of them children predominated; talk of compulsory evacuation was once more heard. The fears of the public seemed justified when only seventy-two hours later – 'The Saturday' – the Luftwaffe struck again. Sidney Chave had expected the raid on Thursday. 'We felt somewhat apprehensive as we were in no doubt that if Wednesday's raid could be repeated nightly for about a month, the civilians would be licked. Fortunately it is not possible to raid on such a scale very often.' This time the main focus of attack moved farther west, though again many parts of the region were affected. Nine Chelsea Pensioners were killed, including one who was 101 years old. There was talk of evacuating the Royal Hospital, but the remaining pensioners scorned the proposition. In Lambeth a bomb fell in the churchyard, blew open a grave more than a century old, and hurled bits of the still decomposing corpse many yards around. The head landed on the roof of the church. 'The stench was horrible,' recorded Canon Don. 'The coffin, with an inner lead lining, must have been air-tight – a horrible thought. The sooner cremation becomes universal, the better!'

London braced itself for another season of heavy raids, as continuous and far more damaging than those of 1940. But though Sidney Chave feared that the civilians would be licked, the authorities felt confident that London was in better shape to resist attack than the year before. The problem of homelessness was being tackled with new vigour; fortunately, given the destructiveness of the latest raids. In September 1940 Sir Warren Fisher, for many years the ultimate civil service mandarin and a man of fearsome energy, had been appointed Special Commissioner with responsibility for clearing away debris, reopening roads and railways, and setting in train a measure of reconstruction. 'Londoners were in a frenzy of rage with the government,' he said, when he left the job two years later. There is no evidence that the public really held the government so badly to blame for the mountains of rubble and gaping craters which disfigured their city, but there was certainly a feeling that more could and should be done. With Fisher there, more was. On 14 October 5000 men of the Pioneer Corps had begun work on clearance and demolition, and thousands of unemployed were drafted in to provide unskilled labour. Within six weeks another 8000 troops, including many engineers, had joined the work. A group of Indians from the Punjab, specialists in railway construction, contributed their skills. By January derelict buildings in the City were being dynamited: 'the noise of the explosion is much sharper than that of a bomb,' noted Charles Graves. Smashed-up bricks and rubble were carted away for use in the building of runways, some was even sent to the United States in ships that would return with food and weapons; reusable timber was put to one side, the rest burned. Soon only the foundations were left and these were quickly covered by grass or brambles. People returning to London would notice the gaps, reflected Leslie Paul, 'but will be spared all sense of ruin and desolation and will wonder what we were so fussy about'.

In a curiously tactless leader the *Evening Standard* exulted in these labours. 'Stand by and cheer!' it advised the Londoner. 'Clean, wholesome, well-directed sticks of dynamite can be the symbols of so much in this great land of ours.' They would sweep away all trace of the 'slum-ridden, smoky, crooked and decaying' streets. 'Henceforth, King Dynamite shall rule in this most famous of cities.' 'Come friendly bombs and fall on Slough,' as John Betjeman saw it. Whether the average Londoner would have taken as positive a view of the demolition may seem unlikely, but Fisher for one felt that there was 'nothing worse for morale than to have this debris untouched for everyone to see'.

One thing was certainly worse, and that was to be left without a home. One Londoner in six was homeless at some point in the blitz of 1940 and 1941. Relatively few houses were totally destroyed, but the people to do repairs were woefully lacking; by November 1940 London needed 6000 tilers, more than were available in the whole country. This was where Willink came into his own as commissioner for the homeless. 'Neither commissar nor liaison officer, merely Coaxer-in-Chief,' he described himself. Artisans were borrowed from the services, drafted in from other regions, imported from Ireland. Repair became an urgent priority. By August 1941 over a million houses had been made weatherproof. In many cases it was only a question of broken windows or cracked slates, but these would quickly have deteriorated if left in disrepair.

Patching up houses was not the full extent of Willink's responsibility. By the end of the year hostels were being opened for bachelors or husbands whose wives had taken the children to the country. The first were in Islington and Hoxton: they offered hot breakfast and evening dinner, take-away lunch, a strongly protected basement and other facilities, all for £1 a week. 'Homes almost as comfortable as the wives had provided,' boasted Florence Horsbrugh, parliamentary secretary at the Ministry of Health. For those more temporarily displaced, rest centres offered comfort superior to anything enjoyed before. By April 1941 only five of the eighty schools, cinemas or church-halls originally designated as rest centres were still both available and habitable, but the Treasury had conceded that all expenditure on centres by local authorities was reimbursable and a new service quickly evolved, staffed mainly by volunteers but with a stiffening of professional social workers and teachers who had lost their pupils.

The Army lent a million blankets and Willink, on his own initiative, authorised structural work to make the centres, if not secure shelters, then at least the source of some protection. Their test came in April, with the influx that followed the two great raids; they proved successful and were never overcrowded, even when things were at their worst. Meanwhile the LCC had begun to organise communal feeding, through mobile field kitchens and the dining rooms at rest centres. By May 1941 there were 170 such canteens – known as the Londoners' Meals Service – and 190 mobile kitchens. These kitchens were particularly close to Woolton's heart. He wanted to call the people who ran the service 'Queen's Messengers' because they were messengers of mercy. When he retailed this piece of unctuous flattery to the Queen she put her hands in the air and said, 'Oh, my Lord, do you think I mean that? It is what I have tried so hard to be.' It is not clear from the text which Lord she was invoking; Lord Woolton, anyway, considered that it was 'a very moving insight into the mind of a great lady'.

The shelters themselves, if not much safer, were far more comfortable and hygienic than in the past. There were dishonourable exceptions, usually stemming from administrative weaknesses. Tooting's hundred public shelters, each holding between fifty and 300, were staffed by only forty wardens. There were reports of 'gambling, bad language, hooliganism, wanton damage and theft'; 100 to 150 electric light bulbs were stolen every week. An East End magistrate expostulated in dismay, 'The things that are going on in these shelters are very dreadful. For a young girl to go into a public shelter now without her father and mother is asking for trouble.' But such orgies are rarely referred to, most accounts describe the good order, even domesticity of the shelters. The worst slums – the Tilbury shelter, the Arches in Watney Street – had been cleaned up beyond recognition. 'Some are even cheerful,' said Jock Colville at the end of March, 'though it is terrible to see human beings living in such cramped conditions!'

Trench shelters had been drained and properly protected; in Poplar, as the days grew longer, the council began to arrange open-air dances in the parks in the hope of enticing participants into the trenches if the alert sounded. In November 1940 a Central Advisory Committee on Entertainment and Instruction had been formed, which organised distribution of books from public libraries as well as more than 200 LCC classes. By the New Year ENSA was providing weekly concerts in about twenty shelters; the first to be broadcast came from an Underground station and featured George Formby seated at a piano on a platform mounted over the track. He was introduced by the ubiquitous Admiral Evans. The Council for the Encouragement of Music and the Arts (CEMA) sent people into the shelters with gramophones and classical records; this was not an invariable success, at a shelter in Enfield there were complaints that the music made it impossible to hear the bombs properly.

Since the beginning of October, Herbert Morrison boasted just before Christmas, accommodation had been found for an extra 105,000 in the Underground – 200,000 bunks had been moved in, and a further 200,000 were ready for installation. New deep shelters were being tunnelled from three stations and sites for seven others had been surveyed. Stoves were being installed and sanitation problems would be solved by the New Year. It was this last point which most struck visitors to the tube shelters. 'There was a pleasant, antiseptic smell and everything was clean and orderly,' wrote a surprised Charles Graves at the end of January. The 'cleanly, normal, domesticated air' impressed George Orwell. 'Especially the young married couples, the sort of homely, cautious types that would probably be buying their houses from a building society, tucked up together under pink counterpanes.' In mid-November the first tube 'Food Train' was provided for shelterers; presumably a hazard to George Formby or any other entertainer suspended over the track, but a boon to hungry or thirsty shelterers.

With better facilities, more space, more time to make friends, a spirit of companionship grew in the shelters. 'You got a real community going after it was organised better,' one habitué recalled. 'Until then everyone had been shifting around and you didn't hardly know anyone. But now you had a regular spot with the same bunks every night, and the people around you became like regular neighbours.' Even in the shelters of the House of Commons Leonard Woolf found the same mood: 'Everyone felt the extraordinary blossoming of the sense of comradeship and good will which settled upon us in London during the blitz.' Nor was it only in large public shelters that such camaraderie prevailed. Leonard and Virginia Woolf once took refuge in a pill-box on Wimbledon Common. They found a couple already ensconced there, who were having a cup of tea. 'We were invited to join them. In two minutes we were all chatting happily like old friends.'

By February 1941 it was estimated that 92 per cent of London's population could be accommodated in public or private shelters. The Morrison shelter, a table of steel with sides of wire mesh, was joining the Anderson as a safety device for those who stayed at home. One in five Londoners could have found room in a public shelter, though even at the worst of times nothing like that number availed themselves of the opportunity. A new halfway house was the Haldane shelter, a reliable but expensive model of flexible size made up of tubes with circular steel girders. The authorities provided these with reluctance. A delegation at the Home Office demanded more but was assured they were of doubtful value. Then a siren went. The Home Office officials said all the shelters in the building were fully occupied and urged the visitors to leave. They refused and were eventually shown into a ministerial shelter. It was a Haldane.

The government's view was still that people should be advised to use their own shelters whenever possible and discouraged from taking to the tubes. They had yielded to the clamour for deep shelters, but pursued the policy without notable urgency. Lord Horder said in March that he knew of a shelter in which 'aged and infirm people have lived for four months without emerging'. The vision of a population of permanent troglodytes still haunted the authorities. 'Public shelters should not be made too attractive,' considered Alderman Charles Key, the Civil Defence Commissioner. Even as sympathetic an observer as George Orwell was disquieted by the contented placidity of life in the tubes: 'What is one to think of people who go on living this subhuman life night after night for months, including periods of a week or more when no aeroplane has come near London?' Such fears were misguided. Though a handful found security and a sense of community underground which they had never enjoyed in their usual homes, 99 Londoners out of 100 returned to the surface with relief as soon as they were satisfied that the coast was clear.

Various less obvious hazards existed. Harold Scott was preoccupied by the risk of floods. If the Serpentine were breached, he calculated, the waters would rush down to Knightsbridge and flood the Underground. The bank was massively reinforced with rubble

and soil, a piece of landscaping which survives to this day. The risk
of a gas attack was always in the minds of the authorities. The public
appeared largely indifferent: in Holborn and Ludgate Circus spot
checks showed that by now barely 5 per cent of passers-by carried
their masks and few of these had been tested in recent months.
Even rumours of a new horror gas – a vicious compound which
made people sick in their masks and seared them with mustard gas
when they took them off – caused no change of heart. The government tried to set a good example. Hugh Dalton ordered that all
civil servants should wear their masks between 12 noon and 12.15
p.m. every Monday: 'Rather a joke, and also quite a good thing
from the point of view of morale,' he wrote hopefully in his diary.
The practice did not spread, even around Whitehall. In mid-February small quantities of a dark-coloured liquid were scattered over a
street in Pimlico to test the responses of the civil defence teams to
a gas attack. The anti-gas units reacted quickly and efficiently; the
public thought the operation at best comical, at worst a nuisance.
Gas was like a ghost – frightening but unbelievable. The same view
did not apply to invasion; a threat which grew more real as the
spring began. By mid-February more than 50 per cent of Londoners
believed an invasion would come soon; two-thirds of these considered it a development to be welcomed.

The violent renewal of the blitz in March and April coincided with
a bleak period for London's food supplies. Before Christmas it had
been a question of individual commodities disappearing, returning
briefly, then vanishing again. Lord Woolton, who was to be
appointed Minister of Food in April 1940, announced that no more
bananas would be seen until the war was over; two or three weeks
later Charles Graves was offered banana fritters for lunch at the
Overseas Club. The more prosaic onion was for a time equally
sought after; a greengrocer placed one in his window mounted on
a velvet cushion and placarded, 'Very rare specimen. Found in Earls
Court 1940.' When they were available prices were high. Woolton
received one through the post with a plaintive message reading, 'I
am sending you the onion as a gift. After paying 6d for it I had not
the heart to cook it. I hope it will bring tears to your eyes as it did
to mine.' Then, in January, home-grown supplies became available
and they were commonplace again. But the first shortage that struck

seriously at the Londoner's traditional eating habits was that of meat; in January the ration was halved to 1/2d a week. 'With rump steak at 2/4d [a pound] we are not running any undue risk of becoming coarse by eating too much meat,' commented Mrs Britton wryly.

The Londoner's diet for the next few months, until lend-lease food began to flow in June, was as restricted and meagre as at any time in the war. A mark of the seriousness with which the government viewed the crisis was its unpopular ruling that no pets were to be supplied with food suitable for human consumption. Horse flesh was in short supply, dog biscuit and jars of dog food disappeared. The National Canine Defence League claimed that this was false economy; by keeping down vermin cats and dogs saved more food than they ate. The government was unimpressed.

General Lee got back to London after a few weeks away and noticed 'a considerable deterioration in many directions . . . There is no question but that the food situation is very much worse.' Rosemary Black, a prosperous inhabitant of St John's Wood, got back to her flat to find a note from the maid, who had been out shopping: 'Madam, there is no honey, no sultanas, currants or raisins, no mixed fruits, no saccharine at present, no spaghetti, no sage, no herrings, kippers or sprats (smoked or plain), no matches at present, no kindling wood, no fat or dripping, no tins of celery, tomato or salmon. I have bought three pounds of parsnips.' Some relief came in March and April. Onions were not the only vegetable to become more freely available; home production soared; in the parks of Croydon alone enough vegetables were produced to provide 15,000 meals a day. The drop in population too helped ease certain shortages. And yet the privations were real and painful. 'The British are doing precious little grumbling at the hardships they're enduring,' remarked Anthony Weymouth. 'Everything, of course, is relative – and after the pounding London has had during the last seven months, the absence of marmalade, for instance, seems a very small matter.' Yet small matters can bulk larger than great.

Food had replaced the weather as the staple topic for conversation, noted Betty Hudson. That the situation was still far easier for the rich than the poor remained dispiritingly evident. Colville lunched at the Turf Club and noticed with relief that the sideboard was slightly less laden with cold meats than it had been on his last visit, but 'certainly the rich can still eat sumptuously'. An attempt was made to reduce the discrepancy by forbidding restaurants to serve more than one main dish per meal. The definition of 'main dish' was open to many interpretations; bacon and eggs could not be served together, nor a poached egg on Welsh rarebit, but the only perceptible difference in most West End restaurants was that it was no longer permissible to have an omelette between the soup and the fish. But the government was concerned about the unfair burden borne by the poorer sections of society. Kingsley Wood's budget of April 1941 increased taxation on the better off and made a serious bid to stabilise prices, which had been rising sharply. Clothes rationing closed another avenue where the rich had been conspicuously better able to protect themselves against the rigours of the war.

Between 'The Saturday' and 10 May London enjoyed a relatively easy ride. The people had braced themselves for an unsurpassed ordeal; instead they experienced a reversion to normality. On 10 May the supporters of Preston North End poured into London for the Cup Final; a crowd of 60,000 was at Wembley to watch an undistinguished draw. As the crowds flowed home they might have reflected that the moon was full that night and the Thames at low ebb – a combination peculiarly propitious for the Luftwaffe. No one, however, seems to have taken any particular steps to prepare for an attack. By next morning more than 3000 were dead or seriously injured. It was the worst raid London endured in six years of war.

The Law Courts, the Tower, the Mint were hit; Marylebone was the only main-line station to remain open; every bridge between the Tower and Lambeth was impassable; Beckton gas works was blown up, 700 gas mains were fractured. Westminster Hall was set on fire and the House of Commons gutted – 'though I don't care about that, I wish it had got most of the members,' commented Sir Alexander Cadogan in atrabilious mood. Big Ben had its face pocked and scarred, a bomb had passed right through its tower. For the policemen on duty the only good moment of the night had come when Big Ben struck two o'clock correctly only a few minutes after the bomb had fallen. 250,000 books were burnt in the British Museum. Westminster Abbey was badly damaged: 'There will not be any service in the Abbey today, sir,' said a policeman to Colville, exactly as if the Abbey was closed for spring cleaning. The fires around the Elephant and Castle were the most serious since 29 December. Source after source of water was exhausted or cut off and the blaze was not brought under control until after daybreak with water carried by nine miles of hose from the Thames and Surrey Canal. One of the most curious incidents occurred at an apparently deserted house in York Terrace, Regent's Park, where ninety-nine members of the Group for Sacrifice and Service (a Californian sect) were worshipping the moon. Some of the dead were dressed as priests; the archbishop, a London oculist, wore a solid gold cross studded with diamonds.

The blaze was watched from Cuddesden Hill, not far from Oxford; to the German bombers the red glow was visible when they were over Rouen, 160 miles away. At Watford an unobservant resident left his house the following morning, stared in dismay at the black storm clouds covering the horizon, and went back for his macintosh. And yet, as has so often been reiterated, life went on. The Temple had been reduced to a smouldering ruin but the pillar box still stood in the centre of the court. The postman threaded his way through the rubble to pick up the letters and even changed the tablet which announced the time of the next collection. The raid killed 1436 – more than the San Francisco earthquake of 1906. Over the next days Larry Rue, an American journalist, noticed with dismay that 'City gents' were going to their offices unshaven. 'I began to realise to what deep depths of their being the 10 May raid had shocked and shaken the people of London. It was just one raid too much.'

'False alert about 9.50,' noted Cadogan in his diary, 'but I suppose we shall get it again tonight.' They did not, nor the next night. Months passed before there was another raid and then it was only minor. Though nobody suspected it, dared even hope it, the blitz was over – 300,000 houses had been destroyed or badly damaged, more than 20,000 civilians killed, fifteen Wren churches wrecked. There was still trouble in plenty to come, still major air-raids as well as the V1s and the V2s, but the intensity of the raid of 10 May was never to be repeated.

The following day Hugh Dalton visited the ruins of the Commons and remembered the last words Churchill had spoken there at the end of a vote of confidence debate a few days before, a vote won by

447 to 3. 'When I look back on the perils that have been overcome, upon the great mountain waves in which the gallant ship has driven; when I remember all that has gone wrong, and remember also all that has gone right, I feel sure we have no need to fear the tempest. Let it roar and let it rage. We shall come through.'

At much the same time the Revd Jimmy Butterworth surveyed the ruins of the youth club and workshops he had laboriously built up in his East End parish over the last nineteen years, broke down and wept. 'Wotcha crying for, Jimmy?' asked a boy. 'Because this is the end.' 'The end, me eye. You've still got us, ain'cha?'

10

Is There a Myth of the Blitz?

IN HIS COMPELLING and judicious study, *The Myth of the Blitz*, Angus Calder emphasises that the word 'myth' does not imply 'untruth'. His contention is not that the stereotypical clichés of the London blitz (gallant Cockneys joking at adversity, 'Are We Downhearted? No!', 'London can take it!', 'We're all in it together') were false, but that, wittingly or unwittingly, they were developed and refined for the purposes of propaganda and accepted by the people as the standard of how they should be behaving and, consequently, how they *did* behave.

Some revisionist historians, however, have interpreted Calder's title as a green light for seeking out every instance of greed, panic, cowardice, snobbishness, prejudice, and to deduce from them that the authorities were callous and inefficient, the people shiftless and uncertain. Supporting evidence for their case has appeared already in this book and more is to come. Much dirt was, indeed, brushed under the carpet by propagandists intent on producing a sanitised and heart-warming picture of London's travail. It is the conviction of this author, however, that the quantity of dirt was relatively inconsiderable; that few Londoners behaved badly, many more conspicuously well; and that the population of London as a whole endured the blitz with dignity, courage, resolution and astonishing good humour.

Londoners manufactured their own myth. It is striking how many spoke and wrote in clichés. 'Although the past week has been very trying with the bombs and sleepless nights,' wrote Henry Penny, a bus driver from Paddington, 'we are still not "Downhearted", for as it has been said, we are all in the "Front Line".' It had indeed been said and, give and take a few capitals and inverted commas, would be said many times again. They acted out their clichés, too. Ed Murrow, on the steps of St Martin's as the alert sounded, held his microphone to the pavement so that Americans could hear

Londoners on their way to the shelter. 'They were impressed by noticing that nobody ran.' This did not show indifference to danger. 'It was not done to run!' recorded Frances Faviell. Londoners made a deliberate effort to seem nonchalant and unafraid.

Ed Murrow and his colleagues contributed as much as anyone to the propagation of the myth. There were over a hundred American journalists in London during the blitz; Murrow the best known to the British, but also James 'Scotty' Reston, Quentin Reynolds, Negley Farson, John Gunther, Fred Bate, Vincent Sheean, not to mention occasional visitors such as Ralph Ingersoll and Raymond Gram Swing, fêted while in the capital and well known in the United States. They tended to be less critical in their assessment of London under fire than any British commentator would have dared be. Anything that contributed to the vision of a society of stout-hearted yet self-deprecating heroes was written up, anything that savoured of greed, cowardice, any sort of baseness, was rigorously eschewed. It was a propaganda exercise conducted with great skill, and one for which the British had cause to be grateful.

There were various totems of embattled London. First was Winston Churchill. In the long haul of 1942 and 1943 his leadership was to be challenged, his iconic role impugned, but during the blitz he was free from question, to abuse him publicly was almost treasonable. To Londoners, even at their most shocked and demoralised, his presence was revivifying. Bernard Kops endured a night of devastation, when the Columbia Market was hit by a land mine. 'The King of England came the following morning, drawn and grey he walked slowly over the wreckage. No one cheered because they didn't feel like cheering. But when Churchill came a few hours later, with a cigar sticking out his fat pink face, a few people cheered and even I felt like cheering.' Kops was no lover of the monarchy, but on less fraught occasions the King, especially if accompanied by the Queen, would have been cheered as well. The fact that he stayed in London by day and sometimes by night as well through the worst of the bombing endeared him to his people.

> The King is still in London, in London, in London,
> And he would be in London Town if London Bridge was
>   falling down!

went a popular song of the period. Frank Lewey, the socialist mayor of Stepney, was immensely impressed by the King's indifference to comfort and safety when visiting the bombed sites. An old woman tapped Lewey on the shoulder and said, 'I bet old 'Itler daren't go among 'is folk like this. They'd pull 'im to bits, some of them!' As he left, one woman wondered aloud whether the King knew how few guns guarded the East End. 'Give 'im time, dearie,' said another. ''E's the right sort. I don't suppose there's no more guns round the Pallis.' Shortly before the outbreak of war the King's private secretary, Hardinge, had asked Euan Wallace and Oliver Stanley whether they thought the King should live at Windsor or in Buckingham Palace. The King himself was strongly in favour of staying in the capital. Both men agreed that the moral effect of this would be invaluable but, 'We made it quite clear that we thought the Queen should not be allowed to stay in London.' If this was ever communicated to the Queen it was ignored; she stayed with her husband throughout the blitz.

Buildings as well as people enjoyed a talismanic significance. The collapse of the dome of St Paul's would have meant far more to Londoners than the loss of any half dozen other churches. But it was Big Ben, triumphantly striking the hours through the most devastating raids, which above all symbolized the will to resist. It never missed an hour throughout the blitz; then after the worst was over in June 1941 a workman left his hammer on the spindle bracket and brought the works to a grinding stop.

The two main elements in the myth of the blitz were the comradeship and sense of unity which it inspired among Londoners and the cheerful good humour with which it was endured. Both these were justified by the facts; both were transmogrified into something more sublime.

The blitz, believed J. B. Priestley, produced a new and improved Londoner. 'In 1940–41, for once, [we] felt free, companionable, even – except while waiting for the explosions – light-hearted. It took bombs to deliver us.' The jealousies and grudges of everyday life were cast aside: 'We all got on very well together,' remembered a young doctor from St Thomas's. 'The occasion has grown so big that petty enmities and dislikes have been forgotten.' Traditional inhibitions vanished. His part of Kensington had turned into a village, an ARP warden remembered in wonder, 'People I never used to know stop me as I walk along and ask if there's anything I want to know.' A woman from Ealing tried to convey the special flavour of blitz society; it was enormous fun, she wrote, 'because people seem to have let down that peculiar barrier that divides them in peacetime so effectively from one another. I should say there was more genuine camaraderie than ever before.' Virginia Woolf in a pill-box on Wimbledon Common was not alone in tasting the pleasure of spontaneous communication. 'It was making people talk to one another,' wrote Frances Faviell. 'They opened up amazingly about how they thought and what they thought – how they felt and what they felt.'

It also broke down class barriers, she believed. Nothing could destroy overnight a system that had grown up over the centuries, but London was more nearly classless at this period than ever before or since. A warden in Ilford marvelled at the ease with which he entered houses which would have been closed to him before the war, and described the relaxed relations which existed between all sections of the community. Ed Murrow and Ralph Ingersoll, the latter in particular much on the lookout for manifestations of English snobbery, were insistent that the raids had set the barriers tumbling; there had been a social revolution, the old structure based on property and capital had broken down. Frank Cockett, a young Australian doctor at St Thomas's, who was equally antipathetic to British snobbery, believed that the German raids were 'doing more to knit England together than anything else would'. Eric James, then a youth working in the docks, found a 'fantastic sense of comradeship'; the dockers almost worshipped Churchill and the royal family and felt no resentment against those who were better off or had escaped the worst of the bombing. Humphrey Jennings, a left-wing iconoclast celebrated for his fiercely realistic film documentaries, wrote to his wife in October 1940 to tell her that the damage in London was heart-breaking, but 'what an effect it has on the people! What warmth – what courage! What determination ... Everyone absolutely determined, secretly delighted with the *privilege* of holding up Hitler. Certain of beating him, a certainty which no amount of bombing can weaken, only strengthen ... Maybe by the time you get this one or two more 18th century churches will be smashed up in London: some civilians killed: some personal lives and treasures wrecked – but it means nothing; a curious kind of unselfishness is developing which can stand all that and more. We have found ourselves on the right side and on the right track at last!'

Yet there were many qualifications. Another effect of the blitz, Eric James believed, was that parochialism had broken down. People from Bermondsey who had never visited the West End, or even crossed the river, now thought as Londoners. But to Graham Greene in *The Ministry of Fear*, London 'was no longer one great city; it was a collection of small towns'. Every district, every street, was a unit preoccupied primarily with its own affairs. The heavier the bombing, the less people cared about anyone except their immediate neighbours, concluded a Home Office report in early October. 'Whereas two weeks ago, a raid on London upset the whole of London, today Streatham or Stepney scarcely worry at all if there have been a great many bombs on Shoreditch or Lewisham.' Local loyalties pulled as never before: a labourer insisted on returning to his badly damaged home from relatives in Fulham only half a mile away because 'I'm a Chelsea man'; a woman found her way back to what was little more than a heap of rubble – 'Why should I let 'Itler drive me out of Poplar?' A conviction that *their* fire was more important than one in the next district led to some of the few angry crowd scenes in the war; in Brixton inhabitants formed a cordon to stop a fire engine moving off to another borough and had to leap aside as it accelerated away.

Though James may have got it broadly right, there was still resentment of the rich to be found in the poorer quarters. Why is there not more destruction done to the homes of those in high places? asked Viola Bawtree. The rich were 'far more responsible for allowing bombers to be created than are the poor people in the East End'. The rich were known to be better protected; even if their houses did not enjoy deep concrete basements they could afford luxury shelters; Leslie Paul wrote indignantly of one that had cost £180 and boasted a lavatory and two bedrooms. They escaped to the country in their cars and scorned to offer lifts to those who were trudging in the same direction. They were better looked after by the civil defence: a family in Greenwich complained that they had been forced out of their house for ten days by a UXB: 'In Mayfair it would have been dealt with after two days.' Frank Mayes, an avowed Communist, visited the tubes while on leave from the Navy and wrote in his diary, '10,000 people at the Elephant and Castle, indescribable squalor and dirt, how I hate those bastard capitalists.' Sometimes resentment spilled over into direct action – or inaction. Maurice Wood pointed out to a warden that Lord Portman's house was on fire. 'Is there anyone in there?' asked the warden. Wood said that it was empty. 'Let it burn then!'

The possibility that such feeling might get out of hand was at its most real in the East End in the early days of the blitz when 90 per cent or more of the bombs were falling on that part of London. An 'aggressive Labour bus-driver' told Hilda Neal that the East End had been left open to the German bombers but, 'when the West End was touched the Government started the barrage'. 'I could see he was a born grouser and trouble-maker,' concluded Miss Neal loftily. 'Class feeling is growing because of worse destruction in working-class areas,' said a Home Office report. When bombs first fell on Stepney Green, Bernard Kops's father asked, 'Why don't they drop them on Park Lane?' The rich, he deduced, had a secret agreement with the Germans. Some believed that the Germans actively fostered this belief. Frank Lewey told of an agitator who fomented trouble by contrasting the fate of the East Enders with 'those parasites at Buckingham Palace'. The agitator had been found floating in a water-filled bomb crater. 'He did not die of drowning,' Lewey added darkly. 'After him, the whispering campaign died away.' Even without subscribing to such lurid fantasies, it is obvious that such ill-feeling was of benefit to the Germans and rightly worried the government. It was the Germans who saved the situation, however, by extending their bombing to other parts of London. There had been a real danger of working-class disaffection, reported the Spanish ambassador, but the subsequent bombing 'of the aristocratic and commercial quarters had . . . strengthened the single-minded determination to carry on the war to the limit'.

One of the very few occasions when the East Enders set out to right their grievances was on 15 September, in the early evening, when about a hundred demonstrators, led by the Communist MP Phil Piratin, marched to the Savoy Hotel and demanded shelter when the alert sounded. 'There is little doubt that the *Daily Worker* and the Communist Party are taking the opportunity of creating trouble,' wrote Euan Wallace in some alarm. Probably they were, but never were national stereotypes better justified. Far from a Jacquerie storming the Tuileries, a slightly embarrassed group shuffled into the lobby, after some parleying were ushered to a shelter downstairs, and asked to leave only when the all-clear sounded – which, fortunately for the management, happened after fifteen minutes. A few placards were brandished and Vic Oliver, who was in cabaret in the restaurant, was asked loudly why he was not performing in the tube shelters, but most of the intruders behaved decorously and some even tipped the hall porter as they left. As a demonstration it might reasonably be called a damp squib, but the protesters had a real point, no less real for being presented so half-heartedly.

The second element in the myth of the blitz – the good humour, even jollity of the victims – was equally well founded in fact and equally romanticised. The Cockney joker, unflappable, master of meiosis, had always been dear to the capital's heart and now became an international figure. His prototype was the Jewish shopkeeper in Aldgate who was sweeping up the glass from his shattered windows. 'If that feller 'Itler keeps on like this, 'e'll get 'isself disliked,' he observed gravely. Defiant slogans adorned blitzed buildings – 'More open than usual'; outside a police station, 'Be good! We are still open'; a barber's, 'Close shaves a speciality'; a church, 'If your knees knock, kneel on them'.

Stories illustrating *sang froid* were especially popular: the nanny who remarked tartly, 'Yes, that was probably bombs, Master James, but that's no excuse for elbows on the table'; the Duke of Devonshire's butler who, asked what he'd thought of the previous night's blitz, replied that he hadn't seen such fireworks since His Grace came of age. John Hope found himself in a railway carriage with a group of elderly Cockney ladies swopping bomb stories. 'The 'ouse next door 'ad a terrible pasting,' said one, 'I found poor Mrs Andrews 'alf one side of 'er door and 'alf the other. Well, you 'ad to laugh!' People really did joke in the teeth of disaster; there was a strange lightness of heart among those who had stayed behind – 'people whom the climate of danger suited,' Elizabeth Bowen called them. 'There was a diffused gallantry in the air, an unmarriedness: it came to be rumoured about the country that everybody in London was in love.' Londoners felt themselves an elite.

Kingsley Martin was exceptional when he wrote of his elation during the blitz, but many considered it an experience they would not have missed. An old man who had been bombed out was asked whether he wished to be evacuated. 'No,' he replied, 'nothing like this has ever happened before and it will never happen again. I wouldn't miss it for all the tea in China.' Michael Jones, a young writer for *Horizon*, went into the thick of the blitz and 'returning with shining eyes, described the streets full of glass like heaped-up ice, the fires making a great sunset beyond the silhouette of St Paul's'. Rosemary Black, living in St John's Wood, found to her amazement that she was enjoying herself: 'I do get such a kick out of finding myself comparatively fearless and also self-controlled and calm.' The bombing was 'like mountains. It seems to make one tireless and wide awake and vital.'

Even the less adventurous congratulated themselves on the way they were coping. 'It's extraordinary how we've adapted ourselves to bombing,' reflected Miss Harrison of Beckenham. 'None of us is foolhardy and sometimes we're frightened, but we've got the feel of raids by now.' Live for the moment, was some people's solution; George Orwell wondered at the contented lunchtime crowds, apparently oblivious of the perils of the night ahead, 'like animals which are unable to foresee the future'. Fatalism was a useful defence. A young woman at the BBC wrote that 'you gradually realise that the whole thing's a matter of luck anyway, so what the hell? One lives under a certain strain, but when you are in London you are unconscious of it . . . so adaptable are human beings.' It was the calmness, the resigned resolution of the Londoner, which impressed those from outside. A Hungarian doctor was at the Bank when the Underground shelter was hit. 'You English cannot appreciate the discipline of your people,' he said. 'I have not found one hysterical, shouting patient. It does not happen in other countries. If Hitler could have been there for five minutes with me, he would have finished this war. He would have realised that he has got to take every Englishman and twist him by the neck – otherwise he cannot win.'

A network of psychiatric clinics had been prepared to deal with the neuroses caused by bombing. After two weeks, one case had been reported, after ten weeks only twenty-three. Dr Edward Glover disbanded his clinic after a month because he had not had a single patient. The number of patients attending hospital with neurotic illnesses declined during the blitz; there were fewer suicides, drunkenness was halved. Anna Freud told Ralph Ingersoll, 'You have never seen anything like these people. They are so calm and they take it all so well.' Not one true case of shell-shock had been reported, nor had she heard of a single breakdown that could be directly attributed to the bombing. Rose Macaulay claimed to be suffering from 'burial phobia'; so great was her fear of being trapped beneath the debris of her house that she admitted she would rather sleep in the street. Yet even this highly rational fear was soon wearing off, 'and may have been a passing disease', she concluded two or three weeks later.

Not that Londoners were unscathed by their experiences. Exhaustion induced by lack of sleep was the greatest threat. At the end of September one Londoner in three was getting less than four hours' sleep a night. In Shoreditch and some of the other poorer areas, the proportion rose to a half. Things got better in October but some still found sleep hard to come by. A woman in south-east London told a Mass Observer that her husband and daughter went to bed as soon as they had had their evening meal in the hope of getting some sleep before the raid began. 'I've got some Phospherine and I make them all take that. We've tried earplugs but we don't like them. We wrap shawls around our heads instead when we hear bombs coming.' 'Sleep!' exclaimed a café proprietress in Fulham in mid-October. 'You can't sleep! We can't go on like this, can we? It can't go on! They'll have to do something about it soon or there'll be a revolution.' People's reactions were diverse and unpredictable. To cite a trio of literary figures: H. G. Wells boasted, 'I can sleep through all that row. I have the gift of sleep'; C. P. Snow dreaded the evening, could not sleep and was glad of any excuse to get out of town; Stevie Smith was unruffled by the bombing, 'Never had such quiet nights – no dogs, no motor cars, no babies crying.'

For some the lack of sleep came from the demands of work as much as bombing. General Lee noticed that the doorman at the American Embassy looked worn out and found that he had been patrolling with the Home Guard the previous two nights: 'There is a form of attrition which war brings and which affects everyone.' Whatever the cause, exhaustion led to mental strain, short tempers, quickness to see discourtesy where none was meant. Everyone in her office was in bad shape, reflected Viola Bawtree in mid-October, 'They seem constantly misjudging me and taking offence, and I mustn't give way to self-pity, and by flaring up at the way they speak

I also am to blame.' Some suffered from mild hallucinations. 'I don't mind not hearing things, but I do mind hearing things that are not,' complained Miss Bawtree, who imagined sirens and the drone of approaching aircraft. Nancy Bosanquet had the same problem, 'When I am tired I hear distant warning sirens continually.' In his novel *No Directions*, James Hanley gives a vivid picture of a city of dazed sleep-walkers, whose frayed nerves and easy irritation betrayed the strain under which they lived.

The Home Office was aware of the perils and urged its staff to take short breaks from London whenever opportunity offered. It rarely did. In the meantime there was nothing to be done except to lower the sensibilities as far as possible and keep going. A middle-aged woman in Kilburn owned to feeling 'not so much depression as bewilderment'. 'I wake up in the morning,' she said, 'and I look around, and I say to myself, "Well, I'm still here, and the house is still here, that means there's another day for me." And I get up and I start my work. I don't seem to think about it any more. It's funny the way you get.' She sleep-walked through life, like the young woman in Elizabeth Bowen's short story 'Mysterious Kor'. ' "I thought girls thought about people," said Arthur. "What, these days?" she said. "Think about people? How can anyone think about people if they've got a heart?" ' For some, it was only fear that could snatch them from their reverie. 'Fear. Paralysing physical fear,' wrote a WVS worker in her diary in May 1941. 'It grips you and you feel contaminated, unclean.'

Under such pressures it would have been extraordinary had a dismayed defeatism not emerged here and there. Leslie Paul was told by a friend that the atmosphere in the heavily bombed Elephant and Castle area was turning against the war. There was anger at the failure of the defences to keep German raiders at bay: 'If people about here were asked,' exclaimed an old lady in a corner shop, 'they would want peace now on any terms.' On almost the same date, in mid-October, Kenneth Clark told Harold Nicolson that he was seriously concerned about the risk of the Germans making an apparently reasonable peace offer. 'The spirit of London is excellent but it would take little to swing this country into cowardice,' concluded Nicolson, who consistently underestimated the fortitude of his fellow citizens. A few weeks before, he had predicted that if night bombing continued the will to resist might be broken: 'One cannot expect the population of a great city to sit up all night in shelters week after week without losing their spirit.' Expect it or not, that is what they did. There were pockets of disaffection, moments of despair, but they were few and far between. A typewriter mechanic told Hilda Neal that the people in the East End were saying they had better give in. 'I told him I had not found those I met like that; but he was full of grumbles, probably over-tired.'

For most people grumbles were a convenient way of letting off steam, a part of life as traditional as conversation about the weather. George Orwell recorded in his diary the discomfort and overcrowding of the public shelters: 'People, mostly elderly working class, grousing bitterly about the hardness of the seats and the longness of the night, but no defeatist talk.' In such a hot-house, rumours flourished, swelling alarmingly as they passed from mouth to mouth. The government believed that as little information as possible should be made available to the Germans; the principle was sensible enough, but it meant that the British too were kept in the dark and thrust back upon their own, often vivid, imaginations. Macabre exaggeration became a hallmark of many Londoners' conversation. Tom Driberg was surveying the ruins of a large house where he happened to know that only one person had been killed. 'They say there's dozens buried down there still,' volunteered a bystander, 'they ought to call for volunteers.' Driberg asked sharply how the man knew there were people buried below. 'He gave me a dirty look, mumbled "Chap who was here just now said so," edged away; a moment later I heard him say to a woman, "They say there's dozens buried down there still . . ."' Naomi Royde-Smith sub-titled her book about wartime England 'A Diary of Rumours' and described a taxi journey in which landmark after landmark said to have been destroyed turned out to be substantially undamaged.

Dreams of the future solaced many. A letter in *The Times* signed by the two Anglican Archbishops, Cardinal Hinsley and the Moderator of the Church of Scotland, launched an energetic debate about the shape of the post-war world. It struck a vein of public consciousness. Leslie Paul lectured in the shelters and elsewhere on the problems of reconstruction, and was met by passionate interest in the kind of world that would be created once victory had been won: 'This is growing like a tidal wave. The harder our circumstances now, the fiercer the bombing, the more ordinary people tend to pin their hopes upon "after the war".'

In the meantime, the Germans should be made to pay a hundred-fold for what they were doing to London. The belief that Berlin was being hard hit was one of the factors which the Home Office identified as sustaining morale in the first weeks of the blitz. Demands for vengeance became less vociferous as the attacks diminished. In Barking, in December, at the burial of a German airman, a woman put a wreath on the coffin inscribed 'To some mother's son'. The crowd not only made no protest, 'but appeared rather to approve'. Yet each major raid rekindled public rancour. After the fire raid of 29 December, Harold Nicolson noted the growing conviction that 'similar treatment of the Germans is the only thing they will understand'. George Britton deplored the rising demand for reprisals, which he believed could achieve little militarily and would bring the British 'down to the level of the Nazi bandits', but recognised that detestation of the Germans had grown to such proportions that it could not be ignored. The final great raid of 10 May exacerbated such feelings; the American journalist Quentin Reynolds sensed 'a new and intensified hatred of Germany in the people of London . . . No matter how long this war drags on, Britain will be inspired and encouraged by her hatred.'

Generalisations about national characteristics are always suspect, but it can be said with some assurance that the English are not very good haters, or, at any rate, not good at sustaining their hatred when the immediate cause of offence has gone. Within a few months of the end of the blitz, the fiercest rage against the Germans had died down. Even in the early summer of 1941 a Gallup Poll in central London showed only 45 per cent in favour of reprisal raids. (Oddly enough, the corresponding figure in Cumberland and Westmorland was 76 per cent.) But while indignation lasted it was potent enough. One of the most often repeated rumours was of a German pilot who had parachuted from his burning plane into the East End and had been torn to pieces by an angry crowd before the police arrived to arrest him. Sometimes, to make the story grimmer still, the pilot was a Pole who could not speak enough English to explain himself. Most people knew a man who knew a man who knew the story was positively true; no eye-witness ever volunteered an account. Very possibly it never happened. But if it *had* happened, few Londoners in mid-May 1941 would have condemned the violence unequivocally. Nor did anyone protest when a man kicked a German bomber pilot who parachuted into Chelsea the night that the Old Church was left a gutted ruin. Equally nobody else joined in; they merely shifted from one foot to another in an embarrassed way and tried to pretend that nothing untoward had happened. Only when the same man grabbed the German's revolver from its holster and seemed about to use it on its owner did the bystanders intervene to hold both parties until the police arrived.

Anti-Semitism was another unattractive characteristic evident during the blitz. It had always been latent, particularly in the East End where there was a large Jewish community. The people wanted someone to blame; the government was impersonal and remote; the Germans even more so; the Jews were there, identifiable, already viewed with distrust. They were the first to scuttle to the country, said their critics; they (somewhat inconsistently) monopolised the shelters; they demanded the full rent for bomb-damaged property; they controlled the black market; never volunteered to work as wardens or firemen; ostentatiously displayed their wealth. The Home Office was sufficiently concerned by the trend to commission weekly studies on anti-semitism; not surprisingly they found that most of the prejudice was based on the flimsiest misconceptions. 'Though many Jewish people regularly congregate and sleep in the public shelters, so also do many of the Gentiles,' read one report, 'nor is there any evidence to show that one or other predominates among those who have evacuated themselves voluntarily through fear and hysteria.'

Orwell thought that there was less anti-semitism than thirty years before, but still denounced it as dangerous and ugly, all the worse for blinding people to the horrors of Nazi persecution: 'Because two days ago a fat Jewess grabbed your place on the bus, you switch off the wireless when the announcer begins talking about the ghettoes of Warsaw.' But there were enough fat Jewesses grabbing places on buses to give anti-semitism an edge of virulence; Orwell himself noted in his diary the high proportion of Jews in a crowd waiting to enter a tube shelter: 'What is bad about Jews is that they are not only conspicuous, but go out of their way to make themselves so.'

There is a note of perceptible surprise in Hilde Marchant's comment when bombs fell on a predominantly Jewish quarter. The police and wardens had expected them to be more hysterical than their Cockney neighbours, 'but even the police said they had been no trouble. They had behaved like good citizens.'

Refugees from Europe were often lumped with the Jews as undesirable and potentially subversive, but – perhaps because no black man could conceivably be a German – there seems to have been little colour prejudice. E. I. Expenyon, an air-raid warden from Nigeria, found everyone most friendly. He was amused to discover that, as a man of colour, he was considered a lucky omen – 'Wherever my duties take me the people listen to my instructions and are willing to allow me to lead them.' Somewhat bizarrely, he found himself preaching the virtues of racial toleration when a group of European refugees in one of his shelters was segregated and abused. They were guests, he told the inhospitable English, they were entitled to 'the protection of the Union Jack', he expected to see a spirit of friendship and cooperation and those who did not agree had better seek another shelter. His homily was accepted meekly and only a few hardened bigots went elsewhere.

Generalising about morale in London is made more difficult by the fact that it was not a constant but fluctuated with the course of the blitz. In the heavily bombed areas for the first two days it came closer than at any other time to collapsing. In dockland areas, said the Home Intelligence report for 9 September, 'the population is showing visible signs of its nerve cracking from constant ordeals'. But even in the worst of times the mood was described as extremely volatile; black depression one day, bold truculence the next. Only a few days after the gloomy report of 9 September the Cabinet was told that in all districts morale had jumped to 'a new level of confidence and cheerfulness'. The anti-aircraft barrage was given much of the credit for the change, but at every point of the war Londoners accommodated themselves with striking speed to whatever was inflicted on them. The government never quite believed that this could last. In October 1940 members of the 4th Battalion of the Grenadier Guards at Wanstead were ordered to hold themselves in readiness 'to help the police in the event of rioting or severe bombing in the East End of London'. Their services were never called upon; on the contrary, Home Office reports indicated 'mild chagrin' in some parts of the capital when the focus of attack moved away in December. Londoners were used to being at the centre of the stage; the heavy raid of 8 December was said to have caused 'no serious upset of morale but rather a sense of excitement'.

By the beginning of March 1941, two months of comparative lull had done much to restore Londoners to good condition. People had lost that 'ghastly tired, haunted look they had, or so many of them,' wrote Hilda Neal, 'with eyes that were sunk in their head, red-rimmed, skin yellow in appearance, caused by fright and sleepless nights'. The renewal of heavy bombing, though in theory expected, took people by surprise. Some young people, said a Home Office report, even welcomed it, but the old age pensioners, particularly the women, felt 'a justifiable hopelessness'. Several Mass Observers, for the first time since September, independently suggested an appreciable deterioration in morale. 'It's bloody. The war seems to be going on for ever,' said a middle-class man of twenty; 'Oh, I don't know, I'm fed up, fed up!' exclaimed a thirty-year-old woman from a slightly lower class. It was the same pattern in April; the erratic incidence of the raids heightened public apprehension and led to deep gloom, yet always after a night or two free of raids there was 'a marked recovery and a restoration of confidence'. The worst morning after came on 11 May when the Luftwaffe had paid its devastating valedictory visit. 'We can't take much more of this,' was a refrain heard more commonly than ever before. They could have if they had had to, but they were spared the test.

Vincent Sheean returned to London from the United States in mid-April. 'You won't find any of the high-spirited we-can-take-it stuff of last year,' he was told. 'We none of us run around the streets during bombings as we used to. People stay at home, they go to the shelters, they are getting a little grim. All the novelty is gone. The epic period is over. Food has something to do with it, too – everyone is probably a little under-nourished. Whatever it is, there's a big difference.' Arthur Marwick, in his engrossing *The Home Front*, has underlined the distinction between 'active' and 'passive' morale – the first the morale of exuberance, gallant and defiant gestures, laughter in the face of adversity; the second 'a grim, if often baffled willingness to carry on'. The first was at low ebb in April and May

1941; there is no reason to doubt that the second was as strong as ever.

Marwick describes how Tom Harrisson, founder of Mass Observation, in his study of the blitz 'lambasted the myths about national unity and heroism, pointing out the snobbish nature of the establishment, the inadequacy of the provisions made for air-raids, and the not unnatural reactions of dismay and even despair among those who suffered the brunt of the bomb attacks'. Most of Harrisson's strictures relate to the provincial cities, which in total were far less severely attacked but individually were devastated in a way inconceivable over the vast area of London. Certainly all the deficiencies Harrisson pointed out were apparent from time to time in the capital. But though the authorities made a faltering start and in some ways misjudged the nature of the threat, they recovered strongly. In most parts of London and on most occasions they made a good job of protecting citizens from the worst effects of the raid and tending to their needs once the damage had been done. Certainly nobody could study the blitz in London without accepting the truth of Harrisson's judgment that 'the final achievement of so many Britons was enormous enough. Maybe monumental is not putting it too high. They did not let their soldiers or leaders down.'

Harold Laski, a socialist ideologue not given to empty heroics, wrote to an American friend, 'The people are simply superb. I know now why Lincoln had his ultimate faith in them. They know all they suffer, yet they take it with a calm and strength I dare not try to put into words.' That, in the sense Angus Calder gave to the word, is the myth of the blitz.

11

The 'enervating lull'

UNTIL THE END of the blitz, the war on the home front fell into neatly defined compartments: the preamble, between the Munich crisis and 3 September 1939; the phoney war; the first perception of real war, beginning with the advent of Winston Churchill and ending with the Battle of Britain; the blitz itself. Between 11 May 1941 and the 'Little Blitz' early in 1944, it becomes a long haul; the progress of the war was defined by events which did not directly affect daily life in London but reflected the war's development in a global arena. Viewed from London – and the view from Moscow, even from Washington, would have been very different – the thirty-two or so months after the ending of the blitz were divided by Pearl Harbor and the entry of the United States and Japan into the war on 7 December 1941; the turning of the tide at El Alamein in October 1942; and the return of the German bombers in January 1944. To abandon these landmarks and the chronological strait-jacket which they imply would be to lose touch with the gradual evolution of living conditions and morale in the capital. Certain themes, however – intellectual life, the waxing role of women, to take two examples at random – do not lend themselves to severance into watertight compartments bounded by precise dates. The next few chapters, therefore, adopt both a chronological and a thematic approach; the themes, so far as possible, being slotted in where they seem naturally to arise in the course of the narrative.

For the first week or so after 10 May 1941 the average Londoner was disposed to give the main credit for the Germans' failure to continue the blitz to the unsuitable weather. That quickly lost credibility, and the increasing strength of London's defences was then taken to be the major factor. Radar had transformed the scene. In the first ten days of May, seventy German aircraft had been shot down, about the same number as in the first four months of the blitz. The Luftwaffe, it was assumed, was licking its wounds or seeking new devices to defeat the improved defences. It was also supposed that some units might have been withdrawn to the Mediterranean. In April 1941 the Germans had overrun Greece and Yugoslavia. British and Commonwealth forces had fallen back on Crete. To attack the island, the Germans would have first to launch an air offensive. On 20 May the attack began. It did not seem far-fetched to see some link between this and the sudden peace over London. Only a month later, when Germany invaded Russia, did it become clear that, whatever the contributory factors, the main cause for the ending of the blitz had been Hitler's decision to postpone the invasion of the British Isles and instead launch a vast operation in the East.

Londoners were slow to believe their luck. 'The next raid is to be the worst ever,' Vere Hodgson quoted an astrologer as saying a week after the great raid of 10 May. She did not necessarily accept the astrologer's views as gospel, but spoke for most of her fellow citizens when she commented, 'This lull bodes something ill. I should not be surprised at a good old blitz on London next Saturday, and I am prepared to see the rest of the Abbey and the Hall go. I don't think anything can save them.' 'A whole fortnight of peace,' wrote the journalist A. S. G. Butler a week later. 'I can't think why they don't try and finish us off.' As the lull continued, the public gradually became more hopeful but did not dare admit as much openly. People talked of it very quietly, as if otherwise the Germans might hear and be provoked into renewed outrage. 'If you dare mention that it's quiet a violent wood-knocking goes on, and you are silenced quite peremptorily,' wrote Betty Hudson.

Churchill was as anxious as anyone to avoid complacency. At a Civil Defence luncheon at County Hall on 14 July 1941 he spoke of the need to prepare for renewed attack in the autumn – 'the same ordeal as last year only rather worse'. London, he declared, was a prehistoric monster into whose armoured hide a shower of arrows could be shot in vain. This particular stegosaurus, if that is what he had in mind, had endured a few bolts over the previous weeks. A land-mine had fallen in Chiswick on 7 June and there had been bombs in Acton the same night. Late in July came a sharp raid, involving some sixty German aircraft. Only about 22,000 Londoners were in the public shelters; the following night the figure had almost doubled. Home Office reports spoke of 'a good deal of wishful thinking' and noted, with what appeared to be some satisfaction, that the raid had been more effective than government warnings in reminding people of what might be in store. But even at 40,000, the number in public shelters was less than half that of an average night during the blitz. Seventy per cent of Londoners still believed there were heavy raids to come, but not, it seemed, just yet. On 4 September, after six weeks of peace, Charles Graves remarked how agreeable it was to go to bed with a reasonable expectation that there would be no raid: 'Never before these last few months has it occurred to me to be thankful for a quiet night. Now it *means* something, it tastes good.' There was no alert in London before 1 November and even then no bombs fell.

Though the numbers of shelterers declined, a substantial hard core persisted, particularly in the tubes. In great part this was for fear of renewed bombing; the numbers increased sharply after any raid on Berlin since it was felt reprisals were likely. In part too it was because many people enjoyed shelter life. 'I don't know how we shall be able to get them all out at the end of the war,' someone remarked to Hugh Dalton as they surveyed the crowds camped on the platforms between Swiss Cottage and Piccadilly. The community spirit noted in the last months of the blitz had largely survived. People treated them as clubs, observed Hamilton Fyfe, an academic from Scotland on a visit to London. 'They like to meet one another, chat and play darts, drink a cup of tea and coffee (so-called) and get a bite at the canteen. They say it saves them coal in the winter as well.'

Above ground, it was the normality of everything that most struck George Orwell, the 'lack of hurry, fewness of uniforms, general unwarlike appearance of the crowds'. Only the absence of cars made an immediate distinction between pre-war and wartime London. One reason for the scarcity of uniforms was that for a while that summer London was put out of bounds to all ranks except those who lived there or could reach their destination only by passing through the capital. The idea was to avoid congestion at the railway stations; the rule was unpopular and only erratically respected. But with or without the soldiers, London resumed with striking speed its traditional tempo of life. George Beardmore returned from Droit-wich at the end of June to find the city 'surprisingly unchanged . . .

sleepy squares with cats yawning on window sills, milk roundsmen brisk as ever, errand boys' bicycles propped against the kerb'.

That people could form such an impression reflected much credit on Fisher's bands of repair and demolition men. Except in the East End and City, where even the least observant could hardly have missed the evidence of war, London was so quickly tidied up that only gaps showed where the bombs had been. Orwell stood on the roof of his block of flats in Bloomsbury and could see no bomb damage anywhere, 'except for a few churches whose spires have broken off in the middle, making them look like lizards that have lost their tails'. But no very close inspection was needed to reveal that those gaps among the houses were not merely building sites awaiting a developer. A glance at Hyde Park, beside Rotten Row, revealed vast mountains of old iron, wood and bricks, each pile four hundred yards or more in length – like Early British ramparts, thought Vere Hodgson, 'I wonder how many homes it represents'. What was left of the parks was unkempt and beset by other wartime needs. Green Park was full of trenches and the paraphernalia of barrage balloons, Hyde Park was cut up into allotments on the southern side.

The parks faced a new threat as railings were removed to turn into weapons or, more frequently, to lie for months in rusting and unsightly heaps. Work did not begin at Hyde Park till early December 1941; three miles of railing which it was thought would produce a thousand tons of scrap. Green Park and St James's Park were expected to yield as much again. The big iron gates of Kensington Gardens were preserved and closed ceremoniously every night; the officials would make the rounds calling 'All Out', even though the park remained open to the world. London's squares were similarly assailed a few months later, a move welcomed by the egalitarians who had long resented these green enclaves reserved for privileged residents. Since the squares were usually converted into allotments the public gained little by the change. There were some spirited battles in defence of certain railings. A proposal to remove those in St James's Square led to cries of dismay from Lords Stafford and Bristol, who feared the gardens would be 'misused' if opened to lesser mortals. 'I regard this ruthless tearing up of old iron railings, which opens up our ancient and historic London squares, as a barbaric piece of Socialism,' wrote the indignant MP for East Dorset, G. R. Hall-Caine. More moderately, the librarian of the

London Library pleaded that the railings were still just as they had been in 1754 and deserved protection on those grounds. Lords Astor and Bearsted, on the other hand, declared that they would resign as trustees of the gardens if the railings stayed. A poll of residents was held and the businesses with offices in the square swung the vote in favour of removal. The Duke of Bedford was more principled if less judicious in his opposition to the removal of the railings in Russell and Bedford Squares. He had already caused a stir by circulating a pamphlet advocating a negotiated peace; now he refused to let his railings be recruited for the war effort. Indignant protesters daubed slogans on the base of the 5th Duke's statue in Russell Square: 'Grandfather of a Quisling! Down with traitor 1941 and his railings – Down with the Duke!' Eventually the railings in Bedford Square were spared because of their historical importance, those in Russell Square taken. The Duke defiantly announced that he would claim the 25/- a ton payable to the owner in such cases.

There were other indications that London had been at war for some two years. People were shabbier; new clothes were a rarity and, when available, worn with a slight air of apology. Though most houses, by the autumn, had unbroken windows, few were freshly painted. Paper saving was in vogue; thirty-five girls working in a City office caused a mild stir when they donated all their old love letters to salvage, from previous admirers as well as husbands. The size of the haul was not revealed. Shops were forbidden to wrap goods, which led to almost twice as many people as usual asking to have purchases delivered.

Home Guard manoeuvres would sometimes disrupt the even tenor of London life. Set to battle in Regent's Park, Charles Graves got permission from the then occupant of Winfield House – now the American ambassador's residence – to go through the grounds and plant his missile launcher on the outskirts of the property: 'This, of course, completely out-witted our alleged enemy.' He was put out by the fact that the Home Guard had to apply to the superintendent before they were allowed to mount exercises in Regent's Park. 'I cannot believe that such a thing would happen in Germany,' he wrote.

In June and July a sudden shortage of cigarettes afflicted London – surprisingly, since more tobacco than before the war was available. 'The real reason for the cigarette shortage is the selfishness of women,' pronounced a Holborn tobacconist severely, 'many of whom have only taken up smoking since the war.' Some tobacconists, sharing this view, refused to sell women cigarettes, or restricted them to packets of ten.

This was only a minor skirmish in the campaign which many men waged to ensure that women did not play a full part in the war. Jill had got out of the Box in the First World War but had been forced back again between 1918 and 1939; now women were on the march again, infiltrating or taking over task after task as it became clear that men were not available to do the work. The idea that women could join the armed services (though very much as junior partners) was well established by the outbreak of war, but the London redoubts of the military proved harder to storm. The War Office viewed with especial dismay the presence of women in the building at night, since many of the senior officials were accustomed to sleep there. When a bomb fell nearby the female staff sallied out in slacks and jerseys. The first sight that met their eyes was 'a revered member of the Administrative Class clad in pink silk pyjamas and a tin hat . . . He was far more perturbed by our arrival than he had been by the bomb and scuttled for shelter at the double.' As for the service clubs, it would have been laughable to suppose that the most redoubtable Amazon would have been tolerated as a member. Even the Home Guard at first declined to accommodate women except in the most mean of ancillary roles. Some women formed private detachments and trained themselves in warlike roles. One Hampstead housewife joined a group who were learning to shoot but did not dare tell her family what she was doing for fear of ridicule. Finally she scored five bulls with five shots and her pride conquered her discretion.

In factories it was the same story: women were initially resisted, then grudgingly accepted, finally taken for granted. In the factory which J. T. Murphy described in his book *Victory Production*, women were at first just one more regrettable necessity, privately considered by the management as 'temporaries' to be dispensed with as soon as possible. But when women made up three-quarters of the work-force and proved themselves quite as capable as the men in all save a few tasks where physical strength was at a premium, they could no longer be treated as poor relations. At one east London radio firm the new order was introduced by a notice proclaiming that, owing to wartime circumstances, smoking and married women would in future be allowed in the office.

'Saw a woman road-sweeper today,' one veteran recorded in her diary. 'Don't think we got as far as that in the last war.' By mid-1940 10,000 women had applied for jobs as London bus conductors; they were kept at bay for a while but were filling the many gaps before the end of the year. Similarly, 25 per cent of London's male bank employees could not disappear without women being called on to take their place and, after a frisson of distaste on the part of management, to serve as cashiers. The Fire Brigades Union had always been a male preserve but by 1943 there were 4300 women driving cars, delivering despatches, working in control rooms. At first they were second-class citizens, denied even uniforms, but the union bravely stood out for equal treatment and won the day. In Hounslow a young woman took over her husband's milk round. Unfortunately she did not know that her husband had always taken a short cut across the Heath, stopping on the way for a mug of tea and some water for the pony. Deprived of its usual treat, the pony refused to budge and it was several days before a milk round was completed to schedule.

As war production got into its swing, and the demands of the armed services became more pressing, it became necessary to employ women with small children. Early in 1942 a 'women's parliament' at Conway Hall demanded the provision of nurseries where small children could be left during the day. The traditionalists, female as well as male, prophesied disaster, but in the end crèches were established. By the end of the war more than three-quarters of London's married women were doing war work, some at home but most in offices, factories or elsewhere.

Milk roundswomen and female road-sweepers signalled to anyone that something strange was going on; only a more educated eye would have noticed how odd it was that the Duke of Kent should journey to Bristol to welcome an incoming American ambassador and that the King should receive him at Victoria Station. It was the first time in British history that a monarch had gone to meet a foreign ambassador. Nothing could have demonstrated more clearly how preoccupied the government was by the need to get and keep the Americans on board in the war against Fascism. It was not only the new ambassador, John G. Winant, who was made much of. Raymond Gram Swing, the broadcaster, enjoyed almost equal attention. 'It is just a little humiliating,' reflected Hugh Dalton, 'that the majority of Ministers of the Crown plus foreign diplomats, British Generals and every kind of notability in the press world have to be collected to help to boost this, I am sure, quite admirable and well-disposed American.' A few days before, on the initiative, it seems, of the *Daily Express*, many Londoners had marked Britain's defeat by the American colonists by flying Stars and Stripes from their roof tops on Independence Day. That same afternoon Winant attended a memorial service in St Paul's for Billy Fisk, an American killed with the RAF in August 1940. He could hardly have shown more dramatically where his sympathies lay.

John Guest returned from a stint in Washington at the end of August 1941. He considered that, in spite of what the papers said, there was little more democratic spirit to be found in London than there had been before the war. When the bombs were actually falling, class distinctions disappeared but they swiftly reappeared once the emergency was over. Morale did not seem much higher than before the war and people's thinking was still 'of the peacetime type'. William Sansom, writer and wartime fireman, thought there had been a change, that people's emotions, once freed, were not so easily put to rest again but that, in the enervating lull that followed the blitz, they had been channelled into directions that might work against national unity and the sense of common purpose.

'Enervating lull' was a harsh description of the relief from brutal bombardment, but a feeling of ennui could be detected in London in the months following the end of the blitz. The old lady who, asked whether she had hated the raids, replied that, on the contrary, she had quite liked them 'because while they were going on they made me forget about the war', expressed a truth of which many Londoners were conscious. The blitz had been terrifying, horrible, but it had been exciting; now there was nothing to do except think about the war and face the long, debilitating drag to victory, up a hill which seemed to be without a crest and with precious few landmarks to suggest that one was even on the way.

The people, Guest judged, were sure that Britain would win in the end but reluctant to make sacrifices which were not strictly essential. The August bank holiday of 1941 found Paddington

Station crowded beyond capacity; the government had urged people to stay at home but many thousands nevertheless travelled towards the west to see evacuated relatives or visit one of England's few coastal resorts that were still open. Those who remained in London flocked to Changing the Guard, the zoo, or what was left of Madame Tussaud's. The allotments were largely deserted, while by 11.45 a long queue had already formed outside the National Gallery for a recital by Myra Hess which began at one o'clock. Every swimming pool seemed to offer a gala, there were thirteen out-of-door venues in the parks where people danced until darkness fell.

A surprisingly large number exercised the dog. After the hecatomb at the beginning of the war few people had their dogs put down, though it was usual not to replace one when it died. By July 1941 only a third of owners admitted to having difficulties in keeping their dog and of these few thought the problem serious. Large dogs obviously required more feeding and pedigree dogs were found to be more susceptible to panic in an air-raid; a small mongrel was the ideal dog to see out the war. The rule that dogs could not be allowed into public shelters caused much distress. 'I make him comfortable, give him a couple of aspirins and hope that he will sleep,' was a typical response. Once the blitz was over, food became the greatest problem, but though securing the necessary supplies was often time-consuming, it was almost always possible to find something for the pet to eat.

Leaving aside the open-air delights laid on for their benefit, the bank holiday crowds had almost a pre-war range of entertainment at their disposal. With the end of the blitz the theatre in particular entered a period of conspicuous prosperity. By the end of 1941, twenty-four were open in or near the West End with old faithfuls like the Penge Empire and the Watford Palace catering to the suburbs. A year or so later theatres were in such demand that offers were made to rent and refurbish the long-closed Lyceum, with an auditorium seating two thousand. Later in 1943 even a Ben Travers farce, starring Robertson Hare – as certain a commercial success as could be imagined – was forced into a lengthy provincial tour until room could be found for it at the Garrick. It seemed that anything would draw the crowds provided it had nothing to do with the war – indeed, *any* war; an epic version of *War and Peace* was a disastrous flop. Even in revues, a modest skit on an ENSA performance was the nearest Hermione Baddeley was allowed to get to the war; at the Windmill van Damm laid it down as a basic principle that members of the services did not want their working life portrayed or even alluded to on the stage. In a spectacularly star-crowded performance of *Heartbreak House*, when Robert Donat as Captain Shotover exulted over the First World War bombing raid and called out, 'I hope they come again tomorrow night', the audience managed only an uneasy titter.

Beverley Baxter, Tory MP and theatre critic of the *Evening Standard*, regularly chided London producers and audiences for contenting themselves with a diet of revues, revivals and American imports, such as *Arsenic and Old Lace* or *The Man Who Came to Dinner*: 'The dreadful indifference of the theatre public to anything unusual, serious or sincere, would make the gods weep,' he wrote in despair. Gradually things improved. There were new plays by Enid Bagnold, James Bridie, Esther McCracken, Terence Rattigan. 'The present school of English playwrights is not yet important,' wrote Baxter loftily, 'it lacks arrogance and the sense of adventure. But it is coming on.' Even Shakespeare was rarely put on during this period. Donald Wolfit's plans for a Shakespeare season at the Scala were frustrated when the theatre was taken over by the Army. He protested furiously and the decision was reversed: 'Will the Secretary of State for War take notice that in the opinion of this House the drama should have precedence over military requirements?' asked an outraged Tory MP. Wolfit responded with a Lear so resplendent that it burnt itself into the minds of all who witnessed it.

To mount a play was a tiresome business. Ernest Bevin refused to rule that stars excused national service must do work for ENSA, but it was privately understood that those who failed to go on one or two ENSA tours a year would be more likely to find themselves in uniform. Good actors, therefore, were hard to find; when he was sued for failing to put on certain plays which he had contracted to produce, Jack Hylton claimed that he could not find a qualified cast. Chorus girls were in short supply too; twenty were needed for a new revue at the Whitehall Theatre, after much effort fifteen were assembled, almost all under the age of eighteen. Costumes and scenery, once lost, could never be replaced; a Gilbert and Sullivan season had to omit *Ruddigore*, *HMS Pinafore*, *Princess Ida* and *Cox and Box* because the necessary material had been destroyed. Wolfit's *King Lear* featured 'a very primitive sort of Stonehenge scenery and ancient Saxon costumes'. Five screens, painted both sides, were all the scenery.

Yet in spite of such limitations, it was a good period for the London theatre. Noel Coward's *Blithe Spirit* opened in July 1941. 'It was just like the old times,' wrote Charles Graves, 'with flashlight photographers, evening dress, pansies and the usual interruption of curtain speech by people from the gallery, one of whom screamed "Rubbish!" and the other "Why did you run away?" ' At the end of 1943 came the return of the American super-stars Alfred Lunt and Lynn Fontanne, in Robert Sherwood's *There Shall Be No Night*, a richly tear-jerking play based loosely on Greek tragedy. But it was the series of revues – *Sweet and Low, Sweeter and Lower,* and *Sweetest and Lowest* – starring the two Hermiones, Baddeley and Gingold, which symbolised London theatre for most of those to whom playgoing was a rarity. Funny, sour and raucously vulgar, these revues had a kind of gallantry to which their audiences responded with passionate enthusiasm. All three were performed at the Ambassador's Theatre; late in the war the doors were blasted in by a V1, but no performance was curtailed or missed.

For every one person who went to a theatre, one hundred patronised their local cinema. The cheaper the seats the more emotional the viewers; the audience at a typical flea-pit cheered and stamped their feet when Churchill featured in a news bulletin. When Hitler appeared, 'they booed and hissed'. War films were not much seen until the turning of the tide at Alamein; with invasion threatening and defeat an obvious possibility, the public preferred to be distracted by *Gunga Din, Goodbye Mr Chips* or *The Wizard of Oz*. But unlike the theatre, the cinema from late 1942 was dominated by a series of war films, most of them romantic or swashbuckling but some, notably Noel Coward's *In Which We Serve*, redeemed by a sometimes harsh realism. What now seems the gross sentimentality of *Mrs Miniver* or *Dangerous Moonlight* – the latter graced by the heady treacle of Richard Addinsell's *Warsaw Concerto* – at the time struck a chord in the hearts of the British public which sent them out into the night proud, exhilarated and resolved to do more to serve their country.

On the whole the government's propaganda films served the same purpose. One of the earliest, *The Lion has Wings*, which showed a German air attack on London frustrated by the defences, was both ineptly put together and made to look remarkably silly by subsequent developments. Things got better, however, and *London Can Take It*, a short documentary about the blitz with a commentary by Quentin Reynolds, was all the more acceptable to the audience because the extravagant compliments on their fortitude and gallantry were paid by a (supposedly objective) American observer. But many disliked too obviously hortatory an approach. *Seaman Frank*, a Ministry of Information film about the Merchant Navy, was enjoyed by 70 per cent of Londoners when it was shown in 1942, but a substantial minority deplored the emphasis on the need to save more for victory. 'There is a feeling that, when you go to the cinema, you expect to be amused and distracted from everyday life and to leave worries behind,' concluded a Mass Observation survey. Half the audience said they left the cinema resolved to increase their savings, but how long the resolution persisted was another matter. 'My idea is that the average person feels like saving more when they see it, but that they forget about it once they are outside,' remarked one sceptical viewer.

A lack of material from the United States led to a substantial cut in film releases. Suburban cinema chains, which till early 1943 received eighty copies of each new film on release, found their allocation abruptly halved. The shortage was made more evident by the practice of providing two main films and a certain amount of supporting material for each performance. Frank Backhouse, a trainee journalist, went to the cinema in Peckham and saw Marlene Dietrich and James Stewart in *Destry Rides Again* and Humphrey Bogart in *The Return of Dr X*: 'These two films, plus two stage turns and an organ recital to complete the programme for the outlay of 6d. Very good value.' The theatre organ was an essential part of all but the humblest cinema; bathed in seductive lights of rose or violet, the organist and his machine rose from the bowels of the cinema and delighted the audience with 'The White Cliffs of Dover' (the number one hit song of the war), 'I'm Going to Get Lit Up when the Lights go on in London', or 'Shine on, Harvest Moon.'

Gone With the Wind remained the undisputed box-office champion, but *Rebecca*, *Casablanca* and *The Grapes of Wrath* survived the blitz and were later joined by *Random Harvest, For Whom the Bell Tolls* and a resurgence of the British film industry with such productions as *49th Parallel, Dead of Night* and *Colonel Blimp*. The last, based on the reactionary buffoon created by the cartoonist David Low, was deemed subversive by the establishment, who at one moment even considered banning it. Mercifully, wiser counsels were heeded and the authorities saved from making total fools of themselves.

The eager queues that formed for Myra Hess's lunchtime concerts at the National Gallery are often cited as evidence that the war released a latent hunger for good music whose existence before had hardly been suspected. These small and elitist gatherings, drawing their numbers largely from the white-collar workers of Whitehall, were not particularly representative of the mass of Londoners. A surer, though still small, indicator of public feeling was provided by the Promenade Concerts, which traditionally took place in the now blitzed Queen's Hall. A fortnight's trial run was held in the Coliseum in May 1941 with six evening performances and three matinees each week. Their success was so striking that in July a season opened in the Albert Hall. Henry Wood conducted, wearing his traditional large carnation; the audience was limited to 4000; every seat was sold. By the end of the season Wood was able to boast that his concerts had been attended by 'the greatest crowds in their long history'. The concert manager admitted that only now was he realising how many people had been turned away from Queen's Hall because of the limited accommodation.

The success was renewed in 1942 and the following year restrictions on numbers were relaxed and 6000 people attended the first night. It was a season distinguished by the first performance of Vaughan Williams's 5th Symphony. The composer was not present; if he had been, pronounced the *Evening Standard*, 'he would have been mobbed by a crowded house, that went wild with delight at one of the loveliest symphonies ever written'. The last night of the Proms, with the BBC Symphony Orchestra and the London Philharmonic combining to mass 160 players on the platform, had been sold out before the season opened nine weeks before. All the traditional patriotic rituals were observed with relish; Henry Wood signalled that his umpteenth encore was final by appearing on the rostrum in hat and raincoat.

The problems for ballet were even more acute than for the conventional theatre. Sadler's Wells had lost the sets and costumes for their productions when they had to hurry home from Holland to escape the German invasion. The grudging allocation of coupons made possible at the most two new productions a year; the surviving costumes became increasingly tatty as the war progressed; their temporary home in the New Theatre was cramped and inconvenient. Throughout 1941 they danced not to an orchestra but to two grand pianos. It made no difference. With Fonteyn, Helpmann and Ashton blossoming into full glory and an apparently insatiable demand for an art form far removed from the grey privations of wartime London, they could have danced in dungarees in a barn and enjoyed packed audiences. Ballet, often with three companies dancing in different parts of town, was an almost invariable feature of London's cultural life. Opera was more erratic. The Carl Rosa company started its first wartime season early in 1943, with Joan Hammond as Violetta in what was said otherwise to be a rather humdrum *Traviata*, but the war was almost over before London audiences saw any opera that was new or more than modestly exciting.

In *World Within World* Stephen Spender claimed that the revival of interest in the arts which he witnessed in London during the war 'arose spontaneously and simply, because people felt that music, the ballet, poetry and painting were concerned with a seriousness of living and dying with which they themselves had suddenly been confronted'. It must be remembered that only a tiny proportion of Londoners cared twopence about serious music, ballet, poetry or painting; as Spender himself ruefully admitted, at his fire station in Cricklewood the radio was switched off only if classical music was being played. The fact that those Londoners who *did* care about such things were starved of concerts or exhibitions meant that whatever was available was eagerly sought after; there was never an empty seat when Myra Hess played at the National Gallery but the queues might have been shorter if there had been three of four other recitals in London on the same day. In qualitative terms the audiences, the visitors to galleries, were more appreciative and attentive than they would have been before the war; quantitatively, any real resurgence of enthusiasm for the arts is harder to establish.

What is more certain is that the intellectuals in wartime London felt themselves to some extent beleaguered and huddled together in a self-protective cocoon, deploring the vulgarities and absurdities of the age. Many were involved in civil defence, the armed services or the government; nearly all believed that the war was necessary, or at least had to be won now that it had started; but they still felt isolated, out of tune with the spirit of the age. The war was waged by reactionaries, wrote Orwell early in 1941; 'at present there is no function in it for intellectuals'. The marginalisation of the intellectuals was the more marked at this period because some were Communist sympathisers and the majority were left wing. As a result they were, or felt themselves, suspect in the eyes of the authorities. With Russia's entry into the war this prejudice lost much of its potency, but the artistic temperament rarely fitted comfortably with a military cast of mind. Graham Greene and Cecil Day Lewis in the Ministry of Information, Stephen Spender and Henry Green in the Fire Service, William Plomer in the Admiralty, Keith Vaughan in the Pioneer Corps, Orwell and Louis MacNeice in the BBC, viewed their wartime occupations with a mixture of sardonic amusement, self-conscious superiority and a usually concealed alarm lest they could not rise to the challenges confronting them.

Coteries formed, around John Lehmann, editor of *New Writing*, in his flat on the sixth floor of Carrington House, or Cyril Connolly, editor of *Horizon*, in Chelsea. These two, with some erratic assistance from the Singhalese poet and harem master Tambimuttu, whose magazine *Poetry London* appeared at intervals from the end of 1940, kept some vestiges of literary life alive during the drear years of war. In fact, literary life in London was, at the best of times, pretty shadowy; British intellectuals, when forced reluctantly to cohabit, tend to talk about royalty statements, literary politics and the sexual excesses of their friends. But the conditions of war, the sensation of being a small band of the partly sane in a world that had collectively gone mad, the need to cling to certain ideals and standards in a disintegrating society, lent these groups a seriousness of purpose, a preoccupation with matters professional or spiritual, which it would have been hard to find in otherwise more propitious circumstances.

Connolly and John Lehmann, the Sitwells, T. S. Eliot, were the
leaders of this world, all trying to preserve still centres of civilisation
where men and women could meet and talk of matters unconnected
with the war. At a socially more elevated, if intellectually more
etiolated level, Sibyl Colefax and Emerald Cunard struggled to
sustain those salons where, before the war, lions of the political and
financial as well as artistic worlds had been accustomed to water
together in cautious if sometimes uncomprehending amity. Lady
Cunard was driven from her palace in Grosvenor Square to temporary lodgings high up in the Dorchester Hotel; Lady Colefax was so
impoverished that she was forced apologetically to bill her guests
after her Wednesday dinners; yet they kept going with a resolution
which, though often snobbish and sometimes absurd, was never less
than gallant.

For those not grand enough to command entrée to these rarefied
redoubts, or who felt inclined to slum, Fitzrovia presented something as near to Bohemia as London was ever likely to provide.
Geographically, Fitzrovia was in north Soho, between Broadcasting
House in Portland Place and the Ministry of Information in the
Senate House of London University. It took its name from the
Fitzroy Tavern, but the Wheatsheaf in Rathbone Place was probably
more celebrated for its colony of artists and writers. It was a world
of pubs: the Black Horse, the Marquess of Granby, the Wheatsheaf
and – if only because it stayed open later than the rest – the High-
lander. Pubs, explained Theodora FitzGibbon, 'were the only places
in wartime London where one could entertain and be entertained
cheaply, and find the companionship badly needed during the war'.
Within them the barriers of class and nationality were broken down.
This individual, embattled world died soon after the end of the war,
the navvy and the shop assistant kept the courts where Tambimuttu
gloried and drank deep, but at the time it had pungent charm for
those who were (or thought they should be considered) brave spirits
set apart from the common herd.

James Maclaren-Ross, talented, louche, a dandy who seemed both
physically and spiritually a little shabby, exemplified the spirit of
Fitzrovia. Tambimuttu warned him that he was in danger of catching
'Sohoitis, after which you will stay there always day and night and
get no work done ever'. Maclaren-Ross did little to prove this wrong.
'Never had the London pubs been more stimulating,' judged John

Lehmann, 'never has one been able to hear more extraordinary revelations, never witness more unlikely encounters.' Alan Ross, then a young and ardent sailor, in search of sensation as remote as possible from his wartime duties, was even more ecstatic. 'It seems to me now,' he wrote in *London Magazine*, 'to have been enormously exciting and savagely happy, to have possessed a gaiety that seems never to have been repeated. Was any of it really as one imagined it . . . ?' The answer probably is that, like the myth of the blitz, Fitzrovia existed primarily in the minds of those who frequented it. However they imagined it to be, it was.

Viewed more objectively and over a distance of fifty years, it seems a little tawdry. Not much great writing emerged during the war, and little of that was produced in London, still less Fitzrovia. There was gallantry in plenty, a defiant and in its way splendid determination to eat, drink and be merry, but the drink – compounded with fornication and tobacco smoke – was the most conspicuous element in the brew, the merriment was hysterical and forced. In no sense did its habitués compose a group with a coherent intellectual or philosophical base, or even a wish to discuss such issues; a Parisian Fitzrovia might have been less stalwart in the face of adversity but it would have been closer to the role which the real Fitzrovians saw themselves as filling.

There were poets, would-be poets, self-styled poets in plenty among those who propped up the bars, but not many of them would have attended the distinguished yet faintly absurd poetry readings at the Aeolian Hall. The first enjoyed particular *réclame* because it was attended by the Queen and the two young princesses. For the assembled poets the success of the evening was T. S. Eliot's rendering of 'What the Thunder said', from *The Waste Land*, 'starting on a deep incantatory note and working up to a climax of superb passion and drama'. The Queen was noticeably less enthusiastic while the princesses crumpled into giggles. John Masefield, the Sitwells and Vita Sackville-West were also deemed successes; the rest ranged between the mediocre and the disastrous. The worst was W. J. Turner, who was inaudible and went on far beyond the six minutes allotted him. He was loudly heckled, to the delight of the princesses, who clearly considered this the best part of the evening.

Those Fitzrovian poets who produced work worth printing found considerable difficulty in getting it published. Many of the established publishers had lost a large part of their stock during the blitz, particularly after the great fire raid of 29 December 1940 which had ravaged the book warehouses in Paternoster Row near St Paul's. With paper allocations cut to a small fraction of pre-war quantities, they were hard put to supply even a part of the demand for classic titles and to keep their regular best-selling authors satisfied. Seventy thousand copies of Michael Sadleir's *Fanny by Gaslight* were printed on the first run, a further 16,000 followed, but this exhausted almost the entire paper allocation for several months. New authors had to try to find a patron among the burgeoning small publishers, who could claim an initial paper ration and profited by the fact that almost anything was selling. Even if a new author's work was well received, prospects for a reprint were bleak.

Starved of new books, the general reader turned to the public library. Here too there were severe shortages, long waits for a chosen title, a failure to meet certain demands, but on the whole Londoners were kept remarkably well supplied. A librarian at West Ham reported an insatiable demand for Trollope – 'he is a most restful man to read'. *The Warden, Barchester Towers* and *Dr Thorne* were the most popular; the majestic *Last Chronicles of Barset* perhaps too bleak for a readership in search of effortless distraction. At Bethnal Green Trollope was low on the list but Dickens was in demand; contemporary favourites were *For Whom the Bell Tolls, Gone with the Wind* and *Random Harvest*. Poetry, too, was sought after; Rupert Brooke the most often asked for; Tennyson, Shelley and Keats the runners-up. Copies were snapped up as soon as they reached the bookshops; demand was three or four times higher than before the war.

Closed museums and empty galleries offered little solace to those who felt culturally starved. A foreign serviceman in London trailed around in the hope of finding somewhere open. He had been assured the British Museum was functioning but found everything closed except the Reading Room, and there only the North Library. Here he found a Polish officer, apparently at work on Byzantine archae-ology, sitting beside a British seaman who was taking notes on Japanese history. Many books appeared in the catalogue but, when asked for, were 'not available'. He continued to the National Mari-time Museum, Imperial War Museum, Wallace Collection and Science Museum and found all closed except the Science Museum's library. Why could nobody warn him before he set off on his pilgrimage? he asked wistfully; 'maybe it's just due to this British habit of secretiveness I heard so much about'.

For some reason he did not try the Victoria and Albert, which he would have found denuded of its most precious contents but still open, with all the clothing and most of the metalwork on display. The director, Eric MacLagen, or one of his senior staff, slept in the museum every night to ensure that someone would know what had to be saved if need arose. There were occasional exhibitions in the National Gallery but virtually all the Old Masters had been evacuated. When the gallery mounted an exhibition of modern art in mid-1941 it was predictably abused by the traditionalists. 'Another bomb there might save posterity lighting a few bonfires in future,' Hilda Neal wrote crossly in her diary. 'Very modern, most of them, intricate splashes of colour, too muddled, we felt, to waste time trying to find out what their painters meant.' She would not have been much better pleased by the exhibition in Bond Street late in 1944 of the paintings of a twenty-one-year-old *wunderkind*, Lucian Freud, all done since he had been invalided out of the Merchant Navy eighteen months before.

Meanwhile the Royal Academy stuck faithfully to the sort of art of which Hilda Neal would have approved. There was never a year without an annual exhibition, though in 1941 the flow of visitors was 'narrow and sluggish'. By 1942 it was in full swing again, enjoying its best year commercially since 1935, and by 1944, with 480 works sold out of a total of 1285, it had broken all previous records, for sales if not necessarily for quality.

Apart from the Ministry of Information, the BBC probably accommodated more of the denizens of Fitzrovia than any other institution. Though many of its departments had been farmed out to the provinces, the BBC felt that it belonged to the capital. Radio meant less to Londoners than to the inhabitants of other cities, let alone country dwellers, but it still bulked large in their daily life. Even when there was a reprieve from bombing most Londoners remained at home and the long nights were made more tolerable by the ubiquitous bakelite box with its mesh of brown canvas covering the mysteries within. The BBC was by far the most potent cultural unifying force in the country, providing in its news bulletins and entertainments a base of shared experience and common reference which linked East Ham and Kensington as effectively as Cornwall and Argyll.

Those who worked for it often saw its defects most sharply. 'Its atmosphere is something half way between a girls' school and a lunatic asylum,' wrote Orwell, after spending six months there, 'and all we are doing at present is useless, or slightly worse than useless.' The BBC could fairly be accused of being bureaucratic, stuffy, unimaginative; but more important, while under almost impossible pressure it provided an unbroken service which both heartened the British people and informed the world of the nation's resolve to battle on. From its building at 200 Oxford Street it organised the broadcasting of news and talks in thirty or so foreign languages and in English to the dominions, colonies and other countries. The directors were at first obsessed by the spectre of some maverick announcer seizing a chance to inform New Zealand or Nova Scotia that the Royal Navy had been sunk or that demands for a negotiated peace were becoming irresistible. The official ruling was, therefore, that nobody should be left alone in a room with a live microphone and that everything said into a microphone had first to be written down and cleared on high. This was soon found to be as impracticable as it was absurd; the discretion which news readers and announcers continued to enjoy was never abused.

There was sometimes a noticeable shortage of material and innumerable repeats, even on the truncated services available. Sandy Macpherson, whose name became virtually synonymous with the hollowly meretricious theatre organ, was once required to broadcast twenty-three programmes in one week and twenty-two in the next. A listener wrote bitterly to the BBC to say that an air-raid would be positively welcome provided 'in the course of it, a bomb would fall on Sandy Macpherson and his ever-lasting organ, preferably while he was playing his signature tune'. But the programmes by which the wartime BBC is above all remembered were of inestimable importance in heartening the nation during the grim, long haul to victory. Of these Tommy Handley's *ITMA* ('It's That Man Again') was by far the best loved.

ITMA was launched in 1939, lapsed briefly, then returned in June 1941 and thenceforward provided a fixed weekly point in the lives of sixteen million listeners. Its characters – surrealistically bizarre, yet possessed of an awful familiarity – and their endlessly repeated catch-phrases, became part of the small change of social intercourse; more people would have recognised a reference to the bibulous Colonel Chinstrap or the German spy, Funf, than could have identified the Chancellor of the Exchequer or the Chief of the Imperial General Staff. Mrs Mopp, with her 'Can I do you now, sir?'; Mona Lott and 'It's being so cheerful as keeps me going'; the Diver's 'I'm going down now, sir', which became a macabre farewell joke for pilots who had been shot down: such slogans possessed a transcendent potency. The knowledge that at the sacred hour almost everyone in London, from Buckingham Palace to a slum tenement in Wapping, was absorbed in the absurdities of Mr Handley's circus did much to foster a conviction of unity and common purpose.

London's own programme, *In Town Tonight*, consisting of interviews with local characters and visitors to the capital, closed after 300 programmes at the end of 1942. By then 3000 people had been featured, for 98 per cent of whom it had been their first broadcast. Mrs Emma Baker, the seventy-year-old flower lady with a pitch outside the Palladium, whose raucous cry of 'Lovely Roses!' featured in the sequence of street noises which introduced the programme, was interviewed on the final episode. Why it was dropped is unclear; an urge for novelty on somebody's part presumably, certainly not justified on grounds of falling audiences. It was anyway soon revived, lingering on until given its final quietus in 1953.

But nationally it was by no means as popular as *The Brains Trust*, that remarkable example of middle-brow didacticism, which opened on New Year's Day 1941 with the intention that it should run for a month or so. It lasted eighty-four weeks without break, then paused briefly and came back for a further period. Its phenomenal success – at its peak twelve million people turned on for the broadcasts – was owed above all to the successful mix of the three wise men who composed the basic team: the acerbic and cynical philosopher, Professor Joad; the brilliantly lucid zoologist, Julian Huxley; and the affable master of the tall story and outlandish fact, Commander Campbell. But the programme also responded to a need of the times which was to become increasingly apparent as the war developed: a hunger for education, for elevation, for some discipline which would equip people for the world to come. There was to be no repeat of 1918. This time Britain had to be, if not a land fit for heroes, then at least a land where everyone would be sure of decent education, health care, accommodation. The national mood which was to respond so enthusiastically to the Beveridge Report, and to sweep the Conservatives from power in 1945, was apparent even in 1941. *The Brains Trust*, with its ingenious blend of iconoclasm, humour and popular instruction, was tailored precisely for an audience that wished to be improved but did not feel disposed to tackle anything too onerous.

Much of the same mix was provided by that other star of wartime broadcasting, J. B. Priestley. Priestley, novelist, dramatist and master of the homespun homily, achieved enormous success with a series of 'Postscript' talks after the news on Sunday night. Robustly patriotic and anti-Nazi, he was also a socialist of the least ideological and most practical turn of mind. His talks abounded in observations on society which to most of his listeners seemed lapidary common sense, but to certain elements of the government were anathema as questioning the sacred rights of property and the fairness of the existing system. A right-wing Tory MP, Walter Liddell, notable mainly for a remarkable resemblance to Henry VIII, put down a motion deploring the BBC's left-wing bias; a counter-force of Tory liberals retorted with an amendment congratulating the BBC on its impartiality. Formally, the government took no line on the issue; but when Priestley's second series of 'Postscript' abruptly came off the air, few doubted that the directive had come from on high, probably from very high indeed. Priestley doubted it least of all. The government did not understand the people, he insisted, *he* did; to suppress his broadcasts was sabotage. At a drunken party he annoyed the young writers William Empson and Woodrow Wyatt by proclaiming that it was his broadcasts which were winning the war. When later that night they were trying to return him to his flat in Albany he passed out in the car. They dumped him in a gutter in Jermyn Street. Wyatt prodded the recumbent writer with his toe and remarked contemptuously, 'He's only a silly old dramatist!'

Of those three great pillars of the extra-parliamentary establishment – the BBC, the MCC and the Church of England – the BBC flourished in the wartime years; the MCC, as will be seen, played a minor role; the Church of England steered an ambivalent course. Long gone were those carefree days when warrior bishops held the borders against whatever rug-headed kerns might assail the state; the modern cleric was required to be patriotic yet to strike an apologetic note – right was undoubtedly on Britain's side, but the whole thing was most regrettable and one should not be too vengeful. Some church notables were deemed to go too far in emphasising this latter point: Bishop Bell of Chichester offended many and probably lost the succession to William Temple as Archbishop of Canterbury by his denunciations of reprisal bombing and refusal to condemn the entire German nation as being as guilty as its leader. Others were indiscreetly pugnacious: Cosmo Lang, who was Archbishop until his resignation in 1942, was felt by many, priests as well as laymen, to be too much the warrior.

Rose Macaulay, who began the war as a confused pacifist though becoming noticeably more belligerent with the passage of time, felt that the church was behaving deplorably in not calling for negotiations, but 'encouraging us to endure the trial of war, and trust that God will defend the right'. (She was quite as much put out by the conduct of certain Roman Catholics. In the Church of Our Lady of the Rosary in Marylebone Road she endured a sermon on the various orders of angels – 'I thought as I sat there, what if the congregation all rose up and mobbed the preacher, and beat him up, and the women scratched his face and the men kicked him, saying "We want something to the purpose, not angels and devils; give us bread not stones." ')

William Temple, who succeeded Lang at Lambeth in 1942, was more successful than any other senior cleric at reconciling the demands of church and state. Even though Lambeth Palace was largely in ruins, he insisted on living there. Temple's wife, Frances, wrote that all their lives they had been used to hearing the phrase 'We must consult Lambeth about that'. 'We thought how hard it would be to feel the same thing about, say, Queen's Gate or Eaton Square! So in our minds it was not so much a case of whether to live there as of how to live there.' Temple's death after only two and a half years in office deprived the church and the nation of a leader whose holiness was never questioned even though to some on the right he seemed too much the socially conscious activist. He was also wedded to ecumenism and rejoiced that out of the blitz had grown a new sense of community between the different religious groups. Worshippers who had lost their churches were welcomed by neighbours of different denominations; when the City Temple was destroyed by fire, its Congregationalist members moved to St Sepulchre, Holborn, with the times of service adjusted so as to allow two different groups to worship their God in different ways; in one parish in south-east London the Anglicans, Baptists, Congregationalists and Methodists took it in turns to hold a united midweek service in their churches.

By the time the blitz was at its height more than one hundred of London's churches were permanently out of action, 500 or more had been at least slightly damaged. With remarkably few exceptions, London's clergy did more than could reasonably have been asked of them to help their parishioners through the air-raids. J. G. Markham was a curate in Walworth at the time. 'We knew that love of our flocks meant not only caring for their souls,' he wrote, 'but for their physical needs as well. We could not simply say our prayers while vital material needs of our parishioners were unsatisfied.' Some, such as Father John Groser or the Revd W. W. Paton (known to all as 'The Guv'nor'), took on the burden which the civil authorities had let fall and for weeks at a time accepted responsibility for the survival of their parishes.

The priest as social worker was already a familiar concept; the priest as air-raid warden became as much a commonplace. Mr Sykes of Holy Trinity was said to be 'not a person but an angel. He put out three incendiary fires last night, and he goes round cheering 'em up in the shelters.' The Bishop of Willesden would cycle to the site of any bomb that fell within his diocese to give what help he could. He joined the rescue services when St James's, Piccadilly, was hit and extricated one of the resident priests. 'I never thought I liked that grubby little man till I had to dig him out,' he later told his daughter. In the East End the worst raids were known as 'Parsons' Particulars' because of the work the vicars did in them, wrote the Mayor of Stepney, Frank Lewey. 'White and coloured, Jewish and Catholic, and Chapel and Church, they seemed so mantled in faith that the malice of men could not hurt them ... Bombs seemed under some potent power which prevented them falling on priests' houses.' The mantle of faith was not always efficacious. There was a fearful toll in dead and maimed among London's clergy. But among the many stories which illustrate the frailties of London's citizens during the blitz, there does not seem to be one which suggests that a priest failed to do his duty.

That this was duly noted, and that the church emerged with enhanced credit cannot be doubted. It does not follow that the population of London turned to God. On the outbreak of war, indeed, they seem if anything to have turned away. A Methodist parson admitted that, for the first few months, his congregations had dwindled; in part at least because people lost faith in a church that could not prevent a war or a God who condoned it. By the spring of 1940, however, attendances were back to normal. In Hoxton, in the East End, it was much the same, though there evacuation was blamed for the initial loss of worshippers. In Kensington, once again in part no doubt due to the decrease in population, congregations remained at little more than two-thirds their pre-war size. But church attendance is not the only test of religious conviction. Theology was one of the areas which enjoyed a marked boom in public libraries. Demand for bibles in bookshops exceeded supply. Travelling by tube Colin Perry was struck by the quantity of passengers reading books about religion. 'It is amazing the number of people who in these times turn to God . . . They try desperately, anxiously, to make up for lost time, putting it crudely. For it is now increasingly obvious that there is only one effective shelter from air-raids – that is the shelter of God.'

The blitz, at least temporarily, seems to have reinforced this preoccupation. Maurice Wood ran lunchtime services for office workers in the area of Portman Square, a prayer service in the crypt shelter every night and prayers for the staff of Selfridge's before work began on Tuesday mornings. He never failed to attract substantial congregations and encountered real religious fervour among his followers. J. G. Markham had similar experiences, and so did many other priests scattered widely around the capital. Such statistics as exist, however, do not suggest that any enduring religious revival was under way. Church attendance rose in 1940, remained high in 1941, but began to decline in 1942. The fall continued. Once the most immediate danger was over it seems that enthusiasm subsided. People continued to describe themselves as Christians but did not do much about it. A survey of religious beliefs in Fulham towards the end of the war showed that 73 per cent declared themselves believers yet 75 per cent had not been to church in the previous six months. Perhaps many of the non-attenders were praying ardently at home; but another poll conducted more or less at the same time, to try to establish what people thought the most important things in life, showed that happiness, or a happy home life came first, then good health, then money, with 'faith' eleventh and last among those items frequently mentioned.

The conclusion of Mass Observation, based on surveys conducted at different periods in widely separated parts of London, was that 'in general the wartime trend is for those with a fairly deep faith to have their faith strengthened; and for those whose faith played little part in their lives before to have had it weakened still further'. When the going got really tough, people turned to God: three-quarters of those who professed themselves atheists or agnostics admitted to having resorted to prayer in moments of intolerable stress. At other times life went on more or less as usual.

12

'The girls here walk out with niggers!'

JAPAN'S ATTACK ON the American fleet at Pearl Harbor on 7 December 1941 and the German declaration of war against the United States a few days later made eventual victory inevitable. They also introduced the blackest period of the war, involving a series of humiliating defeats which cost Britain her South-East Asian and Pacific empire, and included naval setbacks still more damaging to national pride. Of those the most painful came only three days after Pearl Harbor, when the *Prince of Wales* and the *Repulse* were sunk by Japanese bombers off the coast of Malaya. The British public had not yet fully taken in the disastrous weakness of the Allied position, Singapore was still believed to be impregnable, but the scale of the disaster was painfully apparent.

Christmas was therefore unlikely to be conspicuously merry, but at least there seemed little risk of heavy bombing and most of the children had once more drifted back to their homes. 'No Christmas carols at all,' noted Charles Graves, but he did not find the explanation in evacuation: 'I suppose that all the little boys are making munitions.' However concerned they might be about the future, first things came first, and Londoners addressed themselves to the serious business of finding presents for the children. Since scarcely any shops still made deliveries and there was no wrapping paper, customers had to stagger home with whatever loot they had acquired. Some carried suitcases; more, wrote Mollie Panter-Downes, 'looked like harassed and cruelly overloaded camels'. They were the lucky ones who found something to carry away. Gwladys Cox went on a teddy-bear hunt. They were available but only for prohibitive prices; at Hamley's the smallest bear cost 15/6d; at Selfridge's, where she found 'the Xmas decorations very *piano* and, of course, no fandangle, mechanical toy facade, as they usually have', bears were a little cheaper but still 10/- for a small and shoddy specimen. 'A weary-looking woman, with two small children dragging at her skirts, said to me, "Who can afford such prices?" ' But at least there was some pleasure in the hunt and in exchanging complaints with fellow shoppers: 'I noticed that strangers on the bus were chatting unreservedly; the atmosphere was exhilarating, not to say electric.' By Christmas Eve not even the exhilaration remained. Those who had been so ill-advised as to leave their shopping to the last minute found the stores crammed with customers yet almost bereft of goods. There were no turkeys to be had; no whisky, gin or sherry; no chocolates; no fruit; the few remaining toys were shoddy and over-priced.

The New Year brought fresh disasters, in Malaya and North Africa, where Rommel broke through and swept across Libya. Churchill had been paying a lengthy visit to the United States and his return to London was made the occasion for a demonstration of loyalty by Clement Attlee, who assembled almost the entire Cabinet at Paddington to welcome him. The gesture was slightly marred by an over-zealous policeman who failed to recognise either the Lord Chancellor or the Lord President of the Council and tried to shoo them from the station.

Churchill had need of all the support he could muster. In mid-February Singapore fell, a surrender which seemed as abject as it was inexplicable. Only three days before, the German battle-cruisers *Scharnhorst* and *Gneisenau* had escaped from Brest and slipped up the Channel, so far as it was known unscathed and having shot down the Swordfish aircraft which had been sent to attack them. 'The capital seethes with indignation,' recorded Chips Channon, 'and were Londoners Latins there would be rioting. I have never known so violent an outburst.' Few people believed Churchill should be replaced, but there were increasing fears that something was badly wrong with the direction of the war. A poll early in 1941 showed that only 15 per cent of Londoners were optimistic about the prospects for the coming year; better than the 12 per cent who had felt the same a year before but still hardly a resounding vote of confidence in the government.

The only people who seemed to be meeting with any success were the Russians. 'It's a humiliating business having other people fighting for you,' remarked James Lansdale Hodson. Londoners felt they had been left on the sidelines, they were bored and dejected. Hodson noticed an immediate change of mood when an air-raid siren sounded during the day, 'The policeman started wisecracking with me; everybody was smiling.' Gwladys Cox too felt that the zest had gone. In mid-January she saw a newsagent clearing snow from in front of his shop. 'When I laughingly greeted him with "Merry Christmas!" he scowled. How few possess *joie de vivre!*' In this case one's sympathies may lie with the newsagent; *joie de vivre* took some finding in London that spring. The May bank holiday, cold and grey, found huge queues outside every cinema and crowds wandering aimlessly through the streets 'looking as though they didn't know what on earth to do with themselves'.

The fall of Tobruk in June was for the British the nadir of their war. 'Whatever is going to become of us?' wailed a Hampstead housewife. 'Nothing but defeats!' The irrepressible Gwladys Cox reminded herself that Britain always won the last battle, but the thought was not much comfort to her fellow Londoners. 'Browned-off,' was Mollie Panter-Downes's view of the mood in the capital. 'People go about their work and their amusements, queue up in the food shops and buy their pennyworth of bad news, all with complete surface calm,' but they suffered from a vague discomfort, 'a sort of perpetual mental indigestion'. The Home Intelligence Weekly Reports detected apathy, with little interest being taken in the war and even food and the weather not generating noticeable excitement. Londoners realised the dangers of the situation, concluded a report in early August, but 'it does not seem to have inspired the urge towards self-sacrifice that was found after the fall of France'.

On 10 May 1942 the fire services commemorated the first anniversary of the last great raid by a spectacular exercise in the City. Admiring observers were drenched by the power hoses, a small reminder that war did not consist only of newspaper headlines and privations. The retaliatory 'Baedeker' raids on Britain's showpiece provincial cities served the same purpose. When Bath was bombed on 27 April there was an appeal for volunteers from London to help patch up the damage. 'I can feel no sympathy for Bath,' wrote William Regan, from the Isle of Dogs, 'they did not rush to help us in our hour of need, neither did they show any feeling. I have spoken with several people who all express the same feeling.' Regan was an angry radical, who believed that Bath, Norwich, Exeter and other such cities selected as targets were filled with rich and selfish Londoners who had fled the capital to lounge in luxurious safety. Not many people shared his vengeful mood, but Londoners at this time did feel curiously dissociated from the war, as if they had been left behind in a race everybody else was straining body and mind to win.

The authorities reflected the mood by closing public shelters which were costly to maintain. Six West End tube shelters were withdrawn from use, leaving only Green Park, Bond Street, Trafalgar Square and Covent Garden. There was some protest, but most of the public shelters had been deserted. Only one man had stuck it out in a shelter in Barnes, which cost the council a lot to light and heat. The authorities announced that they were going to cut off the facilities. 'This shelter has been my home for more than a year,' protested the man indignantly. 'I shall just sit in the dark and await events.'

As the summer advanced it seemed events might rescue him. In June London had its first night alert for more than seven months. A few hundred incendiary bombs were scattered over a park, but no serious harm was done. The following month there were several minor raids. A new kind of explosive incendiary bomb was introduced, powerful enough to pierce roofs or mattresses stacked double on the top of a car and posing a serious hazard to fire-watchers. Fragments from anti-aircraft shells increased in quantity and threatened anyone who ventured out. Nor was it only those in the open who were at risk from the defences; the only casualty of the raid on 30 July was a foreign refugee, killed when an anti-aircraft shell passed through his window and exploded.

The little spurt of activity died down and London, with most seaside resorts barred to visitors, became a place to which people flocked for holidays, wandering through the streets and peering at the depleted displays in the shop windows. 'I suppose it makes a change for them,' wrote Hilda Neal. She was pleased by the brightly coloured frocks, more often seen than in the previous summers, but less impressed by the hair styles. It was the fashion to peroxide one's hair, usually with a curious streaky-bacon effect, leaving the wearer either skewbald or piebald. Huge clumps of hair in fringes were also in vogue, with the rest of the hair strained back tightly over the ears. 'Even elderly charladies, shoppies, theatricals, wear their hair hanging on their shoulders, many doubtless proud of the beauty it once had. It is grotesque on the elderly, as it makes them look as though they have forgotten to do their hair.'

To promote still further the gaiety produced by bright frocks and peroxided hair, Basil Dean in September organised a grand pageant on the steps of St Paul's – 'An Anthology in Praise of Britain'. It provided an orgy of sentimental patriotism which would have been almost unbearable at any other time or place, but in the middle of a war, in front of the battered cathedral and with the ruins of the City stretching for miles around, was moving, exciting, and admirably calculated to appeal to the United States, to which the broadcast was relayed. 'An offering of British music and drama to stir the hearts of the people by making them conscious of their glorious heritage,' Dean described it. Henry Wood conducted the massed bands of the Guards and Household Cavalry; Edith Evans declaimed Queen Elizabeth's Tilbury speech; Robert Speaight read Julian Grenfell's 'Into Battle'; Henry Ainley gave Henry V's speech before Agincourt; Leslie Howard played the wraith of Nelson; massed choirs sang 'Fairest Isle, All Isles Excelling'; the bands played a pianissimo 'Tipperary'. It was heady stuff.

During the summer of 1942 a dangerous feeling spread among the local authorities, who had to find much of the money for civil defence, that London was over-insuring against what was now a distant threat. In June the *Evening Standard* reported that a third of London's ARP staff were to be assigned to the war factories; one in six firemen were also to be re-employed. Nothing quite so drastic happened, but those who manned the various branches of civil defence were left in no doubt that they were out of fashion. William Regan's wife applied to Poplar town hall for a job as a warden: 'She was told that they don't want any, and are going to sack 200 of those they now have.'

The government grew alarmed at this insouciance. In the House of Commons Churchill warned that the danger of air attack was far from over. Ernest Gowers went even further, making a blood-curdling declaration that 'We may have in front of us raiding of a type which will make you people in London look back upon the memory of 16 April and 10 May 1941 as though they were mere picnics.'

The public paid attention; a Home Intelligence Weekly Report at the end of September found a general expectation that the Germans would dig in for the winter in Russia and switch the Luftwaffe back to the West to renew the attack on London. They also believed that London was vastly better prepared to meet the threat than it had been in 1940 or 1941. They had some evidence to sustain their optimism. The forces of civil defence trained with conspicuous energy as winter approached. On 25 September squads of heavy-rescue workers toiled all day for the honour of being styled the most efficient team in the London region. Blitzed buildings were carefully prepared to present a variety of problems and dummy bodies sown at inaccessible spots amid the ruins to test the ingenuity of the rescuers.

The improved water supply was the most conspicuous sign of London's readiness. All over the capital the basements of blitzed buildings had been converted into giant tanks to supplement the water mains in case of a fire raid. 'They look just like Roman baths and give the ruins an even more Pompeian look than they had before,' noted Orwell. Existing sources were augmented; the Round Pond on Hampstead Heath was surrounded by a high brick wall and raised in level. By the early autumn the supply of static water was ten times as great as at the time of the blitz and twenty miles of steel pipe linked the largest tanks – one of which held a million gallons. 'Fall in Fire Fighters here!' was a notice displayed on the side of several East End tanks; the fire-fighters rarely obliged but small boys did. A seven-year-old was drowned in Wandsworth and the tanks were fitted with ropes and cork belts as a consequence. Many were also surrounded with barbed wire to keep children at bay and to discourage the dumping of rubbish. This served little purpose; seventeen tons of assorted scrap had to be removed from one tank in Langford Road, Fulham. The new reservoirs also encouraged mosquitoes and other insects; in late July Anthony Weymouth noticed that the huge pool which had been created at the corner of Harley and Queen Anne Streets was coated with swarms of flying ants and that the pavements of Harley Street were smothered by the same creatures.

Fire-watchers, who had also been affected by the summer malaise, were now put back on full alert – 3500 were on duty every night in the City alone, each doing a sixteen-hour spell once in ten days.

Early in October the compulsory recruitment of women for such work was announced. Various civil authorities objected on the ground that the task was unsuitable. Their chivalry was ill received; it was pointed out that, in a recent fire-watchers' competition, fourth place had been won by a team of determined women who had scaled walls and roofs like would-be Lady Tarzans.

Gowers also surprised London by announcing that invasion was still a potent threat. A new policy of 'defence in depth' was introduced. The original instruction had been that everybody without a specific task should remain where they were in case of invasion. This was now abandoned: 'We assume that in the event of invasion the stout-hearted among the population will do something anyhow to try to beat the enemy,' said Gowers, 'we think it just as well that they should do something in the right way.' The Home Guards had, of course, been preparing to do something in the right way since the time of their formation. One particularly vigorous exercise, which involved the storming of the BBC, led to three of the defenders ending up in hospital. Their pride was further dented when two medical students entered the building with the help of passes made out in the names of Adolf Hitler and Stanley Baldwin and captured the commander of the BBC Home Guard. By the rest of the population the threat of invasion was not taken seriously. Questionnaires asking what public services people could perform when the Germans arrived produced answers which suggested less than total commitment. One woman volunteered to drive a car, but not on Thursdays, 'as I go down to Kent on Thursdays to see my husband'; another said that she and her maid would be happy to help in any way between five and seven p.m., but that they always went to the country at weekends.

Gas was another distant threat in which people found it hard to believe. At the beginning of the year some tear gas was let off in Holborn to see what happened. Eight out of ten passers-by were found to be without their masks. Then the wind turned, two restaurants had to be evacuated and public irritation was so vocal that the experiment was not repeated. Reports that the Germans were using gas in the Crimea led to threats of retaliation and a warning by Churchill that this could lead to a similar attack on Britain. 'I must get Peggy to make sure that her mask is in good order,' wrote Charles Graves apprehensively, but even if Peggy did something about it, not many followed her example. A rough gauge of how many people were carrying gas-masks was provided by the numbers left behind in trains and buses. At its peak in September 1940 the figure had been 2000 a week, by early 1942 it had dropped to 400. Churchill's warning brought it back up to 550, but by the autumn it was as low as it had ever been.

The death of the Duke of Kent in a flying accident in August 1942 reminded Londoners that the risks of war were shared by everybody. A terrible shock, Gwladys Cox found it, 'out shopping this morning, everyone I met mentioned the tragedy and seemed stunned'. She was more royalist than most, but many seem to have been genuinely distressed by the death of one of the most glamorous and popular members of the royal family. 'The Duchess won't have any difficulty with *her* pension,' said one widow sourly, but she went on to add how sad it would be for the children. A memorial service was held with great pomp in Westminster Abbey. 'The damn thing had no character at all,' wrote Hugh Dalton, 'smooth unctuosities by actor-priests, and beautiful music; but it might as well have been for any notability.' The comment is of interest for showing that in Dalton's eyes the Duke of Kent was not just 'any notability'. The same would have been true for most Londoners; it was the brother of the King who had died in action and in London in 1942 the brother of the King was a figure of great consequence.

The death of a royal prince might cause distress and a glow of sympathy among the people, but it had no appreciable effect on morale. The mere fact that there had been no notable disasters since the fall of Tobruk led to a rebuilding of confidence in Britain. The Germans seemed to have been checked in Egypt, the Japanese on the frontiers of India, perhaps the tide was about to turn? Montgomery's victory over Rommel at El Alamein in October and November showed that the tide *had* turned. In the history of the war, the Russian counter-attack at Stalingrad was of immeasurably greater import, but Alamein was a British victory and there had been so few in the last years that the occasion was gloriously memorable. There was no extravagant jubilation but enormous relief and satisfaction and a feeling that once more Londoners could look their foreign visitors in the face. Dalton recorded that a British general had been seen to rush to the head of a waiting bus queue and leap

The blitz did not stop people eating and drinking at West End restaurants such as the Hungaria (*above*) and if caught by an alert privileged guests could bed down there for the night (*below*) (p. 135)

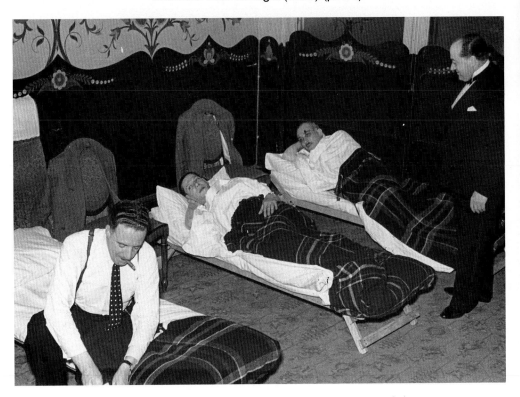

Bert Hardy called this photograph
'East End at War'.
Few images evoke more vividly
the patience and stoicism of the victims
of the blitz

Mrs Charlotte Lister, aged 72, was
bombed out of her home in Battersea.
She took up residence in
the crypt of a nearby church and is seen
here preparing dinner with her friend,
Mrs Rosie Bugden

Salvage Week at St Pancras. The Mayor, no doubt enjoying a good photo opportunity, is shown clambering over the stacks of waste left by munitions workers on their way to their factory

A British Restaurant in the Fishmongers' Hall. 'Brutal in their cooking, brutal in their presentation of food,' stormed Sir William Darling (p. 251)

Many pig clubs opened around London, this one run by the police in Hyde Park. The sty was twice damaged by bombs but there were no casualties among the inhabitants (p. 258)

'Snowdrops' – American military police – patrolling the streets near Leicester Square (p. 215)

'The girls here walk out with niggers!' A scene in Frisco's Club near Piccadilly in July 1943

Rainbow Corner, a vast club for American other ranks, fashioned out of Del Monico's restaurant and the adjoining Lyons' Corner House (p. 216)

Myra Hess playing at the National Gallery. She asked the Director, Kenneth Clark, whether she could give a lunchtime concert. 'You must give one every day,' replied Clark (p. 51)

Women took over many traditionally male roles, including the milk round (*above*), and trained for more warlike activities (*below*). One Hampstead housewife did not dare tell her family that she was learning to shoot until she scored five bulls with five shots and her pride conquered her discretion (p. 184)

The Government urged Londoners to spend their holidays at home. Hampstead Heath was a favourite resort for those who heeded the exhortations – Easter 1943

on the moving vehicle: 'He would not have dared to do this a week before.'

The influx of soldiers from abroad swelled daily. 'Piccadilly is a thrilling place these days,' wrote Vere Hodgson. 'All the uniforms of all the nations jostle you on the pavement.' The Poles and the Canadians were easily distinguished, the Free French not much more difficult, but some baffled categorisation: 'Such varied faces and manners. Girls, too, in their trim service uniforms by the hundred.' Londoners grew blasé and ceased to enquire about the national origins of each new apparition. Curiosity grew too much, however, when what appeared to be a German staff officer strolled through Soho. A crowd collected and eventually he was challenged. An embarrassed Lieutenant Duarte Da Cunha explained that he was the new Brazilian military attaché. To cries of 'Bravo, Brazil' he climbed into a taxi and fled the scene.

For a people which was not famed for hospitality to unknown foreigners, Londoners did not do too badly when it came to welcoming their allies. They were selective, however; those who had homes where they could invite the newcomers generally preferred officers to other ranks and one nationality to another. Mrs Youngman of West Hampstead refused to receive Canadians – 'Common lot!' – but entertained five Polish officers to high tea and bridge from five to eleven p.m. How much pleasure the experience gave the Poles is another matter; problems of food and accommodation limited what even the most open-hearted of Londoners could provide. Usually the visitors entertained themselves: each nationality had its favourite café or pub where they could be sure of finding congenial company; the Free French patronised above all Le Petit Club in St James's Place, where the redoubtable Olwen Vaughan presided over her often quarrelsome flock and where more indiscretions were peddled in an evening than most gatherings could manage in a week.

The diplomats, less glamorous than the military but with more whisky, were stars in the social scene. Winant was by far the most important, but as Russia stemmed the German advance and moved over to counter-attack the urbanely sardonic Ivan Maisky became a particular favourite with the London crowds. He served admirable Russian food and drink at his Embassy in Kensington Palace Gardens. More exotic if less attractive was Wellington Koo, the

Chinese ambassador, who was to be seen at almost every public gathering, unsmiling, unyielding and alarmingly inscrutable. At least the entry of Japan into the war reduced the total of foreign diplomats, though it was several months before their safe return to Tokyo could be arranged. In the meantime twenty of them lived in luxury flats in Kensington, guarded by eight disgruntled policemen who particularly deplored the diplomats' propensity for long walks around Hyde Park. Orwell watched one elderly Japanese, 'with a face like a suffering monkey's', walking along Upper Regent Street in the company of an enormous policeman, 'But whether the policeman is there to prevent him committing acts of sabotage or to protect him from the infuriated mob there is no knowing.'

The foreign presence which grew irresistibly throughout 1942 and soon outweighed all others was that of the Americans. Even before the attack on Pearl Harbor there were more than 2000 people in or attached to the American Embassy, 800 in the Naval Department alone. Within six months that figure had doubled. As well as the permanent presence of Winant and frequent visits from Roosevelt's personal emissary, Harry Hopkins, Averell Harriman was soon in residence to speed up the delivery of desperately needed lend-lease materials, and Anthony Drexel Biddle was a floating ambassador accredited to the Allied governments-in-exile. American journalists were hardly less numerous. At their favourite watering-hole, the Savoy, there was euphoria the day after Pearl Harbor, with (wrote Mollie Panter-Downes) much 'slapping backs and singing "Oh say, can you see . . . ?" ' The hangover followed quickly; within forty-eight hours there was talk only of a war that would be long, grim and hard-fought.

The great build-up began which was to culminate in June 1944 with the invasion. American servicemen had been carefully briefed on what they would encounter. The British, they were told, cared little about size. London, for instance, had no sky-scrapers: 'Not because English architects couldn't design one, but because London is built on swampy ground.' The GIs were given excellent advice about respecting British susceptibilities, showing proper respect to the royal family, remembering the houses would be cold, the tables bare, the cellars empty. Jane Gordon's American cousin came to lunch, took only a small portion of meat and refused a second helping. 'I know what's the matter with you,' said his host, 'you've been reading that little book of instructions handed out to the servicemen coming to England.'

By the middle of 1942 the accents of the East Coast, Middle West or South were as familiar in London as the longer established Polish, French or Czech. American uniforms were omnipresent, with the 'snowdrops' – US military police with white helmets, belts and gaiters – circulating watchfully in their midst. 'They wear on their faces a look of settled discontent,' noted Orwell. 'I don't know how far this may be the normal expression of the American countenance, as against the English countenance, which is mild, vague and rather worried.' If cross-examined, reasons for their discontent became clear. They thought British films behind the times; they didn't think much of the dance halls; they loathed the beer. Above all, they missed their cars. But they found the women 'most hospitable and less sophisticated than New Yorkers', while the restaurants, once they had got used to the cooking and the austerity dishes, were 'Great! We are served before civilians. In the States we come last.'

The American servicemen congregated in the West End, could sometimes be seen in Kensington or Bloomsbury, ventured rarely indeed to Neasden or West Ham. 'The region of Grosvenor Square has been captured – lock, stock and barrel – by the United States,' wrote Anthony Weymouth. 'Large utility vans, with USA painted in white letters on a black background, flash past one at frequent intervals; and outside the houses in the square itself groups of US soldiers and sailors stand about.' In fact the first American troops were housed in Piccadilly, in the former Hotel Splendide and the Badminton Club. Shepherd Market – soon to be known as Eisenhower Platz – was quickly overrun, South Audley Street transformed into a miniature Fifth Avenue, the Washington Hotel in Curzon Street into an American Red Cross Club. London was both military nerve centre and the destination for GIs from all over Britain who had a few days' leave. In April 1942 US troops occupied 10,000 square feet of office space; by June 1944 there were 33 officers' billets (including 24 hotels), 300 other buildings for troop accommodation, 2.5 million square feet for offices, garages, gymnasia and a hundred other uses.

Grandest was the officers' mess at Grosvenor House, ensconced comfortably in the ballroom. Best known and most active was Rainbow Corner, a club for other ranks fashioned out of Del Monico's restaurant on the corner of Shaftesbury Avenue and Piccadilly Circus, and the adjoining Lyons' Corner House. When the club opened in November 1942 the key was thrown away to symbolise that it would remain open twenty-four hours out of twenty-four. It lived up to the promise, serving waffles and other delicacies throughout the night as well as offering two dining rooms which could seat 2000 men. Hot dogs were almost the only transatlantic speciality not featured on the menu, because, it was said, the GIs disliked British sausages. In the lobby three arrows pointed to Leicester Square – 100 yards; Berlin – 600 miles; and New York – 3271 miles. Here the homesick GI, who might well have left his Mid West home for the first time in his life, could dance, read his local newspaper, play pinball machines, or write letters home with the help, if needed, of sympathetic American residents such as Adele Astaire, sister and partner of Fred and married to Lord Charles Cavendish.

When Ernie Pyle, an American journalist, visited London in 1943 he was dismayed by the over-staffing in American headquarters. At lunchtime, 'Floods of American uniforms poured out of buildings. On some streets, an Englishman stood out as incongruously as he would in North Platte, Nebraska.' In principle, the Londoners were grateful that the Americans were there; in practice they sometimes wished that their new arrivals were less conspicuous and rather more widely dispersed about the country. Horror stories circulated about their unruliness, their uncouthness. They were spoken of as if they resembled Gerard Manley Hopkins' dragon, 'A wilder beast from West than all were, more Rife in her wrongs, more lawless and more lewd.'

Charles Graves told of a friend who had bumped into an American in the blackout, apologised, and been knocked unconscious. So many variants of this particular story were recounted that it seemed the US forces were peopled entirely by short-tempered pugilists. They were said to be rapists too: Naomi Mitchison was fed with so many unlikely tales about these lascivious hooligans that when she had successfully crossed Piccadilly Circus without being violated, she said she felt like a Grecian Urn – 'Thou still unravished bride of quietness'. Some of the more sophisticated London girls went out with young Americans from Wyoming or Idaho and contrasted them unfavourably with their Free French or Polish admirers:

'Americans are rather boring, I find,' wrote one nineteen-year-old superciliously in her diary. 'I shan't go out with any more, I don't think.'

The more extravagant of these charges were based largely upon jealousy and the resentment of those who felt themselves supplanted as principal players in a war they considered peculiarly theirs. The often-quoted complaint that the Americans were 'over-paid, over-sexed and over here' (countered by the retort that the British were 'under-paid, under-sexed and under Eisenhower') had just enough truth in it to foster resentment. Both officers and men were vastly better paid than their British counterparts, which gave them an unfair advantage when it came to entertaining women and ensured them the best tables in restaurants, the favour of taxi drivers, and all the other perquisites that money can procure. James Hodson was outraged to be charged 14/- for a carafe of wine. 'American officers, of course, can afford these prices,' he observed. 'An American private receives more money than a Flight Lieutenant in the RAF, when the latter's income tax has been deducted.' But pique at relative poverty is not enough to explain the 'passion of dislike' which Mrs Rosemary Black claimed to have found among almost everyone, 'How can one help resenting the full-fed, candy-pampered, gum-chewing swagger of our invaders?' Arrogance was the charge most often levelled at them: 'bumptious and cocksure'; 'The Americans talk too much before they actually do the job'; 'always boasting about how they won the last war and now are going to win this one', were typical comments from Londoners of very different ages and classes. A Mass Observation poll found 73 per cent of Londoners favourable to the Dutch, 64 per cent to the Czechs, 52 per cent to the Free French, only 33 per cent to the Americans. The government was so concerned about public disaffection that a campaign was set in hand to convince British civilians that the average American was 'a kindly, simple, honourable character' and, even more to the point, an ally and an essential one at that.

The American GI for his part experienced the disgruntled resentment of a knight who had disrupted his career and his family life to come to the rescue of a not particularly prepossessing maiden in distress, only to meet with carping comments about the quality of his armour and the ineptness of his swordsmanship. Orwell talked to a young American soldier who, after two months in London, had still not set foot in an English home. 'Even at their best English people are not very hospitable to strangers,' he reflected, and in 1942, ashamed of the shabbiness of their homes and the meagreness of their rations, they were less welcoming than ever. Orwell detected a 'very bitter anti-British feeling among the soldiers'; contempt for British fighting skills mingled with suspicion that only constant vigilance would save the United States from involvement in a crusade to rescue an imperial system of which they heartily disapproved.

A young American arriving in London asked a US military policeman, 'How's Britain?' 'The girls here walk out with niggers,' was the reply. 'They call them American Indians!' The arrival in London of substantial numbers of black troops was one of the causes of ill-feeling between Americans and local inhabitants. The intention had been that one in ten American soldiers crossing the Atlantic would be black; the bulk of these were posted to the West Country but quite enough found their way to London to pose a problem for the authorities. The Foreign Secretary, Anthony Eden, had tried to avoid the issue by persuading the Americans not to send black troops to Britain, but General Marshall insisted this would be impossible. Oliver Harvey, Eden's private secretary, gloomily set out the alternatives as he saw them: 'If we treat them naturally as equals, there will be trouble with the Southern officers. If we treat them differently, there will be trouble with the "North Americans".' In fact it was Londoners rather than the 'North Americans' who resented any attempt to treat the black troops as inferiors.

At Cabinet in October 1942 Lord Salisbury spoke of the increasing difficulties. A black official at the Colonial Office had recently been refused a table at the restaurant where he habitually lunched because American officers had complained to the proprietor. 'That's all right,' commented the Prime Minister, 'if he takes a banjo with him they'll think he's one of the band!' Neither Salisbury nor Eden was disposed to treat the matter with such levity, but the Cabinet fought shy of issuing any official directive about how black troops should be treated. The nearest approach was a note put out over the signature of Major General Dowler, which advised white women not to go out with black soldiers and, in general, suggested that people should watch how white Americans treated their compatriots and do likewise.

Londoners did nothing of the sort. The girls found them excitingly different, while the men and women in the street took perverse pleasure in maintaining that they were better mannered and more congenial than their white counterparts. Hoteliers and restaurateurs, with much valuable custom at stake, were less liberal. There was an unpleasant scene when Learie Constantine, the great West Indian cricketer and future peer, was asked to leave the Imperial Hotel because American guests threatened otherwise to cancel their reservations. The manager protested that his only purpose had been to please his patrons: 'If they want roast beef, we give them roast beef. If they don't like Chinese visitors, well, we shouldn't have them.' Mr Justice Birkett was unimpressed by this explanation, paying more attention to what the manageress said when she discovered that Constantine and his family were black: 'We are not going to have all these niggers in our hotel. If he does not go tomorrow morning his luggage will be put outside and the door will be locked.' Birkett fined the hotel £5.50 and deplored the fact that, because of a legal technicality, he could not make the amount far larger.

He would have felt quite as strongly about the black sergeant in Home Guard uniform who was turned away from a dance hall much patronised by Americans, or the West Indian assaulted by two white US marines in a Lyons' Corner House. Such incidents abounded and increasingly Londoners began to intervene and to make it clear where their sympathies lay. At one point it was suggested that black Britons should wear a Union Jack to distinguish themselves from the Americans, but this ignoble idea was not pursued. The problem was never resolved and grumbled on rancorously until the invasion of the continent removed the great majority of black troops. The blacks were not above exercising a kind of reverse segregation; Maclaren-Ross remembered passing a pub where a huge black man stood at the door with a glass in his hand, shouting, 'No white folk allowed in here!'

Quentin Crisp, wit and transvestite, described lasciviously how 'This brand new army of (no) occupation flowed through the streets of London like cream on strawberries, like melted butter over green peas – labelled "With Love from Uncle Sam" and packaged into uniforms so tight that in them their owners could fight for nothing except their honour.' Crisp's interest in the invaders was idiosyncratic, but they proved equally irresistible to the girls of London, who saw them both as a romantic novelty and a source of endless goodies. London was full of American soldiers, wrote Evelyn Waugh. 'For their comfort there swarmed out of the slums and across the bridges multitudes of drab, ill-favoured adolescent girls and their aunts and mothers, never before seen in the squares of Mayfair and Belgravia. There they passionately and publicly embraced, in the blackout and at high noon, and were rewarded with chewing-gum, razor-blades and other rare trade goods.'

If Naomi Mitchison had been warned that she might be raped by licentious American soldiers, the soldiers should have been warned that they were at risk of being overwhelmed by a tide of equally licentious women, resolved to bestow their favours on the new arrivals. Two newly arrived GIs got on a bus and asked to be told when it reached Piccadilly. They were perplexed by the conductor's knowing leer, the titters of the other passengers and shouts of 'Have a good time, Yank!' Within two or three minutes they had been propositioned several times and a news vendor had tried to sell them condoms. The *New York Times* described the area around Leicester Square as 'a veritable open market' calculated to shock the most sophisticated New Yorker, let alone country boys from the Mid West. The *Evening Standard* launched a campaign to clean up London's red-light district; an official told them that immorality was not a crime; one hundred so-called 'night-clubs' had been closed but soliciting on the streets was harder to control. When the police did try to clamp down, the prostitutes were most put out. 'First time I've ever had any trouble,' said one when moved from Piccadilly; 'Behavin'' like that for no reason at all,' protested another.

For those Americans who disdained recourse to professionals, the dance halls and other public places offered a rich crop of shopsoiled talents. The only girls who showed any friendliness towards the visitors, noted Vivienne Hall, were 'our most crude specimens of womanhood, who flock around the Americans, doing anything they want them to do and fleecing them in payment – it's disgusting to see our young girls cheapening themselves and screaming about the West End; it's they and not the Americans who are bad.' It was the youth of the girls that particularly offended Hilda Neal, 'Awful little flappers seize on them like limpets; many look about fifteen or younger . . . Judging from the couples I saw in the train on Saturday, the men looked quite a decent class, but the girls were of the factory type and loud at that.' In the Elephant and Castle, Harry Davey remembered, respectable householders looked with disapproval on the behaviour of girls who 'went with the Americans'. 'Going with' did not necessarily amount to much. Some girls specialised in milking their escort for all he could provide and then slipping away, leaving him frustrated and bereft. But to portray the Americans as innocents abroad, victims of a pack of teenage harpies, would be as absurd as to see them all as hardened rapists. Many were certainly looking for sex and ready to take whatever offered without too searching an examination. The theatre critic James Agate, dining at the Café Royal, was asked by two American airmen at the next table whether he thought they could take a couple of girls to the hotel where they were staying. He asked which hotel it was and was given the name of 'one of the most respectable hostelries in London. I told them they could not possibly do such a thing. "Aw," said airman No. 2, "don't get us wrong. We don't mean a coupla women each." '

It was not only the girls who fleeced the affluent GIs. Taxi drivers found them easy game. Charles Graves heard of one who tendered a 2/6d piece for a 1/- fare. The driver offered 6d in change and, when challenged, replied that he had taken the other 1/- as his tip. Most drivers were no doubt honest but a west London magistrate declared that 'there seems to be a regular ramp going on. One hears a great many complaints about American soldiers being overcharged . . . It is not only dishonest but an unsporting thing to do.' Americans who had been in London before were dismayed by the way standards had dropped. In the past, said one, tradespeople had been too proud of their reputation to do one down: 'That's all gone. They're all on the snatch now.' GIs were the prime target, not merely for a host of small boys hoping for chewing-gum but for every kind of professional beggar. Hugh Docherty, with twenty-seven previous convictions, not only solicited from a passing American but clung to his arm when the unfortunate GI tried to walk away. Docherty was given one month's hard labour. 'This pestering of American soldiers must be stopped,' said the magistrate.

So melancholy a catalogue of grievances and misunderstandings gives a false impression. Most Americans most of the time were content in London; most Londoners most of the time were delighted to have the Americans on their side of the Atlantic. When Charles Graves found the GIs 'well disciplined and causing no trouble', 'very charming', and always sensitive to the problems of their hosts, he was speaking for quite as many Londoners as those who complained of arrogance or off-handedness.

Their kindness was never doubted. Hilda Neal saw a flock of children emerging happily from an American mess where they had just enjoyed a Christmas party. 'The Americans are very generous always and have done a tremendous lot for the children. Some of the Yanks were helping carry them.' When the bombing resumed, Londoners were at first inclined to patronise the newcomers who did not know what it was all about but soon played ungrudging tribute to the zest with which they joined in the rescue work. Zest was, indeed, their most conspicuous quality; London in mid-1942 was a grey and battered city; the Americans imported not merely money but also a determination to extract all the fun they could from spending it. In so doing they exercised an admirably liberalising effect on London society: 'Since the Americans did not understand the subtle gradations of British social class (even the obvious ones),' wrote Tom Pocock, 'they ignored them, so sweeping them aside far more effectively than decades of socialist preaching.' Not everyone found this to their taste, but for most people it was a real, if unexpected relief. Elizabeth Bowen's Louie was not alone in her satisfaction when her newspaper assured her that 'we were becoming less stand-offish; the Americans had been agreeably surprised'. Nor did most GIs conclude that London was populated exclusively by beggars, prostitutes and coldly hostile curmudgeons. 'The conviviality of London in wartime was unimaginable,' said one nineteen-year-old from Oklahoma. 'Everyone was real friendly.'

One American attitude which amused more than irritated Londoners was the assumption that their stay would be a brief one; now that they were here the Germans would quickly be overrun and peace restored. The GIs talked, said Mollie Panter-Downes, 'as though they were somewhat doubtful of being able to give the town a quick once-over before leaving to keep a date with von Rundstedt'. Their presence, and impatience to see some action, lent force to the demand for a second front which would relieve the pressure on the beleaguered Russians. The campaign for this had started long before. As early as July 1941 a crowd of some 50,000 crowded into

Trafalgar Square to hear speeches calling for an immediate landing in France. 'In spite of the present Communist line of "all power to Churchill", the Communist speakers in fact attacked the Government very violently,' recorded George Orwell. Similar meetings were held every two or three months; in April 1942 an orator in Home Guard uniform (in fact a Conservative MP) secured the microphone and asked if it were reasonable for those who did not have the full information to tell the government what to do. 'Yes,' came the resounding reply.

'Strike in the West now!' was soon the graffito most prominently displayed on London's walls. Demand for a second front became a frequent feature of the Home Intelligence Reports; in July 1942 it was said that the possibility of a Japanese attack on Russia was being cited as an added reason for urgent action – 'Rumours are rife that it will begin on 15 August or 15 September.' The main argument was military – without a second front Russia would be driven out of the war – but the active participation of the Communist Party lent a sharp political edge to the campaign. 'We shall see how much longer the reactionary semi-fascist section in high places can delay the inevitable moment when we can go to the help of our ally and settle the European question,' wrote the leftward-leaning Mr Britton to his daughter in America.

Sympathy for Russia and a feeling that she should no longer be left to fight single-handed was the most potent force behind the clamour for a second front, but it had taken some time for the strength of her resistance to the German attack to receive the credit it deserved. 'The BBC has discovered that there is a country called Russia,' wrote Britton sourly in August 1941. 'Until a few weeks ago it was only the wicked Communists who had any knowledge of its existence.' But soon Russian successes became the only cheering feature in a disastrous picture; Vere Hodgson consoled herself for the loss of the *Prince of Wales* and the *Repulse* with the reflection, 'The Russians, bless them, are still pushing the Germans back in the snow.'

Russia was soon the height of fashion. When Turgenev's *A Month in the Country* enjoyed so sensational a success at the St James's Theatre that a second box-office had to be opened, James Agate – with a curious indifference to the play's quality – remarked in his diary, 'the motive is purely political and because the play is from

Russia; if Turgenev had been German, Italian, French or even Swedish, the piece would have been played to empty benches'. James Hodson, visiting a factory making shock absorbers on the outskirts of London, asked the workers how they felt about Russia. He found that most of them would rather have worked for Russia than for Britain. A Mass Observation survey in London early in 1943 showed 95 per cent optimistic about the Russian war and widespread admiration for their determination and efficiency. 'Russia knows how to do it. It's time we took a lesson from them,' said a working-class man of thirty-five. Communism was given the credit for much of their success, though, to the relief of the authorities, this did not translate into support for the British Communist Party. 'I don't see that *they're* helping the war effort,' said another working-class man of forty, 'they only create disturbances when there needn't be.'

The Soviet Union was popular at every level of society: the Red Flag flew over Selfridge's, and Ivan Maisky was elected to the Athenaeum. Half the profits from a dinner-dance organised at Claridge's by the International League for the Protection of Horses were to go to Russia. No caviare was served; 'which was a pity,' observed the *Evening Standard* gossip columnist sourly, 'for I can imagine no greater thrill for a Cossack riding against a swarm of Nazi tanks than the thought that men and women eating caviare in London were thinking about his horse.' But such sentimental benevolence did not preclude a measure of paranoia among the upper and upper-middle classes. 'I wonder whether the noticeable decline in saluting in London is due to the growing popularity of Russia?' speculated Charles Graves. 'I bet it is.' Certain Church of England clerics seemed undecided whether the Bolshevik menace was as bad as or worse than the threat from the Germans – 'As an officer in the Guards put it to me the other day, this is a war of religion,' a Paddington vicar told his flock. The Foreign Office, with support from Scotland Yard, anxiously monitored the activities of the various Communist 'front' organisations and successfully rescued the Boy Scouts from the embrace of the Anglo-Soviet Youth Friendship Committee. The Poles in exile, passionately resentful of the country which had joined in their brutal dismemberment in 1939, did all they could to foment suspicion of Soviet policy.

The government, perplexed by the difficulties of reconciling long-

term scepticism about Communist intentions with the urgent need
to bolster resistance to the Germans, mixed covert discouragement
of Communist activities with ostentatious gestures of friendship to
the Soviet Union. The end of August 1941 saw London's 'Red
Week'; with a Soviet play produced by Peter Ustinov at the Vaudeville; Tyrone Guthrie's production of *The Cherry Orchard*; the International Ballet mounting a Tchaikovsky season; and a film of daily
life under the Soviet regime. The hammer and sickle flew over the
Suffolk Galleries, where an exhibition of photographs opened by
Mme Maisky displayed a galaxy of contented cows, still more contented peasants, patriarchal priests and the more grandiloquent
examples of contemporary Russian architecture. One section was
devoted to German atrocities and was judged by 80 per cent of
women visitors to be the most interesting part of the show. 'There
ought to be more really nasty ones,' said one, 'we shouldn't show
the sweet side of war, not to people in this country.' One elderly
lady stood in front of a particularly celebrated picture of eight
Russians dangling from scaffolds. 'She stood gazing at it with an
expression of extreme distress for more than a minute. Suddenly
her face cleared. "No, it's all right, it *is* eight," she said.'

Lady Cripps represented the British government at the opening
of the exhibition; her husband Sir Stafford, soon to return from a
triumphant tour as British ambassador in Moscow, was principal
speaker a year or so later at a demonstration at the Empress Hall,
Earls Court. John Orr spoke for the scientists, Olivier for the actors,
L. A. G. Strong for literature: 'At every mention of the Second
Front the audience applauded like baying wolves,' reported James
Hodson. But all such manifestations were dwarfed by the great Red
Army Rally at the Albert Hall in February 1943. This was another
of Basil Dean's extravaganzas, with fanfares specially composed by
Bax and Walton, an ode by Louis MacNeice set to music by Alan
Rawsthorne, declamations by Ralph Richardson and Sybil
Thorndike, and John Gielgud as the voice of Moscow Radio extol-
ling the heroic defence of Stalingrad. Endless detachments of
workers filed through the hall and Anthony Eden, for the British
government, called on the audience to stand 'and pay a silent tribute
to the glorious dead of the Red Army'.

The object of this exercise was to demonstrate the reality of British
support for Russia. Home Information Reports suggested that some

people scented hypocrisy but most felt it had helped 'to dissipate a suspicion that the alliance between Britain and Russia was artificial'.

In October of the same year thousands of Londoners walked past the Sword of Stalingrad as it lay in state before being shipped to Russia as Britain's tribute to those who had won that crucial victory. The civilians were 'shabby and grubby', wrote Evelyn Waugh. 'Bombing had ceased for the time but the livery of the air-raid shelter remained the national dress.' Dingy decay was the hallmark of London in 1942 and 1943. Even in a rich and relatively undamaged area like Kensington Palace Gardens windows were boarded up, fences broken down, lawns grown rank and wild. The only spruce house was the Soviet Embassy. London's clubs were as afflicted as the homes of the aristocracy and upper-middle classes. Harold Nicolson found that Brooks's had preserved its atmosphere but that the Travellers' had become 'a battered caravanserai, in which the scum of the lower London clubs are served inadequately by scared Lithuanian waitresses'. In winter it was bitterly cold; the windows and curtains failed to keep out the north-east wind.

Elsewhere, there was still a semblance of gracious living. At the end of 1941 Lady Victor Paget gave a party for the American actress Bea Lillie. 'Noel Coward sang "London Pride" in a manner which I found all the more revolting for being sincere,' wrote Charles Ritchie. 'There was a gathering of pansies and theatrical blondes . . . General atmosphere: a *réchauffée* of a gay twenties party with everyone looking that much older.' But as houses grew more bedraggled, food and drink more difficult to obtain, such manifestations became increasingly rare, even unfashionable. Only the public places of entertainment – dance halls, nightclubs, restaurants, pubs – remained as thronged as ever. In 1943 the ballroom at the Regal was still taking £500 a week; the manager remarked how pathetic it was to see so many attractive women, 'whose husbands are apparently in the Middle East and who do not know how to pass the time until their return'. The cream of the establishment still assembled once or twice a year at Buckingham Palace for an afternoon party, but they were cut-price occasions with little if anything in the way of refreshments. Hugh Dalton marvelled to see 'hundreds of male eminences, with their mostly not-very-eminent-looking wives, tramp in Indian file past the King, Queen and the two Princesses', who, he observed, 'both look quite nice little girls'.

Though private entertaining was becoming a rarity, there was no shortage of money, much of it in the hands of people who would not have had it before the war. London was crowded, wrote Hilda Neal in January 1943. The capital had changed greatly, 'all classes and conditions now enter places which formerly would have been considered unsuitable and might even have presented closed portals to them. Expenses *have* to be met by the establishment, and the possession of money gives confidence to the possessor.' The Savoy was said to be filled with rich people from the North – 'Husbands earning good money and wives coming to spend it in London'. By the end of 1942, thanks to bombing and requisitioning, there were 12,000 fewer rooms in hotels and boarding houses than before the war. A quarter of those available were occupied by permanent residents – many of them elderly – whose homes had been destroyed or closed for the duration. At one time some hotel managers contemplated asking these encumbrances to leave, and there was a rule that no room should have more than one light and no double room be occupied singly. If they had been driven out they would have found it almost impossible to rent accommodation; by mid-1942 virtually every furnished flat was full and most blocks had a waiting list. The management of one big block of flats, which had been reduced to six tenants during the blitz, received more than forty applications when a single flat fell vacant late in 1942. The situation was no easier in the suburbs. Kathleen Bliss, who had given up her restaurant in the country to work in a factory in Croydon, tried and failed at twelve addresses and ended up sharing a tiny upstairs room with no bedding supplied and no hope of domestic help.

Some of the money being squandered at the Savoy had been made on the black market. Though this was much gossiped about, it does not seem to have been a really serious problem in London. Commander Reginald Smith of K Division of the police, which covered most of the East End, admitted that there was some thieving in the docks, 'Carcases of meat and crates of tinned fruit disappeared . . . But such petty thefts have always been a fact of life in the docks, and the war didn't particularly change any habits.' Some took pride in meticulously sticking to the rules. Mary Davies, a civil servant, went to dinner with one of her richer friends and was confronted with an off-the-ration haggis. 'My sort of level wouldn't have done any black marketing in clothing coupons or anything like that,' she recorded. 'We would have considered that not really the done thing.'

Done thing or not, it happened sufficiently often for Lord Woolton, in mid-1941, to denounce 'those people who meet at 4.30 in the morning to evade the law' – a reference to racketeers who would bring up eggs, poultry or other foodstuffs from the country and sell them for two or three times the controlled price. On the whole people sympathised with Woolton and might even have agreed with the wrathful Labour MP who exclaimed that his 'way of dealing with such gentry would be to put them up against a wall and shoot them'. But there was a grey area in which systematic black marketing shaded into helping out a friend. Poppet John had a charwoman who worked in a canteen where unlimited butter was available; sometimes she would bring along a few ounces. The Revd J. G. Markham mentioned to one of the barrow boys in his Walworth parish that he was fond of prunes; a box appeared a few days later. In principle he deplored the traffic, but he did not take it very seriously and would certainly never have contemplated denouncing an offender to the police. He would have disapproved of the *agent provocateur* who proffered loose coupons at Swan and Edgar's and was supplied with margarine. The store was fined for not insisting on the would-be purchaser producing a ration book but, as the magistrate pointed out, if the loose coupons had been sent through the post, the transaction would have been perfectly legitimate.

'The Black Market is still rampant, and every day there are prosecution cases, mainly against Jews,' wrote Hilda Neal, a middle-class lady of right-wing views from South Kensington, but probably no more anti-semitic than her working-class equivalents across the river. Some Jews were so concerned by the prevalence of these views that they commissioned a survey from the Royal Statistical Society. In the first five-week period studied, only three out of fifty convicted black marketeers were Jews. Given the heavy concentration of Jews in retail trade, a higher figure would not have been disproportionate. There is no more reason to believe that the black market was run by and for Jews than that Jews were cowards who fled to the country or skulked perpetually in the shelters.

*

It is sometimes claimed that London during the Second World War was peculiarly free from crime. Certainly there was less crime in 1940 than in 1939 and the figures fell again in 1941. Theft from or of motor cars, unsurprisingly, dropped to almost nothing; more impressively, bicycle thefts fell as well. Burglary became less usual, particularly by night – it seems that the blackout deterred criminals, who had no way of deciding whether or not a house was empty. Among the more common crimes only shop-breaking flourished, especially where food and drink were involved. But the improvement did not last. In 1938 ten out of every thousand Londoners were committing crimes, by 1944 the figure was fifteen. Partly, no doubt, this was because the temptation was greater. Items hardly worth stealing before the war were now much sought after. Staff had been cut and purchases could not be wrapped, so it was easier to walk out of shops without paying. Shortly before Christmas 1943 there was a particularly fierce wave of pillage from London toy shops; children were believed to be responsible. 'It is far worse than last year,' moaned one shop manager, 'we are losing big money.'

Scotland Yard were investigating four murders in different parts of London, complained Hilda Neal at the end of 1941. 'Terrible lot of crime coming to light. The prisons are full, and many get off with a fine or a caution, which does not help matters.' In fact, there were fewer murders than before the war but minor violence became commonplace. Towards the end of 1941 the *Evening Standard* reported an epidemic of beatings-up during the blackout in the West End; the following year the journalists themselves seemed to have become a favoured target as they left their offices in the middle of the night. 'The blackout makes for some petty devilry,' wrote James Hodson. 'The papers report the prosecution of two negro soldiers working in conjunction with a decoy prostitute. The unsuspecting fellow is taken along a lonely street and thereupon "bashed" by the soldiers.'

This was violence with a view to robbery; the increase in casual violence was still more striking, perhaps unsurprisingly when so many able-bodied men had been encouraged to develop the arts of unarmed combat. Raymond Savage, a literary agent, bumped into two soldiers outside St James's, Piccadilly, apologised, and was knocked unconscious by a blow between the eyes. Mr Clemence, an American millionaire, emerged from the Grosvenor Hotel and was flattened by a drunk Canadian soldier. When he got up and prepared to defend himself, he was set on by three Americans, knocked down again and violently kicked. He staggered back into the hotel with blood pouring down his face and called for a doctor. 'Get out! We don't want your sort here,' said the hall porter, pushing him violently back into the street. The unfortunate Mr Clemence tottered off, fell into a basement, passed out and ended up in hospital. Such incidents seem to have been concentrated around the West End and confined to male victims. With striking unanimity, women who had reason to walk the streets of London by night insist that they were never attacked or even felt in danger. The church too, it seemed, was privileged. Markham was constantly out at night: 'I was never attacked, never threatened, not even sworn at during those four years, although I had to chase would-be looters, discipline wardens, and was "a bloody parson", possibly, in the minds of many.'

Towards the end of the war nearly one-tenth of London's crime was attributed to deserters. Even by 1942 the number of rootless, homeless men who roamed the streets without proper papers was causing concern. A spectacular raid on a bank in Leicester Square, in which three Canadian deserters pulled guns and held up the cashiers, led to a major police operation in the West End, in which 1400 people had their papers examined and more than 100 arrests were made. A swoop on a dog-track at Walthamstow produced equally rewarding results. For a while the number of violent crimes diminished, but the problem could not be indefinitely contained; there were just too many men – Americans, Canadians, Australians and of a dozen other nationalities as well as British – existing outside the law and dependent for their living on what they could steal or extort from the women they had made their victims. Intoxication added an extra dimension to this turbulent scene. In May 1943 an explosion blew out several windows in Dean Street, Soho. Passers-by looked in dismay towards the skies, then discovered that a French commando had drunk too much, got bored, and thought it would be interesting to let off a small but potentially lethal bomb.

As always, insignificant incidents took up as much police time as serious crimes. In December 1942 an eccentric with a grudge against society prowled the streets of south London spraying ink over the clothes of anyone who came near him. He proved impossible to track down, as did the vandals who destroyed 365 out of 400 young shrubs in Kensington Gardens in a mere three months. Children, surmised the park-keeper, 'They take pleasure in breaking things up. They have even torn deck-chairs apart to make goal posts.' But some of the work the police made for themselves. It can hardly have been necessary to arrest Lord Lauderdale for committing an alleged impropriety in Leicester Square. He claimed that he had been importuned by a twenty-nine-year-old kitchen hand called Robert Willson and had spoken to him in mere politeness. Lady Lauderdale testified to the regularity of their married life and General Ian Hay Beith said that he had never known a more normal person: the case was dismissed.

Some at least of the ill-gotten profits from the black market and other crimes were redistributed at the illegal gambling clubs which abounded in the West End. Since the law provided only that premises should not be used *habitually* for gaming, it was possible for the organisers to shift their base from flat to flat, passing the word around each morning as to where the evening's action would be. The biggest club was run by an under-employed bookmaker. Chemin-de-fer was most often played and stakes were high; at his three tables, the biggest was £100 a game, the smallest £20. With such a turnover it was possible to buy the most lavish delicacies on the black market to tempt the more hedonistic punter.

Early in 1942 Herbert Morrison said in the House of Commons that there were often fifty or more such 'objectionable, pernicious and parasitical' parties taking place every day. Three months later a new Defence Regulation gave the police increased powers and provided that anyone present at such a gathering, whether organising, participating or merely watching, would be guilty of an offence. The clubs were put out of business overnight.

In such an atmosphere those disposed to assume the existence of moral corruption found it all about them. George Beardmore was sent to look for a defaulting rate-payer in Golders Green. He found that the delinquent had deserted his wife and was living with a typist, who had just been dismissed from her job on grounds of promiscuity. The man had recently spent two weeks in prison for non-payment of maintenance. 'None of this would have arisen in pre-war days,' mused Beardmore, 'when neither of them would have dared risk losing a well paid job.'

In the spring of 1942 the Moral Welfare Committee of the Uxbridge deanery deplored the increasing number of illegitimate births. At the Divorce Division of the London High Court, 1841 cases had been brought in the Easter term of 1939. In 1940 the number dropped to 1411 and in 1941, with the blitz raging, to a mere 802. In 1942 it almost doubled to 1565, rose again in 1943 to 2273 and in 1944 to 2923.

The increase was considerable but hardly dramatic. The claim that lower moral standards prevailed in wartime is not proven. If married couples are apart, there is likely to be more adultery. If there is a blackout there is likely to be more mugging. If food is short, people are likely to make a profit by peddling it illicitly. If a lot of money is washing around and there is little on which to spend it, gambling will thrive. Considering the opportunities open to them, Londoners have the right to be astonished at their moderation. There was a lot of crime, more perhaps than those who nursed the version of a uniquely virtuous London would have cared to acknowledge, but even by the standards of the day, let alone the standards of the 1990s, it cannot properly be described as a crime wave. At the most it was a crime ripple.

13

'The lightless middle of the tunnel'

'IT WAS NOW, when you no longer saw, heard, smelled war, that a deadening acclimatisation to it began to set in. The first generation of ruins, cleaned up, shored up, began to weather . . . It was from this new, insidious, echoless propriety of ruins that you breathed in all that was most malarial . . . This was the lightless middle of the tunnel.'

Elizabeth Bowen evoked with characteristic precision the malaise that afflicted London in 1943. After Alamein there were few who believed the Allies could lose the war, but there were many who did not dare predict how or when it would be won. A brief flurry of exultation followed the news of victory.

'London was a city of smiling people who walked as though they were stepping out to the music of a Guards' band,' Mollie Panter-Downes told her American readers. 'Next stop Benghazi!' called the cheerful bus-conductor as he tinkled his bell to herald departure. But even in the moment of triumph there were reminders of the price that had been paid. The church bells, reserved since 1940 for use as a warning of invasion, were authorised to ring out in celebration, but when it came to the point less than half the churches in London rang the victory peal. In the City, only St Botolph's, Bishopgate, was fully up to the task; St Michael's, Cornhill, had bells but no ropes; even in St Paul's the master of the Whitechapel Bell Foundry advised extreme caution since no one knew what damage had been done to the bell tower and to set several tons of metal swinging might have provoked disaster.

'Apart from the uniforms you see in the streets, London might be at peace with the world,' wrote Charles Graves in July 1943, but though nearly all the serious fighting took place in Russia, North Africa or Burma, enough happened in London to remind its inhabitants that the war had not completely passed them by. The Germans were still capable of launching small but damaging raids and did so from time to time, if only to encourage their own people. Frequently such attacks were mounted in retaliation for an Allied raid on Germany, most often for an attack on Berlin. So much was this accepted as the norm that, after a raid on Berlin in November 1942, the steel bunks in the tube stations were more fully occupied than for several weeks. On that occasion the Germans did not come; the popular view was that this was connected with a visit by Mrs Roosevelt to London: 'The President must know that there won't be no raids, or else 'e wouldn't never 'ave let 'er come,' pronounced one matron. Mrs Roosevelt could not stay for ever. In January 1943 there was a heavy raid on Berlin. 'The Nazis are pretty sure to launch a reprisal raid,' noted Anthony Weymouth, and this time the Cassandras were proved right. Two raids on London killed more than one hundred people. Shoreditch, Deptford and St John's Wood were worst hit, Marylebone station was closed and the tube from Hampstead put out of action.

The government half expected that tit-for-tat raids of this kind would lead to a public outcry. Their fears were soon dispelled. Only a tiny minority of Londoners contended – at any rate aloud – that it was foolish to provoke retaliation by bombing the German capital; the great majority, said the Home Intelligence Reports, thought the raids on Berlin should be bigger, better and more frequent. In July 1943 working-class opinion was said to be particularly jubilant over recent raids on Rome. They 'have no time for the people who want to spare Rome', said the Intelligence Report. Their reaction was, 'Take a look at London!'

By May and June the pattern had become familiar, two or three times a week a handful of German bombers – ten or twelve perhaps, a score at most – would attack one or two areas, kill a few people and run for home. At first people feared this might be the preamble to something more serious but they soon adapted to the new threat. For the most part they resorted to ear plugs and a retreat under the blankets rather than the shelters. The number of incidents dwindled in August and September, then picked up again in October. The raids were 'disagreeable because of the suddenness of their violence, which broke up sleep', wrote John Lehmann, 'but considered from the dramatic-aesthetic point of view, they were rather beautiful, and the actual damage they did was comparatively small'.

The dramatic-aesthetic point of view was that adopted by many

Londoners, even though they would not have put it quite like that. In a typical October raid, Vere Hodgson felt temporarily discomfited by the uproar, then 'donned my tin hat – courage returned and I joined the sightseers. All London was doing the same . . . Felt our conduct in being out in the road was most reprehensible, but I did enjoy it.' So, almost incredibly, did many others. Harold Nicolson noted that nobody paid the slightest attention when the warning sounded; indeed, 'It is a strange psychological fact that the sound of the siren gives one a sense almost of pleasure.' Was it because people knew there was little real danger and, anyway, far worse was being done to the Germans? 'If and when raids begin again in earnest, then we shall have feelings of dread and fear.' The authorities were somewhat put out by this insouciance. The public treated the raid of 7 October as if it were a football match, complained an official report, 'advice being shouted to both searchlights and gun crews'. To maintain a dignified calm was admirable; to roam the streets, obstruct the civil defence and court death or injury was irresponsible. Sir Wyndham Deedes, Chief Warden of Bethnal Green, denounced the public's 'stupid negligence'. They were 'helping Hitler by offering themselves as voluntary casualties'.

Once again, anti-aircraft fire was more likely than Hitler to cause casualties. The always serious risk from shrapnel or unexploded shells was redoubled when rocket guns were introduced early in 1943. These added greatly to the hubbub and contributed a new and particularly lethal form of shrapnel formed by jagged fragments from the steel tubes which had held the rocket fuel. Home Intelligence Reports for January 1943 stated that everyone was 'profoundly impressed by the barrage' and had 'great confidence in the defence'. The guns may have made things more hazardous for the German raiders but, in the first serious raid of 1943, six people were killed by shell splinters; an anti-aircraft shell exploded in Enfield, wounding four; a shell in Gipsy Hill severely injured a sailor on leave, while another killed two civilians; one man was killed and two injured when a shell crashed through a wall in Battersea; two more died the same way in Tooting; and a shell fell in the garden of Buckingham Palace, doing irreparable damage to a plot of Brussels sprouts. Things did not improve. During a typical raid in October four shells exploded in Camberwell, killing one and injuring many;

a shell killed a step-father and his two children in Sydenham, and to add to the toll wreaked by the defences, an exploding barrage balloon fell on the Dover Castle pub in Westminster Bridge Road, Lambeth, killing two firemen. The cable from the balloon trailed across the railway tracks near Waterloo and stopped all trains for an hour.

As well as these nocturnal visits the Germans developed a technique of daylight raids in which a handful of light bombers would dart in, attack almost at random and run for home. Little material damage was done and losses among German aircraft were often high, but the inconvenience caused was great and casualties were sometimes serious. On 19 May 1943 a *Te Deum* at St Paul's to commemorate the victories in North Africa – at which virtually every dignitary in London was to be present – had to be postponed at the last minute because Lord Londonderry's butler had thoughtlessly sent a telegram to his employer giving the time and place of the service. The risk that the Germans would mount a strike at this tempting target was thought too great.

Such raids were felt to be worse – or, for some people, better – than the night-time variety, because they seemed more personal; the German pilot appeared to be seeking out individual houses, even individual victims. Joan Veazey, in Kennington, heard a low-flying aircraft and rushed to get her baby out of its pram. 'The straps got tangled and the plane started to fly around. To my horror, I looked up at the black Nazi markings on the wings of the plane and saw the pilot with his leather flying helmet. He was grinning. Suddenly, as I pulled the pram out of the mud ruts, he started shooting his gun at the house, a bullet hit the kitchen wall and he then turned and shot all down the road, where the little children were coming out of school.' Perhaps the German pilot really was grinning and shooting at schoolchildren; anyway Mrs Veazey was convinced he was; the enemy, in her eyes, was wilfully selecting a particular target and aiming to kill – the children, her baby.

Certainly schools seem to have been a favoured target. In mid-March, twenty-four planes came inland; five or six reached London; three trains and a trolley-bus were machine-gunned; two schools were bombed and seriously damaged – though fortunately before the children had arrived. They were less lucky on 20 January. To allow calibration work on the gun-laying radars, the barrage balloons were not flying over south-east London, permitting a Focke Wulf fighter-bomber to sneak past the defences. First it machine-gunned Cooper's Lane School in Woolwich. No one was hurt, but when the plane flew on to the Sandhurst Road School in Catford, Lewisham, it dropped a 1100lb bomb which passed through the side of the building and penetrated the ground floor. It exploded in just over a minute, which allowed some children to scramble through the ground-floor windows but offered no chance to the seventy-five or so eating their lunch in the dining room. Thirty-eight children and six teachers were killed or died in the next few days; many more were seriously injured. A grisly photograph showed the children's bodies covered by tarpaulins outside the school; the authorities not unreasonably concluded that this would be damaging to morale and forbade its appearance.

'Fiendish onslaught of a barbarous foe,' the *Kentish Mercury* described the attack, and Captain Schumann, who had led the raid, did nothing to appease the indignation of Londoners by boasting in a broadcast from Paris that 'the bombs fell just where we wanted them to'. Parents of the surviving children were alarmed and horrified, but when the school reconvened a few days later only a few had decided to take advantage of the official evacuation scheme. 'I think the reason for this is that the mothers feel they cannot bear to let them out of their sight,' said Elizabeth Bear, a domestic science mistress.

There was much criticism of the failure to give warning that the raid was imminent. Archibald Sinclair, Secretary of State for Air, argued in response that one had to choose between sounding the alarm whenever there was the slightest risk of attack – with all the attendant irritation, disruption, and eventually public indifference – or leaving Fighter Command discretion to assess the risk and give the warning only if attack seemed imminent. Parliament had favoured the latter course, which meant that there was a small but unavoidable chance of unheralded disaster. The Sandhurst Road School was one of the worst of these; another came one evening in Putney when a single bomber dropped six bombs and hit the Cinderella dancing club, a milk bar and a crowd at a bus-stop. Eighty-seven people were killed, 200 seriously injured; the heavy dust on the victims' faces made them so hard to identify that the WVS, who set up an incident enquiry point on the spot, had to make one

Putney resident come back three times before they could tell him that two of his sons were dead and one disabled for life.

The most macabre incident of 1943 was, however, only indirectly due to enemy action. It happened in Bethnal Green, on the night of 3 March, during a minor raid in which no bombs fell in the neighbourhood. People were filing decorously into the tube station when a salvo of rockets was fired from nearby Victoria Park. The official enquiry established that there had been no real panic but people outside undoubtedly pressed forward so as to get under cover. A woman near the top of the steep staircase, with a child or bundle in her arms, slipped and fell on to the people in front of her, who in turn lost their balance. The staircase was 'converted from a corridor into a charnel house in from ten to fifteen seconds', said Laurence Dunne, the magistrate who conducted an enquiry into the affair; 178 people were crushed to death or suffocated. 'The disaster was caused by a number of people losing their self-control at a particularly unfortunate place and time,' said Dunne. No individual was to blame, no one had behaved notably badly, not much could be done to stop it happening again except by the use of common-sense and restraint.

This prosaic explanation displeased those who felt that so sensational a happening deserved a more dramatic cause. It was the work of the Fifth Column, said some; a German agent had called out that an oil-bomb was falling by parachute on the street outside. More popular and more mischievous was the theory that it was all the fault of the Jews – again. 'Those East End Jews, they were so terrified, they stampeded,' was the story told all over London except (according to the Home Intelligence Report) in Bethnal Green itself, where they knew the truth. A Mass Observer recorded a middle-aged woman grumbling, 'They lost their nerve. *You* know, like they did in the blitz. They 'aven't got steadiness like wot we 'ave.' Though a poll showed that the percentage of Londoners favourable to Jews had remained steady at 29 per cent, the number of those hostile nearly doubled, to 27 per cent. There was no evidence to suggest that the Jews had been responsible for the disaster, but once spread abroad the story was difficult to silence; even a statement by the Home Secretary in the House of Commons failed to quash it.

Such a catalogue of bloody incidents conveys an impression of

London under constant attack. In fact few people found themselves in immediate danger and this, following eighteen months of relative tranquillity since June 1941, relegated the threat from the air to a distant prospect. Inevitably the local authorities decided to economise by cutting the money spent on ARP. In September 1943 it was announced that the London civil defence bill would be reduced from £14.3m to £8.3m. Largely this was accounted for by reductions in the war debris service, which had tidied itself out of a job, but there were also cuts in the number of ambulances and rest centres. Half the ARP posts in Lewisham were closed between 6 a.m. and 8 p.m. and similar savings were made in Croydon. Morale in the Wimbledon ARP services fell so low that the chief warden considered asking the RAF to bomb the common so as to restore his personnel's flagging spirits. It seems unlikely that the military authorities would have welcomed the idea; the common harboured an ammunition dump by the Queensmere; an army camp near the windmill; a practice ground for Bren gun carriers among the gravel pits and an assault course by Rushmere pond.

The Home Office was dismayed by this wholesale scrapping of the weapons of civil defence. The government knew how quickly the Luftwaffe could address itself to British targets; it knew too how close the Germans were to developing a new generation of unmanned raiders. Against the popular tide, Herbert Morrison in August 1943 issued new fire-watching orders, increasing the responsibility of office workers for safeguarding their premises (though women were exempted from serving in any building 'infested with rats and mice' – a threat evidently considered more dreadful than any mere bomb). In most parts of London, civil defence training was continued vigorously. John Geer enlisted as a messenger. On his first appearance he found himself labelled 'coal-gas poisoning, not breathing' and deposited at the bottom of a derelict house. This was then collapsed around him so that the 'rescuers' could practise digging him out. 'Not a very nice experience,' he observed mildly.

One expense particularly resented by local councils was keeping open shelters which seemed to serve no useful purpose. Supervising them was expensive, leaving them unattended even worse; by the end of January 1943 pilfering from shelters had cost Bermondsey £10,000; 2000 light bulbs had been stolen or smashed in a single night. The council's response was to lock the shelters by day, which caused an uproar when the first daylight raid affected the area. Ernest Brown, Minister of Health, assured the Commons that there had been no case of a shelter remaining locked when the public needed to get in; a condition of keeping them shut was that there should be provision for immediate reopening.

Many Londoners could have cited cases of delays which seemed unacceptably long, but a majority of rate-payers would nevertheless probably have sided with the council. Surface shelters had never inspired great confidence. Many had been shoddily built and were already showing signs of decay, with mortar crumbling in the walls. Orwell wrote one of his articles for *Tribune* to a background noise of drills removing defective bricks from a visibly degenerating wall. He questioned whether such shelters had ever been taken seriously, 'In my part of London there has never been any question of using them; in fact they are kept permanently locked lest they should be used for "improper purposes." ' Public scepticism was increased by cases like that in Hammersmith in November 1943 when the roof of a shelter collapsed and was found to be only three inches thick instead of five and built without the specified crossways reinforcing rods. On inspection, 106 shelters were found to be similarly defective. Two men were charged with defrauding the council of £25,000. The spasmodic raids of 1943 were not enough to drive the public from their homes back into these whited sepulchres.

The tubes were different. By the end of 1941 the number of people sheltering every night in London's Underground had dropped to 16,000; a tenth of what it had been at its peak. A year later the figure was still lower, at about 6000. But there it stuck. In April 1943 Mass Observation conducted an enquiry into this phenomenon. Families had taken root far below the surface, some children of nearly three had never spent a night in their homes. The answer partly was that they had no homes to go to; these shelterers were the bombed-out and dispossessed. But this was not the whole story; almost all of them could have been evacuated or rehoused if they had really wanted it. Mass Observation concluded that a new pattern of living had evolved in London's Underground, new relationships been forged, new laws and rituals established. Some people who had been at odds with society all their lives had for the first time found company and acceptance in the tubes. It was only with reluctance that they would abandon their new-found comradeship.

The war was, indeed, remarkable for building new communities and the way it propelled even the most misanthropic into fresh and – to the surprise of the participants – often congenial relationships. Fire-watching, ARP, the Home Guard – all fostered a sense of belonging, of common purpose, of group loyalty. The Fireman's Art Club, which held its first meeting in Dr Johnson's house in Gough Square in September 1943, enabled people who had previously enjoyed only a tenuous relationship with the arts to listen to Fireman Stephen Spender read his poetry or four professional musicians attached to the station at Hyde Park Corner play a Mozart quartet. Only a small minority of firemen wished to indulge in such pursuits, but they were more likely to do so because the poetry and the music were produced by and for fellow professionals. The traditionally demarcated barriers between man and woman were also shaken if not broken down by shared experiences in new fields. In the tube shelters a woman, whose sphere of influence had until then been confined to the home, could find herself exercising informal authority over total strangers. In the ARP or the fire services, they increasingly shared the risks, the burden and the glory. The price they paid was the acceptance of male rules and inhibitions. In March 1943 the firewomen of No. 35 London area, which included parts of the City, Holborn and the West End, were ordered to remove any brightly coloured nail varnish, adopt a service hairstyle and wear no jewellery except wedding, engagement or signet rings. Women should 'take a pride in their uniform', said Commander K. N. Hoare severely.

Public indifference to air-raids encouraged the authorities to drag their feet on the provision of new and improved shelters. At one point it had been proposed to replace many of the inadequate surface shelters with a superior model designed by Sir Giles Gilbert Scott, the architect of Liverpool Cathedral. Two were actually built in Strutton Ground in Westminster. But they proved expensive and, even though it was claimed that the roof could not be blasted off (one of many flaws in the first-generation shelter), it did not seem that they would provide much extra protection. The programme languished. Progress on the new deep super-shelters was steadier though unspectacular. Work on two of the original ten was abandoned: the one near St Paul's, because it was feared it might destabilise the cathedral; the one at the Oval because it became water-logged as soon as dug. But by September 1942 the first two were ready, 'glistening with white paint and daylight effect lighting', reported an awe-struck *Evening Standard*, and boasting air-conditioning, sick bays, restaurants and first-class sanitation. As if they were presents not to be opened until Christmas, the authorities firmly locked them and said they would be available only in an emergency. Probably they would have remained largely empty in any case; the public mood was against shelters. In September 1943 a man was fined 10/- for dismantling his Anderson. He pleaded that his wife had refused to use it. 'That's got nothing to do with it!' retorted the magistrate. 'You had no business to touch it. Let it be understood by all that there is to be no tampering with any air-raid precautions whatsoever.'

The authorities did some tampering themselves, though on a modest scale. Early in 1943 it was ruled that lights in railway cars without corridors could be left on when a train was standing at a station. Traffic lights came next. First it was agreed that their faces could be exposed fully by day; then their visibility by night was improved. They have ceased to have 'that wretched little hot-cross-bun effect', wrote Charles Graves; now they were half moon, almost like peacetime. As winter approached demands were heard for further relaxation of the restrictions on street lighting and several ministers were said to be in favour. Herbert Morrison did not agree, but grudgingly allowed pedestrians to carry undimmed torches; something they were doing increasingly in any case.

The London which the torches illuminated looked very different from the city of two years before. Elmer Davis, chief of the US Office of War Information, who had last been in England in 1941, noted with approval that 'London is very well manicured and made up indeed'. He must have had some pretty horrific recollections of the blitz. The capital had certainly been tidied up, rubble cleared away, the ruins sometimes turned to good use. In the City a particularly beautiful garden had been made in Gresham Street at the corner of Foster Lane. It was known locally as the Garden of Paradise and was tended by the verger of the demolished St Anne and St Agnes nearby. Another garden had been made within the ruined St Swithun's; a notice posted by the vicar read, 'This is still Holy Ground. I do not think that God will mind if you smoke, but if you leave litter, there is no one to clean it up.' But though there were such oases, closer inspection usually revealed shabbiness and decay. The grass in Leicester Square had been worn away and the only colour came from the variegated berets of the passing soldiers – green for the commandos, maroon for the airborne troops, dark blue for the Poles. 'Regency London is becoming almost ruinous,' wrote Orwell of the terraces around Regent's Park, 'the beautiful but flimsy houses, no longer lived in, are falling to pieces with damp and neglect.'

There were flowers in plenty, but blooming more often in wild profusion than in the well-ordered Garden of Paradise. The Keeper of Botany at the Natural History Museum inspected a bombed site on the corner of Bond and Bruton Street and found four types of willow and a poplar as well as ladyfern, sow-whistle, Canadian fleabane, clover, yarrow, plantains, Oxford ragwort, coltsfoot and funaria. In Thurloe Square there was a Peruvian plant which it was supposed had been blown in from Kew. The ruins around St Paul's were covered by London rocket, a rarity before the blitz. Most common of all was the rosebay willow herb, whose tall flower with purplish petals was to be seen on almost every bombed site. Miss E. M. Alty, who went to work each day in the City, stood with a friend, chewing a piece of grass and contemplating the tassels of buddleia visited by red admiral and peacock butterflies. 'I removed my grass stem to remark in a loamy accent William Barnes might have warmed to, "Crops be riisin". A short and weighty pause, and then without turning her head she answered "Aar".'

The London bus Mr Davis saw on his return was still far from manicured and made-up. Buses borrowed from the provinces struck a jarring note, and even where the original red buses survived they were usually reduced to a muddy brown. Rescue was at hand, however; late in 1943 a supply of the well-known pillar-box red became available and buses began to appear in their familiar livery. Most Londoners would probably have settled for muddy brown and more of them; buses ran rarely and stopped altogether after 10.30 p.m. Those who depended on taxis were often disappointed; only half the pre-war fleet of 8000 was running and these were only allowed to venture five miles outside their licence area. Taxi drivers who could more pleasantly use up their limited petrol allowance by day rarely ventured out at night and those who did were choosy about where they were prepared to go.

Douglas Jay, then a civil servant, believed the main reason for the shortage of transport was that more people wished to travel: 'People have been given a lot of money and this is headed off, by rationing etc, from many normal vents, and thus flows in increased volume towards the unblocked vents, including travel.' This was most true of trains which, particularly at holiday times, were assailed by crowds standing eight to ten deep on the platform. One August bank holiday train left Paddington with more than eighty people in the guard's van. In the case of taxis, however, the sharp fall in numbers was the most obvious factor. Many travellers resorted to bicycles. Members of the Savile Club were celebrated for their cycling prowess. The actor Ralph Richardson was much envied for having a dynamo mounted on the hub of his front wheel which generated its own electric light as he pedalled along.

The absence of traffic, together with the rarity of raids, should have given Londoners some precious silence, but from all over the capital came complaints of a mystery noise which seemed to emanate from the same area but was curiously hard to track down. 'Not only is there almost incessant "hum",' complained Gwladys Cox, 'but a "shaking", for want of a better word; at night my very bed vibrates and I feel intermittent stiff "jerks".' One indignant victim pursued the matter with the police, the Home Office and the Ministry of Health, but got no satisfaction. Eventually he decided he had identified the culprit, a factory in west London, but was met with a bland assertion that, though they *might* be making a little too much noise, this was unavoidable in view of the essential war work on which they were engaged. So far as it could be established, the testing of aero-engines was responsible.

Some parts of the capital were so damaged as to be almost uninhabitable, yet even here a few determined individuals clung on. In what had once been Catherine, Sarah, Alice and Charlotte Streets in the East End only two houses remained in any sort of order: No. 38 Catherine Street where Mrs Barton lived with her husband, and No. 36 where Mr Downey lived alone. By day, when the men went to work, Mrs Barton was deserted except by the soldiers who used the area for training in street-fighting. When the bullets were flying, she would retreat to a room at the back – one of the only two in the house which were weatherproof; if she had to go out during firing, she would creep through a hole in the garden fence. A reporter asked her if she didn't get lonely. 'Just once in a way I get a visit from women who lived somewhere round about here,' she replied. 'It's all so changed that I have to direct them and very often they cry. I'm fifty-two and I've been here all my life. I never thought I should live alone in Catherine Street. I miss the children with their noisy games. But there'll be victory flags flying from No. 38 one day – they're all ready and you can tell them that.'

For company Mrs Barton had a cat called Minnie, a goat called Jimmy, Mr Downing's greyhound and the ubiquitous rats. In 1941, when people's minds were on other, more pressing threats, a survey had shown 'an exceptionally low level of interest' in the rising rat population, but by late 1943 the millions of rats living in London's 3000 miles of sewers were a cause for serious concern. War was declared, and an experimental campaign with gas and poison killed 6000 rats in Kensington in forty-eight hours. Encouraged by this success, the authorities mobilised 300 teams of three men each who laid sixty tons of sausage meat poisoned with two tons of zinc phosphate. By 20 December it was believed a million rats had perished. A month's truce was declared, then the battle was resumed with stale bread painted with barium carbonate as the weapon.

Victory over the rats caused hardly a ripple of excitement. Not much did; after four years of war Londoners were tired and jaded. Most of those who had jobs were overworked; a report prepared in the middle of 1943 predicted that within twelve months a high percentage of civil servants would 'break down or be useless on sheer physical grounds'. Those who were unemployed or under-employed were bored and hard to stimulate; Hilda Neal noticed that a fire at the Charing Cross Hotel (begun by accident rather than enemy action) attracted almost no attention. 'How we should have run to see a fire when we were young. Now, the youth of the town just stare for a minute or two and walk calmly on.'

Appearances by the King, or even Churchill, caused little stir; one of the few people who could attract attention was the victor of North Africa, General Montgomery. When he visited the Hippo-drome Theatre there was so much cheering on his arrival that the audience at nearby Wyndham's could not hear what the actors and

actresses were saying. He was an artist at ensuring that his movements were known in advance. When he lunched with the First Sea
Lord, Andrew Cunningham, at a West End restaurant, he found a
crowd of applauding women, small boys with autograph books and
press cameramen massed outside. 'Dear me,' he remarked in
affected surprise, 'what a lot of ladies.'

Naomi Mitchison visited London in July 1943 and again in mid-
November. 'I got the feeling that morale is worse than during the
tail of the blitz,' she wrote after her second visit, 'worse even than
last time.' There was a new rancour abroad – directed against the
Americans, the generals, the government, even Churchill. The mood
was not defeatist or even pessimistic; Anthony Weymouth found the
public 'unrestrainedly optimistic', even dangerously so, and needing
constantly to be reminded how much grim struggle lay ahead.

Home Intelligence surveys suggested that optimism rose to a peak
every six months or so, but in 1943 the fluctuations seemed to level
out. 'The present complaints of the public are due less to captious
criticism than to the real and inevitable difficulties of the fourth year
of the war,' concluded the report. People were no longer disposed to
make sacrifices which were not thrust on them. They flocked
to Brighton and other recently opened coastal resorts, even though
the government told them that the patriotic thing was to stay at
home. Those who did stay in London were noticeably resentful if
no extra facilities were provided; the Home Intelligence Weekly
Report for 15 June 1943 recorded that Londoners who had to queue
for hours before getting a bus to Richmond Park or Hampstead
Heath were 'in an ugly mood'.

The authorities recognised the need to keep Londoners happy.
Lord Latham, Leader of the LCC, announced that £25,000 (twice
the figure for 1942) was to be lavished on opera, ballet and musical
comedy in the parks: 'We seek to reproduce in London what the
average person might expect to get if he went away to the seaside.'
George Sanger's circus moved from site to site, there was a new
bandstand in Brockwell Park at Herne Hill, a regatta at Hackney,
street-parties with Punch and Judy in St Pancras, evening dances in
six parks. Usually audiences were large and enthusiastic but there
was sometimes trouble: a concert at Burnt Oak, Edgware, had to
be abandoned when unruly children catcalled and threw stones or
fired catapults at the performers.

A few months later Harold Nicolson commented on the extra-ordinary range of entertainment available to Londoners: 'A Tribute to the Soviet Union – organised by the Soviet Unionists (whatever they are), the Centenary of the British Jews' Society, lectures on the Russian Revolution by the Fabian Society, the Rosicrucians on "Individuality", Indian dances, Exhibition of Firemen's paintings.' Even if the events themselves sounded unappealing, he wrote in his diary, it would be interesting to see 'the various oddities who would attend all these weird shows'. Certainly such rarefied delights held little for the average Londoner; opera in the parks was perhaps a little better; al fresco dancing and boxing a definite improvement, but still no substitute for the delights of sand, pier and sea air. The war seemed interminable; Londoners had been cooped up in their shabby city for too long; they were bored and showed it.

Christmas 1943 brought home starkly how little scope was left for celebration. 'We are pretty well on our beam ends as far as Christmas Fare is concerned,' wrote Vere Hodgson. 'No chance of turkey, chicken or goose – not even the despised rabbit. If we can get a little mutton that is the best we can hope for. A few Christmas puddings are about . . . There are shops with three puddings and 800 registered customers.' For those seeking presents the stores were equally barren. Antique shops were the only ones to offer choice, and their wares were usually dilapidated and expensive; old rocking-horses were particularly sought after and commanded ridiculous prices. The New Year offered little relief; there were no bells from the churches, no watch-night services, no late trains or buses, no vacant rooms in hotels. Most pubs ran out of beer and whisky; even the Scottish provision shop which before the war had supplied 2000 large haggises this year had only twelve one-pounders.

Privation and boredom bred a new censoriousness; people who in the past had got on with their own lives, without paying too much attention to whether others were doing better, were now quick to complain and criticise. A letter to the *Enfield Gazette* bore the indignant headline 'Is this total war?' For many months, said the writer, he had had cause to visit the Gordon Hill area of Enfield. 'I have noticed with disgust an apparently able-bodied man who not only plays with his dogs regularly in Hilly Fields, but brings them to this park by car . . . Can such a despicable and unnecessary action be stopped by law?' 'Disgusted of Enfield' was rampant by the end of

1943. People looked furtively at their neighbours, noticed who had new clothes or a bottle of whisky, were jealous and indignant, resented the inequalities in society which had always been blatant but seemed particularly hard to stomach at a time when everybody was supposed to be suffering for a common cause.

Affluent businessmen in large chauffeur-driven cars, slick traders in conspicuously new suits, bibulous merry-makers emerging from smart restaurants: all kindled resentment in the under-privileged, who in 1943 comprised the vast majority of the population. It was food above all which caused ill-feeling. Mrs Britton wrote to thank her daughter in California for a food parcel. She had heard on the radio that she should not be accepting aid of this kind since only the favoured few could receive it, 'but they don't mention the favoured few that are able to go to the big hotels and tea shops and get all kinds of good things'. Those who received parcels from abroad were resented by those who did not; those who ate in expensive restaurants were resented by those who could not afford or did not wish to frequent such places; those who used the black market were resented by those who thought that to do so was unpatriotic, immoral or just too dangerous; those with generous friends on farms were resented by those who had to make do with an egg a week if they were lucky. The subject became of obsessive interest. 'How sick I am of the sound of the word "food",' complained Gwladys Cox. 'Everyone you meet immediately starts discussing the subject.' It was referred to more often than anything else in reports on public opinion. There was grumbling about the exiguous rations, but the system was accepted as fair and inevitable; it was the fact that a few could afford to eat expensively in restaurants, buy luxuries off the ration, secure themselves preferential treatment in shops, which made food the most potent source of discontent.

Nobody starved, but privation was a reality. Richard Brown Baker, an American journalist, looked at himself in a mirror a few months after he arrived in London from the United States. 'The physical change is deplorable,' he wrote. 'It is the more astonishing because I get more milk and eggs, sugar and citrus fruit than most people, and eat in the best restaurants regularly. If such emaciation could occur to me, in five months, how greatly must the health of the British people, after five years of deprivation, be adversely affected.'

Those less fortunate than Mr Baker had to manage on 1/2d worth of meat a week (fourteen ounces more or less), four ounces of bacon and ham, eight ounces of fats and a cheese ration which fell early in 1944 to a mere two ounces. Each person had twenty points a month which could be splurged on some rarity like tinned pilchards (thirty-two points a pound) or spread over less extravagant items like tinned peaches (eight points) or tinned tomatoes (six points). Charles Graves wrote discontentedly that Lord Woolton had just decided to reduce further the sugar allowance, 'This will make it all the more necessary for us to dine out.'

In May 1942 James Lansdale Hodson had supped at the Berkeley on smoked salmon, mushroom pâté, chicken, pudding, a white lady cocktail and red wine. The bill for two was £2.16s.6d. 'It's clear to me that if you have the brass, as they say in Lancashire, you can live in London very well.' The unfairness of the rich being able to ignore food rationing by eating away from home was so conspicuous that the government recognised something had to be done. Hodson recorded rumours that Churchill and Woolton were discussing the imposition of a maximum charge on hotel and restaurant meals; already the trade were protesting that any such provision would mean their bankruptcy. A few days later they were put to the test. Restaurants were forbidden to charge more than 5/- for a meal. They could recoup some of their losses by increasing the cost of wine, but prices were already so high and wine so scarce that there was not much room for manoeuvre.

The limits were applied for the first time on 15 June. The *Evening Standard* sent its reporters around the restaurants and found that many of the better ones had been allowed to add a house charge of 2/6d to 3/6d while six hotels – Claridge's, the Dorchester, Grosvenor House, Ritz, Mayfair and Savoy – were authorised to more than double the maximum by charging an additional 6/- for the privilege of dining on their premises. With coffee at 1/-, smoked salmon an extra at 5/6d and asparagus at 6/-, it was clear the 5/- limit would not prove too rigid for the more creative managements. The system was a complete farce, a waiter at the Dorchester told Graves; the management proposed to charge 5/- for supper, 7/6d as cover charge and an extra 2/6d for dancing.

It was *not* a complete farce. Most restaurants conformed to the new regulations; even those that did not had to avoid ostentatious signs of luxury. Some effort was made to supervise the system: in November Ministry of Food inspectors lunched incognito at the Lord Belgrave Hotel in Whitcombe Street and were served with grilled gammon and plum and apple for 5/8d on one day and duck and plum pie for 6/2d on another. The proprietors were prosecuted for exceeding the permitted maximum. Even the grandest establishments were short of food; at Claridge's nearly every table for lunch was occupied by 12.30, since people arriving later found that most dishes were already 'off'. Inequality was not eliminated – one portly and opulent impresario found the meals so inadequate that he would lunch in one restaurant at 12.30 and move on to another an hour later. But the very fact that he found this necessary shows that the system achieved some success.

Small restaurants that were prepared to stretch a point abounded. When Winifred Lane was doing night work with the ATS, she would often eat at a small Greek restaurant in Tottenham Court Road. 'We had more meat than we'd seen for years and the dark-eyed patron always had a little left somewhere, if you were late in for your supper. He liked us – and we didn't query his sources.' Eve Molesworth found much the same at an Italian restaurant in Jermyn Street, where the manager would conceal steaks under a mound of spinach. The Italian restaurant was prosecuted twice for dealing with the black market and exceeding maximum charges, probably the Greek was too. Such offenders were fined, sometimes quite heavily, but they were rarely driven out of business.

The larger establishments were prosecuted less often, probably because they used more sophisticated methods, possibly because they could buy their way out of trouble. Lord Woolton was relieved when dinner at the Dorchester was cancelled. He did not like it there, he wrote in his diary: 'I'm sure it's one of the places that pays "black market" prices for its food, and many of the staff are suspected of being foreign agents.' It was no easier to control the private hostess who was prepared to use her money to buy provisions from grey if not black sources; long after the worst excesses of the restaurants had been curbed James Agate was able to eat 'a sumptuous meal' in Mrs Belloc Lowndes's house in Barton Street. But the government had shown that it was on the side of fair shares, and even though the system worked erratically and could be manipulated, the fact that the effort had been made went some way to assuage public discontent.

Anthony Weymouth dined at Prunier's with an American friend in December 1942 – smoked salmon, boiled chicken and rice, and chocolate mousse. The American relished it but said that he had eaten quite as well the day before at a local British Restaurant. He was perhaps not the most discriminating of gourmets, but the comment was a striking tribute to an on-the-whole remarkably successful social experiment. By 1943 there were about 200 British Restaurants being run by the LCC, the sites ranging from deserted schools to the banqueting hall of the Fishmongers' Hall or of the Royal Veterinary College. Mayfair's first British Restaurant opened in the drawing room of a Park Lane mansion, Gloucester House. The intention was to provide plain, sustaining and above all cheap meals in a reasonably bright and comfortable environment. Cheapness, at least, was achieved; the average bill was 9d for three courses with coffee and there was no tipping. Basic portions of meat, being controlled, were the same in size as in any luxury restaurant – the difference came in the trimmings and the cooking. The quality, whether of raw materials or of cooking, varied little between British Restaurants, and the response of the customers depended on their expectations.

Many thought the meal excellent; Gwladys Cox, eating in the Finchley Road, thought the food 'passable' but was more concerned about the surroundings – 'the clientele a mixed bag and service somewhat rough and ready . . . A navvy sat beside me in his working clothes!'; the Tory MP Sir William Darling was even more censorious. They were well named, he stormed, 'British to me means barbarian. They are brutal in their cooking, brutal in their presentation of food. One needs to be British to "take it" in a British Restaurant.' Occasionally there were complaints that, even for 9d, the quantities were not value for money: 'One potato, one piece of carrot, and a 2″ x 3″ rectangle of boiled beef, followed by a small piece of boiled pudding, spoilt with evil-tasting sauce,' complained William Regan. Wembley was one of the few areas where the scheme failed unequivocally; local caterers commented, 'although they may have been a little cheaper, we provided a more substantial meal'. In most places the British Restaurants were well patronised, often crowded, and judged a success by everyone except those seeking gargantuan meals, *haute cuisine* or refined surroundings.

The more respectable men's clubs prided themselves on their austerity. Anthony Weymouth, dining with Lord Lytton at the Athenaeum, had to make do with soup and a tiny omelette with half a tomato – 'Wine has of course now disappeared from clubs.' At what was left of the Naval and Military, General Pownall was offered catfish; it might as well have been megrim, dogfish, woofs or ling. Odd new foods appeared, were regarded with suspicion, sometimes won acceptance. The public obstinately refused to agree with Lord Woolton that whale meat or an obscure South African fish called snoek (sometimes snook) was nutritious and agreeable in flavour; horse flesh, however, was widely eaten, *Canapé Cheval* appearing on the House of Commons menu. Rook pie was served in the Grosvenor House Hotel and a Granada restaurant once featured roast eagle.

Food products came and went with disconcerting volatility. Fish was the most remarkable, the vagaries of war and weather ensuring that one week the shops would be empty, the next, if not full, at least tolerably well stocked. Macaroni disappeared overnight. 'A nuisance!' complained Vere Hodgson. 'Perhaps a ship-load will come in. I asked for it the other day, and a man behind me said, "Can I have three bowls of gold dust, please." However, there are some figs, which is an agreeable change.' Onions, too, would vanish for months at a time, then there would be a sudden influx. They were non-existent in the shops, found Mrs Britton in mid-1942: 'By the way, so are a lot of things. Instead of going into a shop and saying "I want so and so", we are all getting into the habit of saying "Have you got . . . ?" '

One of the things they never had got was oranges, until victory in North Africa meant that some were imported. By October 1943 they were appearing in the shops, reserved for children for the first few days, then, if stocks had not been exhausted, available for adults. Lemons never disappeared completely; late in 1941 Sidney Chave noted jubilantly that his mother had secured three, 'the first we have had in the house for many, many months', but this was a rare sighting; they were still almost impossible to find at a time when oranges had become relatively common, and it was cause for jubilation when in 1944 a large consignment meant that customers could buy up to twelve at twopence-halfpenny each.

A reason for the sudden disappearance of certain products was the imposition of price control. Tomatoes had been freely available at 2/6d a pound, then a ceiling of 1/2d was introduced and they vanished from Covent Garden and thus the greengrocers. The same phenomenon occurred in the case of new potatoes and, later, gooseberries. Eventually they would reappear, but the dearth could be lengthy. What happened to the missing commodities in the interval was anybody's guess, but they seemed to be available in the more expensive restaurants. Fruits not subject to price control were more likely to be found in the shops; in July Fortnum and Mason's abounded with grapes and peaches, but the peaches cost 7/6d each. Otherwise the shelves even of Fortnum's usually proved a glamorous delusion: sumptuous chocolates, but on the ration; bright bottles or packets of sauces or chutneys, which availed little without the food they were supposed to garnish; a tactfully printed notice – 'No whisky, no rum, no gin'.

Whether at Fortnum's or less elegant emporia, the Londoner had little chance of securing gin or whisky at the approved retail price. A higher offer was sometimes more successful; a practice deplored by the authorities but not actually black marketing, since Woolton did not concern himself with alcohol. 'Personally, I am not interested,' he wrote with disdain in his diary, 'if people like to be swindled into paying these extortionate prices for spirits, which are totally unnecessary except as a luxury, I should let them be swindled.' Price regulations applied only to newly imported products, such as Algerian wine, limited to 8/- a bottle. When whisky or gin was available, competition to secure them was fierce; a weeping woman was heard protesting that her doctor had ordered her to mix a teaspoonful of whisky in her baby's milk.

Noxious substitutes were sometimes found. 'Hooch' (illicitly distilled whisky) was served often in the West End in 1942 and 1943. Barmen would produce real whisky until they reckoned the customer was befuddled and then switch to a brew of methylated spirits tinted with chemicals. Even a little could produce gastritis and temporary blindness, and a number of young officers had to be treated in hospital for methyl poisoning. Once at least the dose was lethal; an Irish Newfoundlander in the Navy lost all control, leapt through a window, fell twenty feet and died a few hours later in hospital. 'Whisky' was the most common form of adulterated alcohol, but 'gin', made out of one-third pure alcohol, two-thirds water and a few drops of juniper concentrate, was almost as dangerous and even harder to detect.

Pubs and other bars were somewhat better supplied, but nobody could be sure of finding whisky or gin, let alone a favourite brand; even if it was available customers would probably be served only one, or perhaps two glasses. Maclaren-Ross, pubcrawling with Dylan Thomas in the summer of 1943, was relieved to find that, though Scotch seemed to have temporarily dried up, Irish whiskey in abundance was to be found at the back bar of the Café Royal. Beer was more easily procured, though weaker than before the war and often running out well before closing time. Glasses were as likely to be in short supply as the liquid to put in them and pubs sometimes asked their customers to produce their own.

One reason for the liquor shortages, in the eyes of men at least, was the new and unfair competition from women. A survey early in 1943 showed that, whereas before the war women rarely entered pubs and then only under male escort, now they were often to be seen there with other women or even on their own. Most innkeepers welcomed or anyway condoned the invasion: 'Usually when they come in alone, they don't go out on their own, but who am I to criticise?' asked the landlord of a Fulham pub. Male customers were less tolerant. On the whole the elderly were the more shocked but working-class youth sometimes took a robust attitude towards the question – 'If I thought my girl was going into a pub, I'd wring her neck, honest I would,' said a young man of twenty. Certain pubs in Victoria and Covent Garden were notorious as places where girls would go to get drunk and pick up a man; the first being incidental to the second. Champions of British morality complained that American troops were plying London girls with hard liquor and then seducing them; Mass Observation suggested that the girls were making the running and soliciting the men; they were not professional prostitutes but decidedly promiscuous.

In a time of such shortage it was not surprising that any sort of waste was treated as close to treason. The line between the pardonable and the criminal was sometimes hard to draw; the police would prosecute people who fed bread to the birds in Hyde Park but not those who merely emptied crumbs out of a bag. Vere Hodgson complained when she was told off by the Kensington Salvage Council for throwing away a mouldy crust of bread: 'Seems rather hard that I should be singled out when I have nearly poisoned folk with using up ancient food.' She should have had a pig bin; in the Elephant and Castle Harry Davey remembered that every household had a receptacle where anything even remotely eatable was emptied for collection. The authorities urged frugality and offered a plethora of useful tips intended to make meagre rations go further. The Wandsworth Council was particularly active, setting up centres all over the borough where housewives were taught how to make potato soup and cakes without fat or sugar. Using their methods a bean cutlet, large enough to feed a family, cost only 4d. The Ministry of Food's publicising of the need for a balanced diet proved so effective that by the third year of the war two-thirds of London housewives understood the distinction between Energy, Protection and Body-building, and knew which foods produced which. Considering that less than half knew the name of the Air Minister and only 63 per cent could identify a man as powerful and popular as Ernest Bevin, the statistic is not unimpressive. Gert and Daisy, the Cockney comediennes, broadcast briefly every night on behalf of the Ministry and commanded a huge and appreciative audience.

Though the shortage of food was the most severe of London's privations, others seemed little less painful. Soap rationing caused particular concern in the East End, where the Monday wash possessed ritual significance. Grocers in Clerkenwell were besieged by housewives who feared a shortage, while in Finsbury the bath superintendent defied regulations and promised to go on issuing soap until his stock was exhausted. A plea was made for an extra London ration because of the hardness of the water; the Minister's heart proved even harder. 'Nothing can be absolutely fair,' he said dismissively. But rationing, by any rough-and-ready test, *was* fair. To George Orwell it seemed to have a genuinely democratising effect: 'Since no real structural change is occurring in our society, the mechanical levelling process that results from sheer scarcity is better than nothing.' In particular, he felt, this was true of clothes rationing: 'If the poor are not much better dressed, at least the rich are shabbier.'

The ration was exiguous, and though extra coupons were available for those who had lost their clothing through enemy action or other causes outside their control, the stocks available were limited in variety and poor in quality. Vere Hodgson prowled around London trying to buy a pair of socks for a friend; she had the coupons but, 'you can only obtain amazing things in bright red, green and purple'. Bureaucracy made life difficult for those who needed an extra ration. One Chelsea housewife and war-worker lost her only nightdress at the laundry, went to the nearest office three times to seek coupons for a replacement but each time had to abandon the quest and return to work after forty minutes. Rationing proved as damaging to shops as to customers. One after another small traders were forced to close. 'Our main business was stockings and wool,' a Brixton haberdasher told Florence Speed. 'We can get neither. It isn't likely that people will bring their coupons here.' Looking around the drab and barren shop, Miss Speed had to agree. Those that could stay open found staff hard to find or keep; a London shop would take at least three months to repair a pair of shoes because so many qualified cobblers were doing war work.

New books disappeared from the shops as soon as they were printed; second-hand books were almost equally saleable and a bookstall in Oxford Street offered to buy *any* second-hand book for at least half the original purchase price. Newspapers, by 1942, were receiving only 4000 tons of newsprint a week, against 24,000 before the war; it was rumoured that they would soon be reduced in size to two pages, though in the event they never fell below six or four. Old newspapers were on sale at a halfpenny each for use as wrapping paper or fire lighters, and some effort to ease the paper shortage was made by collecting books for salvage. The target of a great drive in London in June 1943 was five million books. 'There are two or three million homes in London,' said an official, 'so we need only two books from each.' Encouraged by this, London boroughs competed in this literary massacre. Boys were offered free seats at the cinema if they collected a hundred volumes. In Kensington, Mabel Constanduros, the actress, toured with a van. People threw more than 2000 books into it, raising the borough's total to 86,700. With a week still to go, Marylebone had amassed 63,000 books towards a target of 100,000, and Paddington 69,000 – though the latter perhaps deserved a bonus point since their haul included a first edition of Gibbon's *Decline and Fall of the Roman Empire*. A late rush took the grand total beyond the target to 5.5 million.

It is unlikely that the paper recycled as a result of this exercise outweighed the value of what was lost. In the case of food it was possible to make a more effective contribution to the war effort. The British passion for gardening blended happily with patriotism and self-interest. 'Londoners dug for victory so manfully,' wrote Mollie Panter-Downes, 'that scarlet runners in every back yard seem to be trying to strangle the house, and there is greater danger of being hit by a marrow falling off the roof of an air-raid shelter than by a bomb.'

Some boroughs fostered the allotment habit with particular fervour; there were 6000 allotments in Wandsworth and the council regularly offered spring cabbage and other plants for sale at cost. Others were more cautious; it was announced early in 1942 that the importance of the royal parks for recreation was so great that no further space would be made available for allotments. In St James's Square allotments were tolerated but no trimming of trees was permitted: 'The trees are more important to us than the allotments,' ruled the Clerk to the Trustees. The Ministry of Agriculture opened a small demonstration allotment between Park Lane and the Hyde Park motor road. It was run by Barbara Tarver, who held a brains trust on site every Saturday afternoon and Sunday evening. She had her problems; in 1942 all her lettuces and shallots were stolen. She inspired jealousy, too. Gwladys Cox reflected sourly that very careful preparation must have gone into the ground; 'it looked in first class condition, the carrots growing splendidly, far better than ours'. Mr Middleton was the Gert and Daisy of the gardening world; his broadcasts were immensely popular and did as much as anything to convince doubters that running an allotment was a pleasant and profitable pursuit.

Nowhere seemed beyond the ingenuity of the would-be gardener. The window boxes of Chatham House, in St James's Square, were turned over from marguerites and geraniums to tomatoes; in the forecourt of the British Museum Mrs Allen, wife of the Keeper of Coins and Medals, had a promising crop of peas, beans, onions and lettuces; on the roof of New Zealand House the caretaker's son, Geoffrey Pleydell, grew wheat (a dozen ears or so) to help nourish his father's Black Leghorn chickens. Nearby, three hives contained the High Commissioner's much prized bees. For Christmas 1942 the gutted shell of John Lewis was transformed into a bower of tents and greenery for the Potato Christmas Fair, sponsored by the Ministry of Food to extol the merits of potatoes as against imported wheat. It was visited on the opening day by Lord Woolton, a baby elephant called Comet, and many members of the public who signed a book pledging that, 'as a Christmas gift to the sailors', they would in future eat more potatoes and less bread.

Mr Pleydell was not the only Londoner to keep chickens; certain suburbs resembled a giant poultry-yard, so great was the concentration of White Wyandottes, Black Leghorns and Rhode Island Reds. Pig-owning, or at least sharing, was also popular. There were pig clubs in many of the parks, including one attached to Hyde Park police station. Twenty men at this station subscribed £1 each, bought eight pigs, built a sty from timbers out of bombed houses (technically, no doubt, looted), collected swill from nearby hostels or other police stations, sold the fattened products after six months and started over again. Each Christmas they were allowed to keep two pigs for themselves. The sty was twice damaged by bombs but there were no casualties among the inhabitants. Other pigs were to be found rootling around to their apparent satisfaction in the basement of bombed buildings; even the swimming pool of the Ladies' Carlton Club in Pall Mall was converted into a giant sty. Cows and sheep were greater rarities but both were to be found in the larger parks. Alfred McGhee, a Scottish shepherd, tended his flock in Kensington Gardens. In July 1943 he was summonsed for beating his dog brutally with his crook. 'I have had to do as I was told all my life,' he pleaded, 'and if my dogs don't do the same, I make them.' This defence was rejected and he was fined £2.

The problem of feeding London was made more difficult by the return of the evacuees. Those who had been moved to other parts of London because of damage to their own neighbourhoods were the first to return. The inhabitants of the Isle of Dogs were flocking back by early 1942. 'They found their suburban neighbours snobbish,' wrote William Regan, 'and seeming to begrudge them the higher degree of safety from air-raids that they themselves enjoyed.' Other parts of London were already beginning to fill up. Gwladys Cox noted at much the same time that she had not seen the streets so full for two years. Many flats in her part of Hampstead had recently been let and prospective tenants were prowling the streets in search of accommodation.

But it was the children whose return caused most dismay to the authorities. By the beginning of 1942 8000 a month were pouring in; 167,000 were at school in London, compared with the 84,000 recorded only eight months before. The mayor of Stepney, John Pritchard, was so worried by the lack of housing and schooling that he invited the councillors of Chertsey – where most Stepney children had been evacuated – to tour his borough in the hope that they might be persuaded to make life more congenial for the exiles. One Chertsey councillor asked a five-year-old boy playing in the rubble why he had come back. 'I like it better here,' the child replied, briefly but conclusively. Most of them felt the same. By the end of the summer seven out of eight had returned. Schools, which had been evacuated en bloc, were forced to return as well because the teachers found themselves abandoned in the country with their pupils back in London. The raids of January 1943 slowed but did not reverse the trend; one mother from the Elephant and Castle said that she had asked her little girl if she wanted to go back to the country, 'and she said "No fear". That's my view too.' Nor was it just the children of LCC schools who were returning; the day after the raid of 17 January the governors of Highgate School announced that at Easter it would return from its country retreat at Westward Ho.

Educating the returned evacuees was an almost insurmountable problem, even when suitable premises could be found. Absenteeism, which had averaged 12 per cent before the war, now ran at 18 per cent or more, in part at least because children were having to do the household chores while their mothers went to work. Books were in short supply and, once lost, irreplaceable; from May 1943 the LCC schools gave up presenting books as prizes to successful scholars. There was a dire shortage of qualified teachers, particularly in the south-east of the capital. The Chief Inspector of Education lamented the fact that half the school life of most thirteen- to fourteen-year-olds had been spent in 'improvised and often unsatisfactory conditions'. Misspellings occurred twice as often in their work as in the work of a corresponding class in 1924; twice as many pupils were unable to read fluently; an alarmingly large hard core was virtually illiterate.

Businesses, too, were moving back; May 1943 saw the return of the London Tin Corporation to Moorgate, the Yorkshire Trust to Old Broad Street, Mawchi Mines came back from Ware. The hospitals which should have catered for the returning hordes were slower to catch up; partly because so many of the young doctors were in the armed services, partly because the hospitals had often been damaged or destroyed. The Royal College of Surgeons had been almost totally demolished, though Charles Graves regretfully noted that 'some of those pathological horrors like double-headed babies in spirit bottles have unfortunately survived in the sub-basement'. St George's, at Hyde Park Corner, was one of the luckiest; it was hit only by one bomb and that did not explode. Matron Hanks, an ardent spiritualist, believed this was because a green light shone over the hospital, protecting it from danger. She liked her nurses to wear pink underwear, since this radiated happiness.

In spite of inadequate hospitals, a shortage of doctors and the wartime diet, the health of Londoners remained remarkably good. The epidemic of typhoid which had been predicted as a result of water pollution never materialised; indeed there was not a single case where the bombing of the water mains led to serious disease. Flu epidemics came and went, particularly in 1943, but flu epidemics had always come and gone, and fears that a population weakened by privation would prove abnormally susceptible were never realised. Tuberculosis was the most dangerous of London's diseases, in the poorer parts of the city at least – cases of pulmonary tuberculosis in Islington in 1943 were 35 per cent up on the figure for 1938, and of non-pulmonary 40 per cent – but though this was serious it did not constitute a major crisis. Venereal diseases also increased, though again not as much as the promiscuity of the age led some to fear. A poll in London in December 1942 showed a welcome readiness to confront a menace hitherto almost unmentionable in even modestly polite society. Three-quarters of those questioned showed no embarrassment and the vast majority were in favour of government regulations over treatment and more public instruction: 'I think it's very good; it ought to be spoken of,' said a lower-middle-class woman of forty.

Though a few of London's factories had assembled their machine tools and decamped for safer parts, the demands for increased production meant that there was more industry in Greater London in 1943 than before the war. At first the authorities had encouraged industry to evacuate, but the lessened danger from air attack and the desperate need to use every available facility for manufacture led to a change in policy. Existing factories were converted to wartime ends: a canning firm in Mitcham found itself producing shell cases; Bryant and May's match factory in Bow adapted its machinery to make fuses for demolition work. An uncompleted tube extension was converted and air-conditioned; five and a half miles of track were put to use as a factory making parts for aircraft; 80 per cent of the workers were women. There was a spirit of dedication and enthusiasm, reported a euphoric visitor, 'they were singing and whistling by their machines'. A small munitions factory was installed in the underground vaults below the Central Lobby of the House of Commons. The Lord Great Chamberlain, perhaps with the precedent of Guy Fawkes in mind, at first resisted the proposal, but was overborne by the insistence of Members of Parliament and the staff of the House. By the end of 1943 the unit, manned entirely by part-time volunteers, was producing several items of some sophistication, including a torque amplifier, part of a predictor unit for anti-aircraft guns. There was 'a fantastic atmosphere in the factory, which was really totally classless', said the welfare officer.

Such reports, suggesting an ideal world in which management and labour selflessly mucked in together, toiling long hours without complaint, were far removed from everyday reality. The bigoted suspicions of the unions, the blinkered meanness of management, were not so easily overcome. Kathleen Bliss and her friend, who in peacetime had run a small restaurant in Hampshire, set off in 1942 to do their bit in a London factory. After training, they found work in Morrison's works manufacturing aircraft parts in Croydon. The employees worked a twelve-hour day and were expected to take off only one Saturday afternoon and one Sunday a month. In a recent crisis they had been required to work all day and all night Friday, all day Saturday and all day Sunday. Their foreman, Stan, had worked seven days a week with only one day off a month for three years, 'so no wonder he looks so desperately ill'. They did not complain about the hours – which they accepted were necessary; nor the pay – which was reasonable; but the food in the canteen was almost inedible; the facilities designed for 150 now served 500, but had not been improved in any way.

Management was quick to exhort labour to greater efforts, but slow to do anything to make working conditions less intolerable or to redress even the most obvious grievances. When snow stopped building work in the Isle of Dogs, all pay stopped too . . . 'What an existence! Will we ever have State Control?' exploded William Regan. 'The end of this war must be the beginning of better conditions for the backbone of the country. Enough of this, it makes me want to kick somebody hard.' Yet the 'somebody' was not uniquely to be found in the board rooms or managers' offices: J. T. Murphy, by instinct and training a champion of the worker against the employer, was appalled by the obscurantist attitude of the union leaders even in the third year of war, their inflexible determination to retain taboos and restraints, their victimisation of anyone who tried to cut corners or do work beyond their prescribed norm.

'Better conditions for the backbone of the country' – William Regan's vision of the future was widely shared. The preoccupations of the ordinary Londoner, wrote C. P. Snow, 'were about equally divided between what they were going to eat today and what was going to happen in Britain tomorrow. It's important to remember how idealistic everyone was in those days, despite the rigours and pressures of war.' It might be said that only by being idealistic was the Londoner able to withstand the rigours of war. The awful disillusionments of 1919 and 1920 were forgotten or, if not forgotten, remembered as a hideous example of what must not be allowed to happen again. This time there *had* to be something better.

The government – or at least its more right-wing members – noted with some dismay the upsurge of what an appendix to one of the 1942 Home Intelligence Weekly Reports described as 'Home-made Socialism . . . During the last six months it is believed that "a new trend of opinion" has gained impetus [in the London region] and is now said to be growing like a jungle plant.' During the first years of the war socialism had taken root among people who had come into contact with the poor for the first time. Now it was spreading 'among black-collar workers who are said to be reading and discussing a good deal'. Employers, most of them traditional Conservatives, were beginning to accept that socialism was inevitable as 'better social opportunities for everyone, and improved social conditions must come'.

An informal programme of mass education was being carried out in London in the last three years of the war. Stephen Spender was only one of many hundreds who gave up their precious spare time to foster a spirit of enquiry and a better understanding of what the future could and should hold. Fireman Spender 'went from station to station, opening discussions on Russia, China, the Law, History, Art and many other subjects'. He admired the seriousness of the participants. 'They liked to discuss a better and juster England. For them "progress" was making a few important improvements in their living conditions, and working for concrete benefits such as better houses and better education for their children.'

The vague resentment which the poor had always felt at the misery of their conditions, and the rules of a society which made it so difficult for them to improve their lot, was now articulated and translated into demands for action. The plight of so many dependants of fighting soldiers, sailors and airmen, whose pitiful subsistence barely provided for the needs of their families; the woman in Bethnal Green who lived on £1 a week after paying rent and fed her daughter by embroidering luxury gloves till late at night; another in Lambeth who had no such skills but eked out her dependant's allowance by occasional prostitution; these stirred pity and indignation among many who would have been unaware of the sufferings of the poor before the war. The release of the Fascist leader, Oswald Mosley, crystallised working-class resentment. It was not just that, as Home Intelligence Reports indicated, there were fears in the East End that Fascism would once again be allowed to flourish; it was the belief that Mosley had been let out because he was rich and well connected. That a Labour Home Secretary, Herbert Morrison, was responsible made little difference. In Hackney, Morrison's own constituency, 8000 signed a petition of protest; 1000 demonstrators gathered outside Parliament and tried to force an entry. Their battle cry was, 'Mosley in, Morrison out!'

Robust, radical, sometimes ill-informed and unfair, but with an unfailing sense of what the public cared about and what they should be told, the *Daily Mirror* was the greatest single factor in creating the national mood at the end of the war. H. G. Bartholomew, the superbly talented and, in professional terms, revolutionary editor;

William Connor, the columnist Cassandra; Philip Zec, the cartoonist: these pricked the nation's conscience and stirred up a discontent
which, if not divine, was at least positive and creative. Jane, the
curiously sexless pin-up who was forever losing her clothes in
unlikely circumstances, was the heroine of the *Daily Mirror* and
Britain's most widely followed strip cartoon. It has often been said
that Jane, drawing in the readers who went on to the news stories
and leading articles, won the 1945 election for Labour. An investigation by Mass Observation casts doubt on this: Jane was dismissed
by a majority of those consulted as 'Piffle', 'Tripe', 'Useless', 'Silly
and stupid', and the general level of interest in strip cartoons seemed
low. But whether Jane attracted or repelled readers, the *Daily Mirror*
could have sold twice as many copies if paper had been available
and it was as successful a crusading force as any newspaper in the
British Isles has ever been.

The spirit of challenge to the established order which the *Daily
Mirror* fostered found an expression in the by-election results of
1942 and 1943. The House of Commons in these years was an
uninspiring scene. The deadening effect of a national government,
the implicit assumption that to be critical was to be unpatriotic, the
absence of serious opposition, created a situation where there was
little scope within the established order for those who felt that things
should be changed or at least that a way towards change should be
prepared. 'The whole thing has a mangy, forgotten look,' wrote
George Orwell of the House of Commons. 'Even the ushers' shirt
fronts are grimy. And it is noticeable that, except from the places
they sit in, you can't tell one party from another. It is just a collection
of mediocre-looking men in dingy, dark suits, nearly all speaking in
the same accent and all laughing at the same jokes.' The American
Albert Viton deplored the 'lamentable paucity of talent' in the Commons; 'pre-war mediocrities . . . too ignorant, too stupid and too
lethargic to realise the need for adjustment'.

An electorate which wished to express concern for the future,
doubts about the readiness of the government to prepare for it, even
a modicum of disapproval about the running of the war, was left with
no resort except to defy the leaders of the Conservative, Socialist and
Liberal parties, defy Winston Churchill, defy 90 per cent of the
national press, defy all the professional patriots in the pubs or
the pulpits, and vote at by-elections for whatever crank or hero was

prepared to oppose the national candidate. Usually this meant voting for Sir Richard Acland's Common Wealth party, which won its first by-election in April 1943 in Cheshire and at the beginning of 1944 achieved the most picturesque of all its victories when a radical cobbler defeated the eldest son of the Duke of Devonshire in what had been regarded as the Cavendish rotten borough in West Derbyshire.

Surprisingly, London stood out against what was close to being a national trend. At Putney in May 1942 a series of disastrous by-election results for the coalition was checked when the National Conservative candidate, vigorously backed by Churchill, defeated the Independent, Captain Bernard Acworth, who stood for nothing very much except a feeling that the war was not being waged to best advantage. 'The result shows that Putney is wholeheartedly behind Mr Churchill,' said the Tory victor. Up to a point it did, though the fact that less than a quarter of the electorate voted took some gloss off the triumph. At West Woolwich in November 1943, by which time the Common Wealth bandwagon was riding fast, the government did still better; the number of voters was equally small, but the National Government candidate won a larger proportion of the votes than the Conservative candidate had done in 1935. Acton a month later had still less voters (16 per cent of the electorate) but an equally convincing government win. The only opposition was from the Independent Labour Party candidate, a left-wing socialist and conscientious objector. The real victor was indifference: 'Frankly, people haven't got the time to attend meetings or vote. It's not all apathy, but they just can't squeeze it all in the day,' said a woman of thirty-five, while a man of fifty explained, 'I've no interest in the election. What have they done for me when they do get into Parliament? Nothing at all. It's self first and last.'

London's voting record cannot be said to have proved much about the electorate's intentions in the longer term. It was, at most, neutral. The electorate was perhaps more sophisticated and sceptical than the fervent radicals of Cheshire and Derbyshire; perhaps Londoners were more preoccupied and had less energy; perhaps the opposition candidates were exceptionally unconvincing. The general election of 1945 was to prove how little comfort the by-elections should have held for the Conservatives. Whenever Londoners were given a chance to show their concern more directly about the destiny of their city, they seized it eagerly. The 'London Re-planned Exhibition' of November 1942 was expected to attract little attention but was packed every day. A gallery of plans showed possible developments of the neighbourhood of Piccadilly, Waterloo Bridge and Covent Garden, the last being designated as a Music and Dramatic Centre. Not for the last time, there was much debate about the surroundings of St Paul's. Should the devastated area be occupied once more by business houses or laid out as an open space with tree-lined avenues? 'Is, in fact, the City to be rebuilt for St Paul's, or St Paul's for the City?' asked Gwladys Cox.

The following year saw another exhibition at Burlington House, this time concentrating on a visionary redevelopment of the slums. 'I could not help feeling a sneaking sympathy for the slum dweller,' wrote Miss Cox, 'who in a neat new prim garden suburb might sigh for the smoky, cosy alley of his former slum, full of "character".' If she had foreseen the tower blocks which awaited the slum dweller, her sympathy might have been less sneaking. The *LCC Plan for London*, with which this exhibition was connected, was an instant bestseller. Mr Britton tried to secure a copy for his daughter in America, visited half a dozen bookshops without success and finally had to settle for a promise of one if and when a reprint came through. It came, but was also quickly exhausted, and only the paper shortage prevented the Plan running into impression after impression.

But it was the Beveridge Report, the blueprint for the welfare state, commissioned by a government whose main objective had been to find a job for an importunate bureaucrat and now viewed with alarmed suspicion by its principal patrons, which most excited and inspired Londoners. In this they were no different from the rest of the country, but London got there first. On publication day, wrote Mollie Panter-Downes, they queued up 'to buy this heavy two-shilling slab of involved economics as though it were unrationed manna dropped from some heaven where the old bogey of financial want didn't exist'. It was endlessly discussed, endlessly extolled. It crystallised an inchoate demand of which the Londoner had till then hardly been conscious. London's reaction to the Beveridge Report, not the Acton or Woolwich by-elections, gave the first true indication of how the capital would vote in 1945.

14

The Little Blitz

IN JANUARY 1944 the Luftwaffe came back to London. Only the most prescient or the most pessimistic had expected it; for most Londoners the blitz had become a distant memory and its renewal an equally distant threat. Large crowds saw the New Year in at Piccadilly Circus; it was 'a peace-time scene but for the blackout', recorded one observer – a pretty significant qualification, one might think, but not one which disturbed the participants' conviction that it was now just a question of holding on for victory. The pantomime season was in full swing; the toy shops were thronged with children trying to exchange their Christmas presents; altogether, wrote Mollie Panter-Downes, it was 'a lively contrast to the days when rusticating mothers smuggled their young into town to visit the dentist, and gave a sigh of relief when the risky outing was over. Nobody claims that it isn't still risky, but at least the mass home-coming is a cheerful sign of greater confidence.'

The weather had resumed its traditional place as the main subject for complaint. The winter of 1943–4 was exceptionally cold and, in spite of the shortage of the polluting coal and coke, London was beset by freezing fogs. The cold weather, following drought the previous summer and autumn, meant that green vegetables and potatoes were in short supply. By the end of January cauliflowers had disappeared, Brussels sprouts were a rarity, only the unpopular 'drumhead' cabbages and gloomy turnips and swedes were plentiful. Wine had almost vanished except from the most expensive res-taurants, and a bottle of whisky was an acquisition to boast about for months; even water was in short supply as a result of the dry season in 1943 and damage to the mains. The public was not showing sufficient care in its use of water, said an official bulletin severely; household supplies would have to be restricted unless there was more economy. 'There are air-raid alarms almost every night,' wrote Orwell, 'but hardly any bombs.' Wild rumours abounded:

that London was to be bombarded by a rocket gun, that a 400-ton bomb had been manufactured in the form of a glider and was to be towed across the Channel by a fleet of German aeroplanes, but the possibility that the conventional air attacks might be renewed was not taken seriously.

Then, on 21 January, 268 tons of bombs fell on London; nothing much compared with the giant raids of 1940 and 1941; trivial compared with what was being dropped almost every night on Germany, but still an unpleasant reminder of a half-forgotten danger. A week later they came again: 161 bombers set out for London (285 said the Germans), only fifteen got through (229 said the Germans). If the British figure was correct it was surprising that more than 300 fires were started, including a major one in the Surrey Commercial Docks. But again, it was nothing compared with what had gone before. Alexander McKee, a soldier on leave with his family in Sidcup, was scornful of the civilians' attitude. 'It was irritating and unnerving to be with people who were afraid of and hiding from a non-existent danger. We only heard one whistle – Norah and I had an argument about it; she said it was a bomb, and I pointed out that the ground had not shaken sufficiently for that.' McKee was right; the explosion had come from an anti-aircraft shell which had landed in a street half a mile away. Almost all the noise and a great deal of the damage was contributed by the guns, though nobody would have dispensed with them.

Another three weeks went by with only spasmodic, almost symbolic, raids. It seemed the worst was over before it had really begun. Things returned to normal; International Woman's Day was celebrated zestfully with a pageant in the Coliseum before 3000 women, speeches by the mother (Lady Montgomery) and wife (Lady Beveridge) of the two heroes of the moment, and a concert featuring Harriet Cohen and Alice Delysia. Then, on 18 February, it began all over again. Six times in the next week the raiders were over in force. 'A short, sharp blitz,' Churchill's private secretary, Jock Colville, described the raid of 20–21 February. From his own vantage point it was certainly sharp – three bombs on the Horse Guards, the windows of Number 10 blown in and a water main burst in Whitehall. The emphasis was on incendiaries; the authorities claimed that all the fires had been put out shortly after the all-clear sounded, but this was not soon enough to save the Great Western

Hotel at Paddington from serious damage. Churchill inspected the ruins the following day. 'It's quite like old times again,' he called out cheerily; a comment that was not particularly well received. Three hundred incendiaries fell on Wormwood Scrubs, and Wandsworth Prison also had a few fires, though these caused less damage and dismay than the descent of the local barrage balloon on K Wing of the central block.

It was still more like old times a few days later, when a Guinness Trust block of flats was hit by a stick of bombs. Rumour said that many people had been trapped and drowned in the shelter. Lord Iveagh, head of the Guinness clan, indignantly denied the suggestion. The shelter had been only half full, he said; all the casualties were among those who had not seen fit to use it. St James's was badly hit on the same night. The palace façade was knocked about and the clock left sadly awry. In King Street several art dealers lost their premises and the roadway was littered with heavy gilt frames. A shop dealing in guns and sporting materials had been blown open, outside a stuffed crocodile lay with jaws open in a pool of water. An equally stuffed wild duck from the same establishment had been catapulted upwards and landed on top of a shattered bureau-bookcase, from where it surveyed its companion with a baleful glare.

The London Library in St James's Square was hit and 20,000 books were lost. James Lees-Milne, the writer, joined in the salvage work. 'It is a tragic sight,' he wrote in his diary. 'Theology (which one *can* best do without) practically wiped out, and biography (which one can't) partially. The books lying torn and coverless, scattered under debris and in a pitiable state, enough to make one weep. The dust overwhelming. I looked like a snowman in the end.' Two hundred yards away the fine art dealers Spinks had their windows blown in. A few weeks before Spinks had been victim of a smash and grab raid; one man armed with a huge hatchet, another in a car. They could have saved themselves trouble if they had waited. The incidence of looting during the little blitz was higher than in 1940 or 1941. In West Hampstead the stock of a wireless shop disappeared within twenty minutes of a bomb falling. 'The looting that went on that night was something hawful . . .' complained a resident of Agamemnon Road. 'When the greengrocer's wife found 'er 'andbag, every penny 'ad been taken out of it.'

Another fortnight of relative calm ushered in the last serious raids in March and April. The worst night was on 14–15 March, when a hundred bombers were over London. The Germans claimed that 'super-heavy' bombs had been used, but the main threat came from incendiaries and casualties were comparatively light. By 18 April, when the last serious attack was mounted, there had been fourteen major raids. Those in February did the most damage, killing 1000 people. In Battersea 3000 houses in an area of twenty acres were destroyed or rendered uninhabitable; there were 1200 homeless in Fulham; St Paul's School was hit, and the bridge over the river at Barnes badly holed.

Most of the time life went on as usual. Air Marshal Tedder, back from the Middle East in March, was surprised to find 'a good old pre-war traffic jam' in Piccadilly. Chips Channon celebrated his birthday in style in Belgrave Square on 7 March: 'There was gaiety, *stimmung*, even some drunkenness; the food was good, oysters, salmon, dressed crab, minced chicken etc. After the brandy had been passed the King of Spain gracefully proposed my health. I counted nineteen cars parked outside my house [for thirty or so guests]. No raid disturbed our revels and we all wished that Hitler could have seen so luxurious a festival in London at the height of the war.' If Hitler had seen it, the occasion would probably have confirmed his worst suspicions about the British.

Those less cocooned in luxury found the little blitz harder to bear. 'London seems disturbed by the raids and less ebullient than in 1940–41,' noted Jock Colville, as did almost every observer. It was the old illusion, thought William Sansom; having once been hit, Londoners felt they had done their bit and were not eligible for a second dose. The debilitating effect of years of hard work on meagre rations was beginning to show. 'Isn't it that we are all getting just a little bit tired of this incessant strain and anxiety?' asked Anthony Weymouth. 'In 1940 we were fresh, well-fed and ready for the fray. Whereas now we are showing the effects of nearly $4\frac{1}{2}$ years of war.' Vivienne Hall in Putney had all her windows blown in. 'We don't like this resumption of bombing a bit,' she complained, 'and it seems to have caught us at the wrong time, we are war-winter-world weary.'

Morale did not break, or anything near it, but the mood had become more sombre. Alexander McKee, who had been so scornful about his family's fear of bombs, was still more censorious when he saw London Street after the warning sounded, 'a panic-stricken pandemonium, crowded with people scurrying arsy-tarsy for the tube. They ran blindly but at great speed, an Olympic runner would have been unable to hold his own . . . A more contemptible rout, I have never seen.' The spirit of the people, he concluded, was almost broken. 'They were weary in soul and body – another Battle of Britain would finish them.' If London Street had indeed been a scene of panic it was most exceptional, but the spirit of adventure and excitement had died. People who had been ready to risk their lives for others in the crisis of 1940 were less enthusiastic four years later when victory seemed inevitable: Lees-Milne, fire-watching in the West End, was disconcerted by the frankness with which his colleagues 'admitted that they were not going to take risks in putting out incendiary bombs, or rescuing people. I said in surprise, "But I thought that was what we were here for!" ' There were more cases of disorder and indiscipline among civilians under bombardment. During a raid in January George Slotin and Annie Wagner stood in the doorway of a pub in Bethnal Green, letting the light stream out. They admitted being drunk and disorderly. 'Disgusting and outrageous behaviour,' the magistrate characterised it.

Various reasons were put forward by those who found the raids of 1944 particularly taxing. They were nastier because more concentrated, suggested Mollie Panter-Downes. 'There are none of those nice ten-minute breathers during which your insides can get back into place.' The raids were worse than those of 1940–1, thought Irene Byers, 'because there are so many at a time and the guns are so fierce'. Vivienne Hall was convinced that Putney had become the Germans' most favoured target, 'It seems quite a sensible thing as we are on the main Portsmouth road.' It was an ill wind that blew nobody any good. Gwladys Cox eked out her sitting-room fire with chunks of wood thrown out from the debris of a nearby block of flats, Buckingham Mansions. But even this, she admitted, gave her 'a sinking feeling, for at this very moment Buckingham Mansions might just as easily have been burning a bit of us!'

People expected that the splendid new deep shelters, constructed with such care since May 1941, would now be available. They reckoned without Herbert Morrison, who announced that they were being held in reserve for certain unspecified 'vital war services'. He was sure, he continued optimistically, 'that these considerations will be understood by the people of London'. Whether they understood or not, the people of London had to make do with traditional shelters. Andersons continued to be most widely used, though many had become waterlogged or turned into store rooms during the previous two years. Morrisons too were in great demand.

Within a few days of the start of the little blitz the population of the public shelters rose from 3000 to more than 50,000. The fact that many tube stations had been closed led to congestion in those still open; by 25 February every bunk was occupied and many families were once more sleeping on the platform. The trouble was that there were more people in London than there had been during the blitz. The authorities struck a note of slightly querulous disapproval in the face of this invasion. The policy was to give priority to women, children and regular shelterers: 'We have been plagued by people who expect preferential treatment, although they are neither homeless nor "regulars".' Grudgingly, extra tube stations were reopened and a thousand bunks put back into the slots from which they had been removed. The nightly trek to the Chislehurst caves, largely abandoned over the last two years, was now resumed. A police swoop revealed that many of these troglodytes were deserters.

A resident of Chelsea recorded that the same tale came from every side – people were jittery and trying to find a place to stay outside London. Among the more prosperous sections of London society this may have been the case, but on the whole people seemed disinclined to move because of what they believed to be a fleeting threat. The Ministry of Health decided not to reintroduce mass evacuation schemes but offered travel vouchers for anyone who was prepared or able to find their own accommodation. Few accepted the invitation; 8000 children were said to have left London in the last fortnight of February, but 245,000 were still at school. On 2 May, only a fortnight after what turned out to be the last raid of the little blitz, the City of London School returned from Marlborough to the Thames Embankment at Blackfriars. Indeed, the imminent second front and the possible need to empty certain areas of the south coast led to reverse evacuation plans being prepared; buildings earmarked for the accommodation of those made homeless by bombing were provisionally reallocated to people moved from the coast. The mechanism for the repair of damaged houses had been allowed to grow rusty. Lees-Milne's charwoman had her house in Battersea badly damaged: 'No ceilings, or rather no plaster left to them, no glass, no light, and dirt and dust indescribable. Mrs Beckwith dares not leave the house for fear of looters. And the Borough says it can do nothing because she is lucky enough to have a roof over her head.'

The raids of the little blitz were usually over by midnight; which meant that people, instead of going to bed after a raid, would wander around looking for a good fire to gape at. 'Sometimes fire-fighters had almost to fight the crowd before they could tackle the flames.' Stephen Spender, in the role of sightseer rather than fireman, prowled around London in search of a blaze which he had spotted from his home. 'As I walked, I had the comforting sense of the sure, dark immensity of London like a warren, continuing a scattered, breeding life concealed in burrows of the ragged, dilapidated streets of Kilburn and Maida Vale. They could be destroyed at one place, but then – the wound sealed off – would flow through other channels and streets and tunnels ... The grittiness, stench and obscurity of Kilburn suddenly seemed a spiritual force – the immense force of poverty which had produced the narrow, yet intense, visions of Cockneys living in other times.'

The dust from the last raid had hardly settled before London showed how quickly things could return to normal: the bus crews stopped work. The strike contained the traditional elements of British labour disputes, a bloody-minded work force determined not to be put upon, an arrogant and insensitive management equally resolved to manage in its own way. The row was over summer schedules – the proposed changes were not unreasonable but the failure to consult those who would have to operate them was unforgivable. The authorities put in soldiers to run the buses, who frequently lost their way and had to be directed by the passengers. No fares were collected, but there was often a whip-round for the military personnel involved. The strike only lasted two days and ended as messily as it had begun; the new schedules were provisionally accepted but there was a promise that consultations would take place as soon as possible. The public on the whole took the side of the busmen. They were equally sympathetic towards the 'Bevin boys', who were selected by ballot to go down the mines rather than do military service. Arthur

Jenner of Bethnal Green, who had been in the Home Guard since he was sixteen, refused to become a coal miner and insisted that he wanted to fight. When he was prosecuted, an indulgent magistrate called him 'public-spirited' and urged the authorities to think again. Ernest Bevin indignantly countered that it was for a magistrate to apply the law, not to pontificate about public issues; the luckless Jenner ended up down a mine.

Even when the little blitz was at its worst the winter programmes of sport continued almost uninterrupted. The same was true throughout almost the entire war. The main protagonists were often soldiers, sailors or airmen on extended leave; the traditional matches were replaced by tourneys between police and fire services, or Army and Navy, yet still much the same people were playing the same games in the same arenas. Cricket was the prime example of how everything could change and yet remain the same. County cricket and full-blooded test matches were abandoned; the Oval was handed over to wartime purposes; almost all the stars, both amateur and professional, joined the services; yet on most summer Saturday afternoons at Lord's the heroes of the pre-war game were to be seen carrying on as before. It was at Lord's that the sacred flame of English cricket was most sedulously kept alive. At the beginning of the war the ground had been handed over to the RAF as a depot to which recruits could report and where they were fitted out and despatched to their training station. Even in the first flurry of excitement, however, the main pitch, pavilion and stands were sacrosanct; the practice ground was surrendered but was soon opened to cricketers for occasional use. A few of the traditional matches – between Oxford and Cambridge, for instance – were never withdrawn, otherwise the ground was at first used almost entirely for one-day matches between groups in some way involved in war work.

In 1939, 330,616 people paid for admittance at Lord's turnstiles; in 1940 it was a mere 53,350. Then came the blitz. A bomb which landed on adjoining Wellington Road damaged some buildings; an oil bomb fell thirty yards to the left of the sightscreen and scorched the sacred turf – out of it tumbled a photograph of a young German officer bearing a scrawled message, 'With Compliments'; incendiaries started fires in the pavilion; but on the whole Lord's survived pretty well. Pelham ('Plum') Warner, high priest of English cricket, maintained his vigil throughout the war. Charles Graves called on him in April 1941: 'It was a hot, sunny day and there was a pleasant sound of ball on cricket bat on the practice pitch. Plum proudly showed me the places where incendiaries, oil bombs and high explosive had been remedied on the cricket ground.' That year those paying for attendance rose to just under 90,000, plus an unknown number of servicemen in uniform who were admitted free. They saw the Royal Air Force *v.* The Rest, a match of almost test quality. The RAF had eight former international players in their side, including such great cricketers as Cyril Washbrook and Bill Edrich, but were still skittled out for fifty-one runs. Later the same year Pilot Officer Edrich was in the crowd when St Mary's Hospital played UCS Old Boys. It was a memorable occasion, for during it Edrich, a professional cricketer, sat down to lunch with Warner and the former England captain, G. O. Allen. To the uninitiated this may not sound particularly dramatic, but to those who knew the immutable shibboleths of English cricket it was as seminal as the ending of apartheid or the storming of the Tuileries.

Another breakthrough came the following year when for the first time cricket was played at Lord's on a Sunday. Even though the match was between two strong teams – the Royal Air Force and the Royal Australian Air Force – it was not advertised for fear of angry reactions from the Lord's Day Observance Society. As a result there were only sixty spectators, including one clergyman; while there were 22,000 on the August bank holiday to watch a combined Middlesex and Essex team play Surrey–Kent. At the time this was held to be a capacity crowd, but by 1943 means had been found to squeeze in an extra 3000 for the first game with a genuine test match atmosphere. An England XI featuring Denis Compton, Ames, Gimblett and R. W. V. Robins played a Dominions team including Keith Miller, Constantine, Carmody and Martindale. Martindale's first over was of eleven balls and yielded nineteen runs. Another England XI playing the West Indies included Denis and Leslie Compton, Ames, Edrich, J. D. Robertson, Trevor Bailey, Godfrey Evans and Alec Bedser. All eight held military rank; Sergeant Bedser got a hat trick and took six for twenty-seven. Attendance fell away in 1944, the summer of the flying bombs, but in 1945 reached 414,000 – well above the pre-war figure.

The crowds at Lord's looked small next to the multitudes who flocked to football matches. The problems posed by London's decision to go it alone were solved in 1941 by an uneasy compromise which saw Aldershot, Reading, Watford, Brighton and Portsmouth included in a London League. It was a simulacrum of the pre-war League: players might appear one week for one club, another week for another; teams were cobbled together at the last minute on the basis of who could or could not get leave from their unit; boys of fifteen and veterans of fifty filled the gaps. But the supporters were as loyal and vociferous as ever and the internationals at Wembley regularly drew crowds of 60–70,000. At first the authorities tried to limit attendances but gradually restrictions were relaxed and soon became almost meaningless. Seventy-five thousand people saw Scotland beaten 3–0 by England on 6 January 1942; the proceeds went to Mrs Churchill's Aid-to-Russia Fund. The Cup Final was almost equally well attended and much of the traditional flummery preserved; at Wembley on 9 May 1942 Portsmouth played Brentford in a match heralded by the band of the Scots Guards and a solo soprano from the WAAF. Less traditional for Wembley was a rugby match between England and Scotland, displaced from Twickenham by the demands of allotments and civil defence. It was the first rugger international to be played at Wembley. In 1945 the London League was enlarged by the addition of Southampton and re-titled the Football League South, but the pattern did not radically change. Attendances continued to grow; 85,000 watched the 1944 Cup Final between Chelsea and Charlton.

In early 1942 London's thirteen greyhound tracks – Haringey, Wembley, Catford and New Cross the most prominent – were limited to one meeting a week, but these could be on Wednesdays, Thursdays or Saturdays. The authorities were unhappy lest midweek sport encourage absenteeism from the factories and in March meetings were restricted to Saturdays only. The tote was discontinued and bookmakers, unless they knew their clients extremely well, insisted on ready money. Crowds were nevertheless huge, too much so in the opinion of Stafford Cripps, the grimly austere Lord Privy Seal. It was Cripps who curbed midweek greyhound racing. He was still more eager to cut down on professional boxing. His anger was kindled by a bout at the Albert Hall which attracted 4500 people who, he felt, would have been better employed on war work. He could not ban boxing altogether, but he succeeded in ensuring

Queueing for fish. Products came and went in the foodshops with disconcerting volatility, but no supply was more inconstant than that of fish

38 children were killed when a German fighter bomber attacked Sandhurst Road School in Catford, Lewisham, early in 1943. This photograph was unsurprisingly marked by the censor: 'Not to be used in Great Britain' (p. 237)

A mobile canteen outside houses damaged by a V1 in Norbury. Extensive damage to roofs was a common effect of such raids

The V2 caused far more devastation, as seen in this photograph of Gordon Hill

People queueing to enter one of the new deep shelters. It took much popular clamour before the authorities agreed to open the doors to the public (p. 300)

Evacuees were pouring back by the autumn of 1944, causing such congestion at Paddington that a ban had to be put on sending luggage in advance

Workmen prepare the lights of Fleet Street for the changeover from 'moonlight' to the full peacetime standard (p. 314)

Tickertape streams from the newspaper office windows in Salisbury Square (*above*) while (*below*) a VE Day crowd celebrates around a bonfire in Wapping

VJ Day. Crowds congregate in Piccadilly

On VE and VJ Days the dome of St Paul's was picked out by searchlights –
looking 'like a marvellous piece of jewellery invented by a magician,'
wrote the critic Desmond MacCarthy (p. 327)

that audiences were limited to about half the capacity of the arena. Haringey, which would have expected to take £8000 for a big fight before the war, was now lucky if it had a gate of £3000. It is a remarkable reflection of the mood of the times that Cripps, instead of being condemned as a prude and killjoy, was hailed as a hero – Londoners in 1942 almost wanted to suffer. Not even Cripps, however, could stop them packing the Tottenham Hotspur football ground to see the British heavyweight champion, Len Harvey, defend his title against the immensely popular Freddie Mills. Mills won in the second round.

If only because of the shortage of facilities, Londoners had always been more likely to watch sport than to take part in it, and more likely to read about it than either. There were few tennis courts in London and most of these were abandoned or dug up for allotments early in the war. Wimbledon kept eight grass courts in action, four of them on loan to the fire services. Seven pigs, poultry and rabbits inhabited the other courts and a donkey grazed on the tea lawn. The tennis club was hit by two bombs, one of which fell near the centre court and pitted it with flying debris; the authorities reckoned that they could have it ready for action within a week but for five years refrained from doing so. Those few members who did turn up to play had to hire reconditioned balls, three at a time. The nets were patched with string.

Golfers did rather better; about sixty courses remained open in the London region. Most had parts of the rough turned into allotments and additional hazards were offered by trenches dug across the fairways and posts of wood sunk in concrete in every large flat space, but they could still provide a game of a sort. Except at bank holidays they were not heavily used. Surveying the almost deserted Coombe Hill golf course, a female Mass Observer surmised that people had a conscience about indulging in this sort of pursuit in wartime. That may have been so, but it seems at least as likely that the problem of covering the seven odd miles from Hyde Park Corner without a car deterred any but the most local of members. The traditional bar at the club house was rarely available and at Hampstead Charles Graves found that 'There were no caddies, of course. Caddies are all getting £5 or £6 a week in munition work.' Lester Pearson, then in the Canadian High Commission, went with a young Foreign Office official, Roger Makins, and another friend to play golf at Roehampton. He was luckier over caddies but encountered other problems. Just as he was about to drive off, his caddy advised him 'to slice well over to the right, "farther over than usual, sir, because there is a time bomb on the left there by that red flag on the 18th fairway". So I gave my slice rein and kept over to the left so successfully that I almost beaned an old goat who had decided to spend the afternoon in one of the tank pits dug on the course to trip up any Nazi aeroplane that might try to land there. Personally I don't think it's a time bomb at all, merely a dud AA shell, but erring on the side of caution is, no doubt, wise in these circumstances. Well, our game progressed without incident for a few holes, I always placing my shots alongside one of those pits – so useful to drop into in case anything should drop down. Then suddenly we discovered an additional bunker in the form of a crater on the 4th fairway, and another, a deep hole, right in front of the 11th tee. As if golf isn't a difficult enough game!'

On 4 June 1944, a large crowd watched the Australians play cricket at Lord's. Few of those present can have thought exclusively of the game. At last it seemed the time had come for the invasion of mainland Europe. People had been pressing for it, talking about it, dreading it for three years or more. In the last three months it had come to seem not merely inevitable but imminent. The demands it would make on the railways and the closure of large parts of the south coast at last persuaded Londoners to put up with the stay-at-home Easter for which the government had so long been hankering. The only important exodus was a day trip to Windsor to see the Derby favourite, Orestes, beaten by a neck. Back in town the public ambled around the streets, joining interminable queues for the zoo or Madame Tussaud's or trying to get a seat in one of the news theatres. 'It is fun to get a nice, unhurried look at one's own town,' said Joyce Benfield, a typist. 'Today we spent the morning seeing St Paul's and wandering about Fleet Street. This afternoon we are going to have an orgy of window gazing. Then, perhaps, we will go to the pictures. We think it's going to be the best holiday of all.'

Throughout April and into May, the place, date and consequences of the invasion were endlessly debated. Vivienne Hall complained of the endless whispering and speculation, ' "It will be hell when it starts", "You'll see, London will be bombed day and night when it starts", "We shall just live in our shelters when it starts", and so it goes on, until I for one feel I could scream, "Well, let it start, and we will see what happens." ' Then, towards the middle of May, as if exhaustion had supervened or a fever burnt out, speculation ended. It would come when it would come, and that would be soon enough. People settled down to wait, like peasants on the slopes of Etna tending their grapes even though an eruption was predicted.

One by-product of the invasion was expected to be an influx of French refugees, perhaps as many as 7000, whose villages would be devastated by the advancing Allies. One side of Onslow Square was taken over, huts built all around and holes cut in the walls of the houses to allow easier communication. Parts of Cranley Gardens and Sumner Place were also converted and large nurseries prepared, distempered and stocked with cots and toys. 'Vast expense,' commented Hilda Neal gloomily, 'wonder if any gratitude will be felt. Doubt it, knowing human nature. Probably think it their due. Suppose it is, if their homes have all been destroyed.'

The refugees never arrived; on the other hand, it seemed that almost overnight, towards the end of May, London emptied of its military personnel. Many were still to be found at the innumerable headquarters buildings, but the great floating mass of those who would be involved in the invasion was suddenly withdrawn. Restaurants and nightclubs were half empty, taxis became miraculously easier to find, the American servicemen's clubs closed – some, it was said, to be converted into hospitals. Some soldiers were still in London, but confined to barracks awaiting the moment to move. One unit was briefed on the invasion plans, issued with French money and then incarcerated in the West Ham football stadium; one hundred or so found this insufficiently amusing, broke bounds and went to celebrate in the West End. For a moment it seemed as if the security of the whole operation might have been jeopardised, but the men were quickly rounded up and the authorities prayed that no word of their indiscretions would get across the Channel.

On 6 June the landings began at dawn. It should have been a dramatic moment in London, the culmination of so many years of waiting and preparation. Instead it was just like any other day – men and women went to their offices, did the shopping, exercised the dog. What else was there to do? And yet it left Londoners feeling curiously flat. Once again they were sidelined, the great issues were being settled far away. 'The un-English urge to talk to strangers which came over Londoners during the blitzes, and in other recent times of crisis, was noticeably absent,' wrote Mollie Panter-Downes. 'Everybody seemed to be existing wholly in a preoccupied silence of his own, a silence which had something almost frantic about it, as if the effort of punching bus tickets, or shopping for kitchen pans, or whatever the day's chore might be, was, in its quiet way, harder to bear than a bombardment.' People queued for their newspapers, turned into the pub to listen to the radio, pondered over the cheerful but uncommunicative bulletins, then went home. The cinemas and theatres were empty; the restaurants had only a sprinkling of customers; taxis cruised the streets in search of fares; the churches, for a time, attracted more than the usual meagre ration of worshippers, but they too soon emptied. People listened to the King's broadcast to the nation, but they did so at home. Long before midnight of D-Day the city was dead.

It was the calm of the Londoners which most struck foreign visitors. Ed Murrow wondered at 'the steadiness of the civilian populace'. As he watched them going about their daily business, he said, he almost wanted to shout at them, ' "Don't you know that history is being made this day?" They realised it, all right, but their emotions were under complete control.' Strong emotions held under rigorous control were also what struck Richard Brown Baker. In his office the only person who seemed aware that anything out of the ordinary was going on was a young colleague named Nora Beloff, who 'was so keyed up that every motion she made was in mad haste, as if victory depended on the speed with which she entered a room or grasped the telephone . . . the name Beloff suggests that she is not a pure-bred Englishwoman, so I suppose ancestry explains her agitation in the midst of all this English calm. The restraint isn't apathy, of course. It's just Britishers being true to form.'

The restraint was sometimes hard to maintain. Almost every Londoner had a friend, a relative, a lover who was likely to be involved in the landings. Heavy casualties seemed certain, a bloodbath possible; who would survive and who die? And suppose the landings failed? The first reports were optimistic, but Londoners were used to cheerful news followed by disaster. If the invading forces were driven back into the sea, how long would it take to assemble another armada? Why should the next invasion fare any better? How many more years would the war continue? Londoners knew that this was the most critical day of the war, perhaps the most critical day of their lives, yet there was nothing they could do to control their destinies. So they did their jobs, ate their suppers, listened to the news and, in due course, went to bed.

15

Doodlebugs and Flying Gas Mains

IN LONDON, warned a Home Intelligence Weekly Report in December 1943, 'it appears that a majority are now giving some thought to the possibility of a retaliatory secret weapon. Indeed, many are anxious about it, though there are still a large number who laugh at the idea.'

In the six months before D-Day horror stories continued to circulate: rockets had fallen on Park Lane; a supersonic beam, directed by aircraft hundreds of miles away, would shrivel up acres of city in a matter of seconds; huge stocks of bleach powder were said to have been delivered at gas decontamination centres. As the moment of invasion approached, such apocalyptic fantasies lost some of their potency. The more quantifiable risk of heavy reprisal raids by the Luftwaffe began to occupy people's minds. Apprehension coupled with a fear that the nightmare would never end seemed to be the prevailing mood; references to war-weariness and depression abound in the intelligence reports. Then came D-Day. The realisation that the landings had been successfully carried out conjured up a dramatic swing in mood. 'The invasion of France has produced a complete change in public feeling – relief from tension, a marked rise in spirits and a feeling that the final phase of the war has at last begun,' declared the Weekly Report. 'There is little mention of war-weariness now.'

Almost light-heartedly London prepared itself for the German counterstroke. Rome had fallen on 4 June, France was invaded on 6 June, the Japanese retreat from Imphal began on 7 June: surely such victories could not pass unchallenged? 'We had all expected the Luftwaffe to mount a massive reprisal raid on London and had steeled ourselves for air-attack,' wrote Alex Savidge, a REME private posted in the capital. When nothing happened it was an anti-climax, a relief certainly, yet in a curious way a disappointment. Then, at 4.13 a.m. on 13 June what was taken by those in the neighbourhood to be a German bomber which had been shot down exploded on a lettuce patch near Gravesend. This incident was hardly heard of, still less thought about in London. Ten minutes or so later there was another explosion, destroying a railway bridge over Grove Road, Bow, and cutting the Chelmsford–Liverpool Street line. This too was believed to be caused by a crashing German bomber. It is now known that Hitler had ordered a mass attack by pilotless aircraft to be launched in February 1944, but that it had proved impossible to get the launch sites ready. Even in June the offensive went off at half-cock; of the ten V1s launched on 13 June, half crashed almost at once and one disappeared into the Channel. It was not till the night of 15–16 June that the first serious assault took place: 244 missiles were fired; 45 exploded on or just after take-off, destroying nine of the launching sites, 73 got through to Greater London.

Sister G. Thomas was on duty at her hospital in Highgate. At midnight, 'suddenly a plane dived, it seemed to come from nowhere. A load of incendiaries or bombs were dropped, then complete silence. It was all over in a moment; everyone thought it was a stray plane, but in twenty minutes the same thing happened again.' By 7.50 a.m. she had begun to smell a rat – 'the "phantom" planes still come, unload and then silence'. William Regan on the Isle of Dogs was equally sceptical. A light aircraft passed over and was shot down; from the noise it must have been carrying a heavy bomb, he concluded. Then it happened again, and again. 'I said to Alf that the gunners were on form, three over, three down. Hardly credible. We began to discuss the possibility of them not being planes, as we could see flames coming from the tails of them, also a light in the nose.'

The thing that most surprised a thirty-five-year-old man recorded by Mass Observation was that within a few minutes of the missiles beginning to arrive everybody seemed to be quite certain what they were. 'I joined a group of people who were staring up at the sky and they were all saying "Pilotless planes". I can't imagine why everyone was so certain so quickly.' Among the last to guess were the anti-aircraft gunners, who congratulated themselves on the extraordinary accuracy of their fire and were too busy preparing for the next plane to have much time to speculate about its nature. Leslie Mann, a teacher living in Sidcup, had a son-in-law who was on duty that night with a rocket-gun in Blackheath. He returned home elated at his crew's success in disposing of a German bomber. Only gradually did it dawn on him that his gun had contributed nothing. 'A competent authority would have warned us, "The enemy is about to send over a lot of high explosives in pilotless, expendable small aeroplanes. Be prepared, as they are due any day or night." No such warning was vouchsafed us,' wrote Mann indignantly.

It could have been vouchsafed if the authority, competent or otherwise, had wished it. The government had a remarkably clear picture of the nature of the threat, though uncertain when the attack would come and how many missiles would be involved. By the end of 1943 both Churchill and Morrison had dropped heavy though guarded hints about secret weapons in the offing. 'In all the chat about whether the Germans will shortly try out something new and nasty,' wrote Mollie Panter-Downes, 'the only point on which everyone seems agreed is that the capital will be the natural and inevitable target.'

In March 1944, when the more alarmist of the intelligence agencies were predicting that as many as 45,000 V1s might be launched, cautious briefings were given to senior members of the civil defence teams and the word was allowed to filter down to the lower ranks. Plans were made for the reactivation of some of the disused shelters. Herbert Morrison thwarted, or at least delayed, a plan to cut down the existing civil defence forces (already much reduced since the end of the blitz) by a further 50,000 men and women. Concrete bases were put in the hills around Sidcup to enable a wall of barrage balloons to be erected. There was heavy bombing of the German experimental station at Peenemünde and of the launch sites. But Churchill was not prepared to take the public fully into his confidence, partly because some of his information had come from wireless intercepts, the secrecy of which he was determined not to jeopardise; partly because the project might still abort, and there seemed little to gain by alarming Londoners before it was necessary. Wiseacres claimed to have known about it all along. Everyone was talking about 'the new German secret weapon', Mr Britton told his daughter in the United States. 'Of course it is neither new nor secret. *We* knew about this sort of thing long ago but the brass hats, the Colonel Blimps, couldn't see its possibilities.' He exaggerated both his own prescience and the brass hats' short-sightedness; if anything, the latter tended to rate too highly the destructiveness of the new weapon. But until the attack began there was not much to be done.

It was curious how many missiles had been dropping on Hampstead or even further afield, commented Anthony Weymouth early in July. Now they seemed to be falling on St John's Wood: 'It almost looks as if they are shortening the range.' Though inhabitants of Hampstead and St John's Wood could have been forgiven for thinking otherwise, they got off lightly. A. P. Herbert was told by Churchill that Tower Bridge had been chosen by the Germans as the focal point of the bombardment; one bomb passed through the central arch and sank the Tower Bridge tug on the other side, and there were other near misses. Due to some miscalculation, however, most V1s fell short and landed in the less densely populated areas south of the river. There was an agonised debate in the Cabinet on whether it would be proper to conduct a deception operation designed to convince the Germans that they were overshooting and should shorten their range still further. Morrison strongly objected – 'We must not play God,' he said – and it was agreed that it would be wrong to 'assume any direct degree of responsibility for action which would affect the areas against which flying bombs were aimed'. But this ruling left some room for interpretation. There seems little doubt that by double agents and other means the Germans were given the impression that their missiles were landing two or three miles beyond the points where they were exploding.

Croydon was the victim of this misconception. It lay in the track of a majority of the bombs. Even if the range had been correctly set a large number of V1s would have been shot down or have fallen prematurely while passing over the borough. It suffered more than any other region; 142 V1s fell on it (Aylmer Firebrace suggests 139, a local historian 143; since some flying bombs were claimed by two boroughs and a few failed to explode an exact figure can never be established); 1000 houses were destroyed, 57,000 severely damaged. The new Archbishop of Canterbury, William Temple, went there on 11 July; bombs fell continually throughout his visit and once at least he had to abandon his archiepiscopal dignity and dive for cover. It was a Croydon woman who was supposed to have uttered the characteristic prayer of those in the track of the V1s, 'Please

God, don't let it explode here, but please don't let it do too much damage when it does explode.' It is unlikely that Temple would have seen much to criticise in this not totally Christian but wholly human petition. It could have been heard as often in other boroughs south of the river. Wandsworth was the next worst hit with 124, then Lewisham and Woolwich.

Though most Londoners seemed to know where the V1s were falling they were given little or no official information. The government took the view that the Germans, even if not actively misled, should be kept guessing about what they were hitting. At first the media were not allowed so much as to reveal that the capital was affected. Londoners were disgruntled about this neglect. The last three days had been one long alert, complained Vere Hodgson on 18 June, and no one had had much sleep. 'Nothing is said on the wireless or in the papers except . . . Southern England! This is us – and we are all fed up.' Ten days later Mrs Byers bemoaned the fact that all she ever heard on official bulletins was, 'Flying bombs came over in the night. Damage and casualties have been reported.' Nobody was ever congratulated on their fortitude or condoled with on their misfortunes. 'I wonder what the rest of England is thinking? If they only knew what poor old London is getting.' It was not just that London earned no sympathy for its suffering; the news blackout made people think that the worst was being concealed. There were rumours everywhere, one man told a Mass Observer, 'and people so nervy and nobody saying an encouraging word – it's not like the old blitz, people are just getting down and disheartened'.

Churchill at least was far from downhearted. The Prime Minister was in very good form, wrote Alan Brooke in his diary, 'quite ten years younger, all due to the fact that the flying bombs have again put us in the front line'. It was also due to the fact that, unlike his fellow citizens, he knew what was going on. He realised that the policy of secrecy was going too far. On 6 July, in a packed House of Commons, he set out in stark but undramatic terms the extent of the threat and made it clear that London had borne the brunt. 'Now Londoners feel that they can put in their places those pushing people in the real Southern England who have been inclined to think that London wasn't getting half such a warm time as they were,' wrote Mollie Panter-Downes.

*

The V1, the 'V' standing for *Vergeltungswaffe* – retaliation weapon – was so-called to give the impression that a long series of secret weapons was on the way. The Londoners called them buzz bombs, bumble bombs, robot bombs, most commonly of all, doodlebugs; the Germans, more colourfully, 'hell hounds' or 'fire dragons'. For the first week the AA guns blazed away furiously, even though the missiles were over central London; thus sometimes shooting them down where they would do most damage. Then a change of tactics supervened; the guns were withdrawn to the south coast where they could try to intercept the missiles before they reached built-up areas. The decision was obviously correct but left people feeling curiously bereft: 'The lack of guns strikes me as an admission of failure in defence,' wrote James Lees-Milne. It was, instead, a harbinger of success. Almost every week a higher proportion of V1s was destroyed before they reached London. In the period between 12 June and 5 September – by which date the launching sites had effectively all been overrun by the advancing Allies – 6725 flying bombs approached the coast of England and 3463 were destroyed by AA guns, fighters or balloons.

Goebbels proudly proclaimed when the offensive started that London was already paralysed and would soon be totally destroyed. 'This is absurd,' commented Harold Nicholson. There was hardly any sign of damage and the traffic flowed as densely as in April or May. Nicolson was more right than Goebbels, but by mid-July, when the pace temporarily slackened, large areas of London had been laid waste. Yet Londoners had adapted, had learnt how to reduce the dangers and to treat the threat with affected if not real nonchalance. As a general rule – though some freakish exceptions were recorded – if the engine of a V1 was still going when it was overhead, those below were safe; when it cut out and began to dive was the time to look for shelter. People in the street would glance up if they heard a flying bomb but would ostentatiously pay no other attention; if any emotion showed, it was as when a wasp is buzzing around a room.

John Lehmann was at a literary lunch at the Savoy when a V1 approached. 'We all became a little more thoughtful,' he wrote, 'conversation faltered, dried up here and there for some seconds, though the thread was never entirely lost; not a fork was lifted to a mouth for a brief span of time that seemed an eternity. When the machine had evidently veered away again, it was satisfactory to observe that no member of the party had actually disappeared under the table.' Literary figures evidently responded well to this particular challenge. Edith Sitwell was in full flow at a poetry reading when a flying bomb passed over. She 'merely lifted her eyes to the ceiling for a moment and, giving her voice a little more volume to counter the racket in the sky, read on'.

The authorities became concerned about the failure of the public to take cover and the Ministry of Home Security issued some helpful hints to citizens urging them not to feel sheepish about being the first to shelter. Nobody paid much attention; sometimes with fatal results. Kenneth Clark was buying a ticket at Waterloo Station when a V1 cut out overhead. He shouted to the others in the queue to take cover and himself went to ground behind a pillar. When he picked himself up he found that several of his fellow queuers were dead or injured. They had remained standing – either from bravado or a determination not to lose their place.

'We are getting used to the buzz bombs and also fewer are coming over,' wrote Charles Ritchie at the beginning of a brief lull in July. 'People are beginning to come to life again – to ring up their friends and to go out to restaurants. I heard my first fresh piece of scandal today – a healthy sign. Life marches on.' Lesley Boyde, who was working with the Free French, attributed the lull to the fact that new shelters had been opened: 'The Jerries seem to realise that they can't kill so many and are maybe giving it up as a bad job – we hope!' The 'we hope!' presumably indicated a measure of scepticism. It was justified. Three nights later the attacks were resumed. Kenneth Holmes from Islington noted that, whenever there was a lull, people assumed it would be permanent, and when bombing resumed, announced that it could not go on for long. 'But I think we have a lot more suffering to come.'

He was right, but though there were still to be many more flying bombs and some particularly bloody incidents, the public felt more and more, and with increasingly good reason, that the threat was being overcome. In the House of Commons on 2 August Churchill spoke of the V1 offensive and gave some daunting figures about the damage done. That night the Germans launched their heaviest attack; 97 flying bombs exploded in the London area. 'It is curious how many people are angry at Churchill,' remarked Richard Brown

Baker. But it was almost the last serious fling. The defences were functioning far better: in June 44 per cent of reported flying bombs had reached Greater London, in July the figure was 33 per cent, in the second half of August it was only 17 per cent. Even more important, the launching sites in the Pas de Calais were being rapidly overrun.

It was high time. In the first fortnight of the attacks the casualty rate was as high as in the same period of the blitz, though the proportion of injuries to deaths was much higher since the V1s as often as not struck by day when the streets were crowded. After a few weeks Churchill claimed that, on a rough average, each flying bomb killed one person. The final tally was almost twice as bad. Lambeth did worse than the norm: 72 flying bombs killed 260 and left 648 seriously wounded; Dagenham did better, 32 bombs for 24 dead. By the time the launching sites had been overrun, 2340 flying bombs had reached London, 5475 people had been killed. One bad incident could transform the statistics for a borough. A bomb which fell outside Bush House in the Aldwych when the street was crowded killed more than a hundred. The trees lost their leaves but were festooned with human flesh; one survivor of the explosion stepped out from the doorway in which he had been sheltering and was cut in half by a sheet of plate glass falling from above. A fifth of Chelsea's fatal casualties were caused by a single V1 which destroyed the sleeping quarters used by American soldiers in Lower Sloane Street.

Minor incidents attracted undue attention because of the targets hit: a V1 which fell in the garden of Buckingham Palace broke a few windows, demolished a summerhouse and damaged the tennis court on which George VI had used to play before the war; a bomb on the zoo killed two pheasants and an adder, which died of the cold after the roof of its high-temperature house had been shattered by blast. In Bermondsey a cereal warehouse was hit and the area around flooded with three feet of grain. A fire started and the firemen's hoses washed the grain into the drains where it swelled and blocked the flow of sewage. An appalling stench and a plague of flies were added to the miseries of those who lived nearby.

The most celebrated incident in the whole campaign came on Sunday 18 June, when the Guards' chapel on Birdcage Walk was destroyed, an event made prominent by the distinction and number of the victims, the conspicuousness of the building and the macabre twist that led to the destruction of a church on a Sunday morning when matins were in full swing. The *Te Deum* was in progress – 'To Thee all Angels cry aloud, the Heavens and all the Powers therein' – when the building exploded; 119 people were killed and 102 seriously injured, of whom some later died. No other V1 attack cost so many lives. On the same day three V1s landed in Streatham, severely damaged 3000 properties but caused only a handful of deaths.

The time wasted by the attacks caused as much annoyance as anything. At the BBC alerts were almost continuous and precious hours of the day were spent running downstairs when the blue light which indicated approaching danger was shown, and back up again when the flying bomb had fallen or gone elsewhere. For a few days it seemed as if Goebbels's boast that London had been paralysed by the V1s might prove justified, but solutions gradually evolved. Heston and Isleworth pioneered a more sensible approach when they introduced their own warning system; three blasts on sirens at the electricity sub-stations indicated that danger was imminent, otherwise people could ignore the sirens and get on with life. The Home Office was indignant and a police inspector warned the official involved that he was breaking the law. The council went ahead regardless, the system worked, and Herbert Morrison accepted the inevitable and instituted local warnings for the whole of London.

The first klaxons were sounded in the City in mid-August, from Whitbread's brewery in Chiswell Street, and soon eighteen more were installed. A week later the system was extended to Westminster, where thirty klaxons were set up at the Houses of Parliament, City Hall, Grosvenor House, Shell-Mex House and other tall buildings. Only the dwindling of the threat in early September prevented the spread of the new technique to the whole of London. By then most big stores and offices had their own systems, which sounded only when a bomb was almost overhead. Meanwhile teams of spotters on the tops of Victoria Coach Station, the London Transport offices in Broadway and other vantage points despatched mobile columns of reserve vehicles and ambulances to places where bombs had fallen. Sometimes they despatched units of the Home Guard as well, to deter looters and keep sightseers out of the way of the fire-fighters and rescue services. In Eltham the Home Guard once took its duties a little too seriously and kept the fire brigade at bay as well, but on the whole they gave the depleted forces of civil defence some much needed support.

For a time the V1s preoccupied Londoners almost entirely. The second front was not forgotten but slipped into second place: 'It was shameful how fear wrenched thoughts home,' wrote Elizabeth Bowen – 'droning *things*, mindlessly making for you, thick and fast, day and night, tore the calico of London, raising obscene dust out of the sullen bottom mind.' The insensibility, the inhumanity was what most obsessed the victims of the V1s. 'No enemy was risking his life up there,' wrote Evelyn Waugh, 'it was as impersonal as a plague, as though the city was infested with enormous, venomous insects.' By the end of June Kenneth Holmes claimed that people were getting used to the raids but that they were still the main topic of conversation, 'We seem to have forgotten the war in France and Italy, and are too occupied with this war on London.' The Home Intelligence Report for the same week recorded that all other war news had been swamped in the minds of Londoners, 'many of whom find it impossible to think of anything else'.

Except in those areas totally devastated in 1940, London reacted to the V1s much as it had to the blitz. An immediate response of defiance, almost exultation, was followed by a period of despondency. Gradually the mood brightened again as people developed new patterns of living to meet the needs of the emergency. In the first few days there was some nervousness and great weariness, but nobody felt the new weapon could affect the outcome of the war. 'I don't expect it to go on for more than a week or two at the most,' said a Fulham man, 'and then, anyway, it's the South Coast they're really after, where all the invasion stuff is.' Mass Observers reported that people were much more cheerful than they had been when the Luftwaffe returned earlier that year; this was Hitler's last fling and it would soon fail. The V1s were clearly more expensive and less efficient than manned bombers; their use proved how desperate the Germans must be. Alexander McKee's only complaint was that the government were playing down the seriousness of the assault, 'If this clap-trap is intended to keep up morale, it's unnecessary – morale is first rate.'

Within a fortnight the mood had darkened again. At least during the blitz it had been possible to snatch a little sleep during daylight hours; the stream of V1s seemed relentless. 'We now live, sleep (when we can), eat and think of nothing but flying bombs,' wrote Vivienne Hall. 'They are always with us – at the office we listen for our warning overhead bell and dash to the store cupboard many times a day as the beauties fly over; the all-clears and alerts follow one another all day long, sometimes as many as fourteen times, and at night I lie and listen as the approaching bomb gets nearer, and as it passes overhead I draw up my knees and cover my head with the bedclothes until it has gone or bursts with a sickening thud.' Sister G. Thomas in her Highgate hospital prepared for the night by packing a small bag with a few necessities which she kept by her bunk. Her torch was under her pillow, together with her spectacle case in which she put a slip of paper with the telephone numbers of a few friends. In her pocket she kept a whistle, in case she should be buried alive under the debris. 'Maybe I will laugh as I read this diary long after the war is over, but there is not much to laugh at now. True, when you are with other people, you keep a grip on your nerves and carry on at least with a pleasant face. But when you are alone you are full of fear.'

Some were relatively untroubled by the flying bombs. John Lehmann admitted that there were moments when it seemed that 'human existence was not much better than beetle or ant life', but did not feel that public alarm was anything like as great as German propagandists painted it. There were some who would joke in the face of any disaster. A neighbour of Mrs Bell, who lived next to a cemetery, woke to find that half a headstone had been blown on to her balcony: 'It said, "In Loving Memory of Maud". I ain't 'alf glad my bleedin' name is Ivy!' But many were pushed almost to breaking-point. Sister Thomas got a few days' leave shortly after her hospital had suffered a direct hit. 'Eventually I reached the station; never have I had a bigger fight to keep from screaming; so at last I reached my friends, and then I broke down. I suppose I knew there was no need to fight any more – I collapsed and screamed and Hilda gave me brandy.' Gladys Strelitz in Ilford found the strain intolerable; she started to walk in her sleep and even when awake needed help to get downstairs. 'I knew I couldn't carry on much longer, that something would have to be done about it. All the tablets the doctor was giving me weren't helping me a little bit, so I ended up with nervous exhaustion.'

Some comforted themselves with the thought that the attack could not last for ever; however many V1s the Germans might possess, sooner or later they must come to the end of their supply. But 'later' might be very late; Churchill in early July made 'one of his fighting speeches', Mrs Byers wrote in her diary, but he offered no hope of an end to the bombardment until the sites had been occupied. 'We in London feel very depressed . . . Well, we must be patient, I suppose.' But the long term seemed to offer little better. 'The Germans can in the future, in complete secrecy underground, prepare more of such things and launch them on an unprepared world,' mused Vere Hodgson. 'Man will perish under the machines that he has made.'

Morale was at its lowest in late June and early July. 'There is not one man I know who's getting used to it; if anything, it is getting everybody down,' wrote William Regan. It was as true in the bus depôt where he worked as in the shops or streets: 'You can see by their expressions, and the way they seem to go – well, sort of, "Let me get out of this". You can feel the uneasiness. Unlike the old days, when everyone wanted to help everyone else.' Field-Marshal Smuts told Sarah Gertrude Millin that Londoners were tired and nervy, 'their food is monotonous, it has been a bad summer. They look worn, and so do their buildings. They're taking it but they're suffering.' London was 'more dirty, more unsociable, more plague-stricken than ever', wrote Cyril Connolly in an article that did not appear until late August but must have been written about this time. 'The civilians who remain grow more and more hunted and disagreeable; like toads, each sweating and palpitating under his particular stone.' Alexander McKee, always scornful of civilians, sneered at those who said that London was hell on earth and wished they could be subjected to an attack by dive-bombers. ' "We ought to get the George Cross", say the Londoners. "You ought to get the Order of the Yellow Streak", say I. 25 per cent can take it, and I give them their full due; the rest are in varying stages of funk.'

Angus Acworth, another Londoner who judged his fellows harshly, told Richard Brown Baker that the mood was entirely different from that of 1940. Then, he said, everybody set their teeth and fatalistically went about their tasks. 'Now people are annoyed and scary. They feel the war is so close to being won that they want to live to enjoy the peace.' They took out their annoyance principally on the government. They could not understand why no steps had been taken in advance to counter the new weapon, and why over-whelming Allied air power was not now brought to bear on the few hundred missile sites responsible for their misery. 'Why didn't they build more deep shelters too?' asked an indignant forty-year-old in Fulham. The clamour for revenge was louder than at any other moment of the war; the *West London Press* assured its readers that the flying bombs had steeled the people to 'a fanaticism that bodes ill for the defeated Huns', while Tottenham Council urged the government to destroy German cities one by one until the V1 attack was halted. Herbert Morrison was booed on a tour of south London; in his memorandum to the Cabinet urging reprisals against the Germans he told his colleagues, 'I have confirmed my hunch that the people are by no means in a good temper.' The Home Intelligence Report for the week ending 4 July recorded wild rumours: 250,000 casualties, two of Churchill's daughters dead. 'Strain, weariness, fear and despondency' were widely reported. People were asking why the government was continuing to claim that morale was unimpaired 'when everyone who knows people in bombed areas knows this is a lie'.

It was reports such as this that led the Home Secretary on 27 June to present to the Cabinet the gloomiest assessment of public morale in the war to date. The public, he said, had so far withstood pretty well the dangers and discomforts of the V1 attacks. But he could not guarantee that this would continue indefinitely, especially if new secret weapons were introduced. 'I have a high degree of faith in the Londoners. But the Government would be wise to be human. This is not 1940–41 . . . the people, not unreasonably, expect a quicker and more decisive defence . . . the people have had nearly five years of war strain – they will resent this new trouble increasingly and want to know what we are doing about it . . . I assure my colleagues that I have done and will do everything to hold up their courage and spirit – but there is a limit, and the limit will come.' Sir John Anderson agreed that the continuous attacks were imposing a heavy strain and prophesied that the public would grow increasingly disaffected. Almost alone in the Cabinet, Churchill refused to be seriously concerned about civilian morale. Provided everything possible was being done to relieve their sufferings, he said, Londoners would remain as staunch as ever.

Churchill was right, and Morrison unduly pessimistic. The worst scenario – in which a rocket offensive began while the flying bombs were still in full spate and together the new weapons overwhelmed the weakened forces of civil defence – never materialised; and the spirits of the Londoners revived while the V1 menace was still at its most ferocious. 'First fears have to some extent died down, and there are now fewer references to terror or greater anxiety,' read the Home Intelligence Report of 11 July. A week later the steadier attitude had been maintained. 'The feeling that the attacks are "just something to be endured" is growing, and most people are now "carrying on as usual".' By mid-August, with the heaviest V1 assault still to come, it was stated positively that 'The majority are now "adjusted", although a few remain nervous.' Henry Willink visited Croydon and the East End and reported that 'on the whole, morale was extremely good and people were withstanding the attacks with more fortitude than in the first week or two'. The petering out of the attacks towards the end of August was not needed to save London from anything near collapse; in terms of morale, victory over the V1 had been won before the advance of the Allies made the threat increasingly unimportant.

In a decidedly ill-judged briefing of the press on 7 September Duncan Sandys, Churchill's son-in-law and Minister of Supply, said that the V1 menace was effectively over; as to a risk of attack by rockets – the V2 – he was not prepared to rule it out but believed that it would not amount to much. 'We do know quite a lot about it,' he boasted. 'In a very few days' time I feel that the press will be walking all over those places in France and will know a great deal more than we do now.' He based his views on a confident report by the Chiefs of Staff which suggested that the airborne launching of V1s was only a remote possibility and that V2 sites in Holland must have been hurriedly improvised. Any rocket attacks would be ineffective and of short duration.

He was wrong on two counts. The technique of launching V1s from aircraft was more successful than had been expected and 79 reached London after Sandys's briefing, while the V2 assault was neither ineffective nor of short duration.

The V2 was the least secret of secret weapons. As early as June an elderly working-class man with no access to inside information was stating as a received truth that the rocket must be the successor to the flying bomb, 'and I can't see how there's going to be any defence against that . . . If he starts sending shells over, we'll be sunk.' About the same time Leonard Woolf was given an informal briefing on the subject by a colonel whose information came from the interrogation of German prisoners. The colonel was talking freely to anyone around, so Woolf assumed it was common knowledge and mentioned it to a friend in the Air Ministry. He was told furiously that he had no right 'to be in possession of – far less talk of – what was a top top secret. I felt that I had only just escaped arrest and imprisonment.' The prisoners involved had no reason to reproach themselves for their indiscretion; for several months before the first V2 landed, German radio had been broadcasting dire threats about the new secret weapon which would rapidly end the war in Germany's favour. The main public debate was about the likely size of the rocket: horror stories told of a gigantic weapon weighing 70–80 tons, with a 10-ton warhead, capable of obliterating 50 acres of London in a few seconds.

At 6.40 a.m. on 8 September London was roused by a thunderous explosion at Chiswick. A little later came a second explosion at Epping. Herbert Morrison rushed to Chiswick, to find a gigantic crater but, thanks to the depth the missile had penetrated, relatively little damage in nearby streets. He had no doubt that this was the first blow in a new assault. A news blackout was ordered, so that the Germans should not know where their missile had landed, or even whether it had exploded. There followed a faintly ridiculous period in which almost everyone knew or guessed what was happening but nobody admitted it publicly. 'All day there have been rumours about the mysterious explosion,' Kenneth Holmes wrote in his diary that night. Some said it was a gasometer, others a boiler explosion in the Express Dairy Works at Chiswick, others again that a munitions dump had blown up, 'but I am wondering is this the threatened Long Range Rocket?' The gasometer theory was the one tacitly, perhaps even actively, propagated by the authorities; at Buck's Club, where people tended to be well informed, it was stated categorically that a gasworks in Chiswick had exploded, perhaps the result of sabotage. After forty-eight hours, by which time four rockets a day were falling, nobody believed a word of it.

Yet to speak of the new weapons was unpatriotic. When an explosion was heard in the Croydon factory where Kathleen Bliss was working, nobody offered any comment: 'Evidently everyone feels that no "Careless Talk" should be allowed to leak to the enemy about the effects of this latest type of attack – eyebrows are raised and shoulders shrugged but nothing said.' Even at the end of October, seven weeks after the first V2 had fallen, Mrs Byers was writing in her diary, 'I wonder when they will be acknowledged? Everyone knows what they are – horrible destructive things.' A few were less discreet. When one of the first V2s fell, a Home Guard asked a GI who was putting a fence round the crater whether it had been caused by a rocket. 'No, man, that's not a rocket. It's one of those flying gas mains.' When the Home Guard suggested that gas mains rarely flew and that this might well be the work of a V2, the GI remained incredulous: 'Rockets! Surely that's fiction? G. H. Wells stuff! It's stupid; I was told at school that nothing could move in the stratosphere.'

It was 10 November before Churchill announced the true nature of the attack; much damage had been and was being done, he admitted, but the weapon was not nearly as destructive as had been feared. The announcement came as a relief; the strain of the self-imposed censorship had been almost as oppressive as the rockets themselves. But it was clear that the weapon could do devastating harm, far worse than the first incident in Chiswick had suggested. A typical V2 landed a few hundred yards from Kenneth Holmes's house in Islington. 'I thought the end of the world had come. The earth trembled, the very air seemed to vibrate, my ears seemed to be deafened and a buzzing sound was passing through them.' The bomb had fallen on Boothby Street. Holmes rushed towards the spot. 'Goodness knows where the houses that had been struck had disappeared to. It looked as though a huge bulldozer had lifted them from the earth and there was quite an open space. Never have I seen buildings so cleanly swept away, and these are 3 or 4 storey tenement houses.' In the final tally an area about 200 yards square had been cleared, at least 50 houses demolished, 200 families rendered homeless and far more damage done in the vicinity. 'It seems incredible that one bomb could cause such devastation.'

Between 8 September 1944 and 27 March 1945, 1054 rockets fell on British soil, about half in the London region. Two to three rounds a day were fired in October, four to six in November, the figure dropped slightly in December, then rose to a peak in January and February. On 26 January, the worst day, thirteen rockets landed. By then the missiles were being picked up by radar but nothing could be done to intercept them and since even the radar operators knew only fifty seconds in advance of their arrival it was decided not to institute any system of warnings. The great majority of the V2s landed in the East End or the outer suburbs to the east and north. Ilford was the worst affected, with thirty-five hits; West Ham, Barking, Dagenham and Walthamstow were also high on the list of victims. This rekindled the old suspicions of the East End, that it had been deliberately targeted for German attack. When Mrs White, Richard Brown Baker's maid, heard that a V2 had fallen near Selfridge's her pleasure was evident; Mayfair had escaped almost all the flying bombs; if it had been immune to V2s as well, those less fortunate would have found it almost insupportable. 'So they've had one up in Oxford Street, have they?' said an elderly East End woman to a Mass Observer. 'Perhaps that'll make them realise a bit what it's like down here.'

The most serious incident – indeed, one of the worst of the whole war in London – occurred in New Cross Road, Deptford, just before Christmas, when a rocket hit a Woolworth's packed with shoppers: 168 people were killed, 120 more ended up in hospital, 11 bodies were never located, including two babies in a pram. One thousand men worked for forty-eight hours to extricate survivors. Almost as disastrous was the rocket on Smithfield Market which fell when crowds of women were flocking to the retail market for their weekly meat ration. Many of the staff were trapped in the cold storage vaults; most of these were got out cold but unharmed; the incident nevertheless cost 115 lives. The Selfridge's V2 destroyed the Christmas decorations; 'the poor little trees, with the ornaments torn from them, lay amongst the broken glass on the pavement,' noted Mrs Robert Henrey. In January a V2 hit the staff living quarters at the Royal Hospital in Chelsea, killing the hospital doctor and causing 140 pensioners to be evacuated.

There was endless debate about which was more disagreeable, the V1 or the V2. Gwladys Cox thought the rockets were worse, 'their entirely silent approach cannot be heralded by sirens and clear weather does not deter them'. John Lehmann agreed; he found their unpredictability particularly disturbing and disliked the thought that, without even a second's warning, he might be 'hurled in fragments into eternity'. More people, however, thought that the unpredictability was an advantage; if one had to die one might as well be enjoying a good night's sleep when it happened, not scrabbling about on the floor in an undignified search for safety. Whatever their opinion, everyone longed to know when the last V2 site would be captured or knocked out. Some feared that rockets, launched from isolated pockets of resistance, might keep coming even after a general ceasefire had been ordered. George Orwell found even more depressing the way that talk of the V2 invariably led to a discussion of the next war: 'Every time one goes off I hear gloomy references to "next time", and the reflection: "I suppose they'll be able to shoot them across the Atlantic by that time!"'

'How much longer does this go on, I wonder?' wailed Vivienne Hall a week or so after the first V2 had landed. 'Are we never to be free of damage and death? Surely five years is long enough for any town to have to suffer?' Her discouragement can well be understood, but most Londoners endured the V2s with remarkable equanimity. Possibly it was because the rockets came so rarely and there were no interruptions to sleep until they landed. Such complaints as there were related mainly to the government's alleged incompetence in providing shelters or organising the repair of housing.

So far as shelters were concerned the public had legitimate grounds for complaint. The knowledge that the V1 and V2 attacks would eventually be coming had led to a reconsideration of policy towards the end of 1943. Even if the new deep shelters were fully operational – and the government privately hoped to reserve most of the space for civil servants driven from their offices – a large number of Londoners would never be within easy range of a public shelter.

The solution was to provide more Anderson and indoor Morrison shelters. Production of Morrison shelters had been stopped a year before but 100,000 were now put on order and reserves of existing stock assembled at Tunbridge Wells and Reading, where they would be easily accessible. Unfortunately, the demands of D-Day slowed this operation and few new shelters had been deployed by the time the first V1 landed. By late August some 26,000 Andersons and Morrisons had been brought in from the Midlands, but few suitable sites were left where the Andersons could be installed and there were not nearly enough Morrisons to meet demand. People within range of the tube station reverted to their old habits; Christmas 1944 witnessed touching efforts to give a festive air to the bleak and unfriendly platforms. The traditional toast – 'Here's to the last war-time Christmas' – was drunk with fervour but a touch of scepticism.

Long before then it had become clear that the civil servants had no need of the new deep shelters. The government was still inclined to feel that the public had no need of them either, but popular clamour induced a change of heart. Between 9 and 14 July four deep shelters were opened. Entrance was by ticket only and priority given to those who were regular users of nearby tube stations or had been rendered homeless. Inevitably there were complaints about the allocation of tickets, but the shelters were never full or even nearly full. Morrison refused to open the deep shelters for the use of night workers during the day. 'We ought not to encourage a permanent day and night population deep underground,' he declared. 'If that spirit gets abroad we are defeated.' In October 1944 he ruled that, as the shelters were never full, two of them – one to the north, one to the south – should be closed. The north London shelterers organised a protest, but though they obtained a stay of execution the shelters were closed before the last rocket fell.

The advent of the flying bombs revived the urgent need to evacuate children from the threatened areas – a task complicated by the fact that 'Bomb Alley', the area between the coast and London over which the V1s habitually passed and where the RAF and AA were trying to shoot down the unwelcome visitors, was equally at threat. Left to themselves, most children would have opted to stay at home; Cliff Beard remembers discussing the matter with his father and mother and staying in Edmonton as a result. Not all parents, however, gave so much weight to their children's feelings, and particularly from the worst affected boroughs a massive exodus began. The official evacuation of mothers and children did not start till early July but by then many thousands had left under their own arrangements. On 7 July 15,000 left on special trains bound for

East Anglia; with characteristic delight in obfuscation, the authorities refused to reveal the destination in advance. 'Perhaps it's Scotland,' suggested one child; 'Or Timbuctoo,' propounded another more ambitiously. By 22 July it was estimated that 200,000 had left. Each mass departure tended to be followed by a smaller but still significant return. 'Do not be influenced by one or two quieter days and nights,' Morrison pleaded. 'The strain on the housewife and her child may get worse before it is finally removed.' Churchill had already announced that those not directly contributing to the war effort would serve their country best by leaving London.

'London is looking emptier each day,' wrote Richard Brown Baker early in July. Thousands had fled the city, children were being evacuated, shops and theatres were half empty. The inhabitants were carrying on as before but the 'air of a boom city, prosperous and gay, which London had early in the spring, has completely disappeared'. The Labour Party annual conference was postponed: the provinces were choked with evacuees, wrote Dalton in his diary, 'and London is not suitable because, apart from flying bombs, there is thought by some to be a risk of rocket bombs'. For the most part, business stayed put. 'Most of the old women have left,' noted Oliver Harvey. 'The only other escapees have been the Soviet Embassy, who have demanded a special train to evacuate their women and children to Blackpool, and the generals at SHAPE, who have decided to seek safety in Portsmouth.' A million people had left London, Vere Hodgson calculated by early August. There were compensations: 'We have plenty of milk now! . . . Managed to get some kippers yesterday without queueing for them.' In spite of some determined recidivism, the net outflow continued. At the beginning of June, the LCC Education Officer announced, there had been 238,000 children of school age in London; by the end of September it was hoped the figure would be 129,000.

The government, knowing that a rocket attack was imminent, was anxious to keep the evacuees away. On 2 August, in the House of Commons, Churchill commended the 'daring and adventurous spirits' of those who had returned to face the V1s, but urged them to rethink their position and discourage others from following their example. At one point there was even talk of evacuating 85,000 of the 130,000 civil servants still working in or around Whitehall. Nearly 16,000 patients and staff were removed from London hospitals; 25,000 beds made ready to receive casualties. Newspapers were urged to support the campaign; in a story about 149 children who were still at a particular London school, the *Daily Herald* referred to them as 'candidates for crippledom'. By the end of August, with the V1 threat dwindling and no V2 yet fired, there was something of a change of heart. The evacuation campaign was not reversed but the urgency went out of it. But Sandys's briefing to the press, with its implication that the dangers were now almost over, was at variance with official policy and with the government's calculations about the risks of a V2 attack.

These made no difference to the delighted Londoners, who at once began to pour back into London. At Paddington on 9 September there was a queue for taxis half a mile long, and rescue workers from civil defence were called in to help clear the congested luggage. Over the next few days 20,000 evacuees were returning each day. 'There's no place like home,' announced Mrs Silver as she arrived at the station, but when she got to Neasden she found that her house had lost its roof. Cases such as hers, even more than the danger from rockets, provided the main reason for the government's refusal to countenance any mass return. The devastation wreaked by the V1s had been fearful, and repair work was only just getting into its swing. In Croydon people were already living in garages, empty shops, Anderson shelters, rest centres. The return of the evacuees compounded an already intractable problem. 'If these people would only stay away for another two months we would be able to cope,' said a desperate Cecil Walker, the Borough Valuer. Fifty-four thousand houses in the borough had been damaged; many could be patched up but the hundreds of building workers drafted in from other areas had to sleep somewhere. Those lucky enough still to have habitable houses were urged to share them with the dispossessed, but the results were not impressive.

'It is nothing short of folly for evacuees to flock back,' expostulated Herbert Morrison on 18 September. 'If you come back now no one but you is responsible for anything that may happen.' By the time he made his protest half the official evacuees were back, their return encouraged by their hosts in the reception areas, who had been none too pleased to accept them in the first place and took advantage of the apparent end of the V1 threat to speed them on their way.

*

Until they got back they had little conception of what awaited them. Large parts of London were virtually unscathed, but the worst affected boroughs were in a lamentable state. 'Casualties not high but housing problem – due to blast – serious,' Alexander Cadogan had noted in his diary on 10 July, and a week later, 'They damage 11,000 houses a day! It's serious.' After the first two weeks of the flying bombs a Home Office statistician calculated that, if the assault carried on as vigorously for another two months, as much damage would have been done as in the nine months of the blitz. In Croydon 54,000 houses had been damaged, including more than 300 food shops; Sutton and Cheam fared almost as badly, with 18,000 houses damaged out of a total of 22,000. 'Damage' did not necessarily mean much; many of the houses affected were still habitable; the vast majority could be repaired; but in almost every case urgent work was needed. Still more inconvenient, the blast of the V1 often ripped off a roof but left the interior intact. The furniture could be salvaged but men to move it and places to store it were hard to find; often it was dumped in derelict buildings where the damp ruined whatever the looter had missed. The V1s and V2s together totally destroyed nearly 30,000 houses in the London area and damaged another 1.25 million.

On 3 November the *North London Press* reported gloomily that the average Londoner faced 'rheumatism, coughs, colds and all kinds of ailments, due to dampness and draught, while he waits for his claim to be paid and a licence for further essential work . . . It is a blessing for Britain and her allies that those who are responsible for the strategy of the war are gifted with more drive and initiative than those whose job it is to care for the bombed and blasted homes of the civil population.' The Home Intelligence Reports described widespread discontent at the slowness and inefficiency of the post-raid services. 'Nothing has been done in two months to make my house habitable, other than block up all the windows. Every time it rains we are deluged,' complained a typical V1 victim in mid-September. 'Paris will be going strong long before London is,' was a bitter comment which was often heard. Wandsworth demanded that its labour force of 5000 should be doubled; Acton said that its 400 builders would have to work flat out until 1947 to complete even minimal repairs. In the House of Commons the MP for Streatham said that tuberculosis was alarmingly on the increase; his colleague for Lewisham complained there were 2800 homeless in that borough alone; the representative for Whitechapel alleged that there were no plans to prepare accommodation for returning servicemen: 'The result will be that we are going to have the worst period of over-crowding in the East End boroughs that has ever been known in the history of this country.'

It is easy to understand the discontent of the homeless or those living in damp and darkened ruins. In fact, however, the government was far from inactive. Labour was the most urgent need and it was provided. Ernest Bevin toured the North. 'The health of London this winter is in your hands,' he told the building workers. 'We are in danger, if repair work is not done quickly, of epidemics of flu and other things breaking out. You must come and rebuild London.' The statistics show that this appeal was heeded. When the V1 attacks began there were 21,000 people tackling repairs in London; by the end of the year the figure was 129,000. More than 45,000 had been drafted in from the provinces. They were lodged in rest centres or shelters or requisitioned hotels, the Ivanhoe in Bloomsbury being the first, and fed in hastily improvised canteens, one of them in the Chinese section of the Victoria and Albert Museum.

All building work in London costing £10 or more was refused a licence unless it was part of the war damage repair programme. In the autumn of 1944 the government pledged that 719,000 houses or flats would have been repaired to a tolerable level by the end of the following March. In December 1944 Duncan Sandys refused to predict when the repair work would be finished, saying that he had learnt his lesson with his ill-fated prophecy that the battle of London was over. By then, however, he knew that the programme was well under way. Christmas absenteeism and bad weather slowed up the work but by mid-January the target seemed once more within reach. Fulham, with 9800 houses to repair, had fulfilled its norm by the end of February; other boroughs did almost as well; by the sched-uled date 800,000 houses had been repaired and attention was being turned to less urgent repairs or to houses damaged by rocket bombs in the last few months.

The pressure on accommodation was further relieved by the pro-vision of prefabricated wooden or metal huts. The wooden huts caused some controversy. The concrete bases on which they were to stand were often not ready in time; Mitcham requested 500 but received only 100; Camberwell, on the other hand, refused to divert workmen from repair work to handle their erection. 'We need accommodation badly,' a local official declared, 'but we are convinced that these temporary huts will not meet our housing needs.' The first wooden hut, in Poplar, was taken over by Mr and Mrs Green and their three young children on 21 October. The Greens had been living hugger-mugger in a badly damaged basement kitchen since their house had been hit by a flying bomb in June, so almost any change would have seemed welcome, but Mrs Green's tribute to her new home – it was dry, it was warm, 'and everything looks so bright and pleasant' – showed real appreciation. There was no bathroom and only an outside lavatory but the large kitchen had ample washing facilities, and the two bedrooms and living room with dining recess must have seemed palatial after what the Greens had experienced.

The metal huts, with most of the panels made from asbestos, were erected first in Lambeth, where the first thirty-eight, in Loughborough Gardens, were given to families living in air-raid shelters. They were designed to last only for two years but, said the borough engineer, 'he would not be surprised if the occupiers developed into such a friendly community that they would want to stay together even in a more substantially built housing scheme'. 850 American servicemen, mainly engineers, took part in the work of erection, and another 225 helped in house repairs. The Americans had already won golden opinions for their part in rescuing victims of bombing; Home Intelligence Reports showed that this new contribution was widely appreciated as 'a fine practical gesture' and that American troops were now more popular in London than at any time since they first began to appear.

The suffering of those made homeless, indeed of all Londoners, was made worse by the harsh winter of 1944–5, the coldest for fifty years. Broken windows, cracked walls, missing roof tiles, combined with an acute shortage of fuel to produce a uniquely uncomfortable Christmas and New Year. Potatoes and other vegetables were in short supply, flowers virtually non-existent; at one school the ink froze in the pots and there was a delay of several hours while they thawed out in front of the only fire on the premises. There was even a shortage of shillings and sixpences to put in the gas meters.

But through the worst of the V1s and the V2s London never ceased to function. Worst affected was the theatre. Bookings had fallen away heavily just before D-Day and the advent of the flying bomb exacerbated the existing trend. Within a few weeks only ten theatres were still open; among them the Windmill, still proudly boasting as it had in 1941, 'We never closed.' Those plays that survived were not necessarily the most worthwhile. Philip Hope-Wallace was at a feeble sex comedy at the St James's Theatre when a V1 cut out overhead. 'How squalid to be killed at this disgusting little farce,' he thought angrily as he dived for cover.

Promenade Concerts in the Albert Hall were suspended too, though not until the end of June and under some pressure from the authorities. Audiences had been averaging 6000 before the V1 offensive; they fell sharply but soon picked up and were back at 4500 when the closure came. Jack Hylton, the impresario, was envious of the concerts' forced demise. Audiences at even the most popular shows had fallen to half the figures of a month or two before. Terence Rattigan's *While the Sun Shines* at the Globe was playing to houses less than half full, even Hermione Gingold in *Sweeter and Lower* attracted only 260 or so against a capacity of 430. Hylton would have been delighted if he had been ordered to close his theatres; as it was he had to stumble on, contractually bound to keep the shows going unless they were patently running at a loss.

In some cases actors accepted smaller salaries but the Musicians' Union refused to contemplate any reduction, with the result that for a time no musical was to be seen. Beverley Baxter roundly denounced this breach of the ancient tradition that 'the show must go on'. Bus workers, cinemas, taxis, even MPs functioned as usual, only the theatre had failed. The musicians in particular had shown 'bad judgment and bad citizenship'. But the failure was a brief one. By the end of August the established shows were returning, the first post-V1 opening was on 1 September and a little later came the dawn of one of the most golden periods of the British theatre. Sybil Thorndike, Nicholas Hannen, above all Laurence Olivier and Ralph Richardson, combined to put on miraculous productions of *Peer Gynt, Richard III, Arms and the Man*. By Christmas nervous parents from out-of-town were venturing up with their children to see *Peter Pan* or Robert Donat's *The Glass Slipper*; and by early 1945 it was clear that neither the V2 nor the occasional air-launched V1 was any longer regarded as a deterrent by London audiences.

The cinema managers took a more robust view of the public's stamina and almost all houses stayed open. V1s had a marked effect on audiences; people tended to leave after the first alert had sounded. V2s were almost entirely ignored – in Edmonton and East Ham, two of the most targeted areas, cinema attendances were 99 per cent of what they had been in 1943. The Granada, Clapham, was one of the few to be damaged, its façade being wrecked and its doors blown off by a V1. It reopened defiantly three days later, still without its doors. 'Anyone could have walked in free but no one did,' said a relieved manager. One of the few cinemas to have closed reopened in late October, when the V2s were growing daily more frequent. 'During the flying bomb attack we decided to close,' explained the manager. 'We thought people would rather stay in their homes. Perhaps it was a wrong decision – I do not know. But there is no question of closing down this time. We are playing to packed houses every night.' One of the performances most regularly packed was Laurence Olivier's *Henry V* – romantic, colourful, swashbuckling and richly patriotic. One line always earned an uneasy titter: when the Duke of Orléans, reminded that the English would fight like devils if given 'great meals of beef and iron and steel', remarked derisively, 'Ay, but these English are shrewdly out of beef.'

But it was neither Olivier's Prince Hal nor even a Windmill girl who provided the most evocative image of London enjoying itself under fire. On July 29 the Army was playing the RAF at Lord's. A flying bomb cut out overhead, dived and seemed likely to land on the practice ground, a hundred yards or so from the pitch. In fact it carried a little farther and exploded in Albert Road. The players and umpires picked themselves up and play resumed. To a rousing cheer J. D. Robertson hooked the first ball for six. It was a rotten ball and deserved such treatment, but it was widely felt that Robertson was equally deserving of a medal.

16

Into the Straight

WITH THE RUSSIANS sweeping across Eastern Europe, the Allied armies on the frontiers of Germany, Athens liberated, the Philippines invaded, the *Tirpitz* sunk, the march to victory in the last quarter of 1944 seemed irresistible and likely to be rapid. The newspapers were filled with references to an imminent end to the war; in mid-September the manager of the Hungaria announced that if victory came on 8 October – the anniversary of the restaurant's opening – dinner and drinks would be on the house. 'I notice that several London shops are beginning to display red, white and blue streamers, and so on, for sale on victory day,' noted Richard Brown Baker in his diary. In spite of the cold, the food shortages, the dereliction, the occasional rocket, Christmas 1944 should have been a happy occasion for the Londoner. It fell, instead, in one of the blackest periods of the war.

There was civil war in Greece, the Russian offensive seemed to have lost its impetus, in the Ardennes the Germans struck back savagely and threatened to break the Allied line. There were some who feared – some, no doubt, who hoped – that these reverses would induce the Allied governments to seek peace on a basis of something less than unconditional surrender. 'I think that the past week has been one of the most trying of the war,' wrote Gwladys Cox on 23 December; 'very bad weather; all the business of Christmas; trying to keep cheerful in spite of grave news about the success of the German putsch [sic] on the Western Front. So many people had hoped that the war would be over by Christmas, and here we are involved in further, unexpected bloodshed.'

The 'business of Christmas' certainly offered little cheer. The toy and cake shops were virtually empty, of goods as well as customers. Turkeys were a rarity. Restaurants were fully booked, but by people who had hoped to be celebrating victory and either failed to turn up or were in sombre mood. Wines, spirits and beer were in exceptionally, even unprecedentedly, short supply. Among the half million inhabitants of Kensington, Hammersmith, Fulham and Chelsea only one was arrested for drunkenness over the Christmas period – a woman, who was fined 2/6d. The statistic says more about the shortage of alcohol than the reluctance of Londoners to drown their sorrows in drink.

The New Year promised little relief. 'This year I am hoping for nothing, expecting nothing – and will doubtless get nothing,' wrote Vivienne Hall. 'Oh, yes, we will win the war, there's no doubt of that, and away from London I imagine one can see the dawn of victory, but here we are tired and depressed. And this week has been a wonderful foretaste of what is before us . . . fog and ice have been the rule and now a biting wind has added its joy. The rockets are falling much faster and the horrible rolling explosions are becoming as frequent as our other familiars.'

'Weariness' is the word that occurs most regularly in the diaries and letters of the period. 'We are ill,' said George Beardmore, 'all of us, at the office, in the shops, and at home – weary of war and its effects.' Things only slowly improved. The German counter-offensive was checked, the Allied advance resumed, but as Leslie Mann, the teacher in Sidcup, remarked, there was 'no spirit of elation or unusual joy apparent in those dreary, wet, grey spring days'. Shortages of goods, restrictions on travel, deterioration of the fabric of life, the endless queueing and waiting – all these crushed whatever instinct to rejoice remained in London.

As if the prevailing gloom were not deep enough, the spring piled up fresh horrors. For most of 1944 a waxwork exhibition featuring alleged German atrocities had been on display in London. Captions outside read: HORRORS OF THE NAZI CONCENTRATION CAMPS. COME INSIDE AND SEE REAL NAZI TORTURES, FLOGGING, CRUCIFIXION, GAS CHAMBERS, ETC. CHILDREN'S AMUSEMENT SECTION NO EXTRA CHARGE. George Orwell was unimpressed, finding the exhibitions 'grubby, unlifelike and depressing' and disgusted by their unabashed appeal to the sado-masochistic instincts of the visitors. A more authentic version soon followed. At the end of April 1945 a film of the Belsen and Buchenwald atrocities was shown in London's news cinemas. Crowds queued for hours, watched in shocked silence, left without applauding or even passing casual remarks. In Kilburn High Street, outside the State Cinema, a woman of fifty-five urged a Mass

Observer to watch the film, 'It'll do you good. It'll make you think.' It had made her feel sick and angry, she said. 'I don't think we could ever be hard enough on the Germans; their behaviour is more like animals.'

These reactions – horror, guilt, a wish for vengeance – were typical of most Londoners. Only in Hampstead, a district, perhaps significantly, with a large Jewish population, was a more sceptical note sometimes struck. 'I do think it's gross misrepresentation to suggest that the prisoners have been treated like that all along deliberately,' said a middle-class man of forty, while a woman of thirty admitted, 'I'm beginning to get fed up with all these pictures; honestly, you can't keep on feeling emotional about it.' For most people the revelations did something to check the anti-semitism, which Orwell for one believed was increasing early in 1945. He listed some of the hostile remarks which had been made to him over the previous few weeks, ranging from the apologetic 'Some of my best friends are Jews . . .' variety to the out-and-out 'These bloody Yids are all pro-German.' One woman, on being shown a book about German atrocities, had exclaimed, 'Don't show it to me, *please* don't show it to me. It'll only make me hate the Jews more than ever.' Among educated people, Orwell concluded, anti-semitism was now something not to be admitted, an active demonstration of solidarity with the suffering Jews was *de rigueur.* 'But it was essentially a *conscious* effort to behave decently by people whose subjective feelings must in many cases have been very different.'

Shortly before the Belsen film was screened in London came the unexpected shock of President Roosevelt's death. 'I don't think I have ever seen London quite so devastated by an event,' wrote C. P. Snow. 'Even my old landlady was crying. The Underground was full of tearful faces – far more than if Winston had died, I'm sure.' This last comment would be hard to justify, but the loss of the man who had been for long regarded as Britain's greatest and staunchest friend came as a severe blow to a city whose morale was only just beginning to recover from the rigours of the winter. There was a service in Roosevelt's memory in St Paul's on 17 April. The King and Queen were present, and three other kings and queens attended. 'The Last Post and Reveille sounded,' wrote Chips Channon, 'and then Winant, dark and romantically handsome, escorted Winston, who was in tears, to the door. After that, everyone in England walked to the exits.' Channon's idea of 'everyone' was circumscribed, but he rightly detected a sense of national grief, and nowhere more so than in London.

Gradually the threat from the air dwindled to nothing. The last serious attack by manned aircraft came on 3 March 1945. Seventy fighter-bombers ventured into British airspace, at least six were shot down and only a dozen or so dropped bombs on London, but it was still an unwelcome reminder of a half-forgotten danger. 'Bombing has stepped up this week, when we thought they could do no more,' wrote Vere Hodgson. 'Rotten! Even at this stage of the war we are having raiding bombers, rockets and fly-bombs – all over at once. I should jolly well think we have had enough. I am fed up.' But it was a final flurry.

The last V2 was launched on 27 March 1945; it fell near Orpington, killing one and injuring twenty-three. Two days later the last air-launched V1 fell on the British Isles. The government still urged caution; the worst must be over, the last known rocket sites had been occupied, but there could be a sting in the German tail. This time there was not, but it took a little time before the public accepted that it was really over. Gradually confidence grew. Complaints now centred on the noise made by Allied bombers pouring towards Germany. In the past the need to avoid the screen of barrage balloons and the fear that German bombers might sneak in under cover of Allied operations had meant that the bomber fleets by-passed London. Now each night they rumbled overhead. Theodora Fitz-Gibbon found as unnerving as the V1s the 'sinister thunderous noise of the death-laden flying fortresses passing overhead on their way to cities such as Dresden'. In the House of Commons an MP demanded that they be marshalled elsewhere. 'Subject to operational considerations,' replied the Air Minister cautiously. He knew that most Londoners, hearing the racket in the skies, merely turned over in bed and thanked God they were not at the receiving end. Some may have felt pity for the German victims, but in London, in 1945, such charity was hard to find.

Curiously, when there were neither German bombs nor Allied bombers, there were complaints about the silence. There was a much increased demand for sleeping tablets; 'It's so quiet at night now that people get restless,' said a chemist. Bus conductors and shopkeepers reported that they were experiencing more rudeness and bad temper among their customers; park keepers detected increased vandalism and litter; truancy was more marked in LCC schools. It seemed that the relief of tension carried its own perils; the transition to peace might in some ways be as disagreeable as the experience of war.

But though there were setbacks, doubts, unwelcome tensions, the period between the New Year and the end of the European war on 8 May 1945 was one of steady return towards peacetime conditions. In no field was this more conspicuous than in London's blackout. The first steps towards its relaxation had been taken in the autumn of 1944. Richard Brown Baker went to a cinema with a friend on 9 September. 'When we emerged after dark Leicester Square and Piccadilly were seething with the usual Saturday-night throng. It seemed to me sinister to have so many people shuffling around in blackness. In another ten days the London blackout is to be partially lifted, so perhaps never again will I behold such a curious, shadowy spectacle.' Four days later Eric Thompson was fined £1 for letting light show from his business premises in Creek Lane. The magistrate, presumably to cheer up Mr Thompson, observed that this would probably be the last case of its kind.

Anti-climax followed. The 'dim-out' introduced on 17 September was supposed to legalise improved street lighting which would not be of pre-war strength but would achieve more or less the brilliance of moonlight. When it came to the point, however, the equipment did not exist and, anyway, could only be deployed in London subject to special restrictions. It was a bitter disappointment 'to find the streets as pitch-black as they have ever been', wrote Anthony Weymouth. 'In Marylebone, at any rate, there is no street lighting yet, except the microscopic starlights which are quite useless.' Marylebone was not alone; it was several weeks before Westminster modified its lighting, while Croydon was obstinately dark even in the middle of November. Householders who took down their blackout found that they were still liable to prosecution if they threw beams or pools of light across the street. Most of them left their curtains as they were. In Lambeth there was a higher proportion of lighted windows than in most parts of London but as soon as a siren sounded, even though the cause was almost certainly an unmanned flying bomb, the curtains would hurriedly be put back in position.

The change from blackout to dim-out had proved a washout, Mollie Panter-Downes told her American readers.

Londoners felt that they were particularly ill-used. Other cities had been bombed less severely during the war, complained Vivienne Hall, and now they would be able to see in their streets at night: 'But not London – oh no, *we* can't expect anything like that! We must wait until this or that authority has moved and argued and then maybe, after the war, *we* shall have a dim-out!! How tired we are of it all!' Relief came in early November, when Herbert Morrison ruled that the higher level of street lighting allowed in the rest of the country could now be extended to London. This, he emphasised, did not mean that all risk from manned aircraft had passed, merely that it had dwindled so far that further relaxation would not be unduly dangerous. One problem was that a halfway house was difficult to achieve in districts lit by gas; it was ten days or so before Paddington and outlying areas like Ruislip and Wanstead devised a technique for giving the moonlight effect tolerable to the authorities. Southwark and Chelsea took a high line and announced that they did not intend to waste rate-payers' money by messing around with compromise solutions; they would do nothing until full lighting was restored. Southwark stuck to its guns; Chelsea gave its inhabitants a welcome surprise by introducing moonlight in the King's Road and other main thoroughfares just before Christmas.

The authorities insisted that street lighting must revert instantly to full blackout in an alert. Some boroughs had a master switch which made this possible; others did not, and had to defer any improvement until a new system had been introduced. The result was that for some months London had a piebald appearance, the pedestrian blundering from areas of comparative light to total darkness and back again. 'All the bombs we have are robots or rockets, so what the —— does it matter whether we are lit up or not?' asked Mr Britton crossly. In fact there were still several manned attacks to come, but even if there had not been Britton's discontent would not have been shared by all. For Gwladys Cox it was a magical transformation: 'It is no longer inky black, but all softly lit up and shining, and all the little beams of light are reflected most charmingly in the wet street. I can now see what is in the street, people coming and going, without torches. It is *Life* again!' Prostitutes were among the few who found the new lighting an irritant. In the blackout they had plied their trade more or less inviolate; now they found the authorities taking an unwelcome interest in their activities. 'I suppose the police think the purification of Piccadilly the most appropriate manner of honouring the new lights,' concluded Baker.

The next phase was delayed until the end of April. LIGHTS UP! announced the *Evening Standard*. As a matter of economy full street lighting would not be restored for a few months, but all other restrictions would be removed on 23 April. Either from habit or because they wished to preserve their privacy and had no other curtains, householders blacked out much as they had done for the last five and a half years. A few hotels lit up, but even these were muted. Almost the only buildings which daringly left their windows uncurtained, noted Mollie Panter-Downes, were the West End clubs. 'Passers-by stopped and stood on tiptoe to peep at the old gentlemen sedately reading their *Times* and sipping their coffee in what was to Londoners a wildly fascinating setting – a lighted room which was throwing its brightness far into the streets without attracting the attention of a warden.' One symbolic moment was the illumination of Big Ben. This was supposed to happen on 24 April, but it took a few days longer to repair the battered faces. The lights were switched on on 30 April – five years and 123 days since the clock had last shone out over London.

Final liberation did not come till after victory in Europe, in July, when the lengthening nights justified the restoration of full street lighting. Even then, it took a little time before everyone came into line: the Edgware Road was a blaze of light, Park Lane unchanged, Piccadilly Circus brighter than noonday, Piccadilly itself as tenebrous as ever. For Harold Nicolson it was a moment of almost sublime satisfaction: 'For years I have crept out of my Club with my torch,' he wrote, 'seeking and peering for the little steps on the threshold. Tonight I emerged into a London coruscating with lights like Stockholm. My old way along the embankment was lit up by a thousand arc-lights. Meanwhile all the sticky stuff has been removed from the buses and undergrounds, and we shall no longer remember how we used to peep out through a little diamond slit in the texture to read the names of the stations as they flashed by.'

The dismantling of London's wartime services began to gather pace. First to stand down had been the Home Guard. A grand parade, with representatives from every London unit, was held on Horse Guards' Parade on 30 October 1944. Sir John Anderson inspected the motley ranks and then addressed them, remarking, 'We may be thankful that you were never called upon to go into action.' The ambiguity of this observation delighted Alexander Cadogan. 'Sense of humour not John's strong suit,' he noted in his diary. Early in December units from all over the country marched through Hyde Park and a dinner for the grander members was held in the Mansion House. As the Lord Mayor neared his peroration, a V2 exploded in the Thames a few hundred yards away. For some, the disbandment of the Home Guard ended one of the most fulfilling periods of their lives. The wife of a chartered accountant confessed that her husband was broken-hearted, 'You see, he met men he would never have mixed with in peacetime – the local butcher, the fishmonger, the newsagent, not to mention a couple of influential company directors. They still like getting together one evening a week.' Many such old-boy gatherings were organised, some persisting for decades after the war was over.

On 1 February 25,000 part-time fire-fighters were released from their duties; they were allowed to keep their dark blue uniforms with silver buttons and red piping as a memento of their activities. About the same date the barrage balloon in Regent's Park was lowered for the last time. The first major cut in a wartime ministry did not come until May, when 3000 men and women from the Postal and Telegraph Censorship Department were laid off; that left 7000 at work so the safety of the realm still seemed assured.

The Home Guard, the fire services, ARP – all these had cut across traditional class structures. With their passing a degree of social flexibility passed as well. People who had worked together, drunk together, risked their lives together, now passed in the street with an affable nod or a brief exchange of pleasantries. The rich man was on his way back to his somewhat battered but still inviolate castle; the poor man settled more or less resignedly at the gate. There were other signs that things were reverting to normal. Evening dress began to be seen again at the more formal functions; the distinction between first and third class on the railways was enforced with greater vigour; railings reappeared around London's parks and squares. 'My démarche about St James's Park is bearing great fruit,' wrote Jock Colville triumphantly on 3 May. 'Iron railings are appearing to preserve the grass and the unsightly paths trodden by the side of the lake are being dug up and resown.' To rail off a park affected all alike and was necessary for regeneration; to rail off a square – even though the rails were at first usually of wood – was more divisive. 'So the lawful denizens of the square can make use of their treasured keys again; and the children of the poor can be kept out,' commented George Orwell bitterly.

The closure of the public shelters and the removal of bunks from the Underground destroyed another wartime culture. There were still about 6000 sleeping in the public shelters in April 1945; a quarter of these had no homes to go to, the rest just liked it. 'It's not that we're in the least frightened of more bombing,' explained Miss Skipton, a seventy-three-year-old filing clerk from Peckham, 'it's just that, well, we have grown so used to being there after all these years.' Mrs Martyn, who had been deputy chief warden at Holborn since 1940, almost broke down when told that the shelter was closing for good, 'I don't know what I shall do when I haven't got to come here every night. I think of all the people as my children.' But though the local authorities were determined to close the shelters under their control, they seemed equally resolved to make the public keep up those on private property. Anderson shelters were not to be touched, Kensington householders were instructed in mid-March. Morrisons might be dismantled, but the components must be kept for possible future use. A few street shelters which obstructed traffic were removed and some trenches in Kensington Gardens filled in.

These were just early items in a programme of tidying up that was to last for the next twenty years or more. It was badly needed. Leslie Mann surveyed Sidcup with a critical eye. Everything had become shabby, dirty and unkempt. 'Several years of complete neglect had desolated the cheaply built property. Windows were boarded up or otherwise blinded, broken or obscured. Roofs were patched. Paintwork especially was ravaged as no paint was obtainable and the peeling and rotting woodwork everywhere had become a standing eyesore. Gardens were weed-grown, paths broken, fences broken down or missing and, I think, more noticeable than anything else, hardly a gate in the whole street functioned as it should.' The same could have been said of almost every London suburb; the only difference between them was the number of vacant sites where bombs had demolished some building. Here nature had often run rampant. Willow-herb had by now invaded almost every bombed site in London; it seemed to need neither soil nor water and would shoot its long, straggling roots into rubble and walls. Its rich rosy flowers were picturesque enough, but it was an infernal nuisance to those who tried to cultivate allotments among the ruins. Its other name was fire weed, because it was popularly believed to flourish wherever there had been a fire. Fireman E. H. Osman, who kept an allotment where once had been a City bank, remarked ruefully, 'It's a bit hard. When we put out fires we never thought we'd get a comeback like this.' It was a myth, said the spoilsport secretary of the Royal Horticultural Society; the weed grew anywhere, after a fire or not.

As well as the surface shelters, the concrete block houses erected here and there for use in street-fighting also began to disappear. A particularly obstructive one at the bottom of Kingsway was the first to go. The last barrage balloons were hauled down by the spring of 1945; the sand bins jutting from shop windows were swept away; by April fire service pumps were emptying the 5800 brick water dams and 3000 steel tanks installed to provide an emergency water supply. Two and a half thousand allotment holders abandoned their territory early in 1945. The LCC was non-committal about how long the areas turned into wartime allotments would be available – the willow-herb-ravaged plots on the sites of bombed buildings would probably be secure until redevelopment began, but choicer locations in parks or playing fields might well have to be surrendered before the year ended.

The government continued its largely unavailing efforts to keep evacuees out of the capital. On 12 April Churchill appealed to the half million or so who were still believed to be in the reception areas to stay where they were. Even on 2 May, when 1500 local authorities received the long-awaited telegram, 'Operate London return plans', delay was still hoped for. 'Those who have no London homes should stay where they are for the time being,' urged Willink. 'Those who are tempted to take a chance will only add to their own and London's difficulties.' Nobody paid much attention. London had never been more crowded, wrote one observer. 'From 10 a.m. to 6 p.m. it is impossible to walk with any comfort down Oxford Street, Regent Street, Piccadilly or, indeed, any of the main streets in the

West End of London.' Hotels were fully booked for months ahead, the shortage of rooms exacerbated by the fact that many – the Carlton, Royal Palace and Rubens among them – had not yet been derequisitioned. The special trains that ran in July to ferry back the last of the evacuees were as often as not half empty, the intended occupants long back in what was left of their homes. 'Whatever else they were, these people were not docile,' remarked Professor Titmuss in his seminal *Problems of Social Policy.*

Other returns were viewed less askance by the authorities. The busts of Byron and Bulwer Lytton were put back on their plinths in the entrance hall of Albany in the autumn of 1944. Joshua Reynolds did not return to his pedestal in Burlington Court until the following April, and even he was well ahead of the rush since he had spent the war in the vaults of Burlington House. Eros, Charles I and others from farther afield were promised for shortly after the end of the European war. Kenneth Clark visited North Wales, picking the first fifty pictures to be restored to the National Gallery: Raeburn, Turner, Reynolds and other British painters were favoured, or perhaps deemed less precious than Piero's 'Nativity', Titian's 'Bacchus and Ariadne' and Van Eyck's Arnolfini portrait, which were to follow in the next consignment. It was estimated that two-thirds of the National Gallery would be open within six months; some paintings were to go on a provincial tour until repairs were complete.

It was announced that Clark was retiring as Surveyor of the King's Pictures and would be replaced by a young art historian now in the Army whose name was Anthony Blunt. Major Blunt, the gossip columnist of the *Evening Standard* revealed, 'now holds a hush-hush job at the War Office. This, he tells me, will claim his attention for some time.' The pictures at Buckingham Palace were safely home by the time he took up his duties; so were the royal horses, which returned from Windsor to the palace mews at the end of 1944. A team of four with coachman and cockaded postilion appeared on the London streets, delivering messages, it was said, so as to save petrol.

The public expected that such economies would soon be unnecessary, but the basic petrol ration was not restored until the middle of 1945. Confirmation of the date led to a hectic rush on London's second-hand car dealers, since no new models were likely to be available for eighteen months or more. Every mechanic in town was refurbishing cars which had been sitting idle in their garages for three years or more. Other garages provided shelter for the dispossessed. In April Sir Malcolm Trustram Eve, head of the London Repairs Executive, declared that an enormous task lay ahead: 200,000 houses still needed the most basic repairs. An LCC survey showed that the number of homeless in central London had doubled over the last year. On a typical day Miss Scott, housing officer for Chelsea, arrived at her office to find two women with their eleven children camped on the doorstep demanding accommodation. Their husbands were respectively a corporal in the RAC, on service abroad, and a dock worker in Deptford, living in lodgings. Their homes had been destroyed but in Manchester they had been assured (or so they said) that flats would be found for them on their return to London. Miss Scott put them into a hostel, but though this answered in the short term the pressure on the hostels themselves was becoming intolerable. As buildings were abandoned by the military the problem was slightly eased – the hostel in which Miss Scott placed her unfortunates had been occupied by Dominion troops a few weeks before – but many of the derequisitioned buildings were irrelevant to the housing shortage. It was nice for Selfridge's to be able to reclaim its fourth floor from the Censorship Department, but not much consolation to the homeless.

In the longer term, prefabricated houses offered some hope. The first prefab, Mollie Panter-Downes reported in May 1944, had 'like a squat mushroom, suddenly sprung up in the shadow of the Tate Gallery. While its aesthetic appeal is limited, lots of housewives who go to see it will think its labour-saving devices are much better looking than anything in the Tate.' The specimen house, with two bedrooms, a sitting room, kitchen, bathroom and separate lavatory, had buff-coloured walls and windows of a tasteful green. Harry Crookshank, the Postmaster General, was 'very struck' by this new technological miracle, which seemed to him excellent value at £450. The carpets and furnishings added £44 to the basic cost, exclusive of the two modern paintings lent by Lord Portal, who was the driving force behind the scheme.

Throughout May Londoners tramped through the rooms, encouraged to criticise what they saw. They did so too: the low ceilings, poor ventilation, absence of back door and size of fireplace, all came in for hostile comment. The first of the 250,000 houses to roll off the assembly line was to be stamped 'Designed by the people of London'. If enough people wanted something then it would be provided, whatever the Ministry of Works architects might think about it – or so, at least, was the official line. In the event, shortages of time and materials meant that the final version was rather closer to the original than its critics would have wished. In fact the first prefabs, put up at the beginning of June 1945 in Weirhall Road, Tottenham, were made of wood and came from the United States; the first semi-permanent prefabs went up in Alnwick Road, Woolwich, about three weeks later.

Things were made a little easier in the spring by the exodus of foreign refugees as their homes were liberated. One thousand people a day were applying for exit permits in April and May, but since shipping for civilians was extremely limited most had to wait. They were confronted by frequent reminders that, though their own countries might now be free, there was still much fighting to be done. In Battersea, an area which had been devastated by a landmine in October 1940 was turned into a training area for soldiers destined for the Japanese war. Amid the ruins of Porson Street, Power Street, Stockdale Road, Corunna Road (the last named the only survivor of redevelopment), instructors dressed in Japanese uniforms and carrying Japanese weapons introduced young soldiers to the techniques of street-fighting. Meanwhile in Battersea Park Road, a few hundred yards away, the first Stop-Me-And-Buy-One ice-cream salesmen seen for five years jingled their bells and did a flourishing trade in choc-ices at 9d each. The ban on making ice-cream had been lifted the previous November. Richard Brown Baker was offered one at L'Apéritif. 'A middle-aged lady in Air Force uniform at the next table was most excited: "It's five years since I had any. I shall certainly have a dish." The white-haired colonel with her grunted, "I hate the stuff!" '

Though the return of ice-cream was a hopeful sign it did not presage the relaxation of other restrictions. Most rationing remained as severe as ever, some got worse and everything seemed in short supply. Even if the coupons could be secured, a Savile Row suit, which had cost fourteen guineas before the war, now cost twenty-five and could not be made in under a year, though some firms surreptitiously offered immediate delivery for an extra ten or fifteen guineas. When it was announced that Pontings had a supply of sheets, hundreds of women were outside the shop by 5 a.m. and police had to be called to control the queues. The first coconut ice at Harry Davey's local sweet shop caused as much excitement. A Croydon housewife, if she found that lavatory paper was available, would alert favoured neighbours with the coded advice: 'Boots have stationery in.'

But no amount of austerity could check the growing realisation that normal life was on the way back. At the beginning of May it was announced that no more sirens would be sounded. There were protests that the all-clear would be the only appropriate way to signal victory. Too late, retorted the authorities triumphantly, the system had already been dismantled. Boosey and Hawkes reclaimed Covent Garden for opera and ballet. The Mecca Dancing Group, which had operated it throughout the war, argued that this would penalise the 25,000 people a week who had danced there during the war. Boosey and Hawkes won the day but were too late to stage the first night of Benjamin Britten's *Peter Grimes*, which opened in June to the almost awe-struck approval of the critics. The barbed-wire cages for prisoners-of-war were removed from the Oval cricket ground and the staff began to comb the grass for particles of barbed-wire clippings. It was regretfully decided that no play would be possible before 1946 but at Lord's more than 100,000 spectators saw Australia beat England in what was a three-day test match in all but name. Wimbledon partially reopened but only for three days and for the championship of the American forces in Europe. Why could not something similar be done for the British forces at the headquarters of British tennis? asked the *Evening Standard* indignantly. 'It is incomprehensible!'

London's shopkeepers had got off to a false start the previous autumn with premature sales of flags and bunting but by the late spring of 1945, as German resistance crumbled, it became certain that the end could be only a matter of weeks away. Gwladys Cox's tobacconist in West End Lane told her that he was doing a roaring trade in Union Jacks and expected to sell as many as he could get.

Consignments of whisky and gin, equivalent to a month's quota, and marked 'Not To Be Sold Until Victory Night', were delivered at hundreds of London pubs. The King ordered that the Buckingham Palace balcony, damaged by bombing, should be reinforced;

it would, he felt, be an unfortunate end to the war if he and Churchill plunged to the ground in front of the rejoicing crowds. There were to be some irritating delays before it was all over, but the count-down to victory was under way.

17

Finishing Posts

THE LAST FEW days of the war in Europe proved infinitely frustrating. German resistance had ceased except in a few isolated pockets, it was known that negotiations were in progress, yet the Allies were still at war. People began to fear that when the great moment arrived it would prove an anti-climax. Mass Observers reported that hope had been so often deferred and expectations so often disappointed that the capacity of Londoners for rejoicing had largely dissolved. It seemed that even the materials would be lacking.

Only a tenth as many flags would be available as had been seen at the Coronation; Kenneth Flinn, works manager of a flag-making firm, said that the display would be tawdry and the flags of poor quality, just coloured cotton. 'We do not consider a flag to be a flag at all unless it is made of wool bunting,' he said severely. Demand for Russian and American flags was reported to be almost as great as for Union Jacks. At the end of April the buyer for the flag department at Selfridge's said that sales were picking up, but had not yet reached the level recorded for the liberation of Paris. 'Welcome Home' flags were moving more briskly than Union Jacks or coloured streamers. It was not till the eve of the great day that Barkers reported queues of 150–200 people, while Derry and Toms announced that not a flag was left.

The authorities seemed to take a perverse pleasure in damping down anticipation. The Ministry of Food ruled that no extra food would be released to restaurants and the 5/- limit on the price of a meal would not be waived. Leading brewers said that a *little* more beer might be available but supplies were low and they could promise nothing. There was no chance of last-minute deliveries of gin and whisky. Pub hours would not be extended. 'This is a time for thanksgiving, not for mafficking,' pronounced Dean Inge of St Paul's – not for nothing known as the 'gloomy dean'. A memorandum was even sent to all managers of Granada cinemas ordering them not to light up their buildings since government permission had not been given under the fuel-rationing order and illuminations might cause crowds to collect. Owing to a fortunate misunderstanding, the ukase was issued too late and cinemas blazed with all the lights available. In the last hours of peace, early in the morning of 3 September 1939, London had been visited by a spectacular storm which had sent some of the more nervous citizens running to the shelters. 'Early this morning, too, I was awakened by the rain – intense Wagnerian rain, which lasted for a long time,' wrote Chips Channon in his diary for VE Day, 8 May 1945. The rain was accompanied by violent thunder. It was the worst storm since the outbreak of war, said some commentators. The judgment would be hard to prove or disprove, but the minds of many thousands switched back almost six years to that moment when the great venture was just beginning.

The police had been instructed to concentrate on traffic control and to keep an eye on the entrances to tube stations; otherwise so far as possible they were to leave the crowds to their own devices. Revellers were to be treated 'in a fatherly manner', unless something more drastic proved essential. Taxis were to be barred from the Piccadilly area and, if the congestion became too great, buses would also be excluded. The police followed these orders punctiliously; almost their only interventions were aimed at stopping revellers from destroying themselves by tumbling from lamp-posts or window ledges. Somebody even climbed the gates at Buckingham Palace and energetically conducted the crowd in community singing, but when the police got him down they merely gave him an affable rebuke and sent him on his way.

'An aimless wandering of great crowds,' was Naomi Mitchison's recollection of VE Day in the West End. 'Almost everyone was tired and wanting to look rather than do. They were sitting where possible, lots of them on the steps of St Martin's. Most people were wearing bright coloured clothes, lots of them red, white and blue in some form. Most women had lipstick and a kind of put-on smile, but all but the very young looked very tired when they stopped actually smiling.' Sometimes, like wildebeest in the Serengeti, a migratory urge would impel everyone in one direction or another, usually towards Buckingham Palace or Downing Street; more often they surged to and fro in aimless eddies. Sudden bursts of more purposeful activity from time to time supervened: a Belgian flag was paraded, followed by a group of the faithful; a procession of students raced through Green Park, exploding squibs, clashing dustbin lids like cymbals, waving a giant Jeyes Fluid poster as a banner. American sailors with their girls formed a conga line down the middle of Piccadilly; the locals struck back by linking arms in the Lambeth Walk.

In so far as there was a focal point it was Buckingham Palace. There were never less than a thousand people packed in front of the railings, from time to time erupting into shouts of 'We want the King!' Every so often, for no evident reason, the crowds would grow denser and more vociferous; presumably some footman was on lookout duty, for it was at such moments that the royal family would appear on the balcony. Sometimes the waiters grew restive; 'Is anyone at home?' Susan Andrews remembers one wag shouting. 'Then suddenly there they were: Queen and Princess Margaret in electric blue, King in naval uniform, Princess Elizabeth in ATS uniform.' A group of Americans were as clamorous as anyone in calling for the King; a Canadian soldier was less enthusiastic. When a girl beside him called, 'We want the King,' he retorted, 'Some of us don't!' 'What you want to come here for, then?' she asked fiercely. He shrugged and made no reply.

But more than the King's, it was Churchill's day. The crowds first fully took in his presence when he walked at the head of a procession of MPs returning from the thanksgiving service at St Margaret's to the House of Commons. The people surged around, held back by the police but pressing to see, perhaps even to touch him. Proud fathers held aloft their babies so that, in years to come, they would be able to boast that they had seen Churchill on the day of victory. 'Winnie! Winnie!' they shouted, over and over again, as if this incantation would somehow secure them a measure of personal attention. Mollie Panter-Downes was standing almost in his path when one of 'two happily sozzled, very old, and incredibly dirty cockneys, who had been engaged in a slow, shuffling dance, like a couple of Shakespearean clowns, bellowed, "That's 'im, that's 'is little old lovely bald 'ead!"'

Before this at No. 10, he had broadcast to the nation, then emerged again, got into his car, and was pushed the whole way to the House of Commons by cheering admirers. If there was one moment of apotheosis it came when he appeared on a balcony in Whitehall to say a few informal words to the multitude. 'My dear friends, this is your victory . . .' he told them. Ernest Bevin, standing beside him, beat time as the crowd sang 'For He's A Jolly Good Fellow', and then called for three cheers for victory. The cheers were for victory, but they were for Churchill too; when he drove off, 'rosy, smiling and looking immensely happy', the almost hysterical crowd mobbed the car and ran with it shouting until its lungs were bursting.

Throughout the evening and far into the night the throng was dense, noisy and enormously good natured. The amount of drunkenness depended on the view of the observer: Naomi Mitchison saw 'a lot more drunks and broken bottles than earlier and a few people crying or having hysterics or collapsing', but most felt that there were few real drunks, the intoxication was in the air rather than derived from alcohol. One reason was that the pubs were beginning to run out of beer by eight o'clock or so; those few that had supplies to last until closing time did their best to ration customers to a pint a head. Nor was there much by way of debauchery. The elderly Norman Douglas was taken by acolytes around the West End and described wistfully the wild lovemaking he had seen in these same streets at the end of the First World War. On 8 May there was much kissing and embracing but the outer bounds of decorum were rarely breached. In Piccadilly Circus Douglas's coterie observed Augustus John striding angrily from the scene. 'Not enough licentiousness, I would assume,' remarked one of the party. Harold Nicolson, walking through the West End, was repelled by the streamers, paper whisks 'and, above all, paper caps. The latter were horrible, being of the comic variety. I regret to say that I observed three Guardsmen in full uniform wearing such caps: they were *not* Grenadiers; they belonged to the Coldstream.'

Certain images recur in the eye-witness reports of those who roamed the West End that night: Humphrey Lyttelton, borne on a hand cart, blasting jazz through his trumpet; a Soviet officer carried in triumph through the streets while everyone rushed to shake him by the hand or pat his legs. He sat there, torn between delight and extreme embarrassment. On the roof above Scott's oyster house, recalled Tom Driberg, 'an airman and a Yank did a fantastic Harold Lloyd act, elaborately sharing a bottle, tossing coins down to the people, who screamed each time they swayed over the parapet'. An ambulance was called and waited, but their life seemed charmed, as did that of the naval cadet who reeled tipsily in the scaffolding high up the side of Swan and Edgar's. For many it was the flood-lighting – a rarity even in 1939, unseen since then – which was the most memorable part of the night. The dome and cross of St Paul's were picked out by searchlights, looking 'like a marvellous piece of jewellery invented by a magician', wrote the literary critic Desmond MacCarthy. The National Gallery floodlit was the sight which most impressed Tom Driberg; the Cenotaph was surprisingly left in darkness.

Where the floodlighting was absent, bonfires often filled the gap. In Green Park a vast blaze set a tree on fire and was fed by anything inflammable which the crowd could find, including the park benches. Inevitably some of the fires got out of control and it was one of the most active nights for the fire service since the great times of the blitz. A bonfire in the middle of Oxford Street was tended by a Cockney in a top hat waving a large Union Jack and leading the crowd in dancing and singing. The authorities evidently felt that this was going too far and soon, wrote W. W. Mitchell, who had come up from Ipswich for the day, 'an engine arrived and extinguished the fire to the sound of hoots and boos from the crowd'.

Further from the centre the bonfires were a still more important feature of the celebrations. At Hammersmith a for the most part elderly and highly respectable crowd danced reels and snake dances around the fire. 'Roll Out the Barrel' and 'There'll Always Be An England' were sung with much gusto; 'There'll always be an *Ireland*,' sang two dissidents defiantly. Not everyone was happy; a scout troop in Poplar lost its fence to the pyromaniacs, and might have lost its hut too if the police had not intervened. One peacetime nuisance was painfully revived. There were over 200 false fire alarms, most of them no doubt made in good faith, some of them malicious. At Edmonton the need for a bonfire was reduced by a benevolent resident connected with the Electricity Board who fitted up a pole with four vast arc-lights. Everyone was surprised that he could afford to pay for the power; only much later did it transpire that he had linked up with the mains high-tension cable.

Whether in the West End or the suburbs, by day or late into the night, the feeling of a family outing prevailed. The children came too; right down to the babies with red, white and blue ribbons in their hair, sleeping peacefully or, more probably, complaining crossly as midnight approached. Having done Downing Street and Buckingham Palace, the family groups trudged on in search of fresh diversion. One small boy wanted to be shown the trench shelters in Green Park. You don't want to see shelters, his father assured him; they would never be needed again. 'Never?' asked the child, showing rather more grasp of the vicissitudes of history than his father. 'Never,' came the confident response. 'Never! Understand?'

In the more rarefied atmosphere of Chips Channon's house in Belgrave Square the mood of domesticity was lacking. Harold Nicolson was among the guests. 'I loathed it,' he wrote. 'There in his room, copied from the Amalienburg, under the light of many candles, were gathered the Nurembergers and the Munichois celebrating *our* victory over *their* friend Herr von Ribbentrop. I left early and in haste.' Nor were there many enquiring children or sleepy babies at the Savoy where the special menu, still at 5/- with a 3/6d cover charge, consisted of *La Tasse de Consommé Niçoise de la Victoire, La Volaille des Iles Britanniques, La Citronneuse Joyeuse Délivrance, La Coupe Glacée des Alliés* and *Le Médaillon du Soldat*. Ernest Bevin was in the hotel at the same time, addressing the Institute of Wallpaper Manufacturers. 'Wallpaper!' exclaimed Tom Pocock, 'nobody had talked about wallpaper for six years, let alone covered their walls with it. This *was* an omen of peace.'

The Archbishop of Canterbury had circulated forms of service for use on VE Day. They were not invariably well received. The vicar of Mapledurham, Dr E. L. Macassey, denounced them as most unsuitable. 'There is nothing manly or British about them. They are in the tone of a whining mendicant. The general trend is, "Let us be kind to the Germans." There is no note of virility at all.' Such considerations did not trouble the congregation at St Paul's. Vere Hodgson was so pleased to see all the choristers back in their stalls that the words of the prayers passed her by completely. Besides, there were other ways of manifesting patriotism: 'We sang all three verses of the National Anthem with great firmness, confounding their politics with tremendous enthusiasm.' Some people had hoped that there would be a midnight service at St Paul's to complete the day, but in the end only 150 slightly dejected revellers joined hands to sing 'Auld Lang Syne' outside the deserted church. The fact that there was no terminal flourish to the day did indeed render the rejoicing slightly pointless. The crowds were still thick at 1 a.m., but when the searchlights were switched off they had no clear idea what to do. They drifted aimlessly away, until at last the streets were empty.

There was one obvious reason why joy was not unqualified – Japan was still unconquered. That it would be defeated in due course was certain, but, wrote Channon, 'at what cost no one could reckon. This thought, I believe, was at the back of the minds of the crowds happily but not quite full-heartedly celebrating all over London that Spring evening.' Henry Treece, up for the evening from his bomber station, found the gaiety simulated and the revelry curiously depressing. 'The war is only half-over, and many who are dancing and singing tonight will dance and sing no more.' The government had done its best to play down the significance of VE Day; the national holiday, it stressed, was for 'relief and relaxation', a brief pause before the next part of the task. Their words seemed hardly to have been heeded, and yet the message was understood by all.

As with D-Day a year before, there were few indeed who did not have a friend or relative involved or likely to become involved in the war against Japan. How long would the fight go on, how many of them would die before it was completed? 'Everyone in London is feeling flat and cross after the VE celebrations,' wrote Harold Nicolson a few days later. 'The Japanese war arouses no interest at all but only a nauseated disgust. We must expect human nature, after having risen to such heights of feeling and resolution, to deteriorate into petty meanness and rancour.' Nicolson was unduly or at least prematurely gloomy. Londoners were intensely interested in the Japanese war; not with the sense of immediate involvement that had coloured their view of the war in Europe but in the conviction that the job had to be done and done thoroughly. But flat and cross they did feel, and their discontent contributed at least one element to the political revolution that was about to happen.

The most surprising thing about the general election of July 1945 is that almost everyone was surprised by the result. With the benefit of hindsight, a Labour victory seems inevitable. An indication of the lines of battle had come in May 1944 when Harley Street declared war on the proposals in a White Paper for a state medical service. One hundred doctors from Marylebone, mainly specialists, attended a meeting to discuss the plan; not one spoke in favour. A resolution was passed declaring that the suggested changes to the health service were a breach of the undertaking that no controversial legislation would be introduced in wartime. The proposals would create a vast and unworkable bureaucracy, stifle medical progress and damage the interests of the public. It made little difference in the popular mind that the White Paper was the product of the coalition government and that the Minister of Health at the time was a Conservative: the medical establishment had come out against the health service, the Tories were the party of the establishment, the health service would not be safe in their hands.

A by-election at Chelmsford in April 1945, the first to be held on the new register that would operate in a general election, saw a Conservative majority of 16,600 overturned by a Common Wealth candidate who won by 6400 votes. And yet the received wisdom, held by the pundits of the left as well as right, continued to be that if a general election were held shortly after VE Day, the Conservative Party with Churchill at its head would gain a crushing victory.

Left to himself Attlee would have been satisfied to let the coalition continue until victory had been won over the Japanese, an event which most people did not expect for another eighteen months or so. He was overborne by his own rank and file and the Conservatives insisted that, if the coalition were to be broken up, it must happen immediately. On 23 May Churchill resigned, returned at once at the head of a caretaker government of almost entirely Tory ministers, and asked for a dissolution preparatory to a general election on 5 July. His triumphal tour of the great cities of the United Kingdom was the most conspicuous element of the campaign. The press reports and cinema coverage of the time give an impression of undiluted adulation, vast crowds thronging the streets to hail the conquering hero and in due course, it was assumed, send him back to Downing Street. The *Evening Standard* followed his progress through the East End of London, with stops in Hackney, Bethnal Green, Shoreditch. There was naturally some organised heckling in this Labour heartland, but, judged the reporter, it was mild in tone, almost affectionate. It rained and a woman shouted, 'Keep your lid on, Winnie! You'll catch cold'; another called out, 'We all love you, Winnie!' He won much sympathy among the women at least by looking tired and, at times, being almost inaudible. CHURCHILL TOUR WRECKS SOCIALISTS, was the headlined summary of the visit; as the reporter looked at the depleted meetings of the Labour candidates he thought, 'Pity the poor Opposition!'

In fact, in London at least, the heckling was sometimes far from friendly: in Walthamstow the reception was hostile and Churchill had difficulty making himself heard; in East Fulham, where Bill Astor was defending a small majority against a young Labour hopeful, Michael Stewart, the Prime Minister was loudly booed. But the pockets of hostility were few and far between; on the whole the tours really were triumphal. The people were fond of Churchill, felt grateful to him and wished to show it. That they intended nevertheless to vote Labour occurred to almost no one.

For those more concerned with statistics than the emotional appeal of Churchill to the masses, hard evidence was difficult to come by. London's constituencies had changed greatly since 1935: Westminster's two seats had lost 40,000 voters and were down to only 63,000; Kensington had lost 20,000; Marylebone's electorate was less than half the size it had been at the previous election. No one knew how the absent servicemen would vote; it was supposed that patriotism would lead them to vote for Churchill, but the proposition was untested. When a Gallup Poll on 18 June showed 45 per cent intending to vote Labour, 32 per cent Tory and 15 per cent Liberal, the figures were dismissed as freakish, an aberration – out of line with everything that experience and common sense suggested would be the result. Even leading Labour politicians defending seats in the House of Commons were held to be at risk. The *News Chronicle* regretfully considered that Ernest Bevin was facing 'a determined challenge' from Brigadier Smyth VC in Central Wandsworth: 'The Tories are making a great effort to unseat Bevin and it is probably going to be a very near thing indeed.' Herbert Morrison at East Lewisham was held to be equally vulnerable. Churchill visited the constituency on the eve of the poll and accused his old colleague of deserting his former seat because he feared being beaten by a Communist. He got a rowdy reception but the experts considered that the attack had been effective.

No exit polls were taken in 1945; if they had been they would not have reflected the many postal votes. Even after the election was over, during the three-week wait for the services to register their voices, the press persisted in its belief that the Conservatives had won and speculated only on the size of the majority: between sixty and a hundred was the usual estimate. The Labour Party claimed to have polled heavily in London and professed to have high hopes for St Pancras, East Islington, North Kensington, South Hammersmith and South Battersea (all Tory held since 1935), but it was generally felt that they were whistling in the dark to keep their spirits up. Harry Crookshank found the mood in the Carlton Club the day after polling 'rather pessimistic', but he was one of the very few senior Tories to predict disaster. On 26 July, an hour or two before the first results were announced, odds of three to one were being offered against a Labour victory and finding few takers.

By that evening a hundred to one might have been offered against a Tory win and found not a single taker. The swing to Labour in London was 18 per cent, one of the highest in the country; 23 seats were captured from the Conservatives, giving Labour 48 out of a total of 62. Far from losing his election, Herbert Morrison won by over 15,000 with the biggest individual vote in any London constituency. Bevin also cantered home. Their party polled better than the Tories everywhere except in the business areas of the centre. Even where the Tories held a seat their majority was fiercely reduced: from 21,300 to 1400 in Hampstead; 33,500 to 16,200 in Kensington. Brendan Bracken, believed to be the Conservatives' most effective campaigner and defending a majority of 7200 in North Paddington, lost by 6500 votes. Tom Driberg quotes a senior naval officer, when told of the result, as exclaiming indignantly, 'The country will never stand for it!' Others ascribe the remark to an old lady in Claridges, or even to a dispossessed Tory minister. Probably it was apocryphal, but it reflects the shocked consternation of those who felt that it was their right to rule Britain.

At Lord Rothermere's declaration-of-poll party at the Dorchester an offended Tory came up to the journalist Tom Hopkinson and said accusingly, 'It's your bloody *Picture Post* that's responsible for this.' Hopkinson mildly replied that he thought the bloody *Daily Mirror* was just as much responsible. The *Daily Mirror*, *Picture Post*, the radical intelligentsia, the Army Education Corps, left-wing propagandists in the BBC – all played their parts and deserve a measure of the blame or praise. But they did no more than orchestrate the instinctive conviction of the British people that it was time for a change and that the rebuilding of Britain would be better done by Labour. Nowhere was more in need of rebuilding than London, and nowhere was that conviction more deeply held.

As London awaited what it was feared would be the protracted death throes of the Japanese empire, the erratic and sometimes painful return to peacetime conditions edged on its way. Immediately after VE Day the BBC broadcast the first weather forecast since 1939; to no one's surprise a deep depression was said to be approaching. Little by little, pomp and circumstance reappeared, though still shorn of much of its former lustre. There was a State Opening of Parliament by King George VI, but the procession lacked the State Coach ('it's not ready for use') and the Windsor Greys ('not enough survivors in the royal stables') and the Household Cavalry escort wore neither breastplates nor plumes ('there's still a war on').

There was only limited flummery, too, when Eisenhower was made a freeman of the City of London. He greeted the crowd from the balcony of the Guildhall, 'I've got as much right to be down there yelling as you have,' he told an accompanying Churchill. Sadly for the London driver, such ceremonies were accompanied by a police campaign against illegal parking. Over the last years those lucky enough to drive a car had grown used to the idea that they could leave it anywhere and for as long as they liked. Now there were stern rebukes for a first offence, fines for those who sinned a second time.

Those who had deluded themselves that the end of the war in Europe would mean a rapid end to rationing were quickly disappointed. In the very month of victory the bacon ration was cut from four to three ounces, and lard from two to one. In London the anyway exiguous bacon ration was not always to be found and queues for potatoes, vegetables and fruit were longer than ever. A fruit salesman in Romford was so short of cherries that he kept them for regular customers and refused to serve a soldier who had lost a leg. The public showed their opinion of his behaviour by overturning his stall and pelting him with his own fruit. A shop-to-shop hunt was necessary to find salt or vinegar and the demand for fish far outstripped supply. The Ministry of Food professed themselves baffled; more than enough extra food had been provided to cover the needs of returning evacuees.

The influx of evacuees was blamed by some for a shortage of bread that afflicted London in May and June. The head of a large bakery thought that a failure of the potato crop was even more responsible, but most of all he blamed the Ministry of Food for advising people to lay in an extra loaf as a reserve against possible trouble: 'We have 12,000 customers. If all of those took the Ministry's advice we should have to provide 12,000 extra loaves. It is out of the question.' The difficulty was eased by seventy army bakers and a number of Italian prisoners-of-war who were assigned to help out in London bakeries. The same emergency aid was not forthcoming when cigarettes almost disappeared at the end of May, though it was officially stated that there was abundant tobacco leaf in the country and machinery standing idle. This time the Whitsun holidays were blamed: factory workers who normally bought cigarettes in their canteen were turning to the shops and exhausting supplies. When there was talk of scrapping British Restaurants, as well as the day nurseries where working mothers had been able to leave their children, it began to seem to some Londoners as if they had been better off when still at war.

The problem of accommodation eased only slowly. People became increasingly resentful at the number of large, begrimed, dilapidated but still habitable houses standing empty in central London, particularly in Paddington, Kensington and Chelsea. The Kensington Council, rather gingerly, began to take over a few of these houses, convert them into flats and let them to the homeless from their own or other boroughs. The pace was not quick enough to satisfy the activists. A group of vigilantes had begun to operate in Brighton, resettling the homeless, particularly returning servicemen, in vacant property. Now they extended their work to London. On 13 July Mrs Topping, who had been perching uncomfortably in her sister's house, was translated to premises in Lewisham. 'I was puzzling where on earth I was to go when out of the blue these Brighton vigilantes turned up,' she told the press. 'I don't even know the names of these men, but I must say how grateful I am to them.'

The idea caught on. A day or two later Mr John Prean, at the head of the Paddington vigilantes, was moving Mrs Wareham and her seven children into a large house in Fernhead Road. He pledged that he would continue in this way until the local council got a move on. Within a few days there were eighteen groups operating in London. A judge in Epsom declared that the seizure of houses by vigilantes was the law of the jungle and could not be tolerated in a civilised community, but the new Labour Cabinet discussed the issue and concluded that, though the right of property had to be observed, it was not necessarily sacred. Councils were given extended powers to requisition property if the owner appeared to have no intention of making use of it. St Pancras Borough Council took over sixty empty houses and posted warning notices on the doors of 240 more. In Battersea, where the council had been receiving a new application for housing every minute, there were no habitable houses standing vacant by the end of July. The vigilante movement, having done its work, softly and suddenly vanished away.

On 6 August an atom bomb was dropped on Hiroshima. In London there was little pity for the Japanese; the new weapon seemed likely to speed the ending of the war and save Allied lives; it must be a good thing. Few contemplated the horrors of radiation. The *Evening Standard* featured a picture headed 'If an Atom Bomb fell on Tower Bridge'. The circle indicating total destruction covered four square miles, from St Paul's in the west to Southwark Park in the east, from Shadwell in the north to the Old Kent Road in the south. It was all very dreadful but it seemed no more than an extension of what had happened in Dresden, Hamburg and Berlin. And it worked.

Harold Nicolson was walking down Piccadilly on 10 August with Victor Cunard when they 'saw some idiot girls leaning out of the windows of an office and sprinkling passers-by with torn-up paper. "They think the war is over," said Victor. "No," I answered. "I expect that they have been demobilised." ' Then he met Harold Macmillan, who told him that the Japanese had surrendered. One thousand people converged on Downing Street to cheer ministers as they arrived for a Cabinet meeting. 'Stay at work,' urged the government; there had been nothing official yet. The people paid little attention. In Fleet Street the office staff on the upper floors began to tear up old papers and throw them out of the windows. George Orwell's bus travelled for a couple of miles through a rain of paper fragments. 'It annoyed me rather,' he wrote. 'In England you can't get paper to print books on, but apparently there is always plenty for this kind of thing. Incidentally, the British War Office alone uses more paper than the whole of the book trade.' In Piccadilly traffic was brought to a standstill. A policeman tried to get it moving again, but a party of Americans, led by a bearded submariner, seized him and carried him shoulder high around the Circus, tossing him from time to time into the air. Nicolson was unimpressed. 'How different it all was on VE Day,' he commented. 'I meet a small procession of American soldiers carrying Old Glory and followed by a few urchins. It is not inspiring at all.'

The fact that the surrender was not official put a damper on the celebrations. There were four days to wait before all was signed and sealed. In the meantime London filled up. Every hotel room was taken and could have been booked twice over. This time, unlike VE Day, it was promised that when the moment finally came, the pubs would be given an extension until midnight; as no extra allowance of beer and spirits was on offer, however, the concession was not of great significance. The announcement finally came late on the evening of 14 August. Once again the West End was taken over by the crowds. Bruce Lockhart went on to the balcony of the Ritz to look down on the revels. There was much noise but no drunkenness: 'What impressed me most was the restraint and amazing good temper of everyone. I felt a glow of pride in the thought that only the English could behave so well without police control.' Alexander Cadogan took a more jaundiced view: 'London not at its best, with scores of thousands of morons wandering about and not doing much more than obstruct traffic,' he wrote crossly. He objected particularly to their habit of letting off fireworks and petards: 'Surely we've had enough bangs in the last six years?'

The VJ celebrations in Braemar Avenue, Wimbledon Park, struck a cosier note. The entertainments committee, 'ably led by Mrs Delphine Speight', organised a tea party for twenty-five children. It was 'a truly magnificent spread. Housewives, laughing at the rationing and almost bare larders, produced an abundance of good things.' Tea for the adults followed and 'the fun was resumed at dusk with dancing and singing around a big bonfire in the middle of the road. Numerous fireworks added to the merriment and a running light buffet supplied refreshments. A piano, moved into the street for the occasion, provided non-stop dance music, and Mrs Baker is to be congratulated on her grand playing and untiring efforts. A surprise feature in the evening's entertainment was a fine display of acrobatic dancing by a young but well-known local girl.'

Next morning in South Kensington there was a long queue of dishevelled and weary revellers outside the ABC hoping for a little breakfast. The many who had tried to sleep in the park picked themselves up and eased aching limbs. The dust carts began the laborious business of gathering the paper and other refuse shed over the last few days. London returned to work. The war was over. Now it was time to do something about the peace. 'I have said many times that when it's all over I will have a night and day in bed so as to enjoy it,' wrote Mrs Britton after VE Day. 'But I haven't. We haven't even had a drink to celebrate, we can't get it. But it's all over now and we must all hope and strive for better things.'

What sort of better things? And did Mrs Britton get what she hoped and strove for? The city in which she lived had endured a long and gruelling ordeal, far worse than anything suffered by other cities of the British Isles. 'London was on duty for most of the war,' wrote Richard Titmuss. 'Between the first and the last incident the alert was sounded on 1124 occasions. If these are averaged, it may be said that Londoners were threatened once every thirty-six hours for over five years, threatened at their work, having their meals, putting their children to bed, and going about the ordinary business of their lives.' London had endured 101 daylight and 253 night attacks; no other British city had more than 125 in all, that one being Dover. Fort-one per cent of the flying bomb attacks were on London, 49 per cent of the rockets. Out of an estimated total of 147,000 fatal or serious casualties in the British Isles, 80,000 were in London. In the rest of the country only Birmingham and Liverpool suffered more than 5000. Thirty per cent of the City had been virtually destroyed, 20 per cent of Stepney and Southwark; 80,000 buildings had been wrecked beyond repair, another 700,000 had suffered more than minor damage. Now, surely, was a time for recompense.

There were grandiose plans to repair the desolation and conjure a new and splendid city from London's ruins. 'The devastation of war has given us an opportunity that will never come again,' proclaimed the *Architectural Review* in 1944. 'If we do not make the

City of London worth the spirit of those who fought the Battle of Britain, posterity will rise and curse us for unimaginative fools.' The government paid lip service to the sentiment. 'Let us deal with the planning of Greater London as a great adventure,' urged the Minister of Town and Country Planning, Lewis Silkin. 'What is being attempted is nothing less than the creation of conditions in which ugliness and dreariness are ended.' Lord Latham, the Leader of the LCC, pledged an all-out campaign to overcome London's four main defects, which he identified as traffic congestion, inferior housing, the confusion of business and residential areas and lack of open space. Bold new road works would be undertaken; areas such as Poplar and Stepney entirely redeveloped; land purchased so as to add to the parks, ensuring that there would be at least 2.5 acres for each thousand people and that this figure would eventually rise to four acres. Professor Sir Patrick Abercrombie, whose visionary plans for the rebuilding of the County of London and Greater London had kindled the excitement of many thousands, called for the immediate setting up of a commission with powers to buy land, build satellite towns, negotiate with industry, so as to reconstruct rationally and efficiently. It would take fifty years to complete the grand design, he said, but 'unless something is done very quickly things will go all wrong'.

Fifty years have passed, and things have gone wrong; if not all wrong, then at least badly wrong. *Si monumentum requiris, circumspice* – 'If you need a monument, look around you' – Wren's great epitaph in St Paul's Cathedral must haunt those who have been responsible for London's restoration. There were many excuses. The money was never there. The urgent need to provide accommodation and office space always got in the way of more reflective long-term planning. No one could fully comprehend the demands of the future. The populations of Battersea, Bermondsey, Camberwell were down by nearly half, of Chelsea and Fulham by a third, should not final decisions be postponed until it was clear whether they would return to their former levels? The stifling growth of motor transport was a threat not yet fully comprehended. But whatever the reasons, planning failed. In material terms at least, Mrs Britton did not get her better things. She was betrayed, and London with her.

But material things are not all. On 1 May 1942 a major working in the War Office wrote to a friend, 'The greatness of war is the greatness of death and danger; it presents overriding circumstances which remove altogether for the time being the motives of selfish people – the immediate prospect of advantage over others. These people realise at once that in the face of death we are all equal, and only then do they let the false pretences drop and become real, ideal human beings. What a pity it lasts for so short a time – not war, but the change of heart that it brings.' Londoners under the stress of war had found a sense of unity, of common purpose, a readiness to sacrifice themselves for the community and their neighbours, an indifference to the social and financial inhibitions which had ruled their lives in peacetime. They had not miraculously been transformed into saints: snobbery and selfishness were still too often seen, crime and corruption flourished. But war had brought a change of heart for all that. Would it last as short a time as the major feared? Would human nature once more 'deteriorate into petty meanness and rancour', as Harold Nicolson had predicted?

Some things seemed likely to last for a while at least. The worst excesses of inequality, with all that they bred in jealousy, resentment, discontent, had been dramatically reduced. In 1939 7000 people had net annual incomes of £6000 and over; by the end of the war the figure was less than a hundred. The lower-middle income group earning between £250 and £500 a year had increased by three million. Under a Labour government the rich would continue to be curbed, the privations of the poor would be further relieved. London, for the greater part of its population, would develop into a more congenial, more sympathetic, better place to live. Perhaps this would have happened anyway; it is not necessary to pay so dreadful a price to secure a measure of social justice. Certainly Londoners could not claim all the credit; they had shared much of the suffering with their fellow countrymen and must share the glory too. But without the war the progress enjoyed between 1945 and 1950 might have happened more slowly and less decisively. Without the Londoners it could hardly have happened at all.

But the major from the War Office was not concerned primarily with schools and hospitals, with pensions and fairer shares. The greatness of war lay in the spirit that it created. Did anything of this survive? Did the 'motives of selfish people' once more prevail? There were some at least who were marked for ever by their wartime experiences, who did not retreat into pre-war redoubts of isolation and class-consciousness. Some institutions never resumed the implacable rigidity which had been the hallmark of their earlier existence. There was a new flexibility in society, the shibboleths of caste and income were shaken if not destroyed, the worst excesses of formality, pomposity, privilege were eliminated. 'Social and sexual distinctions were swept away,' wrote Theodora FitzGibbon, continuing hopefully, 'and, when a dramatic change such as that takes place, it never goes back in quite the same way.' More nearly the same way than she and many others would have wished; but not quite the same way. To that extent London was changed and for the better. So, for a while at least, were Londoners.

Yet though the structure of society may be modified, human nature is not so easily changed. The generous impulses that had sprung up under the impulses of war were soon to wither; the instincts of self-interest, self-aggrandisement, self-preservation resumed their habitual sway. War soon became a memory: fearsome, horrifying, boring, depressing, sometimes glorious, sometimes even beautiful; but a memory which less and less shaped the thoughts and actions of those who had endured it. The comradeship, the courage, the self-sacrifice, were not forgotten; they were enriched by nostalgia, exalted into myth; but as guidelines for the conduct of daily life they became ever more irrelevant in a materialist world where the securing of advantage for oneself and one's family seemed the most if not invariably the all-important consideration.

So only the memory is left; not the memory of a golden age perhaps, but still one deserving much congratulation. There is much that Londoners can look back on with pride, remarkably little about which they need to feel ashamed. The war had been a test unexampled in its relentlessness and its ferocity. Its legacies did not prove as potent as had once been hoped, the opportunities that it created were frittered away, but no one looking back on those dreadful years can doubt that the test had been passed with honour.

Bibliography

Manuscript

The most valuable archive, mainly of contemporary letters and diaries, is at the Imperial War Museum. I list below the collections which contained material of relevance. Of these I would signal out as particularly helpful the letters of George and Helena Britton of Walthamstow to their daughter in California; Irene Byers, who lived in West Norwood and worked in the Central Telegraph Office; Gwladys Cox from West Hampstead; Vivienne Hall, a secretary from Putney; and Hilda Neal, who ran a typists' agency in South Kensington.

Miss E. M. Alty; Miss S. M. Andrews; Mr Frank Backhouse; Lieutenant F. S. Balch; Mrs R. Balister; Miss Viola Bawtree; Miss Valerie Beck; Mrs P. Bell; Miss Kathleen Bliss; Miss N. Booker; Miss Nancy Bosanquet; Mrs Winifred Bowman; Mrs Lesley Boyde; Mr Francis Brakespear; Mr George Britton; Mrs Helena Britton; Flight Officer B. C. Bullard; Mrs Irene Byers; Mr Sidney Chave; Mr Robert Chipperfield; Miss Pamela Clewett; Mrs Margery Cossins; Miss Gwladys Cox; Mrs Cecilie Eustace; Miss B. J. Fisher; Mr Charles Gayler; Mr John Geer; Mrs Anne Maxtone Graham; Mr H. F. Grey; Miss Vivienne Hall; Miss H. A. Harrison; Mr Kenneth Holmes; Mrs Betty Hudson; Mr G. W. King; Miss Winifred Lane; Mr Derek Lord; Revd James Mackay; Sergeant Alexander McKee; Mr E. Leslie Mann; Revd J. G. Markham; Mr W. W. Mitchell; Miss Shelagh Morrison-Bell; Miss Hilda Neal; Miss Nora O'Connor; Mr Henry Penny; Mrs Ivy Price; Mr William Regan; Miss Vera Reid; Miss Jessie Rex; Mr B. J. Rogers; Miss Barbara Roose; Miss Doreen Roots; Mr Stanley Rothwell; Mr Alex Savidge; Mr William Smith; Mrs Florence Speed; Miss Delphine Speight; Mrs V. J. Staunton; Mr J. L. Stevens; Miss Marion Stevenson; Sister G. Thomas; Miss

Joan Thompson; Mrs E. Varah; Mrs Joan Veazey; Mr S. M. S. Woodcock.

In the Public Record Office the Daily and Weekly Home Intelligence Reports (PRO INF1/264 and PRO INF1/292) provide an excellent picture of public morale as seen through the eyes of officialdom. Certain Cabinet papers (mainly on PRO CAB or WP) are of use, as are also the Home Office papers on HO 203.

The Mass Observation Archive in the University of Sussex contributed much to the Home Intelligence Reports and has been used widely in many books – specifically in Mass Observation titles such as *War Begins at Home, Britain* (1939) or *Puzzled People* – and in many others, particularly those by Tom Harrisson and Angus Calder. A pioneer social survey organisation started in 1937 by Tom Harrisson, Charles Madge and Humphrey Jennings, Mass Observation contrived to be both endearingly amateurish and notably effective. It continued its activities energetically throughout the Second World War. Its archive contains a treasure house of unused material, especially in MO Files A Series and Main Series and Home Propaganda Bulletin of the Advertising Service Guild No. 2, 1941.

Among other archives, the Lambeth Palace Library contains the diaries of Canons Ian White-Thompson and A. C. Don, both chaplains to the Archbishop during the wartime period. Also in the Library are the Recollections of Archbishop William Temple written by his wife Frances. The unexpurgated text of Harold Nicolson's diaries is in Balliol College, Oxford, while the diaries of Euan Wallace and Lord Woolton are in the Bodleian Library.

I have been allowed to see and, where desirable, quote from many individual letters or fragments of diaries which survive in private hands. I do not list these collectively for the same reason as I have not identified all those to whom I have spoken. When I have quoted directly from such sources I identify the author.

Printed Sources

The *Evening Standard* is the only newspaper I have read through, day by day, for the whole period covered by this book. Others I have consulted for periods when it seemed likely that they would contain material of interest or when steered in their direction by references in other books. Those which have in some way or another directly contributed to my text include: *Barnet Press*; *Bromley and Kentish Times*; *Chelsea, Westminster and Pimlico News*; *Croydon Advertiser*; *Croydon Times*; *Enfield Gazette*; *Kensington News*; *Lewisham Borough News*; *North London Press*; *Sidcup Times*; *South London Observer*; *South London Press*; *Streatham News*; *Sydenham, Forest Hill and Penge Gazette*; *Tooting and Balham Gazette*; *Tottenham and Edmonton Herald*; *Wanstead Express and Independent*; *Wembley News*; *West London Press*; *Wimbledon Borough News*. Magazines which have proved valuable include *Horizon, Lilliput, The Listener* and *Picture Post*.

I planned at first to break down the books cited in the bibliography into different groups, but soon realised that so many titles would recur under two or more headings as to render an already long list insupportable. Even then certain books would have defied classification. It might, however, be of some use if I mentioned under various categorisations those I found of particular importance.

General studies of the civilian war, whether of Britain as a whole or of London in particular. Angus Calder's two studies of wartime Britain, *The People's War* and *The Myth of the Blitz*, pioneered a new approach to the history of the period and put in his debt all who subsequently worked in the same field. Richard Titmuss's *Problems of Social Policy* is as weighty as it is humane. Terence O'Brien's *Civil Defence* is almost equally important. Arthur Marwick's *The Home Front* is a model of readable and lucid sociology. Other books which provide particularly useful material are Susan Briggs's lively and evocative *Keep Smiling Through*, Jonathan Croall's *Don't You Know There's A War On?*, Peter Lewis's *A People's War*, Joanna Mack and Steve Humphries's *London at War* and Leonard Mosley's *Backs to the Wall*. Of books based exclusively on Mass Observation material *Speak for Yourself*, edited by Angus Calder and Dorothy Sheridan, is a particularly rich source. Norman Longmate has contributed signally to the history of the civilian war in Britain; among his more wide-ranging titles *The Home Front* and *How We Lived Then* deserve special mention.

Blitz books. Pre-eminent in this category is Constantine FitzGibbon's *The Blitz*. Tom Harrisson's *Living Through the Blitz* makes excellent use of Mass Observation material. There are innumerable more or less ephemeral studies written, mainly by journalists, during the war. Ed Murrow's *This is London* is one of the best of those contributed by Americans in London, and Ritchie Calder's *Carry on London* the most interesting of those by indigenous writers. For the period of the V1 attacks Norman Longmate's *The Doodlebugs* is an agreeably written and comprehensive study.

Local histories abound; I have tracked down a large number but fear there may be more that I have missed. William Sansom's *Westminster at War* (a study not really fitting happily in this category) is the best written; Berwick Sayers's *Croydon and the Second World War* the most extensive and detailed.

Biographies and autobiographies that contain substantial sections devoted to London during the war are of varying value. I would pick out Fenner Brockway's *Bermondsey Story. The Life of Arthur Salter*, Bernard Kops's *The World is a Wedding*, John Lehmann's *I Am My Brother*, Harold Scott's *Your Obedient Servant*, Stephen Spender's *World Within World* and, for a more idiosyncratic approach, Theodora FitzGibbon's *With Love*.

Cultural life in London is well illustrated by the memoirs of Lehmann and Spender mentioned above. Other books dealing with this subject include Robert Hewison's *Under Siege*, Andrew Sinclair's *War Like A Wasp*, and most recently Peter Stansky and William Abrahams's *London's Burning*. J. MacLaren-Ross's *Memoirs of the Forties* provides a stimulating picture of Bohemia, London-style.

Diaries and collections of letters fall into two categories: those written by professionals for publication and those for personal or private consumption. Among the first, two are pre-eminent. George Orwell's letters to the New York *Tribune* and his diary extracts (the latter not written for publication) are to be found in Volumes 2 and 3 of his *Collected Essays, Journalism and Letters*; and Mollie Panter-Downes's letters to the *New Yorker*, brought together in her *London War Notes*, are unrivalled for their intelligence, wit and perception.

Other diaries written by journalists with a view to immediate or later publication and containing much of interest are three volumes by Charles Graves, five by Charles Lansdale Hodson, two by Anthony Weymouth and one (confined to the period of the V1s but excellent on that subject) by the American journalist Richard Brown Baker. Diaries or collections of letters written – so far as one can tell – for private ends and which I have found of particular interest are those of George Beardmore, published as *Civilians at War*; F.

Tennyson Jesse and M. M. Harwood (*London Front*); the American general Raymond Lee (*The London Observer*); the Canadian diplomat Charles Ritchie (*The Siren Years*); and Rose Macaulay's *Letters to a Sister*.

Novels and short stories that in some way touch on London during the Second World War must be countable in hundreds, perhaps even thousands. Above all I would pick out Elizabeth Bowen's *The Heat of the Day* and certain of her short stories, and Henry Green's novel *Caught*, for their marvellously evocative and exact depiction of wartime London. Of those that are a delight to read as well as a source of illumination, I would recommend particularly novels by Graham Greene, James Hanley and Evelyn Waugh.

In the list that follows, an asterisk indicates a work of fiction. (Except where specified, London is the place of publication.)

Addison, Paul, *The Road to 1945*, 1975.

Agar, Herbert, *Britain Alone*, 1972.

Agate, James, *Ego 6*, 1944.

——, *Ego 7*, 1946.

Allison, George F., *Allison Calling*, 1948.

Anderson, Verily, *Spam tomorrow*, 1956.

Anon., *Front Line. The Official Story of Civil Defence in London*, HMSO, 1942.

Anon., *35th City of London Battalion, Home Guard*, 1944.

Baker, Richard Brown, *The Year of the Buzz Bomb*, New York, 1952.

Balchin, Nigel,* *Darkness Falls from the Air*, 1942.

Barry, F. R., *Period of My Life*, 1970.

Beardmore, George, *Civilians at War*, 1984.

Beaton, Cecil, *The Years Between. Diaries 1939–44*, 1965.

Benney, Mark, *Over to Bombers*, 1943.

Bishop, P. M. F., 'Guy's and the German War', *Guy's Hospital Gazette*, 21 July 1945.

Bisset, Ian, *The George Cross*, 1961.

Blake, Lewis, *Bromley in the Front Line*, 1980.

——, *Red Alert. South East London 1939–45*, 1982.

Bloch, Howard (ed.), *Black Saturday. The First Day of the Blitz*, 1984.

Boorman, John, *Hope and Glory*, 1987.

Bowen, Elizabeth,* *The Collected Short Stories*, 1980.

——, *The Heat of the Day*, 1949.

Briggs, Susan, *Keep Smiling Through*, 1975.

Brittain, Vera, *England's Hour*, 1941.

Brockway, Fenner, *Bermondsey Story. The Life of Alfred Salter*, 1949.
Bell, Reginald, *The Bull's Eye*, 1943.
Butler, A. S. G., *Recording Ruin*, 1942.
Cadogan, Alexander, *Diaries 1938–45* (ed. David Dilks), 1971.
Calder, Angus, *The Myth of the Blitz*, 1991.
——, *The People's War. Britain 1939–1945*, 1969.
Calder, Angus and Sheridan, Dorothy (eds), *Speak for Yourself. A Mass Observation Anthology*, 1984.
Calder, Ritchie, *Carry on London*, 1941.
——, *Lesson of London*, 1941.
Channon, Henry, *Chips. The Diaries of Sir Henry Channon* (ed. Robert Rhodes James), 1967.
Chernow, Ron, *The Warburgs*, 1993.
Christiansen, Arthur, *Headlines all my Life*, 1961.
Churchill, Winston S., *The Second World War*, vols I–VI, 1948–54.
Clark, Kenneth, *The Other Half*, 1977.
Cockett, Frank, 'Medicine and War. The Bombing of St Thomas's', *British Medical Journal*, 22–29 December 1990.
Collier, Richard, *The City That Wouldn't Die*, 1959.
Colville, John, *The Fringes of Power*, 1985.
Compton, Denis, *Playing for England*, 1948.
Conway, Peter, *Living Tapestry*, 1946.
Cooper, Duff, *Old Men Forget*, 1953.
Coppock, J. T. and Prince, Hugh C. (eds), *Greater London*, 1964.
Crisp, Quentin, *The Naked Civil Servant*, 1968.
Croall, Jonathan, *Don't You Know There's A War On?*, 1988.
Cross, Arthur and Tibbs, Fred, *The London Blitz*, 1987.
Dalton, Hugh, *Second World War Diary* (ed. Ben Pimlott), 1986.
Darwin, Bernard, *War on the Line*, 1946.
Dean, Basil, *The Theatre at War*, 1956.
Delderfield, R. F.,* *The Avenue Goes To War*, 1958.
Delmer, Sefton, *Black Boomerang*, 1962.
Driberg, Tom, *Colonnade*, 1949.
Eckersley, Roger, *The BBC and all that*, 1946.
Ekpenyon, E. I., *Some Experiences of an African Air-Raid Warden*, 1943.
Fairbanks, Douglas, *A Hell of a War*, New York, 1993.
Farrer, David, *The Sky's the Limit*, 1943.
Farson, Negley, *Bomber's Moon*, 1941.
Faviell, Frances, *A Chelsea Concerto*, 1959.
Ferguson, Howard, *Myra Hess by her Friends*, 1966.
Ferguson, Rachel, *Royal Borough*, 1950.
Fine, Simon, *With the Home Guard*, 1943.

Firebrace, Aylmer, *Fire Service Memories*, 1949.

FitzGibbon, Constantine, *The Blitz*, 1957.

FitzGibbon, Theodora, *With Love*, 1982.

Forbes, Patrick, *The Grenedier Guards in the War of 1939–1945*, vol. 1., Aldershot, 1949.

Fyfe, Hamilton, *Britain's War-Time Revolution*, 1944.

Gallacher, William, *The Rolling of the Thunder*, 1947.

Gardner, Juliet, *'Over Here'. The GIs in Wartime Britain*, 1992.

Gielgud, Val, *British Radio Drama 1922–1956*, 1957.

Gillam, Geoffrey, *Enfield at War 1939–45*, 1985.

Gordon, Jane, *Married to Charles*, 1950.

Gorham, Maurice, *Sound and Fury*, 1948.

Grafton, Pete, *You, You and You*, 1981.

Graves, Charles, *Off the Record*, 1942.

——, *Londoner's Life*, 1942.

——, *The Home Guard of Britain*, 1943.

——, *Great Days*, 1944.

——, *London Transport Carried On*, 1947.

——, *Women in Green. The Story of the WVS*, 1948.

Green, Henry,* *Caught*, 1943.

Greene, Graham,* *The Ministry of Fear*, 1943.

Haldane, Charlotte, *Truth Will Out*, 1949.

Hamburger, Michael, *A Mug's Game*, 1986.

Hampstead, Borough of, *Hampstead at War*, Oxford, 1945.

Hanley, James,* *No Directions*, 1953.

Hardy, Clive and Arthur, Nigel, *London at War*, Huddersfield, 1989.

Hargreaves, E. L. and Gowing, M. M., *History of the Second World War. Civil Industry and Trade*, 1952.

Harrisson, Tom, *Living Through the Blitz*, 1976.

Harrisson, Tom and Madge, Charles (eds), *Mass Observation. War Begins at Home*, 1940.

Harvey, Oliver, *War Diaries* (ed. John Harvey), 1978.

Hasker, Leslie, *Fulham in the Second World War*, 1984.

Henrey, Robert, *The Incredible City*, 1944.

——, *The Siege of London*, 1956.

Herbert, A. P., *The Thames*, 1966.

Hewison, Robert, *Under Siege. Literary Life in London 1939–1945*, 1977.

Hibberd, Stuart, *This Is London*, 1950.

Hodgson, Vere, *Few Eggs and No Oranges*, 1976.

Hodson, James Lansdale, *Through the Dark Night*, 1941.

——, *Before Day-break*, 1941.

——, *Towards the Morning*, 1941.

——, *Home Front*, 1944.
——, *The Sea and the Land*, 1945.
Holden, Inez, *Night Shift*, 1941.
Holliss, Barry, *The Forgotten Front Line. Station 40, New Cross*, Tadley, 1987.
Hopkinson, Tom, *This Our Time*, 1982.
Idle, E. Doreen, *War Over West Ham*, 1943.
Ingersoll, Ralph, *Report on England*, 1941.
Ironside, Robin, *Painting Since 1939*, 1948.
Jackson, Stanley, *The Savoy*, 1964.
Jennings, Mary-Lou, *Humphrey Jennings*, 1986.
Jesse, F. Tennyson and Harwood, M. M., *London Front*, 1940.
Kavanagh, Ted, *Tommy Handley*, 1949.
Kee, Robert, *The World We Left Behind*, 1984.
Kendal, Alan, *Their Finest Hour*, 1972.
Kendrick, Alexander, *Prime Time. The Life of Edward R. Murrow*, 1970.
Knowlden, Patricia, *The Long Alert*, 1988.
Kohan, C. M., *History of the Second World War. Works and Buildings*, 1952.
Kops, Bernard, *The World is a Wedding*, 1963.
Lambert, Derek, *The Sheltered Days*, 1965.
Lancum, F. Howard, *'Press Officer, Please!'*, 1946.
Lee, Raymond E., *The London Observer*, 1972.
Lees-Milne, James, *Prophesying Peace*, 1977.
Lehmann, John, *I Am My Brother*, 1960.
Lewey, Frank, *Cockney Campaign*, 1944.
Lewis, Peter, *A People's War*, 1986.
Lockhart, Robert Bruce, *Comes the Reckoning*, 1947.
Longmate, Norman, *How We Lived Then*, 1971.
——, *The GIs. The Americans in Britain 1941–1945*, 1975.
——, *The Doodlebugs*, 1981.
——, (ed.), *The Home Front. An Anthology of Personal Experiences*, 1981.
Macaulay, Rose, *Letters to a Sister*, 1964.
McDonald, Iverach, *History of The Times 1939–1966*, 1984.
Mack, Joanna and Humphries, Steve, *London at War*, 1985.
Mackintosh, J. M., *The Nation's Health*, 1944.
McLaine, Ian, *Ministry of Morale*, 1979.
MacLaren-Ross, J., *Memoirs of the Forties*, 1965.
Macleod, Joseph, *A Job at the BBC*, Glasgow, 1947.
Macmillan, Harold, *Winds of Change*, 1966.
McMillan, James, *The Way It Happened. 1939–1950*, 1980.
Marchant, Hilde, *Women and Children Last*, 1941.
Martin, Kingsley, *Editor*, 1968.

Marwick, Arthur, *The Home Front*, 1976.

Mass Observation, *London Survey*, 1940.

——, 'The Tube Dwellers', *The Saturday Book*, 3, 1943.

——, *Puzzled People*, 1947.

Mathew, David, *Catholicism in England*, 1948.

Matthews, W. R., *St Paul's Cathedral in Wartime*, 1946.

Mayhew, Patrick, *One Family's War*, 1985.

Millin, Sarah Gertrude, *The Pit of the Abyss*, 1946.

——, *World Blackout*, 1946.

——, *The Sound of the Trumpet*, 1947.

——, *Fire Out of Heaven*, 1947.

——, *The Seven Thunders*, 1948.

Minns, Raynes, *Bombers and Mash*, 1980.

Mitchison, Naomi, *Among You Taking Notes*, 1985.

Morgan, Guy, *Red Roses Every Night*, 1948.

Mosley, Leonard, *Backs to the Wall*, 1971.

Mountevans, Admiral Lord, *Adventurous Life*, 1946.

Murphy, J. T., *Victory Production*, 1942.

Murrow, Ed, *This is London*, 1941.

Myers, Rollo, *Music Since 1939*, 1948.

Nicolson, Harold, *Diaries and Letters 1930–39* (ed. Nigel Nicolson), 1966.

——, *Diaries and Letters 1939–45*, 1967.

Nixon, Barbara, *Raiders Overhead*, 1980.

O'Brien, Terence, *Civil Defence*, 1955.

Ogilvy-Webb, Marjorie, *The Government Explains*, 1965.

O'Leary, John, *Danger Over Dagenham*, 1947.

Orwell, George, *Collected Essays, Journalism and Letters* (eds Sonia Orwell and Ian Angus), vols II, III, 1968.

Padley, Richard and Cole, Margaret (eds), *Evacuation Survey*, 1940.

Panter-Downes, Mollie, *London War Notes*, 1972.

Parkes, James, *An Enemy of the People. Antisemitism*, 1945.

Pearce, K. R., *Uxbridge at War*, 1989.

Pelling, Henry, *Britain and the Second World War*, 1970.

Perry, Colin, *Boy in the Blitz*, 1972.

Pickles, Wilfred, *Between You and Me*, 1949.

Plastow, Norman, *Safe as Houses. Wimbledon 1939–45*, 1972.

Pocock, Tom, *1945. The Dawn Came up Like Thunder*, 1983.

Ponting, Clive, *1940. Myth and Reality*, 1990.

Powell, Dilys, *Films Since 1939*, 1948.

Priestley, J. B., *Margin Released*, 1962.

Prisons, Commissioners of, *Reports 1939–45* (Cmnd 6820, 7010, 7146), 1946–47.

Quennell, Peter, *The Wanton Chase*, 1980.

Radford, Frederick, H., *'Fetch the Engine'*, 1951.

Reston, James, *Prelude to Victory*, New York, 1942.

Reynolds, Quentin, *The Wounded Don't Cry*, 1941.

——, *Only the Stars are Neutral*, 1942.

——, *Quentin Reynolds*, 1964.

Richardson, Maurice, *London's Burning*, 1941.

Ritchie, Charles, *The Siren Years*, 1974.

Robertson, Ben, *I Saw England*, 1941.

Robertson, Diana Forbes and Capa, Robert, *The Battle of Waterloo Road*, New York, 1941.

Roosevelt, Eleanor, *This I Remember*, 1950.

Ross, Alan, *The Forties. A Period Piece*, 1950.

Rothwell, Stanley, *Lambeth at War*, 1981.

Royde-Smith, Naomi, *Outside Information*, 1941.

Salmon, D. M., *To, For and About You. The People of Streatham*, 1945.

Sansom, William, *Westminster at War*, 1947.

Saunders, Hilary St George, *The Left Handshake. The Boy Scout Movement during the War*, 1949.

——, *The Red Cross and the White*, 1949.

Sayers, W. C. Berwick, *Croydon and the Second World War*, 1949.

Schimanski, Stephen and Treece, Henry (eds), *Leaves in the Storm*, 1945.

Schweitzer, Pam (ed.), *What Did You Do In The War, Mum?*, 1985.

Scott, Sir Harold, *Your Obedient Servant*, 1959.

Scott, Mark, *Home Fires. Bexley at War*, 1986.

Seth, Ronald, *The Day War Broke Out*, 1963.

Sevareid, Eric, *Not so Wild a Dream*, New York, 1946.

Shakespeare, Geoffrey, *Let Candles Be Brought In*, 1949.

Shaw, Anthony, *'We Served'. Wartime Wandsworth and Battersea*, 1989.

Sheean, Vincent, *Between the Thunder and the Sun*, 1943.

Simkins, Peter, *Cabinet War Rooms*, 1983.

Simmons, G. W., *Tottenham Hotspur Football Club*, 1947.

Sinclair, Andrew, *War Like A Wasp*, 1989.

Smith, Graham, *When Jim Crow met John Bull*, 1987.

Snow, C. P., *The Light and the Dark*, 1947.

Spender, Stephen, *Citizens in War and After*, 1945.

——, *World Within World*, 1951.

——, *The Thirties and After*, 1978.

Spier, Eugen, *The Protecting Power*, 1951.

Spinks, G. Stephens, *Religion in Britain Since 1900*, 1952.

Stansky, Peter and Abrahams, William, *London's Burning*, 1994.

Strachey, John, *Post D*, 1941.

Street, A. G., *From Dawn to Dusk*, 1942.

Tabori, Paul,* *They Came to London*, 1943.

Tanfield, Jennifer, *In Parliament 1939–50*, 1991.

Taylor, Philip M., *Britain and the Cinema in the Second World War*, 1988.

Thomas, Leslie,* *The Dearest and the Best*, 1984.

Thompson, Laurence, *1940. Year of Legend, Year of History*, 1966.

Timoleon (Sir William Darling), *King's Cross to Waverley*, 1944.

Tiquet, Stanley, *It Happened Here. The Story of Civil Defence in Wanstead and Woodford*, 1947.

Titmuss, Richard M., *Problems of Social Policy*, 1950.

Turner, E. S., *The Phoney War on the Home Front*, 1961.

Unwin, Stanley, *The Truth About a Publisher*, 1960.

Vale, George F., *Bethnal Green's Ordeal*, 1945.

Wallington, Neil, *Firemen at War*, Newton Abbot, 1981.

Warner, Pelham, *Lord's 1787–1945*, 1947.

Wassey, Michael, *Ordeal by Fire*, 1941.

Waugh, Evelyn,* *Put Out More Flags*, 1943.

——,* *Men at Arms*, 1952.

——,* *Officers and Gentlemen*, 1955.

——,* *Unconditional Surrender*, 1961.

West, Rebecca, *Black Lamb and Grey Falcon*, 1942.

Westall, Robert, *Children of the Blitz*, 1985.

Weymouth, Anthony, *Journal of the War Years*, vols 1, 2, Worcester, 1948.

Williams, Francis, *Nothing So Strange*, 1970.

Wilson, H. A., *Death Over Haggerston*, 1941.

Winant, John G., *A Letter from Grosvenor Square*, 1947.

Woolf, Leonard, *The Journey Not The Arrival Matters*, 1969.

Woolton, Earl of, *Memoirs*, 1959.

Woon, Basil, *Hell Came to London*, 1941.

Wyatt, Woodrow, *Confessions of an Optimist*, 1985.

Wyndham, Joan, *Love is Blue*, 1986.

Young, Ken and Garside, Patricia L., *Metropolitan London*, 1982.

INDEX

NOTE: Ranks and titles are generally those at the time of latest mention